IROQUOIS
IN THE
WEST

MCGILL-QUEEN'S NATIVE AND NORTHERN SERIES
(In memory of Bruce G. Trigger)
Sarah Carter and Arthur J. Ray, Editors

IROQUOIS
IN THE
WEST

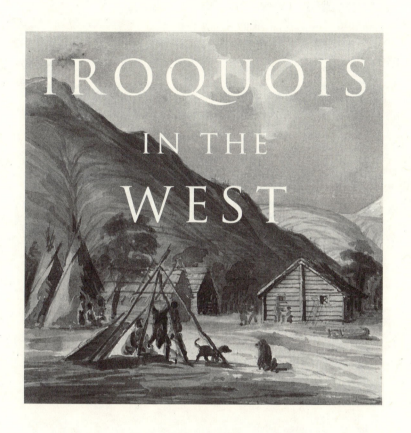

JEAN BARMAN

MᴄGILL-QUEEN'S UNIVERSITY PRESS

Montreal & Kingston · London · Chicago

© McGill-Queen's University Press 2019

ISBN 978-0-7735-5624-9 (cloth)
ISBN 978-0-7735-5625-6 (paper)
ISBN 978-0-7735-5751-2 (ePDF)
ISBN 978-0-7735-5752-9 (ePUB)

Legal deposit first quarter 2019
Bibliothèque nationale du Québec

Printed in Canada on acid-free paper that is 100% ancient forest free
(100% post-consumer recycled), processed chlorine free

This book has been published with the help of a grant from the Canadian
Federation for the Humanities and Social Sciences, through the Awards
to Scholarly Publications Program, using funds provided by the Social
Sciences and Humanities Research Council of Canada.

We acknowledge the support of the Canada Council for the Arts, which
last year invested $153 million to bring the arts to Canadians throughout
the country.

Nous remercions le Conseil des arts du Canada de son soutien. L'an
dernier, le Conseil a investi 153 millions de dollars pour mettre de l'art
dans la vie des Canadiennes et des Canadiens de tout le pays.

Library and Archives Canada Cataloguing in Publication

Barman, Jean, 1939–, author
Iroquois in the West / Jean Barman.

(McGill-Queen's Native and northern series ; 93)
Includes bibliographical references and index.
Issued in print and electronic formats.
ISBN 978-0-7735-5624-9 (cloth).–ISBN 978-0-7735-5625-6 (paper).
–ISBN 978-0-7735-5751-2 (ePDF).–ISBN 978-0-7735-5752-9 (ePUB)

1. Iroquois Indians–Canada, Western–History. 2. Iroquois Indians–West
(U.S.)–History. I. Title. II. Series: McGill-Queen's Native and northern
series ; 93

E99.I7B37 2019   971.2004'9755   C2018-906247-9
                                                   C2018-906248-7

Contents

Figures

Acknowledgments

My engagement with Iroquois in the West originated with a descendant whose research on his family uncovered an Iroquois forebear living in British Columbia. Carey Myers was determined to learn everything he could about "The Iroquois," as he affectionately termed his great-great-grandfather Louis Oteakorie. It was our many conversations over the years that grew my interest in the larger topic of Iroquois in the West.

My biggest debt of gratitude is to Carey Myers, who along with other descendants validated my interest. Long before I met Carey, Edgar Des Autel shared with me his family's intriguing story respecting Iroquois descent during a visit to the Colville Reservation in eastern Washington State. At a time when I was still only moderately curious, Sharilyn Calliou put up with my turning the conversation to her Alberta family during our discussions respecting her University of British Columbia doctoral dissertation.

Others have also generously shared information about their forebears. Charles Doy Farrington and Lynda Farrington helped me to sort through the life of Charles's grandfather Frederick Alexie, also known as Alexcee, as did fellow descendant Barbara Sheppard. Bénoit Thériault of the Canadian Museum of History gave me access to Alexcee's letters, paintings, and other materials in the Marius Barbeau papers. Val Napoleon introduced me to the Napoleon Thomas family, whose landholdings were ferreted out by Carolyn van Huizen and Sharon Keen of the British Columbia Land Title and Survey Records Distribution Service. If not for the generosity of Ann Cameron, I would not have known about the complex life of her antecedent George Tewhattohewnie. Bobby Mercier generously responded to my questions respecting prominent early families on the Grande Ronde Reservation in western Oregon, including his forebears Joseph Sanagratti and Frank Norwest.

I am very grateful to Richard Ouellet for encouraging me to research the cluster of Iroquois families, including his own, who made their lives in what would become Jasper National Park in Alberta. Following up on leads that he shared with me, which are detailed in his fine Simon Fraser University master's thesis and University of British Columbia doctoral dissertation, I consulted the South Peace Regional Archives for taped interviews from the Kakwa/Two Lakes Oral Histories project and the British Columbia Archives for taped interviews respecting early guides, including Iroquois descendants, who worked out of Jasper National Park. Andy Kilmach of the Jasper-Yellowhead Museum and Archives made available the transcript of an interview with James Shand-Harvey.

Many others have also given assistance along the way. Chris Hanna's research was fundamental to my disentangling Vancouver Island families. The Glenbow Archives in Calgary, Huntington Library in California, Jesuit Oregon Provincial Archives at Gonzaga University, Kansas Genealogical Society, Missouri Historical Society, National Archives Research Facility in Seattle, Oregon Historical Society Research Library, Sacred Heart Mission among the Coeur d'Alenes, and K. Ross Toole Archives at the University of Montana in Missoula each unearthed critical documents, as did Diane Lamoureux, Angie Friesen, and others at the Provincial Archives of Alberta. Brother Francis McDonald provided access to records of the St Joseph Mission, Williams Lake, British Columbia. Trudy Nicks of the Royal Ontario Museum gave her blessing to my drawing on her primary research as explicated in her doctoral dissertation and in her publications. Dennice Goudie and Elida Peers explained the large cross-border cluster linked to Louis Shaegoskatsta, Frances Haines located information respecting the William Laing Meason family, Antonia Mills shared insights at critical moments, and Donald Smith and Rob Foxcurran kept me grounded. Roderick J. Barman sustains me, as do Rod Barman and Emily Barman. I thank you all.

My two principal research supports have been Bruce McIntyre Watson and Nicole St-Onge. Bruce's three-volume biographical compendium, *Lives Lived West of the Divide*, has eased research for many descendants and others, including myself. The invaluable Voyageur Contracts Database, constructed by Nicole St-Onge of the University of Ottawa and others, and now available on the Société historique de Saint-Boniface website, was fundamental to my understanding.

A Social Sciences and Humanities Research Council grant facilitated the publication in 2014 of my *French Canadians, Furs, and Indigenous Woman in the Making of the Pacific Northwest*, where Iroquois were introduced, and then this volume, where they are the focus in a broader setting. I am extremely grateful for the opportunity that the grant gave me to collaborate with Bruce McIntyre Watson, for Geneviève Lapointe's fine research assistance, and for the encouragement that the council's support gives scholars to persist through to the end of their work despite sometimes difficult points along the way.

My thanks to Bill Nelson for drawing the map and to Alexandra Peace for the index. For making the images available, I am grateful to staff at the Glenbow Museum, Jasper-Yellowhead Museum, Library and Archives Canada, Minnesota Historical Society, Oregon Historical Society, Royal Ontario Museum, Smithsonian Institution, Sooke Regional Historical Society, University of Montana Archives, and Washington State University Libraries, as well as to Alana Collins, Karen Duffek, May Edwards, Bill McLennan, and Carey Myers. The UBC Emeritus College Scholarly Reimbursement Fund covered the cost of the images and map.

Above all, I thank the scholars who have over the past century put into print aspects of the history of Iroquois in the West. I have learned from, and am grateful to, Fred Bruemmer, Alexander Chamberlain, John C. Ewers, Jack Frisch, James Gibbons, Jan Grabowski, Vincent Havard, Theodore Karamanski, Trudy Nicks, Nicole St-Onge, and Allen Trelease, along with fine graduate scholarship by Richard Ouellet and Jennifer Jameson, each of whom is acknowledged in the bibliography. My intent is not to erase or supersede others but to take the slivers of stories from the shadows of the past that have variously come my way and put them into a whole that reflects my particular interests.

At McGill-Queen's University Press, my thanks go to executive director Philip Cercone, to acquisition editor Mark Abley, who was perceptive and persuasive, and to managing editor Ryan Van Huijstee and copy editor Robert Lewis, who were encouraging and astute. I could not have had a more supportive team. The manuscript's two readers were observant, knowledgeable, and helpful. I am in your debt.

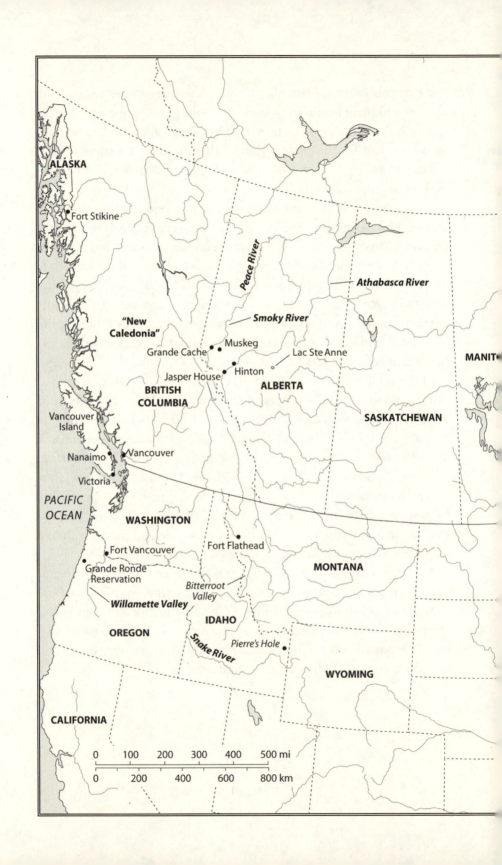

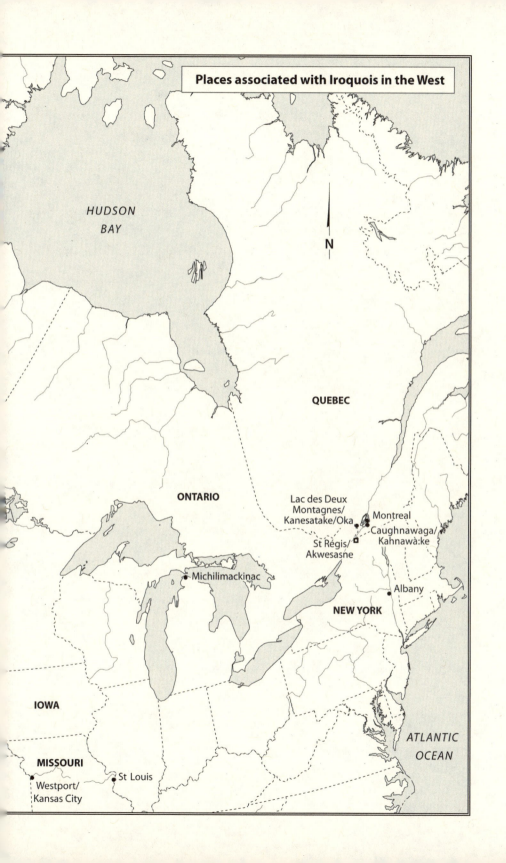

Places associated with Iroquois in the West

HUDSON
BAY

N

QUEBEC

ONTARIO

Lac des Deux
Montagnes/
Kanesatake/Oka

Montreal

Caughnawaga/
Kahnawà:ke

St Régis/
Akwesasne

Michilimackinac

Albany

NEW YORK

IOWA

ATLANTIC
OCEAN

MISSOURI

St Louis

Westport/
Kansas City

IROQUOIS
IN THE
WEST

Introduction

"Much of this book is about the labor to live a good life": so Audra Simpson begins her powerful *Mohawk Interruptus*, published in 2014. "The people of the Mohawk nation of Kahnawà:ke do this work with great verve and equanimity, while enduring and pushing against the ongoing stress and structure of settler colonialism."[1] Simpson's contemporary description applies equally well to their forebears who two centuries ago left home without leaving behind their ways of life. Iroquois principally from Caughnawaga, to use the terminology of the time, were enticed west by a rapidly expanding fur trade. Although some soon returned to today's Quebec, others never did. Making their way across time and place, they – so far as was possible – self-determined their lives. This is their story.

But wait. Being Iroquois has not always meant the same thing. The past is particular, as suggested by the many recent books with Iroquois in their titles, subtitles, and subject matter.[2] The term "Iroquois" embodies five centuries of complexities. General agreement exists that the word originated as the name of the family of languages spoken by five, and later six, Indigenous peoples living south of Lake Ontario who prior to contact with non-Indigenous outsiders formed a league or confederacy.[3] Iroquois who early on disengaged from this powerful league, or Haudenosaunee Confederacy, figure not at all or marginally in most accounts. Those who departed for then French territory are for the most part ignored or reduced to an aberration.

It is these independent-minded Iroquois who interest me. From 1667 onward, Iroquois settled across the St Lawrence River from the fur trade enclave of Montreal at the Jesuit mission of Sault St Louis, later known as

Caughnawaga and today as Kahnawà:ke. Two small groups subsequently splintered off. Some headed to the St Régis mission at Akwesasne, located on the St Lawrence River near today's Cornwall, Ontario.[4] Others left for a Sulpician community at Kanesatake, known by virtue of its location as Lac des Deux Montagnes, or Lake of Two Mountains, and today as Oka.[5]

My interest in Caughnawaga, St Régis, and Lac des Deux Montagnes relates to their residents' adventurous spirit. During the early nineteenth century, at least 600 Iroquois, and likely many more, from the three communities took a chance on the West, being that vast region of the North American continent then lying beyond newcomers' grasp. The fur trade based in Montreal was so hungry for capable employees that it hired Iroquois on a par with non-Indigenous employees as paddlers of the large canoes underpinning the economy. Some Iroquois glimpsed the West only from the water, others stayed away for years on end, and others never returned home.

Iroquois engaging the West, be it briefly or forever, were ambitious and determined. They were never more so than in facing down the divide that non-Indigenous newcomers erected to distance themselves from, and to render inert, "Indians," as Indigenous peoples were then termed. Among newcomers' justifications for usurping Indian lands and overturning ways of life were their paler and thereby supposedly superior skin tones. They were white, whereas others were not. As explained by Jason E. Pierce respecting the American West, "largely a social construction, shaped, defined, and contested by those claiming whiteness and those arbitrating it," whiteness became "the standard by which others were to be judged" and found wanting.[6] Premised on physical separation from supposed unequals, this constructed Indigenous-white divide goes someway to explaining the apparent ease with which settler colonialism was effected and long survived.

Iroquois in the West refused to be set aside. They knew who they were and acted accordingly. Hired alongside white employees, Iroquois possessed self-confident dispositions and useful work skills. They were hardworking, ambitious for the future, and determined to set the direction of their lives. They had long since become Catholics and so were not easy objects of conversion to other Christian denominations. They were self-confidently "Iroquois," a name that they held on to as a self-description, whereas their counterparts back east described themselves as "Mohawk" after the largest of the Indigenous groupings that had earlier come together into a confederacy. Today, Iroquois in the West continue to call themselves "Iroquois," as I do here.

To whites' refrain that "Indians are not like us," Iroquois in the West responded, "Not so fast; what is it you do that we cannot also accomplish if it should be in our interest to do so?" And Iroquois did do so time and again. By their outlook and their actions, they repeatedly unsettled the assumptions of superiority that whites took west with them. Iroquois's strong senses of right and wrong led, on the one hand, to their being respected as employees in the fur trade and, on the other hand, to their sometimes challenging that economy in the interests of fair play for all employees, whatever their skin tones.

Iroquois's outlook and actions put them at cross-purposes with the Indigenous-white divide as it was constructed and intended to be effected in the West. By virtue of being away from home, Iroquois were not indigenous to the places they headed, and did not make that claim, but rather held on to ways consistent with the places from which they came. They were bound together by strong senses of self that were predicated on their identity as Iroquois. They were self-confident and self-reliant, hardworking, respectful of the family life they shared with local Indigenous women, unwavering in their Catholic faith, and committed to place. In their everyday lives, Iroquois in the West minded themselves as opposed to exploiting others. For their living, they utilized natural resources, notably animal pelts, which were for the most part renewable.

For the first generation of Iroquois in the West, the divide effected between whites and Indigenous peoples was more often a nuisance than a barrier to their everyday lives. The principles of right action that they took from home did not directly threaten whites' taking for granted that they were in charge. Apart from potentially deadly disputes over trapping, Iroquois might find acceptance among the Indigenous groups from which came the women with whom they "partnered," this term being used to describe relationships comparable to marriage that existed prior to access to a priest. From the perspective of Iroquois in the West, land was not a commodity to be wrested away from others but, as with an Iroquois cluster crossing the American West and another setting down at Jasper in today's western Alberta, a means to live as best they could in relation to the environment. The closest that Iroquois in the West got to colonizing was a cluster whose members shared their Catholicsm with the Montana Flatheads among whom they lived.

With the passage of time, which was marked by growing white settlement, Iroquois and then their offspring were increasingly slapped down. The intermediate space they occupied along the Indigenous-white divide was harder and harder to sustain. Iroquois who settled in the American Pacific Northwest alongside their white neighbours were dismissed out of hand as Indians and, for that reason, had no place in the new order of things. Iroquois who made their home at Jasper in today's Alberta were turfed out, their descendants again displaced.

Iroquois in the West accommodated themselves to their circumstances even as they held on to their senses of self. They repeatedly challenged the assumption of an Indigenous-white divide, doing so not as an end in itself but so as to live as they would. Iroquois in the West were not, except by choice, confined in the first or subsequent generations to reservations or reserves. The decisions that Iroquois made across time and place, if increasingly constrained and sometimes undone by the dominant society, were their own as opposed to being forced on them. That Iroquois in the West so acted across time and place cannot be overestimated.

My larger argument is straightforward. The principal depiction of Indigenous peoples as bit players in North America's past overlooks the many ways that, despite the obstacles put in their way, they have, in different ways, self-determined their lives in whole or in part. Iroquois's circumstances were not unique to them but echoed across time for other Indigneous groups. As for their responses, to generalize from Audra Simpson, "The Mohawks of Kahnawà:ke are nationals of a precontact Indigenous polity that simply refuse to stop being themselves."[7]

IMPETUS

As with so much of my writing, happenstance played a role in the advent of this book. Almost as soon as Carey Myers, thanked in the acknowledgments, introduced me to the story of his Iroquois forebear Louis Oteakorie, the three of us, vicariously so in respect to Oteakorie, became fast friends. A Protestant minister's son and by occupation an air traffic controller,

Carey grew up not far from where I live in Vancouver and would drop by each time he discovered something new. Carey was a consummate researcher for whom each find was as magical as the first inkling of his distinctive descent. As well as listening appreciatively, I was soon putting aside whatever I came across in my own reading and research on related topics that might add to our conversations. My doing so began to fill in the larger pattern of events that had prompted Oteakorie to leave his home village of Caughnawaga in the late 1840s.

The pathway that Louis Oteakorie took west had by then been followed many times over by Iroquois similarly intent on living as they would. Initially employed at the principal Pacific Northwest fur trade post of Fort Vancouver, near present-day Portland, Oregon, Oteakorie was soon dispatched north to Vancouver Island. There, he was among those constructing Nanaimo, where recently discovered coal seams were to be mined to service Royal Navy ships plying the West Coast from their home base in Valparaiso, Chile. At nearby Fort Rupert, he partnered with a Kwakiutl chief's daughter, with whom he had half a dozen children, their son Alex eventually becoming chief through the female line of descent. Like many other Iroquois in the West, Oteakorie did not look back.

Quite remarkably, Louis Oteakorie's decision to head west survives in his own words. It does so through Oteakorie relating his story to an old friend settled at Quatsino Sound on northern Vancouver Island. A visitor there that day later put the story on paper. Some refashioning and likely romanticization do not negate the core of its authenticity. That day, Oteakorie along with his wife, Mellas or M-las, and their son, Alex, came for a visit from 50 kilometres, or 30 miles, away bearing gifts of dried wild strawberries and cranberries. Arriving in "a long cedar canoe," Oteakorie was described as "a tall well built native of another race, his finely chiseled features; those broad shoulders; long tapering limbs: told me he belonged to some far away, fast travelling tribe." At the time, "he was nearly 85 years old, and yet he was as straight as an arrow, and as nimble as the boy and so that evening was spent with the story."[8]

The conversation began with Oteakorie being asked to recount how he had gotten to the Pacific Northwest. First came the short answer: "Oh, on rivers and some big lakes; and I walked a lot, too … It's a long way from where my people lived. The coming of many people drove some away, amongst these myself." Urged on by his wife and son, Oteakorie detailed the beginning of what would be a three-year trip west with two Iroquois companions:

> Waiting for the new moon in May, we swung our new birch canoe up the St. Lawrence. There was no hurry or excitement over my starting this long journey; there were only just another day, not thinking about ever arriving at our destination or what it would be like. We were just going to a place where the trappers had not taken the furs and there was lots of country to trap in. Then I had nothing to think about; only the graves of my people. The white man had taken our lands, overran our forests, and given us nothing but lead bullets in return ... Soon deer, bear and moose, and wild turkey were gone, they took possession of the great trees from which we made sweets (maple) ... And I was on my way, each day towards the setting sun.[9]

Many adventures later, wintering along the way with friendly Indians, the trio reached Fort Vancouver: "We drew to the landing, tied up the canoe, and, walking up to the gate, we knew the custom; all arms must be left at the gate. When we were accosted, proudly I answered in English, 'Trappers from Montreal.'" Eventually, "I with others were sent up the coast to help establish a place known now as Fort Rupert."[10]

There, the account ends, perhaps because the evening was late or possibly due to Oteakorie having reached his place of being. Although Carey was unable to uncover his great-great-grandfather's past in its entirety, Oteakorie's recollection gives every indication of a life well lived on his own terms.

Carey Myers's death in June 2012 left a void in my life. "The Iroquois," as Carey called Oteakorie, was no more. Or was he? On reflection, I could think of no better tribute to Carey, to "The Iroquois," and to the friendship that grew up between the three of us than to share what I have learned.

SLIVERS OF STORIES FROM THE SHADOWS OF THE PAST

The history of Iroquois in the West comprises slivers of stories from the shadows of the past. It inevitably does so given that almost all of the first generation and most of the second were illiterate. The good news is that

Iroquois left traces with others who wrote about adventures in which they played a role and with descendants into the present day.

Iroquois also figure in records and accounts of the fur trade and of religious and government bodies. Although men in charge were inevitably influenced in what they wrote by their positions and prejudices, their journals and letters are often the only sources of information respecting what occurred. Their writings speak to Iroquois's ambition and determination in sometimes difficult circumstances. With the passage of time, Iroquois sons and daughters found their way into newcomers' lives, the former less so than the latter, who were much sought out by newcomer men at a time when white women were in short supply.

Although they are but slivers from the shadows of the past, the stories that survive are all the same powerful, testifying to the self-confidence of Iroquois and their descendants who shared their selves with others. Among aspects of their everyday experience that can be tracked across time and place are self-definition and pride as Iroquois, a spoken language described as Iroquois, first names and surnames consistent throughout their lives, an active and enduring commitment to Catholicism, hard work as a matter of course, men's considerate relations with each other and with the women in their lives, and a sociability that included a preference for clusters and bands.

ORGANIZATION

The eight chapters that follow are divided into four parts. Part 1 explains how, now two centuries ago, Iroquois came to head west. Parts 2, 3, and 4 follow four clusters of Iroquois who made their way across time and place.

Part 1, "Becoming Their Own Iroquois Selves," backgrounds Iroquois's reasons for leaving home. As explained in chapter 1, which draws on wide-ranging secondary literature, Iroquois intent on "Self-Determining Their Lives" broke away from the large Iroquois Confederacy early on. Some of them, as described in chapter 2, took a chance on paid employment in an expanding fur trade when it came their way. The consequence was their "Heading West, Maybe Forever, Maybe Not."

Part 2 follows two clusters of Iroquois "Daring to be Adventurous." Chapter 3 originated in my longstanding curiosity respecting Iroquois's relationship with Montana Flatheads, which goes back to a marvellous travelling exhibition that visited the Vancouver Museum in November 1993 entitled "Sacred Encounters: Father De Smet and the Indians of the Rocky

Mountain West." At the exhibition's opening, I was privileged to receive a large poster depicting an outdoor chapel described in the accompanying book by Jacqueline Peterson and Laura Peers.[11] The poster's place of prominence on the wall of my university office chided me for years on end to live up to my promise to myself to learn more about "Bringing Catholicism to the Flatheads." In order to do so, Iroquois and their Salish contemporaries, then known as Flatheads, repeatedly travelled 2,800 kilometres, or 1,740 miles, from their Montana home to St Louis, Missouri, and back again.

Chapter 4 follows an equally adventurous Iroquois cluster. This chapter has its impetus in research for my book *Abenaki Daring* (2016). The younger brother of the book's Abenaki protagonist, Noel Annance, was among a cluster of Iroquois "Challenging a Fur Monopoly" upon realizing that the pelts they provided were being undervalued by those in charge. Abandoning the organized fur trade, these Iroquois variously made their way across the middle United States.

Part 3 attends to Iroquois "Sticking with the Fur Trade." Following on from my *French Canadians, Furs, and Indigenous Women in the Making of the Pacific Northwest* (2014), chapter 5 tracks Iroquois "Committing to the Pacific Northwest" as paid employees. Chapter 6 follows their offspring "Disappearing into a Changing Pacific Northwest" subsequent to the large territory being divided in 1846 between the United States and Britain, later Canada.

Part 4 has its impetus in my *Stanley Park's Secret* (2005), which tracks families who lived in Vancouver's future park, to be evicted upon its becoming such. My search for comparative cases led me to an Iroquois contingent "Banding Together" in the Rocky Mountains. Chapter 7 tracks their attempts over the course of the nineteenth century at "Becoming Jasper Iroquois," which was not to be. Chapter 8 follows Iroquois dispossessed upon their homeland becoming Jasper National Park and subsequently "Persisting in Jasper's Shadow." Iroquois and their descendants would again be dispossessed, even so retaining their senses of self into the present day.

My goal in reconstructing persons and events in past time is not to tell others what to think. It is rather to provide, so far as is possible, the voices, outlooks, and actions of Iroquois in the West as they shared themselves with others.

PART ONE

Becoming Their Own Iroquois Selves

Part 1 follows an Iroquois cluster "Becoming Their Own Iroquois Selves." Accommodating themselves to the presence of the Catholic Church in their midst, they moved toward "Self-Determining Their Lives," as described in chapter 1. Iroquois's principal community of Caughnawaga survived and matured because its residents were determined that it would do so.

Chapter 2 tracks Iroquois "Heading West, Maybe Forever, Maybe Not." During the first two decades of the nineteenth century, Iroquois from Caughnawaga and the two smaller communities of St Régis and Lac des Deux Montagnes were recruited on a par with whites by a rapidly expanding fur trade based in nearby Montreal. They were hired principally to paddle the large canoes that took trade goods west in the spring and returned with animal pelts. In the course of doing so, Iroquois glimpsed the West, a vast region of the North American continent lying beyond newcomers' grasp. Whereas most Iroquois returned home, some did not.

Self-Determining Their Lives

Iroquois did not head west in a vacuum. Prior to Europeans' arrival, five Iroquoian-speaking nations came together into a confederacy to protect their common interests. In the later 1600s, some from among their numbers were enticed away by the missionizing Jesuits to settle at Caughnawaga, known also as Sault St Louis and later as Kahnawà:ke, on territory claimed by France. There, over time, they became their own Iroquois selves with the confidence to self-determine their lives. Among their numbers were at least 600 and possibly many more who would head west with the fur trade when the opportunity to do so came their way. It was for good reason that the editor of the multivolume *Jesuit Relations*, which a century ago brought together documents related to that religious order's interactions with Iroquois, characterized them as "the craftiest, most daring, and most intelligent of North American Indians."[1]

CAUGHNAWAGA BEGINNINGS

Westward Iroquois's principal home community of Caughnawaga originated in the tumult following Europeans' arrival in northeastern North America at the beginning of the 1600s. Three countries played principal roles. France centred itself along the St Lawrence River between today's Quebec City and Montreal, and England did so to the southeast along the East Coast. Holland, which was interested mainly in trade and would depart North America in 1664 to return briefly in 1674, had its commercial depot at what the English would rename Albany, located in future New York State. None of these swaths of territory directly intruded on the five

Iroquois nations formed prior to contact. Moving from west to east, the Iroquois Confederacy comprised Seneca, Cayuga, Onondaga, Oneida, and Mohawk peoples, to be later joined by Tuscaroras.[2]

Iroquois, along with other Indigenous peoples, were repeatedly and persistently drawn into conflicts whose impetus lay in political events in Europe. As a French official put it possessively to his English counterpart, "You are wrong, Sir, to hold as indisputable that the Iroquois savages, whom you call your Indians, are yours … You know we have been more than 20 years in possession of the Five Iroquois Nations."[3] Once it became possible from the 1620s for Iroquois to acquire guns and ammunition in Albany, the consequences magnified. According to an early Dutch missionary, "the Arms used by the Indians in War were formerly a Bow and Arrow with a Stone Axe and Mallet, but now they get from our People Guns, Swords, Iron Axes and Mallets."[4]

Much as occurred generally wherever newcomers encountered Indigenous peoples, a principal imperative was religious. A French-Iroquois peace treaty negotiated in 1666, at a time when the non-Indigenous population of New France did not much exceed 3,000, included a provision for "two Black gowns (that is to say, two Jesuit Fathers)" to establish Catholic missions among the Iroquois.[5] The Society of Jesus, whose members were known as Jesuits, had been founded in France a little over a century earlier, in 1540, as an order of priests committed to converting Indigenous peoples around the world to Catholicism. Located on the south shore of the St Lawrence River across from the then small village of Montreal, with a newcomer population of 600, the Jesuit mission moved several times prior to finding a permanent site in 1716 at Caughnawaga in the Seigneury of Sault St Louis, which had been ceded to the Jesuits in 1680.[6]

Several hundred Iroquois were admitted to this "mission to the Iroquois" upon agreeing to abstain from drunkenness, participate in daily Catholic religious practices, and give up their traditional practice of acting out dreams, as well as promising that the men would not abandon their wives.[7] Among their number was Kateri, or Catherine, Tekakwitha, who shortly after being baptized in 1676 slipped away to Caughnawaga. There, she died four years later at age twenty-four, possibly due to her preference for extreme physical penance, to be canonized by the Catholic church as a saint in 2012.[8]

Most Caughnawaga recruits were from the five Iroquois nations. The Jesuits had already been active, and it was earlier converts, along with others dissatisfied with the state of things, who found their way there. A Jesuit described how the mission's location made it "a place where a great many people pass, hardly a band of Savages stops at it without some of their number being induced to remain."[9] Gretchen Green refers to arrivals as comprising "a mosaic of ethnic origins," which included goodly numbers of Mohawks, who were the easternmost and thus the most proximate of the Iroquois peoples, as well as Oneidas, Onondagas, and Hurons.[10] Audra Simpson aptly describes early Caughnawaga as "a refugee community."[11]

Two other sites attracted some of those initially heading to Caughnawaga. Lac des Deux Montagnes, also known as Kanesatake and today as Oka, was begun in 1676 by the Montreal-based Sulpician religious order, which was granted land about 60 kilometres, or 35 miles, northwest of Montreal. As of 1685, the population of Lac des Deux Montagnes stood at 222, compared with Caughnawaga's 682, growing by the end of the century respectively to 273 and 790.[12] Lac des Deux Montagnes long continued to be divided between founding Iroquois and Algonquins, each with their separate missionaries, languages, and ways of life. The latter lived, by one account, "principally by the chase," whereas Iroquois "cultivate the soil, and engage as voyageurs, or in any other capacity as may yield them the means of subsistence."[13] A second group splintered off from Caughnawaga in 1754. Some thirty families, said to be looking for more fertile land, formed their own mission community at St Régis, 100 kilometres, or 60 miles, upriver along the St Lawrence at the junction with the St Régis River.[14]

CAUGHNAWAGA AS A MISSION SETTLEMENT

The relationship between the Jesuits and their Caughnawaga charges was more complex than it might appear upon first consideration. The Jesuits' initiative survived and thrived not because one entity imposed itself on another but because it suited both parties. Kelly Yvonne Hopkins makes the perceptive observation that "many Iroquois accepted the Jesuits as diplomatic hostages who would ensure the good will of New France and its Indian allies and so prevent enemy attacks."[15] In the course of everyday activities, as put by David Blanchard, "these priests served important functions for the Iroquois, acting as interpreters, teachers, and mediators between the Europeans, both English and French."[16] Gerald Taiaiake Alfred astutely reminds us that Indigenous persons at Caughnawaga and elsewhere "became Christians for a number of reasons, not the least of which was political."[17]

Jesuits played another very important role, which was to fix individual and family names. Bestowed at baptism and reinforced at marriage, first names were limited to those in the Catholic lexicon of acceptability. The distinctive surnames appended to first names appear to have been those already at play in the community and, more particularly, in the family. Although impossible to know with precision, the consequence was almost certainly that these surnames gave individuals greater senses of self than they would otherwise have possessed. They were each distinct persons and family members.

Jesuits were more accommodating of Indigenous ways than were their Protestant counterparts. Blanchard states that "the Jesuits were generally supportive of Iroquois culture."[18] With their own interests in mind, "black robes," as they were known for their dress, learned Indigenous languages and to some extent adapted to Indigenous ways of life. Hopkins points out that "Canadian Iroquois villages practiced traditional Iroquoian values of hospitality and entertained visitors with large receptions and plenty of food."[19] The Iroquois comprised a matrilineal society where descent passed through women and roles were carefully delineated. The membership of the Turtle, Wolf, and Bear clans organizing living arrangements and other aspects of everyday life was, Audra Simpson explains, "determined through matrilineal descent lines."[20] As had occurred at the mission's earlier locations, Caughnawaga's permanent site was laid out in a traditional Iroquois pattern, its growing numbers of longhouses, which averaged 18 by 6 metres, or 60 by 20 feet, being positioned close together, their front and back doors aligned north to south.[21]

Religious practices incorporated Iroquois preferences, as with the strong emphasis on music during the celebration of mass: "The savages Sing through nearly the whole of it, the men on one side and the women on the other."[22] By a second account, "All their prayers are set to music … Their voices are both mellow and sonorous, and their ears so correct that they do not miss a half-tone in all the church hymns, which they know by heart."[23] As explained by Jean-François Lozier, "the vocabulary of the new religion ... provided the social and cultural cement which generated a shared sense of belonging in the mission villages and allowed the formation of cohesive communities out of culturally heterogeneous fragments."[24]

Accommodation had its rewards. As early as 1676, a young Indigenous man who had been sent to France for his schooling, as was Jesuit practice for a select few, "constituted himself the Schoolmaster of the village" and "gathered all the Children of the village in his Cabin, in the evening after prayers."[25] According to Green, the early Jesuits did not encourage use of the French language, be it for schooling or the liturgy, and most inhabitants spoke the Mohawk variant of the Iroqouian language due to Mohawks' numerical predominance and to Caughnawaga's closer geographical proximity to their homeland than to that of any other of the Five Nations.[26]

This range of factors encouraged a sense of separation from other Iroquois, on the one hand, and from the oversight of the French and English, on the other hand.[27] As gleaned by Daniel K. Richter, "when Christians divorced themselves from ceremonies that had previously ratified their bonds to fellow villagers, they began to define themselves as a distinct people."[28] By the early eighteenth century, in the view of Jan Grabowski, a "shared sphere of common activities and interests" had made the Iroquois settlement "an integral part of the colonial society" in a "partner-like relationship."[29]

Owing also to proximity to Montreal, residents of Caughnawaga functioned, in Green's words, as "a quasi-independent middle group between the French and Five Nations, defying a dependent status."[30] By so doing, in the view of Lozier, they became "a military and diplomatic force to be reckoned with."[31] Gilles Havard describes how, "during the negotiations for the Great Peace of 1701," which ended almost a century of conflict between the various Indigenous peoples and France, "their diplomatic role ... was essential." Havard explains that, "marking the importance of this diplomatic site," delegates from the Five Nations and the Great Lakes who were on their way to Montreal for the peace talks separately stopped off for a day at Caughnawaga to be ritually welcomed and to hold a council. Havard makes the extremely important point that, by virtue of signing the resulting treaty, a chief from "the Sault," or Caughnawaga, and a chief from "La Montagne," or Lac des Deux Montagnes, were "making a de facto affirmation of their sovereignty despite the fact that they lived in the "colony" of New France.[32] They were self-determining their lives.

Another indication of the mission settlement's distinctiveness was coming into play. The English referred almost as a matter of course to "the praying Indians of Canada" and to "French praying Indians" in order to indicate, as one official put it, "Indians … instructed by the Jesuits."[33] The term became so commonplace that some of the Five Nations referred to visiting "the praying Indians of Canada" on their way, in the fall of 1692, to "Mount Reall" on a peace mission.[34] English officials became increasingly consternated by how the French "very much court the Five Nations of Indians to submit to the government of Canada, and by their Jesuits strangely allure them with their beades, crucifixes and little painted Images, gaining them many converts."[35] Although conflict would not cease, a more self-confident, less contentious way of life was coming into being.

A MATTER OF ECONOMICS

The Jesuits were not all about crucifixes and beads. What they sought for their charges, as did missionaries generally, was a settled economy based on agriculture. This goal was assisted by Iroquois already living in semi-permanent villages where they grew the precontact staples of corn, or maize, squash, and beans, sometimes planted together in small mounds.[36] As of 1682, according to the approving Jesuits, "We have here a large farm, on which we keep oxen, cows, and poultry, and gather corn for our subsistence … The men hunt, in order to obtain a provision of meat; The women go to the forests, to obtain supplies of wood," as well as to attend to the food crops.[37] From Jesuits' perspective, their charges obliged, but something more was going on. At the same time as "our Iroquois … are sedentary," the men departed at the end of September, "each taking his own road to the hunting grounds of the deer and beaver, nor do they return to the village before the month of february."[38]

This acknowledgment, almost in passing, that Iroquois incorporated beaver into their yearly round is revealing for its linkage to one of the principal means by which Indigenous peoples more generally accessed newcomer goods.[39] The importance early on that was attached to beaver, consumed fresh and dry in France, as well as to the sale of their pelts, with the matted underfur becoming the felt used for men's hats, long preceded

Caughnawaga and continued to be critical.[40] Even as early French arrival Samuel Champlain was heading up the St Lawrence River in 1603, prior to founding Quebec City, he appraised that route's utility for getting pelts to market.[41] Iroquois's frustration at being repeatedly caught between the French and the English related, on one level, to larger differences between the colonizers but, on another level, to access to "the place where we goe a Beaver hunting."[42]

Economics, more specifically beaver, was the underside, or rather the upside, of colonialism as enacted both by and respecting Caughnawaga. The French, English, and Dutch each proceeded as they did in good part because of the profits to be had thereby. Beaver pelts were the principal commodity having to be acquired for the colonial enterprise to be worthwhile, whatever the cost to Indigenous ways of life. Pelts were the currency of the day.

ALBANY'S CENTRALITY

Within this frame of mind, Iroquois along with other Indigenous peoples found it advantageous to trade the much sought beaver pelts where prices were highest and goods the most reasonable, which was at Albany. Skirting the Indigenous-white divide in order to do so was taken for granted, seemingly by all the parties.

Albany was located a very manageable 350 kilometres, or 215 miles, south of Caughnawaga via the appropriately named Iroquois (later Chambly and then Richelieu) River, which led to Lake Champlain and down the Hudson River.[43] As early as 1632, by one count, the Dutch traded in total "15000 Beaver Skynnes, besides other commodities."[44]

Earlier controlled by the Dutch, but by now an English possession, Albany was long the only site in the centrally located New York colony whose merchants were legally permitted to trade with Indigenous peoples. Albany had every advantage over its principal competitor of Montreal, whose merchants were tied to a monopoly company that exported beaver pelts to France on which a high duty was levied and acquired trade goods perforce from France. Prices offered per pelt were two or three times higher at Albany, and goods were of superior quality. England had been the earliest country to experience the Industrial Revolution. Particularly desirable was the woollen fabric known as strouds after the English town where it was manufactured.[45] Caughnawagas were at least once said to have "stated flatly they would rather be dead than deprived of English goods."[46] It was trade with Albany that honed the Caughnawagas' formidable skills and high reputation, which they would eventually extend across the North American continent as paddlers and trappers.

Albany depended on trade to survive, making the travel prohibitions against outsiders entering English territory that accompanied the intermittent warfare hard to abide. The finest skins originated in French territory, be they beaver, caribou, or muskrat. Caughnawagas, and more particularly the pelts they brought with them, were for that reason welcome, whether they arrived licitly or illicitly. Two English officials who had come by canoe from Albany to Montreal in 1698 for preliminary negotiations leading to the 1701 Great Peace, which was agreed between New France and Indigenous peoples, took pains to record that on the way there "we met a canoe, with French Indians, loaded with beavers, on their way to trade at Albany."[47]

While in Montreal, the English delegation quietly "encouraged some French Indians ... to accompany us and settle among us, promising to have them instructed in the Christian religion." Caughnawagas turned the invitation to their economic advantage, for what was awaiting the English upon arriving at the designated meeting point on their way back to Albany but "forty, including men and women, with five to six hundred beavers."[48] By virtue of travelling in the company of the two English officials, the entourage was not stopped along the way south, as it might have been, but rather slipped through to Albany with its furs.

IROQUOIS INITIATIVE

It has been estimated that by the turn of the eighteenth century half of the pelts originating in New France went through Albany as opposed to its economic hub of Montreal, where any consumer item cost two to four times as much as it did in Albany.[49] In June 1700 "the Sachims of the Canada praying Indians," a reference to Caughnawaga chiefs, had no difficulty in cementing a relationship with the English for trade in beaver skins.[50] It seems the French did not quite know what to do in response for fear of alienating the principal group of Iroquois on which they could potentially count in times of crises. As explained by Jean Lunn based on detailed primary research, "attempts were made, of course, to control the mission Indians, but the authorities never dared go so far as actually to forbid the savages, as they forbade the French, to trade at Albany."[51]

As described in records consulted by Lunn, Caughnawagas adopted varied trading strategies as circumstances warranted. In 1722 it was with tomahawks raised that they informed guards along the way of their destination and plans to return the same way. In 1731 empty canoes were sent past the checkpoints to distract the guards while pelts were portaged around them. In 1738 such small quantities of pelts were taken on each of many trips past the guards that it was not worthwhile for them to do anything. The same year, 200 Iroquois got permission in advance to take their cargo to Albany by threatening otherwise to settle among the Six Nations.[52]

The consequence was that, as well as trading pelts on their own behalves, which became more difficult as numbers of furbearing animals were depleted close to home, Caughnawagas functioned as middlemen.[53] A Montreal merchant's three daughters who ran a store in Caughnawaga from 1727 to 1752 were almost certainly complicit in the store's practice of accepting in payment beaver pelts that never made it to Montreal but rather found their way to Albany.[54] Caughnawagas were the conduit through which Montreal merchants were able, despite prohibitions on their trading in Albany, to access superior trade goods absolutely essential to their economic wellbeing.

Employing the characterizations of her time, Lunn described in 1939 how furs "in the town [of Montreal] were smuggled out to Caughnawaga in the baskets of the squaws." Women were sufficiently important that an Albany merchant's letter book distinguished two of the most "regular and faithful" traders as Marie Magdelaine and Agnese. In exchange for a considerable 10 to 12 per cent of the value, trusted Caughnawagas transported the furs to Albany and returned with the requested goods. To avoid pelts' owners being implicated in case of a mishap, the letter of instructions accompanying the cargo used a code word agreed upon in advance with their Albany counterpart as the means of identification. Summarizing the above merchant's letter book, Lunn stated that "the Indians usually arrived with the bulk of the shipment intact, but with five or ten pounds of fur missing," which was attributed to someone along the way taking out a beaver skin and making up the weight by wetting the furs or by adding sand to the pack, all of which caused Lunn to editorialize about how "it seems curious that large packs of valuable furs and goods should have been entrusted to anyone as notoriously untrustworthy as the Indian."[55] The author's need to do so, despite her amazing research, is a powerful reminder of how assumptions can intrude on one's findings.

The informal alliance between Caughnawaga and Albany lost its purpose with France's departure from North America in 1763. Not only could English goods now be got in Montreal, but Albany merchants also had a far greater territory in which to trade. The lessons that Caughnawagas took away from a half-century of challenging both the English and the French over access to Albany had to have been considerable. Iroquois had long been hunters and boatmen, but their paddling skills in particular must have been measurably improved by virtue of negotiating the perilous course between Caughnawaga and Albany.

FUNDAMENTAL POLITICAL CHANGE

These same years of the eighteenth century witnessed fundamental political change directly impacting Caughnawaga. Initially, it was more of the same. For all of the attention accorded the Great Peace of 1701, the initiative was short-lived. The next decades witnessed ongoing wars between France and Britain that had their origins in European conflicts, during which, as phrased by Blanchard: "The Iroquois sometimes sided with the French, other times with the English, but never against themselves. They supported no side, by supporting every side, and thus were insured of always being on the winning side." Quoting a Caughnawaga, Blanchard characterizes the Iroquois stance in the intermittent warfare extending from 1688 to 1763 as "aggressive neutrality."[56] Blanchard's perspective echoes an interview conducted in 1947 with a Caughnawaga who, on being asked about this long-ago time, responded similarly: "They were on both sides. They could not lose. One side had to win."[57]

Times were changing generally. By the 1730s, Richter argues, "the Six Nations were sinking into irrelevance in a region more and more dominated by Euro-Americans."[58] That Caughnawagas' numbers declined less rapidly than did those of some other Indigenous groups, even as newcomer totals grew, was due in part to the ongoing practice of adopting into the community Indigenous and non-Indigenous captives.[59] Acknowledging in 1735 that "the majority of the adults whom we instruct for baptism in the village are slaves taken in war," the Jesuit in charge at Caughnawaga observed that, except for their presence, numbers "are visibly on the decrease."[60] That year, the longstanding and ongoing fur trade between Caughnawaga and Albany, with its concomitant of everyday knowledge of the English language, was formalized in a treaty.

By the mid-eighteenth century, Caughnawaga's population was a thousand or more, and with its freestanding shops and residents possibly conversant in English, the community was both the bane and the envy of its Six Nations counterparts.[61] Indicative of the continuing priority accorded economics was a report prepared for William Johnson upon his being given oversight of the Six Nations in 1755, to be followed a year later by his appointment as British superintendent of Indian affairs. Johnson was well aware of how, to the distress of the Six Nations, "the Cognawagas who were absolutely in the French interest were permitted to trade openly at Albany."[62] Johnson's correspondence indicates that he had a grudging respect for their initiative and did not want it discouraged, hence his order of 1755 that "the Cagnawaga Indians who may come to Albany, receive no disturbance or Injury" or "ill usage of any kind."[63]

As a consequence, in the ensuing global military conflict between France and Britain, with its North American reach, William Johnson found it "most provokingly Insolent" that the Caughnawagas had "taken up the Hatchet against us."[64] The war's conclusion was fundamental in both its immediate and longer-term consequences. In a 1759 battle, and formally in 1763, France lost New France to Britain, and two decades later Britain would cede thirteen of its colonies along the East Coast, which became the independent United States. Overseen by William Johnson, the Indian Department thereupon took charge of Quebec, including its Indigenous peoples.

ENGAGING THE NEW ORDER OF THINGS

Caughnawaga was, Green reminds us, well situated to take advantage of the new order of things:

> They maintained their identity in the face of strong pressure from both the Iroquois League and the French. Although overseen by Jesuit missionaries, the Kahnawakes managed to retain much of their

independence and self-determination … The Kahnawakes forced the French, the English, and the Iroquois League to deal with them as a separate power in the geopolitics of northeastern North America. They are an example of a native group which adapted to changing circumstances but kept control over the adaptations they made and changed in ways which kept their identity and autonomy intact.[65]

Caughnawagas continued to do well. Consistent with his earlier interest, a gathering assisted by William Johnson in September 1763 in the aftermath of New France's demise included both "the Six Nations, and Indians of Caughnawaga, in Canada," among the eighteen Indigenous peoples invited.[66] Caughnawaga, whose population Johnson described as "emigrants from the Mohocks," along with "a few at Aghquissasne [Akwesasne]," accounted for 300 of the adult males under his charge.[67] The Caughnawagas did everything right at this key event and got their reward. Taking the initiative in the morning of the second day,

> The *Caughnawagas* acquainted Sir William that, since they had unexpectedly found the Six Nations there, they judged it necessary to have a Meeting with them; which was accordingly held that morning, with the general meeting only subsequently convened. Johnson addressed them privately at the end of the general proceedings.

>> "Brethren of Cagnawaga. I have heard with satisfaction the speech you made to the Six Nations in general, and to the Senecas in particular. The manner in which you expressed your disapprobation of their Conduct Convinces me of your sincerity and good sense, and in justice to you, I shall … send it home, that the Great King may know your good disposition and honest intention."[68]

Caughnawaga appears to have prospered during the second half of the eighteenth century.[69] In 1773 the Catholic Church suppressed the Jesuits worldwide, and although the bishop of Quebec refused to accept the decision, the order atrophied with secular priests in charge. The land on which Caughnawaga sat was now managed by the Indian Department on its residents' behalf. One of the department's obligations was to collect rents on parcels that, from the beginning of the century, the Jesuits had ceded to non-Indigenous peoples. The sums collected were to be distributed to the Iroquois but in practice were mismanaged or used for church repairs.[70] All the same, Caughnawaga remained its own entity to the extent that it was neutral during the hostilities that led to the formation of the United States not long afterward.[71]

During these same years, the Iroquois League atrophied. Already weakened by population decline and growing numbers of newcomers on its territory, members' involvement in the war whereby the United States gained its independence left the league, in William J. Campbell's apt characterization, "tattered" and "splintered."[72] The Mohawks' close alignment with the British, due in part to their leader Joseph Brant being Johnson's de facto brother-in-law, led in the war's aftermath to their being granted territory in the remaining British possession, which comprised former New France, now divided between Lower Canada, or future Quebec, and Upper Canada, or future Ontario.[73] Other parts of the once proud Six Nations lying in what was now the United States got on with the new order of things as best they could.[74]

ENTERING THE NINETEENTH CENTURY

As the eighteenth century drew to a close, in the assessment of long-time English trader and interpreter John Long, Caughnawaga had "about two hundred houses ... chiefly built of stone" and a population of "about eight hundred."[75] A much higher estimate puts the total at 1,800.[76] In Long's view, Caughnawaga "is considered the most respectable of all the Indian villages, and the people are in a great degree civilized and industrious."[77] The residents' way of life and clothing differed little from that of their white neighbours.

Caughnawaga and the two smaller communities of St Régis and Lac des Deux Montagnes, the latter of which, according to Long, had "about two hundred inhabitants, who are very industrious," were at turning points.[78] On the one hand, residents of all three continued to be marked by strong senses of self and, reinforced by intermarriage, of community. Referring to St Régis, another trader was struck by how "these people have been instructed in reading and writing in their own language, and are better instructed than the Canadian inhabitants of the country of the lower ranks."[79] There from 1768 to 1788, Long early on had learned "the Iroquois and French languages." Indicative of Iroquois's independent character, the residents of Caughnawaga, Long reported, "have a French priest … who instructs them, and performs divine service in the Iroquois tongue."[80]

The three communities were as distinctive physically as they had ever been. One of the Jesuits in charge at Caughnawaga described how "side by side with the Iroquois other savages seem dwarfed," given that "nearly all the men of our mission are nearer six feet in height than five." By his measure, "their stature, and their features are regular," and "their complexion is of an olive tint that is not so tawny as that of other tribes, not differing much from that of the portuguese."[81] A later observer evoked Caughnawagas' "angular features, piercing black eyes, the guttural accents of the native language, the swarthy bronze complexions in evidence everywhere."[82]

At the same time, the three communities' self-containment facilitated by trapping and hunting was becoming a thing of the past. Not enough animals could be had close at hand or at a near distance to provide food and pelts to trade for needed goods. In 1790, as explained by Long, they still "kill beaver and deer, but not in such great abundance at present as they did formerly, the country being better inhabited … It is not improbable, that in a few years there will not be many good hunters among them."[83] The alternative increasingly became wage labour drawing on familiar skills.

TO SUM UP

The many writers who have described and interpreted Caughnawaga agree that the community was distinctive. Rather than existing since time immemorial in the pattern of indigeneity as it is conceived generally across North America, at some point persons chose to live there. For all that the Jesuits were long nominally in charge, Caughnawaga was essentially a self-creation, which caused its residents to be more self-determining than they would likely have become in other circumstances. Their trapping and trading skills were well in place, alongside confident dispositions. They were their own Iroquois selves.

Heading West, Maybe Forever, Maybe Not

During the first two decades of the nineteenth century, life changed for some Iroquois from Caughnawaga, St Régis, and Lac des Deux Montagnes. Over 600 men from the three communities are recorded by name as heading west to areas of North America beyond white settlers' grasp. Iroquois's skill as paddlers, and also as trappers, going back in time to the Albany trade, caused them to be recruited into a westward-expanding fur trade. Whereas most soon returned home, a minority stayed away, maybe forever, maybe not.

Persons perceived as Indigenous could not in general easily find workplace niches in non-Indigenous economies, whereas Iroquois were in demand. Their history made them aware that they needed to take the initiative as opportunities came their way, and they did so. Men and their families, and also the communities from which they came, were as a consequence a little better off.

A FLUID ECONOMY

The North American fur trade was by its nature a fluid economy. As areas became trapped out, it was necessary to move into parts of the continent not yet overwhelmed by newcomers. From the time of New France's beginnings in the early 1600s, France claimed exclusive rights to trap and trade in a vast swath of territory extending west and south from today's Quebec. Initially not in direct competition, the Hudson's Bay Company (HBC), formed in London in 1670, was given exclusive rights to trade in the vast area to the north drained by Hudson Bay. England's defeat of

France in 1760 rearranged the fur trade. Not only was New France now in English hands, but the economy that sustained it was as well.

English-speaking traders, who were increasingly dominant in Montreal, looked ever farther afield for areas not yet exploited and for employees, both officers in charge and everyday workers, sometimes termed servants. The economy was able to expand as rapidly as it did due to the area from Montreal as far west as the Rocky Mountains being navigable by water, hence the demand for paddlers. In 1783 Montreal traders joined together to form the North West Company (NWC), a loose coalition in which men were allotted shares and in practice continued to operate largely independent of each other, establishing their own trading posts, as also did the HBC. The consequence was a free-for-all with, to quote Charles M. Gates, "almost no restrictions."[1] Six hundred trading posts, mostly ephemeral and fleeting, were constructed between 1774 and 1821, 350 by Montreal traders and 250 under HBC auspices.[2] The HBC's takeover of the NWC in 1821 closed down the competition and ended Iroquois's sustained recruitment. By then the fur trade had crossed the Rocky Mountains and was firmly in place in the Pacific Northwest.

RECRUITING IROQUOIS

Unlike the HBC, which had long hired from Scotland and England, companies based in Montreal relied on French speakers. Men of the first generation were known as Canadiens and their children born in the fur trade by Indian women as "Métis," being the French word for persons of mixed Indian and non-Indian, usually white, descent. Eventually, the Canadian Constitution of 1982, section 35(1), would expand the then preferred term of "aboriginal peoples" to include "the Indian, Inuit and Métis peoples of Canada," to be followed by a 2013 federal court ruling in *Daniels v. Canada* that both Métis and others of mixed Indigenous descent should be considered "Indians" under subsection 91(24) of the Constitution Act of 1867.[3] A consequence has been that the term "Métis" is applied ever more generally and generously to encompass all Canadians, past and present, not wholly Indigenous but laying claim to some Indigneous descent.[4]

Carolyn Podruchny puts the number of French speakers in the fur trade at a thousand or more at the turn of the nineteenth century, a total that would double and possibly triple over the next two decades.[5] Thus Iroquois come into view as being not so very different from Canadiens and Métis in sharing paternal origins in New France, the Catholic religion, including first names so derived, and to some extent language.[6] There was at the same time a fundamental difference in that the second and subsequent generations of Iroquois in the West who were born to local Indigneous women did not embody the white descent commonly associated with being Métis. Iroquois descendants would not define themselves as Métis, or be so defined by others, but would be known, as were their forefathers, as Iroquois.

It is impossible to know with certainty when Iroquois began heading west. As early as 1794, "3 Iroquois" are said to have deserted an independent trader on the North Saskatchewan River, which cuts across today's Saskatchewan and Alberta, in favour of the NWC.[7] Another contemporary account describes "a small colony of Iroquois, emigrated to the banks of the Saskatchiwine, in 1799, who had been brought up from their infancy under the Romish missionaries, and instructed by them at a village within nine miles [15 kilometres] of Montreal," which was Caughnawaga.[8] By 1800, unnamed Iroquois, sometimes termed "Mohawks," were noted as a matter of course in post journals.[9]

Some claims come across as grandiose, pointing more to Iroquois distinctiveness than to numbers per se. A NWC partner asserted in 1795, "You will meet with an Iroquois from Montreal at the foot of the Rocky Mountain; and a Chipewean from Hudson Bay" who "have their families and properties with them." Their independence awed him: "They have it in their power to settle where they please – Or continue their course to Asia or Greenland, if they find it passable and suitable to their convenience and fancy."[10] In 1802 the officer in charge of Cumberland House, an HBC post on the Saskatchewan River in northeast Saskatchewan, ranted against the NWC for having brought in over 300 "Eroquees or Mohawk Indians" on three-year contracts who left "nothing wherever they Come," meaning "the destruction of the beaver" at the HBC's cost.[11]

A counterpoint to these assertions are the contracts that prospective employees signed, almost all with their marks, as searched out and made accessible by Nicole St-Onge and her colleagues. Differing not at all from those agreed upon by Canadiens and others, surviving contracts are accessible on the website of the Société historique de Saint-Boniface and are used with permission.[12] Among the Voyageur Contracts Database's over 35,000 contracts negotiated between 1714 and 1830 in the presence of Montreal notaries are 1,100 signed between 1800 and 1821 with Iroquois from Caughnawaga, Lac des Deux Montagnes, or St Régis.[13] The year 1800 signals Iroquois's appearance in numbers in the database, and the year 1821 marks their receding from view after the HBC, based elsewhere, took charge.

By a matching process described in the research note at the end of this volume, these 1,100 contracts were attached to 530 named Iroquois from one of the three communities, half of whom signed a single contract and the others two or more. To this total were added another 85 named Iroquois from the three communities who were identified in other primary sources, including the surviving NWC ledger for 1811–21,[14] as working in the fur trade during these years. The total number of named Iroquois rounds off to 600.

The just over 600 named Iroquois who engaged with the fur trade between 1800 and 1821 are a starting point as opposed to the unknowable total number who did so over the two decades or across time. Another 200 contracts in the Voyageur Contracts Database that are not included in the 600 were signed in Caughnawaga by named persons unable to be identified as Iroquois, some or all of whom may have been non-Iroquois residents or may have come there only for the purpose of signing a contract.[15] Other contracts have almost certainly not survived or were oral agreements, and some Iroquois appear to have headed west on their own volition. Iroquois also worked in the fur trade prior to 1800 and subsequent to 1821, including Louis Oteakorie, discussed in the introduction, and those heading to the Pacific Northwest through 1858, profiled in chapter 5. The total number of Iroquois who engaged the fur trade is impossible to know.

It is also the case that larger totals are demographically hard to sustain given the populations from which Iroquois came. The minimum number of 600 named Iroquois who engaged the fur trade between 1800 and 1821 is feasible, given that it cuts across generations, but just so. Caughnawaga, the home parish of 9 in 10 of the 600 named Iroquois extracted from the Voyageur Contracts Database, had in 1800 a population, depending on the estimate, between 800 and 1,800.[16] As of 1815, Caughnawaga is said to have had 900 houses.[17] A government census taken in 1825 put Caughnawaga's population at 1,003, Lac des Deux Montagnes's at 248, and St Régis's at 441.[18] Unless otherwise specified, the minimum total of 600 named Iroquois signing contracts between 1800 and 1821 is used in the text.

TO BE A PADDLER

Paddling was at the heart of Iroquois's participation in the fur trade. Almost 9 in 10, or 950, of the 1,100 contracts with the 600 named Iroquois were agreements to paddle back and forth between specified destinations on behalf of one of the numerous companies involved in the fur trade. The other 150 contracts were for a period of employment ranging from one to six years, which might centre on paddling or alternatively on trapping.

To be a paddler was to head west with men and trade goods along well-travelled water routes and, usually within a week of reaching their destination, to return east with men and animal pelts. It was generally accepted by this time that Iroquois were excellent paddlers: "There they are! Yes, there they were. Coming along with the full swing of eight paddles, swept a large North-west canoe, its Iroquois paddlers timing their strokes to an old French chant as they shot down towards the river's source."[19] Iroquois sometimes formed the majority or even entirety of a canoe's crew, and at other times they comprised a minority among men who were likely but not necessarily Canadiens.

The tasks accorded the eight to twelve paddlers of the large canoes, 7.5 metres, or 25 feet, in length, that headed west from Montreal as soon as the ice receded in the spring were sharply differentiated. A "devant," or bowsman, at the front manoeuvred through what lay ahead and set the pace for paddling, whereas a "gouvernail," or steersman, at the stern had overall responsibility for the canoe. These two "boutes," also known as endmen, used paddles 2 to 2.75 metres, or 6.5 to 9 feet, in length to get purchase while standing so as to see what lay ahead, below, and around. Their capacity was repeatedly tested by rapids and falls that needed to be navigated or alternatively portaged, which entailed men carrying the canoe, along with its contents in packs on their backs, to the next accessible waterway. There might also be a guide with overall responsibility for several canoes travelling together. The routine paddling was done by "milieux," or middlemen, who had short paddles around 1.25 metres, or 4 feet, in length.

Roughly 600 of the more than 1,000 paddling contracts that Iroquois signed over the two decades were as middlemen, another 60 as seconds apprenticing to be endmen, just over 180 each as bowsmen and steersmen, and 15 as guides. Among Iroquois who paddled more than once, as many

Figure 2.1
Paddling a canoe, by Carl W. Bertsch, 1931

Figure 2.2 *Opposite*
Managing a canoe, by Carl W. Bertsch, 1931

Figure 2.3 *Above*
Portaging a canoe, by Carl W. Bertsch, 1931

rose in position as remained the same or fell back, suggesting that an opportunity to be employed may have mattered more than did the particular
position in a canoe.

Iroquois and others paddled by set routines that differed only in their
destinations.[20] Each day began well before dawn, with breaks for meals
along the way. For up to sixteen hours, middlemen paddled forty to fifty
strokes a minute, with canoes averaging 7 to 9 kilometres, or 4 to 6 miles,
an hour. Speed was of the essence given that only five months separated
the ice breaking up and the water freezing again on northern waterways.

The starting point was Lachine on Montreal's south shore, with a req-
uisite stop at the Catholic mission of Ste Anne to ask for the priest's blessing on the hazardous voyage about to be undertaken. Men and canoes
headed up the St Lawrence River to the Ottawa River and then to its junction with the Mattawa River. There, a choice had to be made, depending
on the final destination, about whether to continue on the northward-
turning Ottawa or go west on the Mattawa.

Those opting for the Ottawa River in due course reached the NWC post
of Fort Temiskaming on the lake of the same name. That area had a long
association with the fur trade and with Iroquois from Lac des Deux Montagnes, consequent on a trader from there in the late 1700s making that
community his base of operations to trap in the vicinity. Ongoing tensions
with local Indigenous peoples and the reluctance of Canadiens to be employed contributed to a reliance on Iroquois.[21] A remarkable 230 contracts,
or 1 in 5 of the total number signed over the two decades between 1800 and
1821, were agreements to paddle to and from Temiskaming. Among those
doing so, Louison (or Louis) l'Iroquois from Lac des Deux Montagnes
signed five contracts beginning in 1797 and extending to 1807 to paddle
principally there and back, initially as a milieu but after the first two trips
as a devant. René Caraquanon paddled eight times between 1800 and 1811,
Thomas Comontesa three times in 1802–03, Joseph Choritéa three times
in 1809–10, and the list goes on.

From Temiskaming, it was possible to continue to the long-established
HBC post of Moose Factory on James Bay at the southern end of Hudson
Bay and, from 1800, also to a nearby NWC competitor. Between 1800 and
1808, Iroquois made seventy trips to Moose Factory, which repeatedly
agitated nearby competitors. In 1804 came an HBC report of "three large
canoes mann'd by Iroquois chiefly … arrived at our Opponents Settle-

ment," a year later three more canoes "manned by 18 Iroquois" arrived, and so it went.[22]

Most canoes, on reaching the junction of the Ottawa and Mattawa Rivers, continued not on the Ottawa but rather up the Mattawa through a combination of small waterways and portages to Lake Nipissing, from which the French River led to Lake Huron. The Jay Treaty, signed in 1794 in the aftermath of American independence, ran the boundary between Britain and the new United States through the Great Lakes to Rainy Lake on the way to Lake of the Woods. To the west at Lake Huron's junction with Lake Michigan lay Michilimackinac Island. Although the post was surrendered to the United States in 1796, it was long given as many Iroquois's paddling destination.

The 250 contracts having Michilimackinac as the final destination were never more significant than during the War of 1812 between Britain and the young United States. "The struggle for the fur country," as it was termed, centred on Michilimackinac Island, which if nominally American had been, in the words of Pierre Berton, "an economic no man's land, where British traders operate easily."[23] British forces captured the island early in the war and were determined to hold it, even after their supply lines running through similarly captured Detroit were cut when Americans retook Detroit in the fall of 1813. Americans wanted the island back, but by the time their forces arrived the next summer, British defences fortified by Indigenous volunteers were at the ready and won the day.

Iroquois appear to have helped provision the British troops. Berton's reference to American efforts during the summer of 1814 "to intercept the great fur canoes of the North West Company" and his reference to "two American schooners … seeking the North West Company's fur canoes" tally with large numbers of Iroquois and others signing contracts to head there.[24] The NWC hired 50 Iroquois from Caughnawaga on 15 May 1814 and more on other dates. During the week of 9 to 17 September, the government hired, along with over 200 Canadien paddlers, 75 Iroquois, some of them returnees from the earlier trip, to head to British-held Michilimackinac. The notary witnessing the contracts applauded, as he had done earlier, Iroquois's willingness to so engage.

Not far from Michilimackinac lay the NWC trading crossroads of Sault Ste Marie. More than a hundred contracts sent Iroquois there between 1815 and 1819. In 1817 a cross-country brigade heading east passed a NWC officer along with thirteen soldiers and "twelve well-armed Iroquois" on their way to Red River in the aftermath of a dispute with HBC interests.[25]

Some destinations were still farther on. On the north shore of Lake Superior lay the NWC's principal rendezvous and storage site of Grand Portage, whose origins went back to 1681 as New France's Fort Kaministiquia, named after the river of that name. Since Grand Portage had landed in American territory by the terms of the Jay Treaty of 1794, the NWC replaced it in 1803 with Fort William at the northwestern end of Lake Superior, safely on British soil.

It was at Grand Portage and later Fort William that those managing the large Montreal canoes exchanged trade goods for pelts before turning back. Along with their trade goods, those going farther west transferred to smaller canoes with half the capacity and crews of five or six.[26] Some 30 contracts had Iroquois heading to Fort William via Michilimackinac. Another 175 Iroquois contracts had men stopping at Fort William on their way west. Possibly due to their numbers, Iroquois are said to have had their own encampment there, separate from those of Canadiens and other employees.[27] North and west of Lake Superior lay what was known, enigmatically and sometimes almost idyllically so, as the Northwest or alternatively as "pays sauvages," or wild country. One or the other was named as the destination on 100 contracts, mostly for fixed time periods.

Paddling contracts had advantages for men agreeing to them, and for their families, as they specified in advance the amounts, means, and timing of reimbursement. Contracts for the spring were often negotiated far in advance of departure to ensure that companies acquired their full complement of personnel and thus could head out as soon as it was possible to do so. Recruiters went from location to location throughout the winter searching out prospective employees. Indicative of what generally occurred are fifteen identical contracts by which Caughnawaga Iroquois agreed on 4 December 1800 to paddle to Moose Factory and back, which were followed two weeks later by three more such contracts. Men's wages ranged from 250 to 300 livres, being the French currency of the day. There was usually an advance on signing, which could be shared with others, and in some cases sums could be made available to a wife, mother, or other person while the employee was away. The final payment was made in Montreal following his return.[28] Not only could men make provisions in advance to support those left behind, but the moneys entering local economies were substantial.

In a good year for hiring, some men made two or even three trips a season. Initially contracted in St Régis in February 1801, Jacques Tawanthus was rehired that November to head out in the spring, returning in time to contract in August for what must have been a late-summer trip given that he signed on again in November 1802 to paddle the next spring. Following a four-year hiatus, possibly due to the tiny handfuls of Iroquois then being hired, Tawanthus contracted in August 1807 and thereby appears to have gotten in a short late-season trip given that he was hired again the next March and the next year in both March and August, followed by August 1810 and January 1811. Tawanthus's last paddles on record were during the War of 1812 and then in its aftermath, for a total of a dozen trips between 1801 and 1816 as a clearly dependable milieu. Thereupon he disappears from view in the records that were located. As with Tawanthus, Iroquois's decisions about whether to persist as paddlers in the fur trade were not necessarily, but possibly, of their making.

However short or long, each trip was its own adventure, with all of the comradery and hardships that ensued. For some men, once was enough, or perhaps their skills were such that they were not rehired. For others, paddling gave a rhythm, a routine, and an economic base to their lives. The work had a comforting certainty about it, as did the sociability ensuing between men in close proximity for days, weeks, and months on end. Paddling with others gave them a kind of assurance that the way of life they knew was comfortably in place and that they would soon be returning home more self-confident and better off than they would otherwise have been.

MAKING INDIVIDUAL DECISIONS
WITHIN CONSTRAINTS

For half of those signing more than a single paddling contract, the time period between their first and last agreements was two to five years, for another third it was six to ten years, and for the remaining quarter it was as long as the full two decades. Uneven access to employment meant that many, if not most, Iroquois made decisions within constraints not of their making.

The intermittent nature of men's contracts is explained in part by the differing opportunities available but also by individual choices. Lazard

Anthonytenwash contracted on 4 March 1808 to paddle to and from
Temiskaming as a milieu. Although impossible to know with certainty, he
may well have returned home to raise a family given that he does not turn
up again until ten years later, agreeing on 12 March 1818 to a three-year
contract to head to the Northwest as a devant. He is recorded in the NWC's
ledger and account books as being employed from 1819 to 1821 in
Athabasca, today's province of Alberta, with cash from his wage going to
his wife.[29]

Friendships may help to explain how some Iroquois approached the fur
trade. In what was a typical hiring, between 29 January and 3 February
1809, notary John Beck hired eight Caughnawaga Iroquois, together with
four Canadiens from various Quebec locations, on identical contracts
to paddle to Fort William, on to Lac la Pluie on the border between today's
Ontario and Minnesota, and then back to Montreal. The gouvernails and
devants were promised 400 livres a month after returning to Montreal,
and the milieux received 250 livres, with small advances upon signing that
would be deducted from the total amount. The men would be provided
with "a 3-point blanket," the number of points denoting its size, "3 yards
of cotton, a pair of leather shoes, and a tumpline" for carrying goods over
portages.[30] Just two of the eight, one of whom was on his first trip, had not
previously paddled together. Devant Pierre Ounaratier, gouvernail Thomas
Osarakwa, and milieu Thomas Yocantez had already paddled at least five
times with one or more of the others, as had gouvernail and subsequently
devant Thomas Tecatariacon three times and two others twice. Following
the 1809 trip, Ounaratier, Osarakwa, Yocantez, and Tecatariacon would
each paddle another four times with one or more of the others. Paddling
was for these men a way of being and of belonging.

Familial ties also played a role in decisions. The presence of numerous
similar or identical surnames argues for relatives making decisions together
or similarly. Antoine, Étienne, and Michel Hotesse were hired on together
as milieux in the first years of the century, with two of them later signing
multi-year contracts. Michel and Paul Ouamtany were each contracted for
six trips as milieux between 1801 and 1809, half of them together, whereupon Paul seems to have gone on to other things whereas Michel stuck
around, being dispatched in 1816 to the Pacific Northwest, where he died
in 1828.

However short or long Iroquois paddled, the experience had to have altered their outlooks. For the most part, they travelled routes already familiar to those in charge, but their doing so did not take away from the newness of glimpsing the West for the first time and then again each time they went.

Whereas some men held on, others did not do so through no fault of their own. Indicative of what happened more generally, on 22 October 1803 an HBC clerk reported from Fort Alexandria on the Assiniboine River about 200 kilometres, or 125 miles, northwest of today's Brandon, Manitoba, that "this afternoon one of our Men (an Iroquois) departed this life, and it is thought what harried him out of this World was, his having forced too much in carrying in the Portages on his way in a circumstance that occasions the death of many of our People yearly."[31] Some Iroquois never returned home not by choice but by circumstance.

STICKING WITH THE FUR TRADE

Three factors encouraged some Iroquois to do more than glimpse the West as they passed by on the water. The first was agreement to a term contract, which was a wholly different proposition from a paddling contract. Of 1,100 surviving contracts signed by Iroquois between 1800 and 1821, just 150 were for time periods ranging from one to six years. Two-thirds of them were for paddlers and the other third for "chasseurs," being hunters and trappers. Term contracts put their holders, be they paddlers or chasseurs, on the ground as opposed to almost solely on the water. Most term contracts were a function of distance, stipulating only a broad destination. In almost half of them, it was the Northwest or the North, and in others it was the "pays sauvages." The Northwest had an enigmatic quality, being described by a NWC partner early on as "all that extensive Country which lies between Lake Superior and the Frozen ocean, between Hudson's Bay and the river of the West – many parts of which are very little known except from Indian Reports."[32]

Chasseurs's contracts were distinctive in that, rather than a salary, they enumerated the goods and equipment that would be provided at a cost, the prices paid for the pelts they were expected to deliver, and the locations to which they were to be taken. Chasseurs were not employees as such but rather engaged the fur trade on their own recognizance. The contracting of chasseurs was limited to Iroquois, whose reputation was enhanced by their employing the latest trapping technology. The process had been revolutionized toward the end of the eighteenth century on the realization that the iron or steel traps used to catch larger animals would be effective with the much-prized beaver when baited with a twig dipped in the castoreum of the female.[33]

A second option for Iroquois wanting to do more than glimpse the West was to sign or renew a contract while away from home. Those that survive, which are few, argue that paddlers might be from time to time implored to do so. We do not know the means by which fifteen named Iroquois under the leadership of Charles Kanawata, described as "an Iroquois chief," got to the West, an earlier contract being located for only one of them, but in 1805 they all agreed at the NWC post of Fort Vermilion on the Peace River in today's northern Alberta to trap over the next year.[34] A clerk reported from there in 1808, very possibly referring to the same men, that "a few Iroquois from Canada hunt hereabouts."[35] A decade later the rival HBC attributed Fort Vermilion's success to "sixteen freemen Canadian Iroquois, men partly worn out in their service whom they have, without making them quite free, permitted to go and kill furs on their own account and these people apply themselves to killing Beaver with an application unknown to the Indians."[36] "Freemen" was the term used for men who, upon a contract's expiry, had opted to live on their own resources, trading pelts for needed goods.

Similarly, in the fall of 1819 an HBC officer instructed his junior on the ground respecting four unnamed Iroquois and a Canadien,

> As the contracts of some of the above mentioned Servants expire in May, and as they cannot come to [the NWC post of] St. Mary's [located at the confluence of the Smoky and Peace Rivers in today's central Alberta] to effect an engagement at this place, you will consider the services of these individuals necessary to accomplish the desired objects, re-engage them on their former terms, but should they insist on an advance of wages, you will not exceed what you conceive their Services will fully warrant.[37]

Indicative of Iroquois ambition and determination, back in due course came the reply that the men would "not engage unless I gave them seventy-five pounds."[38] The junior officer was thereupon instructed "to re-engage the Iroquois and Hunters on the most advantageous terms without delay, in which I trust you will find little difficulty."[39] Back came the complaint that "the Iroquois who undertook to conduct and introduce us to the Natives will not re-engage until all doubts are removed as to his safety."[40] From the HBC's perspective, the situation was no better a month later when it was reported that "the Iroquois intended for New Caledonia [today's central British Columbia] do not renew their Engagements."[41] Iroquois knew their own minds and used them to advantage.

A third possibility was simply to stay on in the West at a contract's end. Whether as paddlers or especially as chasseurs, their time there gave them a preview of what lay ahead if they did so. Given that no records follow men home, it is impossible to know how many Iroquois were enticed by this option, but it was certainly feasible.

IROQUOIS ON THE GROUND

Iroquois on the ground, as opposed to paddling canoes, faced their own challenges, much as had *coureurs de bois*, independent Canadiens active early on in the fur trade. One of the earliest recorded references to named Iroquois resulted from NWC officer David Thompson in November 1800, at the initiative of his superiors, successfully negotiating with a Peigan chief in today's southern Alberta "about introducing a number of Iroquois and Saulteaux into the country about the mountains." Thompson requested permission for them "to cross Peigan territory and trap beaver in the mountains."[42] A few days later, in a conversation with another chief, Thompson "again introduced the subject of the Iroquois and Saulteaux, which met with a better and more ready reception here, indeed they were well pleased with it."[43]

Likely as a consequence of the news travelling, on 21 February 1801, as recorded in the Voyageur Contracts Database, "four Iroquois" named as Charles Simonet, Joseph Théawaygatay, Louis Tzouraquize, and Charles Annaharrison signed two-year contracts in Caughnawaga with the New North West Company, also known as the XY Company, "to leave their village in the spring as soon as it was possible to travel to the high country or the vast interior known as the Northwest and there for two consecutive years to hunt for wild animals and collect all the skins and furs they can."[44]

The Montreal notary's first language was English, which Simonet trans-
lated into French for the others, having likely picked it up during his earlier
one-year contract signed in 1798 as a milieu. An advance may have gone
to his family, given that four years later, on 20 February 1805, the long-serv-
ing Simonet would sign a contract alongside his son Jean Baptiste Anoniata. While away, Simonet would have money paid to his wife in 1815 and
to a daughter in 1816.

According to these four Iroquois's identical 1801 contracts, they were
each to be furnished with unspecified goods and food rations and to have
payments deposited into their accounts based on an agreed price per pelt
depending on whether it came from a beaver, marten, muskrat, or some
other animal. The pelts, which they were explicitly prohibited from selling
to anyone else, were to be delivered to agents of the company that had hired
them, either directly or at the long-established fur trade post of Grand
Portage. "They put their marks only after having had everything explained
in their language by the said Charles Simonet."[45]

Likely due to news spreading of the opportunity to be had, six days later
two more Iroquois, Pierre Atthéhiton from Caughnawaga and Louis
Awhona Karah from Lac des Deux Montagnes, joined the others. On 13
March 1801 so did two more Iroquois from Caughnawaga, Joseph Jotzen-
hohané and Ignace Ranazatirchon. In line with their principal obligation
over the two years of their contracts, one of their number, Charles Annaharrison, was described on his contract as a second gouvernail capable of
having charge of a canoe, likely the one taking them westward, the others
doing the paddling.

Even as the New North West Company was recruiting, so was the North
West Company, which on 23 February 1801 signed two-year contracts with
eight Lac des Deux Montagnes men, named as Ignace Caiatonie, Louis
Cassaquontie, Philip Chinaquina, François Choriohwarrie, Alexander
Nashotha, Jean Baptiste Quontietie, Joseph Sassanowanany, and Louis
Thoweagarat. "The so-called Iroquois Indians wishing to go hunting in
that part of the Wild Country called the Northwest under the protection
of the said North West Company"[46] had identical contracts that described
in detail which animals they were to hunt for what recompense. Equipment and food would be provided, but it appears that this would be only
during the trips west and back.

The contracts as usual favoured the company. "The said Iroquois Indians" were "to hunt and collect fur pelts" in their exchanges with local Indigenous peoples who had pelts to trade, drawing on "a small assortment of Goods" provided by the company on credit at "a quarter below" their market value. As for the pelts so acquired, "each and every one of" the men were obliged "to reserve them and to preserve them and to deliver them" to the NWC at preset prices, with their accounts to be so credited in Montreal. Not only were the hires forbidden to trade with anyone else for any purpose, but "none of them may remain in the said lands of the North West after the said 3 years" of their contracts.[47] That such conditions were repeated in other Iroquois's contracts likely did little to stop those deciding to stay in the West from doing so.

Four years later, in 1805, the same Charles Simonet was among a clutch of Iroquois contracted to head to the Northwest as chasseurs. On 20 February he signed with the NWC for two years, alongside his son Jean Baptiste Anoniata, who was hired as a milieu. Whereas the two Simonets signed for two years, four other Caughnawagas – Guillaume Ganerérogen, Louis Taritha, and Charles Teharongatha, along with Pierre Tonenitogan, described as a chief – had just done so on 3 February for three years. They were followed by Louis Karakontie and Ignace Kayenthoway from Lac des Deux Montagnes on 4 April, who each also signed for three years.

Just under half of this cluster of term employees appear at least once in other sources. "Simonette, Charles & son," so named in the NWC ledger, were employed in 1811–12 and again from 1815–18, as were "Ignace Kayenthoway (& associates)" from 1812–18, with no indication of who the associates were. In 1815 Simonet's son Jean contracted with the HBC to paddle as a devant. Louis Tzouraquize was employed from 1811–13 and possibly in 1822, and Philip Chinaquina was hired as a paddler in 1815.

Chief Pierre Tonenitogan, who was contracted in 1805, was almost certainly the Pierre Tevanitagon listed in the NWC ledger for 1812–20 who thereupon headed to the Pacific Northwest,[48] where he would directly challenge fur trade pricing for pelts prior to engaging the American West, as narrated in chapter 4. One of the Iroquois joining with Tevanitagon would be Charles Annaharrison. He was among those signing two-year contracts in 1802 and must have returned home given that he agreed to seasonal paddling contracts in 1813–14 prior to a two-year term contract in 1818 that took him to the Pacific Northwest. By 1821 Ignace Kayen-howay along with Louis Karakontie, who figures prominently in chapter 7, were based at the fur trade post of Dunvegan on the Peace River in Alberta. Charles Teharongatha would be home at the latest by 1831, having completed eight paddling contracts and one term contract between 1808 and 1817.

Charles Simonet can very unusually be tracked back home, consequent on his seeking to recover his way of life: "The Petitioner was 21 years absent from his family in the North West Country, previous to his return to the Village in the year 1822 ... From so long an absence, his wife had given up all hopes of seeing him again. Under these circumstances the Chiefs declare that, according to the Custom of their Nation, Petitioner's Wife was justified in disposing of her Husband's Property."[49] Not keeping in touch, however impossible that might be in practice, had its consequences.

These partial chronologies speak to the hard work and determination that marked men's lives as they decided whether to head west, maybe forever, maybe not. That records have not been located for some of them, apart from a single contract, does not mean they did nothing more, only that their lives, like so many others, were not documented in a manner that survives. Well past the Hudson's Bay Company taking over in 1821 from the North West Company, Iroquois would, as described in chapter 5, continue to be hired. An 1858 government report lamented that they "still cling to their roving habits, and many of them are Voyageurs and Canoemen in the employment of the Hudson's Bay Company."[50]

IROQUOIS RESOURCEFULNESS

The stories that do survive respecting the fur trade repeatedly speak to Iroquois resourcefulness. Iroquois were not unaware of their ambivalent circumstances, doing the best they could to look after themselves within their intermediate space between whites in charge and other Indigenous peoples. One such account comes from the NWC post of Lac la Pluie lying west of Lake Superior. Called Rainy Lake House in English, it was the destination of ninety Iroquois paddlers in 1802–03. Whereas most of them came and went, some did not. Among the post's thirty-three employees as of 1805 were gouvernail Thomas Tiosaragointé (or Thacharacointe) and milieu Ignace Canawatiron. Three years earlier, the pair had been among nine

Caughnawagas who signed paddling contracts on the same day, 5 November 1802, very likely together.[51] The pair recontracted locally, being persuaded to do so almost certainly because they had proven themselves. In Lac la Pluie's post journal they were treated not as outsiders but on a par with other, almost wholly Canadien, employees. Sometimes described as "the 2 Iroquois," suggesting they were the only two there, they were most often part of larger groups charged with manning canoes, getting wood, cutting "hoops, & Keg Wood," seine fishing, collecting animal skins from the local Ojibwe people, and doing whatever it took to keep the post in operation throughout the year.[52]

Tiosaragointé and Canawatiron acted as they did with the long term in mind. They were among just four of the thirty-three Lac la Pluie employees with credit balances as opposed to debts that had to come off their future wages. Tiosaragointé's and Canawatiron's credit balances were by far the largest of any of the men.[53] The two may have been anticipating their return home. Whereas no further information has been located respecting Canawatiron, who perhaps did return east soon thereafter, Tiosaragointé is listed in the NWC ledger as variously employed through 1821,[54] whereupon he also disappears from view.

Another case of resourcefulness comes from the fall of 1819. The Fort Edmonton journal related in passing, as if it was commonplace, that North West Company "Iroquois 20 came over in consequence of bad treatment & offered their services if the HBC would pay their Debts to the N.W."[55] Hinting at what may have ensued more generally is the case of Eustache Orackwatiron, variously posted at least from 1811 across the vast Athabasca District centred on the large lake of the same name. Despite "deserting" in 1818, hence forfeiting his pay, he had as of 1822 an amazingly large credit balance along with the notation "Montreal" after his name, indicating he was about to return home wealthy indeed.[56]

CAUGHT IN THE MIDDLE

Other Iroquois were not so fortunate. Encounters with local Indigenous peoples could turn deadly, never more so than at Chesterfield House, located at the confluence of the South Saskatchewan and Red Deer Rivers in present-day Saskatchewan. It was there that Iroquois's engaging the Indigenous-white divide caught them up. The impetus was the arrival in

1801 of fourteen unnamed Iroquois "from Montreal."[57] Thirty Caughnawaga Iroquois had recently signed term contracts to head to the
enigmatic North or Northwest, and some or all of them were likely among
the fourteen.

Beaver trapping was most productive in the winter, and so in January
1802 the "fourteen Irroque Indians," accompanied by four Canadiens,
headed up the South Saskatchewan River, where they had been told beaver
were plentiful. Four of the Iroquois went ahead "to make friends with the
Falls Indians," also known as the Gros Ventres, whose trapping territory
they were entering. In response, the Gros Ventres "killed two of the Irroques who went to their tents to give presents." Subsequently, "the two
[other] Irroques gave several presents to the Fall Indians, [who] said that
they were very sorry for killing the two men and that they might go to the
house with great safety, and further that they would conduct them safe
thither; but they had not left ... about ½ mile when they were killed and
scalped also by the Falls Indians, and their bodies very full of stabs."[58]

Learning what occurred, Chesterfield House's head, Peter Fidler, sought
the remaining men's safety, and so "gave the Fall Indian chiefs a big keg of
liquor and one fathoms of tobacco to let the others come safe to the house,
which they solemnly promise to do." By another version, also in Fidler's
hand: "We told them that when the other 10 Irroques and two Canadians
came here that they will be admitted into the house & Trade as usual. This
is done with the intent of keeping the fall Indians from falling upon the
other Irroques, as they are very much irritated at present by the great losses
they have met with in the Summer & this Winter."[59]

Three days later, on 25 February, the situation seemed to have eased, and
Fidler sent eight men out from the post "to bury the two Irroques that was
killed nearest the house." His description of what had occurred was
graphic: "In the evening they returned, they say that they have been used
in the most shocking and barbarous manner, being nearly cut to pieces ...
This morning a number of Fall Indians came to trade which we did trade
with them as usual, after they had solemnly promised to let the other two
Canadians and ten Irroques arrive safe. They also appeared much down-
cast at what they had done before."[60] Fidler's attempt at a resolution fell
flat. A week later, on 3 March, with the situation still unresolved:

At 2 ½ a.m., the watch gave the alarm that all the Falls Indians was coming to attack us, when immediately all hands were under arms in the bastions, but it proved that they were going down the river to meet the ten Irroques and two Canadians to kill them; it was absolutely not in our power to prevent it. Our hunter a Blackfoot being at the house, we sent him to them and he spoke with several of the Fall Indians, and they said that they had killed the ten Irroques and two Canadians about sixteen miles [25 kilometres] from the house, and they told them that had we all been there ... they would have served us the same. They carried the scalps of the poor men on the end of poles when they passed the house in a very insulting manner, signifying that ere long they would have ours as well.

Fidler's rewritten description was even more graphic:

Every one of which was scalped & several they cut into pieces limb from limb, their Nose, Private parts, & mangled them in the most Shocking manner ... they hung their scalps upon long poles & all passed up the river near the house singing & dancing, some of them was even eating the part of the heart of one. They Pillaged those they killed of 1 Keg of Powder, 70 lbs. of Ball & 60 lbs. of Shott, upwards of 50 Steel Traps & all their Guns and other articles.[61]

This description is significant for listing the items the Iroquois had carried with them.

It took only two days for the Gros Ventres, having made their point, to return to the practicalities of trade: "This morning two men came to our house, and to learn when we would admit them to trade ... We told that we should not speak to them; but when several of the great chiefs came in, then we should speak of them but not before."[62] The chiefs' return caused Fidler to revisit the motives for the attacks: "They said that it had from the first been their fixed determination to kill the Irroques, as they well know from their hair and heads that they were not Europeans."[63] Iroquois's intermediate status, neither white nor Indigenous from the Fall Indians' perspective, had been their undoing.

IROQUOIS TAKING THE INITIATIVE

One of the most vivid cases of Iroquois in the West taking the initiative, and being so recognized, comes from David Thompson's journal chronicling his crossing of the Rocky Mountains in 1808–10 at the behest of the NWC in search of a western water route for getting pelts to market. Thompson's journal recounts his reliance on eight Iroquois he identified only by their Christian names: Charles, Ignace, Jacques, Joseph, Louis, Martin, Pierre, and Thomas.[64] Despite over half of the Iroquois in the Voyageur Contracts Database sharing one of those eight first names, none are probable, much less certain, matches.

Five of the Iroquois can be physically glimpsed courtesy of Jack Nisbet, who teased out from Thompson's manuscript journal the items advanced to them based on their specific and extensive requests. Ignace received three steel traps, a "fine Capot," being a long coat with a hood, "fine Cord trousers," two "Callicoe shirts," a black handkerchief, and 2 pounds of soap. As well as two steel traps being given to each of the others, Jacques got a blue capot, two "fine Cotton shirts," a black handkerchief, a "3 pts striped" blanket, and 3 pounds of soap; Joseph got a capot, a cotton shirt, cord trousers, a black handkerchief, a red striped blanket, and 2 pounds of soap; Martin got a black silk handkerchief, silk stockings, and 4 pounds of soap; and Pierre got a capot, two calico shirts, cord trousers, a 3-point blanket, and "1 Par a Fleche," being a hide saddlebag.[65] The detail speaks to the care that Iroquois took with their physical appearance and to their self-confidence.

Thompson chronicled his reliance on these eight Iroquois, who almost magically turned up whenever he was in need of advice and counsel. While he was at Salish House in western Montana in February 1810 making "two Canoes, for the transport of the Furrs, Provisions, &c., ... six Iroquois Indians (who had come this far to trap Beaver) assisted by looking for Birch Rind fit for large Canoes, we found none."[66] Thompson used the opportunity to hire "Pierre Iroquois, devant," and "Joseph Iroquois, guide."[67] Alerted that the Pacific Fur Company, based in New York City, was approaching the mouth of the Columbia River by sea to establish the trading post of Astoria, Thompson sped up his goal of reaching "the mouth of the Columbia before the month of August" 1811.[68]

Finding the relatively easy Howse Pass through the Rocky Mountains blocked by Indigenous peoples angry over the fur trade's entry into their territory, Thompson headed north in October 1810 to search of an alternative route. An Iroquois freeman rescued him: "With Thomas an Iroquois Indian as Guide, our route lay over the high ground."[69] Thompson, along with eleven employees and Thomas, headed off on 29 December to make the final dash over the Athabasca Pass, located about 250 kilometres, or about 150 miles, north of the preferable Howse Pass.[70] It was an Iroquois who took charge. On 10 January 1811, "Thomas told us, that although we could barely find wood to make a fire, we must now provide wood to pass the following night on the height of the defile [i.e., narrow valley between two mountains] we were in, and which we had to follow."[71] A day later, during a steep descent, "Thomas came to us, he had, thank Heaven, killed two Buck Moose Deer."[72] Thomas thereupon left to take letters to Thompson's NWC superiors recording the accomplishment.[73]

Come the spring, Iroquois again took the lead. Thompson hired "Charles a fine, steady Iroquois to accompany us as Bowsman, being an excellent Canoe Man," and "Louis to hunt & be the foreman or Steersman of a Canoe."[74] Upon Thompson and his men overnighting with the Kootenay people, he got another acquisition: "Ignace an Iroquois Indian was in this camp. I engaged him as Steersman for the voyage before us."[75] Indicative of Ignace's status as a freeman living by his own resources, as the others may also have been, Thompson hired him in exchange for "550 livres & the ordinary equipment" of clothing and perhaps other goods.[76] As Thompson prepared for the final sprint down the Columbia River to the Pacific Ocean, he named as accompanying him, along with five NWC employees and two local Indigenous men as interpreters, "Charles and Ignace, two good Iroquois Indians."[77] Thompson and his men reached newly constructed Astoria on 14 July 1811, departing eight days later along with "my men as before, two Iroquois Indians, four Canadians," for the trip back across the mountains, for which they were "well armed, each man had a Gun and a long knife."[78]

The presence of Iroquois had by now become so usual for Thompson that at an agreed rendezvous stop six weeks after leaving Astoria, upon unsuccessfully "examining every where to find a Letter, or some marks from some of my people, whom I expected here, nor from my Iroquois I hung up a letter for the latter." Thompson explained in his journal that "we set up a few lines in Iroquois as we supposed only those people would be here."[79] The Iroquois encountered by Thompson were, in other words, literate in their own Iroquois language. This ability may not have been that unusual. An American trapper in the Rocky Mountains in the early 1830s recalled an Iroquois who had left home about 1815 to work for the North West Company before becoming a freeman, noting that he "could read and write in his own language, was upright and fair in all his dealings, and very generally esteemed and respected by his companions."[80]

LIVING A CONTRADICTION

Whatever their capacity, be they paddlers or on term contracts, Iroquois in the fur trade lived a contradiction. Despite being hired on a par with whites, they were alien to the usual operation of the fur trade. They did not belong from the perspectives of many of the men in charge and also of local Indigenous peoples. Even as Iroquois were valued as paddlers or trappers, they were all too often disliked for daring to engage the Indigenous-white divide.

Iroquois independence of character did not accord with the deference that those in charge expected from their supposed inferiors. David Thompson griped that "they considered themselves superior to all other people, especially the white people of Canada, which they carried in their countenances, being accustomed to show themselves off in dance and flourishing their tomahawks before the civilized people of Canada, and making speeches on every occasion, which were all admired and praised through politeness to them, gave them a high opinion of themselves."[81] Iroquois did not, despite being good Catholics and thereby fellow Christians, know their place. American writer Washington Irving described them, based on early fur trade journals, as "first-rate hunters, and dexterous in the management of the canoe" so long as they were kept "in proper subordination." From his perspective as a New Yorker committed to a particular social structure, "these half-civilized Indians retained some of the good, and many of the evil qualities of their original stock."[82] No question exists that an Indigenous-white divide was from whites' perspectives firmly in place, or at least that it ought to be so.

Fur trade officers, being almost all Scots or English, were at best ambivalent. On the one hand, there was acceptance of Iroquois's capacity.

Ross Cox, a NWC clerk who was part of a cross-country brigade heading east in the spring of 1817, had no qualms about poling a raft across a river alongside "Louis, an Iroquois Indian" and a couple of others. Approaching rapids, Cox pinned his hopes on "the long experience of the Iroquois, accustomed from his infancy to similar scenes" and "took care not to separate" himself from Louis.[83] On the other hand, Cox could not countenance "the Iroquois, Nipissings, and others of the native tribes of Canada" as being on a par with white employees like himself. Despite the identical wording of contracts, he took for granted that "they engage ... on lower terms than are usually allowed to the French Canadians." For all that Iroquois "are strong, able-bodied men, good hunters, and well acquainted with the management of canoes," they "are rather quarrelsome, revengeful, and sometimes insubordinate."[84]

Fellow NWC officer Alexander Ross was similarly ambivalent. He was admiring of Iroquois as "expert voyageurs, and especially so in the rapids and dangerous runs in the inland waters, which they either stem or shoot with the utmost skill." Ross had at the same time an ensemble of frustrations: "They are brought up to religion, it is true, and sing hymns oftener than paddling songs; but those who came here (and we are of course speaking of none else) retain none of its precepts: they are sullen, indolent, fickle, cowardly, and treacherous."[85]

The longevity of Caughnawaga, by now over a century old and characterized by clear expectations for the conduct of everyday life, much as also were Lac des Deux Montagnes and St Régis, may have made Iroquois appear more knowledgeable about the expectations for their behaviour than was actually the case. No one may have thought to pass onto them, perhaps owing in part to different first languages, the assumptions of those in charge regarding employees and how Iroquois might attempt to deflect them if they chose to do so.

RETURNING HOME

Iroquois heading west, maybe forever, maybe not, made a difference not only to the fur trade but also to the communities from which they came. It seems likely that some of Caughnawaga's decline in population from a possible 1,800 to 1,000 between 1800 and 1825 was due to Iroquois being tugged away by the West. As explained in a published history of Caughnawaga, "Sometimes their engagements were of longer direction, lasting ten, fifteen or twenty years; sometimes they did not return at all ... [and] long absences from Caughnawaga was the reason given in 1843 for the dwindling population of the village."[86] For the vast majority of Iroquois, their engagement with the fur trade was a part of their life course as opposed to its entirety. Although it is impossible to make a full determination of numbers, the 1825 census of Caughnawaga and the 1831 census of Lac des Deux Montagnes are filled with familiar surnames.[87] Comparing these names with those located on contracts or elsewhere in fur trade records shows that over 100 men returned to the places from which they came. Some of these men continued to be intermittently employed by the NWC nearer to home for short-term tasks.[88]

Men returning home had to cope both with reintegration and with managing changes effected while they were away and subsequently. Internal politics were complex, whether families sought prominence or just a reasonable living.[89] It was also the case that men's time away may have caused them to return with more confidence than they would otherwise have had. Although some farmed a little, wage labour became the principal means of earning a living alongside families' fabrication of moccasins, snowshoes, and beadwork. Some trapping was ongoing, as with "a party of St. Akwesasne [i.e., St Régis] Indians from Canada" recorded in 1815 as crossing the border into the United States and returning "with three hundred beaver skins."[90] Paddling long distances on hire was possible from time to time with exploring expeditions and otherwise. What began as exhibitions of traditional crafts and of paddling and other physical skills led to openings in stage shows across North America and Europe. Bridge building close to home during the 1880s provided opportunities for employment as steelworkers at various sites, including New York City, where some settled from the 1920s.[91]

Whatever the specifics, which are part of another story, life went on.

TO SUM UP

Iroquois responded in large numbers to their being welcomed into the fur trade on a par with whites. As evoked in a history of Caughnawaga published a century after the event, "their love of adventure, their physical strength and power of endurance, their skill as hunters and trappers, their dexterity in handling the paddle, made them valuable aids in the thriving commerce which was then spreading over the continent." The consequence was that "their services were constantly in demand."[92]

The vast majority of Iroquois heading west left home in order to return, perhaps a bit better off than when they had departed, and to get on with the lives they had left behind. A minority, considered in the next chapters, acted differently. They were determined not only to glimpse, but also to be, of the West.

PART TWO

Daring to Be Adventurous

Iroquois's "Daring to Be Adventurous" while in the West was consistent with their strong senses of self. Chapter 3 turns to a cluster who enacted their religious sensibilities. "Bringing Catholicism to the Flatheads" describes four trips by Iroquois and Flatheads from future Montana in the northwest United States to St Louis in the middle of the country in search of a missionary to the Flatheads, or Salish, among whom an Iroquois cluster had found a place of being. The missionary was got, only to depart for fresh fields of conversion, leaving the Iroquois to resume their mentorship.

Chapter 4, "Challenging a Fur Monopoly," attends to an Iroquois cluster whose members looked out for their own self-interest and by doing so the interests of others. Hired on term contracts as trappers, they became so aware of the fur trade's economic inequality that they effected permanent change. In the aftermath of their doing so, they animated the American West to become a model for adventurous Iroquois stereotypes favoured by authors of the time and to some extent subsequently.

Bringing Catholicism to the Flatheads

Among Iroquois in the West was a cluster in today's Montana, home to, among other Salish peoples, the Flatheads, as they were then known. Iroquois found among them a place of belonging and reciprocated by sharing their commitment to Catholicism. The consequence was that four times during the 1830s Flatheads together with Iroquois travelled 2,600 kilometres, or just over 1,600 miles, southeast to the longtime fur trading centre of St Louis on the Mississippi River in search of Jesuit missionaries patterned on those who had long resided in Caughnawaga. Iroquois were ambitious on the Flatheads' behalf, determined to do right by them.

By so acting, Iroquois repeatedly challenged the Indigenous-white divide, which was intended to prevent Indigenous peoples from playing any role in the changes being foisted on them by white outsiders. Guided by Iroquois living among them, Flatheads took their future in their own hands.

THE FLATHEADS

For reasons that are inexplicable given that Flatheads did not flatten their children's heads, such was the name that white newcomers gave to Indigenous peoples living in southwestern Montana's Bitterroot Valley, a location secluded by mountain ranges on both the west and the east. Not only did their setting protect Flatheads to some extent from outsiders, but a mild climate and abundant foodstuffs also contributed to the valley's appeal.[1] Flatheads' acquisition, likely in the early eighteenth century, of horses descended from wild herds originating in Spanish Mexico initiated a yearly migration eastward to open plains populated by buffalo. The large animals were hunted for meat, with their bones formed into utensils and their skins used for clothing and for shelter in large tents known as lodges.[2] Numbering about 500, Flatheads were not particularly influential or warlike compared to the Blackfeet to the northeast.

Flatheads used their contacts with white outsiders strategically. The cross-country exploratory expedition led by Meriwether Lewis and William Clark on behalf of the US government passed by the Bitterroot Valley on its way west in September 1805, at which time horses were purchased.[3] North West Company partner David Thompson also acquired horses there, describing the "Saleesh," his name for the Flatheads, as "a fine race of moral Indians, the finest I have seen."[4]

IROQUOIS'S ARRIVAL

The earliest narratives of Flatheads' encounters with Iroquois were by Jesuit missionaries Pierre-Jean De Smet, Gregorio Mengarini, and Nicolas Point.[5] When these narratives are used alongside other contemporary sources and a history written by fellow Jesuit Lawrence B. Palladino, which incorporated contemporary documents and testimony acquired since his arrival in the area in 1867, we can begin to tease out what occurred.[6]

In 1839, based on conversations with Flatheads, the bishop of St Louis described how between 1812 and 1820 a band of two dozen Iroquois led by Ignace La Mousse, known familiarly as Big Ignace or Old Ignace, had arrived "from Canada."[7] Peter Ronan, who later in the century was in charge of the Flathead Reservation, to which Flatheads had by then been confined, may have been drawing on local knowledge in explaining how an Iroquois band "in their hunting and trapping excursions had penetrated into the Bitter Root valley from their homes in the British possessions," today's Canada.[8] By another account, "it is said that about 1820–1825 a small party of Iroquois, originally from around Caughnawaga, Quebec, under the leadership of Ignace La Mousse (or big Ignace), reached the Flathead country, and being well received there, married and became members of the tribe."[9] None of the Iroquois named as interacting with the Flatheads appear in the Voyageur Contracts Database, leaving unanswered how they travelled west.

"The wandering band" of Iroquois, to use Palladino's phrase, found among the Flatheads their place of being. Relationships grew in two ways.

First, by virtue of partnering with local women, "these Iroquois became members of the Salish or Flathead nation." Second, Ignace La Mousse acquired a leadership position emanating from the Catholicism inculcated in him as a child. Palladino described how La Mousse "would speak to them of the Catholic religion, its teachings, its prayers and its rites, the conclusion of all his discourses being always the same, namely, the advantage and necessity of having the Black Robes or Catholic missionaries among them, by whom they could be instructed and taught the way to Heaven."[10] As paraphrased by a Canadien living with the Flatheads for a time, Ignace took care not to represent himself as more than he was: "All that I say is nothing. If those dressed in black should come here they would know, for it is from them that I learned all of this which I tell you."[11] La Mousse, and possibly other Iroquois, taught the Flatheads the sign of the Cross, Lord's Prayer, and other aspects of Catholic devotion, to which they responded by praying together morning and evening, observing the Sabbath, baptizing children, and marking graves with crosses.[12]

Iroquois acted on their religiosity. In 1825 Ignace La Mousse took his son Baptiste to St Louis, possibly on the way visiting an older son back home. At St Louis, Baptiste met with General William Clark of the earlier Lewis and Clark expedition that had visited the Flatheads. As to the reason for the meeting, according to Ronan, writing in 1890,

> During the stay of the explorers in the Flathead camp Captain Clark took unto himself a Flathead woman. One son was the result of this union, and he was baptised after the missionaries came to Bitter Root valley and named Peter Clark. The half-breed lived to a ripe age, and was well known to many of Montana's early settlers. He died about six years ago and left a son, who was christened at St. Mary's mission to the name of Zachariah, and pronounced Sacalee by the Indians. The latter has a son three years of age, whom it is claimed by the Indians, in direct descent, to be the great grandson of the renowned Captain Clark.[13]

Then the superintendent of Indian affairs, based in St Louis, Clark arranged for the admission of Ignace La Mousse's son Baptiste to St Régis Seminary at nearby Florissant, where he remained for two years before disappearing from view.[14]

FIRST FLATHEAD DELEGATION TO ST LOUIS, 1831

The Flatheads wanted "black robes" and repeatedly discussed in council how to acquire them. The returned La Mousse suggested that some of them might go to St Louis with their request, and at a general assembly four men volunteered to do so on what would be the first of four Flathead delegations. Two heading off were Flatheads, and two were Nez Percés who lived among the Flatheads.

The four set out in the spring of 1831, reaching St Louis in early October by established trade routes.[15] Their behaviour on arriving makes clear the full extent to which the Iroquois had mentored them in the Catholic faith. Writing for publication, the Catholic bishop of St Louis, Joseph Rosati, described the visit: "Some three months ago four Indians who live across the Rocky Mountains near the Columbia River (Clark Fork on the Columbia) arrived in St. Louis. After visiting General Clark who, in his celebrated travels, had visited their country, and has been well treated by them, they came to see our church and appeared to be exceedingly well pleased with it. Unfortunately there was no one who understood their language."[16] Given imprecise notions of geography at the time, it is not surprising that the Flatheads were so sited by the bishop.

Bishop Rosati described approvingly how the arrivals already knew how "to make the sign of the Cross and to pray."[17] Writing in 1839 to the head of the Jesuits in Rome, Rosati had a more precise understanding of how his visitors came to know about Catholicism: "Eight or nine years ago some of the Flathead nation came to St. Louis. The object of their journey was to ascertain if the religion spoken of with so much praise by the Iroquois warriors was in reality such as represented and, above all, if the nations that have White skin had adopted and practiced it."[18] This account is revealing for its reference to "White skin" and hence to whiteness as a marker of difference.

St Louis was not kind to the four visitors, whose language no one understood. The bishop explained that "some time afterwards two of them fell dangerously ill." He was away from St Louis, so others acted in his stead:

Two of our priests visited them and the poor Indians delighted with the visit. They made the sign of the Cross and other signs which appeared to have some relation to baptism. The sacrament was administered to them; they gave expressions of satisfaction. A little cross was presented to them. They took it with eagerness, kissed it repeatedly, and it could be taken from them only after death. It was truly distressing that they could not be spoken to. Their remains were carried to the church, and their funeral was conducted with all Catholic ceremonies. The other two attended and acted very becomingly.[19]

The two men did not die at the same time, as the absent bishop assumed. Records of burial in the Catholic parish cemetery in St Louis indicate that Keepeellelé, or Pipe Bard, who may have been baptized as Narcisse, died on 31 October. He was described as forty-four years old and both Flathead and Nez Percé. Paul, as he was baptized, died on 17 November and was described as a Flathead.

In the spring of 1832, the two remaining visitors started for home. American painter George Catlin, then in his mid-thirties and using St Louis as his base, described how "two old sad and venerable men of this party died in St. Louis, and I traveled two thousand miles [over 3,000 kilometres], companion with these two young fellows, towards their own country, and became much pleased with their manners and dispositions." Along the way, Catlin painted two young men whom he described as Nez Percés wearing Sioux outfits presented to them and whom he named as "Hee-oh'ks-te-kin (the rabbit skin leggings), and H'co-a-h'co-a-h'cotes-min (no horns on his head)."[20] They may or may not have been the two men from Flathead country. Catlin recounted what happened to the pair:

The last mentioned of the two, died near the mouth of the Yellow Stone River on his way home, with disease which he had contracted in the civilized district; and the other I have since learned, arrived safely amongst his friends, conveying to them the melancholy intelligence of the deaths of all the rest of his party; but assurances at the same time, from General Clark, and many revered gentlemen, that the report which they had heard was well founded; and that missionaries, good and religious men, would soon come amongst them to teach this religion, so that they could all understand and have the benefits of it.[21]

Such optimism was ill-founded. The Catholic bishop noted how a clergy-man had offered to go with the returning pair, but nothing ensued and they left alone.[22] De Smet's biographer suggests that the St Louis Jesuits did not follow up because it was a time of missionary contraction, marked by the closure of the Indian school at nearby Florissant, in which La Mousse's son had been enrolled in the 1820s.[23]

This first Flathead delegation to St Louis had the unexpected conse-quence of attracting not the much-sought Catholics but rather Protestant missionaries offering their services. The impetus was a Methodist confer-ence held in St Louis at the time that the four visitors were there, during which a letter published in the *Christian Advocate and Journal* on 1 March 1833 emphasized the Flatheads' desire for Christianity.[24] As word spread, various groups responded.

In August 1833, Methodists Jason Lee and his nephew Daniel Lee were appointed missionaries to the Flatheads, and on their way west the next April, they made a point of visiting William Clark in St Louis to find out more.[25] Two versions exist as to why the pair ended up, as they did, in the Willamette Valley in Oregon rather than in Montana. The Catholic ver-sion has the Flatheads, during the Lees' stop there, letting them know in no uncertain terms that "their services were not wanted, and that it was Catholic Black Robes whom the Indians desired and had sent for." As described by Palladino,

> The missionary gentlemen who stood before them did not tally with the description of the Black Robes given by their adopted brethren, the Iroquois. The missionaries spoken of by the Iroquois wore long black gowns, carried a crucifix with them, prayed the great prayer (the Mass), and did not marry. But the newcomers wore no black gowns and, upon inquiry, had no cross to show, prayed not the good prayer, and, besides, they married. They surely could not be the teachers they had sent for. Consequently, they made the Lee party understand that the Flat Head tribe did not care for them nor their ministrations.[26]

The Methodist version has the head of the Hudson's Bay Company post of Fort Vancouver persuading the Lees that the Willamette Valley was a more advantageous site than among the Flatheads, where "it was too dangerous for them to establish a mission."[27] In both versions, Iroquois influence was telling.

SECOND FLATHEAD DELEGATION TO ST LOUIS, 1835

The Flatheads became increasingly aware that the St Louis expedition had not had the desired outcome. Possibly aware of Protestants poking around, Ignace La Mousse offered to head off in search of Catholic missionaries and departed in the summer of 1835 on what would be the second Flathead delegation. He initially proposed to travel to Quebec, where he was born and where he expected that priests were to be got, but he then decided on St Louis. La Mousse took with him his fourteen- and twelve-year-old sons for the purpose of having them baptized, and at St Louis on 2 December 1835 they were bestowed the Christian first names, respectively, of Carolus, or Charles, and Franciscus, or Francis.[28] As described by Rosati, "The Flathead nation sent again one of the Iroquois nation to St. Louis. There he came with two of his children, who were instructed and baptized by the Fathers of the College." Having the immeasurable advantage over members of the predecessor delegation of being able to speak French and thereby to communicate, La Mousse requested "missionaries for his countrymen."[29] Assured that they would be sent as soon as possible, La Mousse returned home with his sons.

In the meantime, more Protestant missionaries, being this time Samuel Parker, R.H. Spalding, W.H. Gray, and Marcus Whitman with his bride, Narcissa, all dispatched by the American Board of Commissioners for Foreign Missions, coveted the Flatheads, only to be rebuffed in a manner similar to that experienced by the Lees. As Parker described in his memoir, the Iroquois's influence on the Flatheads was very real: "The night of our arrival [11 May 1836] a little girl, of about six or seven years of age, died. The morning of the twelfth they buried her ... They had prepared a cross to set up at the grave, most probably having been told to do so by some Iroquois Indians, a few of whom, not in the capacity of teachers, but as trappers in the employ of the fur companies, I saw west of the mountains." Indicative of the missionaries' dismissive attitude toward others' religious practices, Parker proceeded to break "the cross of wood" into pieces, telling the Flatheads peremptorily that "we place a stone at the head and foot of the grave, only to mark the place."[30] Such an action could not have endeared Parker to his hosts and might well have precipitated the missionaries' departure.

THIRD FLATHEAD DELEGATION TO ST LOUIS, 1837

The passage of eighteen months with no Catholic missionaries, but with encircling Protestants, prompted Iroquois stalwart Ignace La Mousse to head out again in 1837 on what was the third Flathead trip to St Louis. This time, Old Ignace was accompanied by three Flatheads and one Nez Percé, and on the way they met up with others heading in the same direction.

The group was attacked, and its members killed fifteen Sioux before being themselves overpowered. According to Palladino, the whites were ordered to stand aside and not be killed, with Old Ignace being counted among their number since he was dressed like a white man, but "he spurned the command, and preferred to share the lot of his adopted brethren." In Palladino's words, "thus perished the one who may justly be called the apostle of the Flat Heads."[31]

FOURTH FLATHEAD DELEGATION TO ST LOUIS, 1839

The death of all five members of the third delegation did not deter a successor. Based on local knowledge, including that of Ignace La Mousse's son Francis, Ronan described what occurred:

> In 1839 two young Iroquois announced in council of the Flatheads, that notwithstanding the fate of the two [sic] previous delegations who had been sent for St. Louis, they were ready to repeat the trial and conduct Catholic missionaries to the tribe. Soon after this offer, it was learned that a party of Hudson Bay employees were going to make the voyage in canoes, from the head waters of the Missouri to St. Louis, and the two Iroquois made application to accompany them and were accepted. Within the year the Indians arrived in St. Louis and held audience with the Catholic bishop of that city the Right Reverend Rosati.[32]

This fourth delegation comprised two Iroquois French speakers: Peter Gaucher, known in English as Left-Hand Pete, and Young Ignace, so named to distinguish him from Ignace La Mousse.[33] Along the way, the pair passed St Joseph's Mission at Council Bluffs in future Iowa. There, they stopped to confer with the priests in charge and, in so doing, met Jesuit Father Pierre-Jean De Smet, who would thereupon volunteer to minister to the Flatheads.[34] Writing at the time, the thirty-eight-year-old De Smet recognized the Iroquois for who they were and accepted the truth of what they told him:

> On the 18th of last September [1839] two Catholic Iroquois came to visit us. They had been for twenty-three years among the nation called the Flatheads and Pierced Noses, about a thousand Flemish leagues from where we are. I have never seen any savages so fervent in religion. By their instructions and examples they have given all that nation a great desire to have themselves baptized. All that tribe strictly observe Sunday and assemble several times a week to pray and sing canticles [i.e., hymns or chants]. The sole object of these Iroquois was to obtain a priest to come and finish what they had so happily commenced. We gave them letters of recommendation for our Reverend Father Superior at St. Louis. They thought nothing of adding three hundred leagues to the thousand they had already accomplished, in the hope that their request would be granted.[35]

As described by De Smet, their goal was to secure a "Black-gown, to conduct them to heaven."[36]

Reaching St Louis, the two Iroquois laid their request before Bishop Rosati, who assured them a priest would be dispatched the next spring. Writing to the head of the Jesuits in Rome, the bishop recounted the visit of this delegation in some detail, the third to make it all the way to St Louis:

> It was composed of two Christian Iroquois. These Indians, who talk French, have edified us by their truly exemplary conduct and interested us by their discourses. The Fathers of the College [later St Louis University] have heard their confessions and to-day they approached

the holy table at high mass in the Cathedral Church. Afterwards I administered to them the sacrament of Confirmation, and in an address delivered after the ceremony I rejoiced with them at their happiness and gave them the hope of soon having a priest.[37]

Bishop Rosati's letter of 20 October 1839 lauded the Iroquois as teachers and mentors of the Flatheads. Based on information that the pair had told him, he reported that, "of the twenty-four Iroquois who formerly emigrated from Canada, only four are still living."[38] The number did not take into account the second generation, including Ignace La Mousse's and others' offspring. Rosati could not resist a swipe at his non-Catholic counterparts that was almost certainly based on what the two Iroquois had shared with him:

> Not only have they planted the faith in these wild countries, but they have besides defended it against the encroachments of the Protestant ministers. When these missionaries presented themselves among them, our good Catholics refused to accept them. "These are not the priests about whom we have spoken to you," they would say to the Flat Heads: "These are not the long black-robed priests who have no wives, who say mass, who carry the crucifix with them."[39]

Rosati concluded with a plea to his superior: "For the love of God, my Very Reverend Father, do not abandon these souls."[40]

When the men had accomplished their task, Rosati explained, they made ready to head home: "They will depart to-morrow; one of them [Peter Gaucher] will carry the good news promptly to the Flat Heads, the other [Young Ignace] will spend the winter at the mouth of Bear river, and in the spring he will continue the journey with the missionary, whom we will send them."[41] In the event, Young Ignace spent the winter at Florissant, northwest of St Louis.

ENTER DE SMET

Pierre-Jean De Smet, who had met the two Iroquois on their way to St Louis and was now planning to extend his missionary work among Indigenous peoples, accepted a mandate to survey the situation that the Iroquois had described to determine how best, or whether, to proceed. The Jesuits did not have the capacity to be everywhere and had to make choices.

Guided by Young Ignace, who had remained behind for that purpose, De Smet left St Louis on 27 March 1840 about the same time that fellow Iroquois Peter Gaucher reached the Flatheads with the good news. After travelling by steamboat to Kansas City, they joined about thirty men of the American Fur Company who were heading to its annual fur trade rendezvous site of Green River in central Wyoming.

When he reached Green River on 30 June, De Smet was met by ten Flatheads, whom the chief had dispatched upon getting Peter Gaucher's news that a priest was finally on the way. A little over a week later, they got to Pierre Hole on the border between Wyoming and Idaho. Mostly Flatheads were encamped there, and they welcomed De Smet for responding to their deputations, as the principal chief there put it, "to the great Black-gown [the bishop] in St. Louis, to obtain a father."[42]

The very next day, 12 July 1840, De Smet got a taste of how fully the Iroquois had taught the Flatheads about Catholic practices. In the evening, following the recitation of night prayers under De Smet's oversight, "a solemn canticle praise, of their own composition, was sung by these children of the mountains to the Author of their being." Taking note of how "the Flatheads had already had for some years a custom of never breaking camp on Sunday," De Smet set a routine in which the Iroquois continued to play an active role:

During all my stay in the mountains, I said the holy mass regularly Sundays and feast-days, as well as on days when the Indians did not break camp in the morning; the altar was made of willows; my blanket made an altar cloth, and all the lodge was adorned with images and wild flowers; ... they took assiduous part with the greatest modesty, attention and devotion, and since various nations were among them, they chanted the praises of God in the Flathead, Nez Percé and Iroquois languages.[43]

The Flathead peoples whom De Smet encountered numbered, by one estimate, about a thousand.[44]

De Smet spent six weeks ministering to the camp before leaving for St Louis on 27 August to urge the establishment of a permanent mission. Told funds were in short supply, De Smet visited several American cities to secure the needed monies and personnel, with whom he set out from St Louis on 30 April 1841.[45] De Smet had with him two priests and three lay brothers, including Gregorio Mengarini, who later published an account, and Nicolas Point, who left many sketches of his activities.[46] Upon De Smet's departure the previous summer, the Flatheads had promised to meet him the next year on 1 July at the foot of the Wind River Mountains in western Wyoming.

DE SMET'S 1841 WELCOMING PARTY

It is indicative of respect for Iroquois among the Flatheads that De Smet's 1841 welcoming party in the Wind River Mountains included three Iroquois, being Young Ignace and the two sons of Old Ignace baptized in St Louis as Charles and Francis. On the basis of conversations with him, Palladino noted that "Young Ignace traveled four whole days and four whole nights without a bit to eat, that he might be among the first to welcome the missionaries."[47] Ignace La Mousse's son Francis then guided De Smet and the others to the fur trade post of Fort Hall in today's eastern Idaho, where the missionaries replenished their depleted supplies. In a letter to his superiors written on 16 August, De Smet described how, while travelling by horse over "the highest chain of the Rocky Mountains … the young Francis Xavier was my only companion."[48]

From the outset, De Smet was cognizant of the Iroquois's influence on his Flathead charges: "In compliance with the counsels of some poor Iroquois, who had established themselves in their tribe, they had conformed, as nearly as they could to our creed and manners, and even to our religious practices. In what Catholic parish was the Sunday, for example, ever more religiously observed?" De Smet described how, "during the ten years just elapsed, four deputations, each starting from the banks of the Bitter Root, on which they usually assemble, had courageously ventured to St. Louis, over a space of 3,000 miles [4,830 kilometres] – over mountains and valleys, infested by Blackfeet and other hostile tribes." Not only that, but in anticipation of his arrival, "they themselves had traveled upwards of 800 miles [1,290 kilometres] to meet us."[49]

De Smet especially commended the two principal Iroquois for their roles in bringing the Jesuits to the Flatheads. About Young Ignace, whom he

knew as Ignatius, he wrote: "Ignatius, who had advised the fourth deputa-
tion, and had been a member of it, – who had succeeded in his mission,
and introduced the first Blackgown into the tribe, – who had just recently
exposed himself to new dangers, in order to introduce others, had crowned
his zealous exertions by running for days without eating or drinking, solely
that he might reach us the sooner." De Smet described Francis, whom he
knew as Francis Xavier, as a mission mainstay:

> Francis Xavier was the son of old Ignatius, who had been the leader
> of the second and third deputations, and had fallen a victim to his
> devotion to the cause of religion and of his brethren. Francis Xavier
> had gone to St. Louis at the age of ten, in the company of his coura-
> geous father, solely that he might have the happiness of receiving bap-
> tism. He had finally attached himself without reserve to the services
> of the mission, and supplied our table with a daily mess of fish.[50]

Leaving Fort Hall at the end of August 1841, the missionary group
headed to the Bitterroot Valley, which they reached a month later. On the
first Sunday in October, at the site selected for what was named St Mary's
Mission, they planted a wooden cross hewn from two cut trees.[51] Construction of a church and a couple of smaller structures followed. It was as the
church was being finished that one of the Flatheads exclaimed that the site
was where little Mary had foretold it would be built.[52] De Smet had told a
version of her story in his August letter, penned prior to his reaching the
Bitterroot Valley, that is revealing both of Iroquois initiative and of his
approval of their actions: "A girl about twelve years of age, seeing herself
on the point of dying, had solicited baptism with such earnestness that she
was baptized by Peter the Iroquois, and received the name of Mary. – After
having sung a canticle in a stronger voice than usual, she died, saying: 'Oh,
how beautiful! I see Mary, my mother.'"[53] De Smet asked rhetorically,
"What were the Iroquois before their conversions, and what have they not
since become?"[54]

The transformation process envisaged by the Jesuits began in earnest
the next year, 1842, when grain brought to the Bitter Root Valley was sowed.
As put optimistically by the first Indian agent there, "The first year the crop
yielded rich, to the great enjoyment and delight of the Indians, who learned
for the first time how to till the soil and force it to yield a manifold crop."[55]

IN FOR A FALL

De Smet's hopes for the Flatheads and their Iroquois counterparts were too high not to come in for a fall. His charges had every reason to think that they were special, that they mattered, and they treated De Smet with the consequent respect, but for him they were a steppingstone to growing numbers of Catholic missions. As was the case generally at this point in time, the thrill lay in conversions, more conversions, and yet more. De Smet spent most of his time travelling back and forth to raise funds, acquire more personnel, and expand his missionary field, so much so that by the mid-1840s the Flatheads, who hardly ever saw him, were openly disillusioned. The editors of De Smet's papers astutely observe that he was not a stayer but always seeking new adventures: "Father De Smet was now again in his element – exploring regions new to him; jotting down the experiences of each day in order that he might send them forth to the world where they would bring new workers to his vineyard."[56]

Relations between the Jesuits and the Flatheads, by now down to sixty lodges and 350 people, according to Iroquois Peter Gaucher, became so strained that St Mary's Mission was shut down in 1850 and sold to an enigmatic Major John Owen to become a trading post that he named for himself.[57] Catholic missionaries returned five years later to establish a single large mission that they named St Ignatius in the forlorn hope that the Flatheads would forsake their Bitterroot Valley home to move nearby, which they refused to do. Flatheads similarly refused to move onto an Indian reservation unless it could be established so that they remained where they were. In 1872 the US Congress both ordered Flatheads' removal and opened the coveted Bitterroot Valley lands to white settlers. The Flatheads still refused to leave and remained in the valley in absolute poverty until 1891, when they finally agreed to move onto the Indian reservation.[58]

A CONTINUING IROQUOIS PRESENCE

Through all this dislocation, emblematic of what was happening generally during these years to Indigenous peoples with the complicity of missionaries, half a dozen Iroquois and Iroquois offspring buttressed the Flatheads, by their examples nudging them toward a market economy. Two complementary sources tell us something about them. The first source originated with John Owen, whose acquired mission site became a trading post. Alongside other settlers and passersby, five Iroquois or offspring patronized Fort Owen, whose ledger survives for the 1850s, along with Owen's journals. The second source is thanks to US army enlistee Gustavus Sohon, who was part of a railway survey that wintered in 1853–54 in the Bitterroot Valley. Sohon not only learned to speak Salish but between 12 May and the end of June 1854 also pencilled sketches accompanied by characterizations of three of the Iroquois, along with nine Flathead and nine Pend d'Oreille leaders.[59]

Taken together, these and other sources vividly evoke how two Iroquois of the first generation and four Iroquois offspring made livings for their families in a setting where subsistence was replaced by a cash economy in a dominant white society. Descriptions of these six Iroquois speak to selective adaption, personal strength of character, commitment to family life, and religious, physical, and moral tenacity.

Two of the Iroquois depicted by Sohon, being Peter Gaucher and Ignace La Mousse, were part of the original band. The characterization that accompanies one of Sohon's spring 1854 sketches reads admiringly, "Pierre Kar-so-wa-ta. An Iroquois who came to this country thirty years ago, and settled here. He is the most industrious indian in the valley, cultivates a small farm raising wheat, oats, potatoes, etc. and owns a large band of cattle; he speaks the mountain french and english, besides several Indian languages."[60] Peter Gaucher twice patronized Owen's trading post, once in 1854 for such luxuries as looking glasses, a comb, and pepper, for which he paid cash, and a year later to buy gunpowder and clothing, for which he traded a whole or part of an ox.[61] As were some of the other Iroquois, he was friendly with Owen, who noted on a trip away from his trading post that "Old Pierre an Iroquois Came into Camp this Evng being out hunting Cattle."[62]

Likely because Peter Gaucher was the only Indigenous person then in the village, all the others being away hunting buffalo east of the Rocky Mountains, he was front and centre in 1855 when Isaac Stevens, the governor of Washington Territory, met with the Flatheads to seek to convince them to move from the Bitterroot Valley to the site of the new mission. Referring to Gaucher, whom he called "Pierre the Iroquois," Stevens asked, "Can he raise crops there?" Pierre responded, "I think so." Stevens anticipated that Gaucher would back up his position: "I ask Pierre again, which

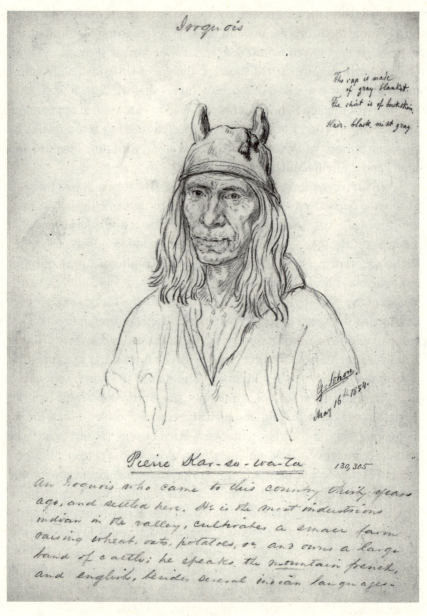

Iroquois

The cap is made
of gray blanket.
The shirt is of buckskin.
Hair, black, mixt gray

Pierre Kar-so-wa-ta   130,305

An Iroquois who came to this country thirty years ago, and settled here. He is the most industrious indian in the valley, cultivates a small farm raising wheat, oats, potatoes, &c. and owns a large band of cattle; he speaks the mountain french, and english, besides several indian languages.

Figure 3.1
"Iroquois, Pierre, Kar-so-wa-ta," by Gustavus Sohon, 16 May 1854

is the best, this valley or the Mission? He has tried both." To this inquiry came the diplomatic response, "I do not know." The governor was adamant in his position: "The labor Pierre has put on his land will be paid for. You can gather your crops. You will not be required to move for a year and a half or two years."[63]

Gaucher's strength of character was such that John Owen truly lamented his death in May 1856: "Old Piere's [*sic*] wife retd to the fort to day; she left here in company with her husband on the 17 Inst. & retd a Widow. Old Pierre from what I could understand was thrown from his horse in big hole [a valley in southwestern Montana] running an Elk & had his Neck broken; he was an Iroquois & an old trapper been a long time in the Country."[64] A Jesuit had a similar response: "Ignatius is settled here, as well as the family of Iroquois Peter. The death of this venerable old man is a great loss to the mission."[65]

The other Iroquois of the first generation was named as Aeneas, whom his grandson Baptiste Finley attested was Young Ignace, the Iroquois who had gone to St Louis on the fourth delegation and returned with De Smet.[66] Indicative of Young Ignace's versatility in accommodating himself to the changing times, a Catholic missionary encountering him in 1845 said that he was "clothed in the fashion of the whites, but wearing his hair long, after the manner of Indians."[67] By the 1850s, the appellation Aeneas was in common usage as Young Ignace's name. It was by this name that he paid cash for the ammunition he purchased at Fort Owen in 1851, two years later trading "1 yoke steers" for clothing, flour, and "grinding 3 ½ bus Wheat," indicating that he was farming.[68] Sohon described Aeneas less favourably than his counterpart Peter Gaucher: "Iroquois – 'Aeneas' – Came to this country with Pierre, but has not the industry or forethought of his comrade Peter. He is poor but an honest and reliable man."[69]

At about the same time, Aeneas stood out from the perspective of a US army officer exploring the area: "I learned through an old Iroquois Indian called Aeneas, now resident in the Bitter Root valley, whose wanderings amid the mountains had often thrown him with parties travelling with wagons at the southward, thereby rendering him capable of judging of the requisites for a wagon road, that a line could be had through a gorge-like pass in the Core d'Alene mountains."[70] Although the immediate dispatch of a topographer with Aeneas as a guide to check the route was thwarted by snow, the route was subsequently proven out, so much so that he was

Figure 3.2
"Iroquois, Aeneas," by Gustavus Sohon, 16 May 1854

named in the official report. The father of two children, Aeneas would die in 1880.[71]

Charles Lamousse, the third purchaser of goods at Fort Owen, was the third Iroquois sketched by Sohon. Charles Lamousse was one of three sons of Ignace La Mousse, who had early on taught the Flatheads elements of Christianity. Charles, along with his younger brother Francis, had accompanied their father on the second delegation to St Louis in 1835, where they were baptized. Both brothers had been among the ten lodges whose members had gone to meet De Smet on his return west in July 1841.[72] A story goes that in 1842 an HBC trader arrived with an array of goods that he promoted by arranging a women's race, with an assortment of them going to the winner, who was Charles Lamousse's wife, thereafter known as "race woman."[73] The description on Sohon's sketch of Charles Lamoose made in June 1854 reads, "Lamuh (Indian name) Charles (in baptism) Charles Lamoose – ½ Iroquois and ½ Pend-d'oreille speaks English and French and lives with the Flatheads."[74] Over the decade for which accounts survive, Charles Lamousse purchased from the trading post not only essentials ranging from clothing to gunpowder but also little luxuries like playing cards, sugar, coffee, and tobacco, at a total cost of $40.50, which he paid with livestock, bear skins, and his labour.[75]

John Owen considered a fourth Iroquois, Ignace La Moose's son Francis, also known as Francis Saxa, to be an "old friend and voyageur," describing him in his account book as an "Engaged Man," or employee.[76] On a trip from Fort Owen to Walla Walla in April 1851, Owen recorded in his diary, "went out a hunting today with Lamoose," who "Killd a Doe Elk & 1 Goose; for myself I failed to Kill any thing."[77] A week later, "Lamoose was in the lead" chasing down and killing buffalo.[78] The next day, bear were sought: "We got under cover of the ridge when Lamoose dismounted tied his horse and approached the animal within about 100 yds ... Lamoose took deliberate aim and fired."[79] Although at one point he was debited for "goods stolen," it did not prevent him from being a steady purchaser of luxury items alongside food and other essentials.[80]

When Francis Saxa's wife died in 1865, John Owen, who himself had an Indigenous wife to whom he was devoted, memorialized her in his journal: "Had a coffin Made for the Wife of Francois Lamoose who died last Night after a Most lingering illness from Cancer of the breast. She had suffered intensely for Months. Poor Woman her trials are Now over on this sphere

Figure 3.3
"Charles Lamoose," by Gustavus Sohon, June 1854

& it is to be hoped that she has gone to seek repose in the Celestial hunting grounds of her people."[81]

The fifth Iroquois was Louis Lamoose or Saxa. Ignace La Mousse's youngest son, Louis, may have been making his living elsewhere, given that he does not turn up in the Fort Owen ledger. When Jesuit priest Lawrence Palladino, who wrote the history of the Flathead mission, arrived in 1867, one of his two guides was "Louis Saxá, a younger son of Old Ignace, the famed Iroquois who brought the faith to the Flatheads."[82]

The sixth and final Iroquois was Pierre Baptiste. Like the La Mousse sons, he was described as a "half-breed Iroquois," but further identification has not been possible. Employed by Owen during the early 1850s as a horse guard, Pierre Baptiste used up what may have been a good part or all of his wages on the usual trio of gunpowder, clothing, and tobacco.[83] His work as a packer with his own horses and mules meant that he thereafter purchased items elsewhere. In June 1856 Owen noted in his journal that Pierre had "arrived from the Mission on his way to hunt in the big hole," for which he had left two days later.[84]

These remains of a contingent that had long since been Iroquois were caught up not only in a changing economy but also in changing perspectives toward Indigenous peoples, in whose numbers they were included. In 1859 De Smet, now chaplain to the US minister of war, was ordered "to St. Mary's or Bitter Root valley, to revisit my first and ancient spiritual children of the mountains, the poor and abandoned Flatheads," for the purposes of their signing a treaty handing over their land. Among those De Smet encountered on his duplicitous mission was "Francis Saxa, or Iroquois," whom De Smet called a "Flathead chief."[85] In 1890, likely referring to the same person, local Indian agent Peter Ronan described "Francois, a worthy and wealthy Indian, who at this date is still a resident of the Bitter Root valley and is well and favorably known by the settlers."[86] In census enumerations, "Francis LaMouse Saxà" and "Peter LaMouse Poé," the last word being their "Indian name," turn up, along with family members, from 1886 onward.[87]

Jesuit priest Lawrence Palladino, who was personally acquainted with Charles, Francis, and Ignace Lamoose, described all three as still alive as of 1894.[88] Francis was the longest lived of the brothers. The editors of De Smet's letters noted about him, "Still living (1903) near Arlee, Montana, where his ranch may be seen from passing trains. He is commonly called

François Saxa (meaning Iroquois) or Lamousse, and is a most respected citizen."[89] As recorded by Palladino, "at the time of our writing, in this year of grace 1910, the whole story in its substance can still be learned from the lips of Francis Saxá, one of the two lads whom their Father, Old Ignace, took with him to St. Louis in 1835 ... [He] has been a personal friend of the writer for very many years; and perhaps in the whole of Missoula County there is not a man more respected by White and Indian than François Saxá, the name by which he is known."[90] By then he was "entirely blind" and "living with his son, Peter."[91] Two later historians note that "Francis Lamoose, also known as Francis Saxa, lived to old age among the Flathead and was a well-known and respected informant on Flathead cultural history."[92]

Just as the Iroquois served the Flatheads well, the Flatheads did so in reverse.

TO SUM UP

The Iroquois who from the early nineteenth century threw their lot in with the Flatheads did their job well. Ignace La Mousse acted as a de facto priest, providing a level of care that the Jesuits, who flitted back and forth once they had been secured, could not reach. The small cluster of Iroquois and Iroquois sons had no other end in view than to share their version of Catholicism, whereas De Smet and the others viewed the Flatheads as simply one more step in their larger goal of religious conversion. For almost a century and perhaps longer into subsequent generations, Iroquois and Iroquois offspring mediated changing times by determinedly navigating the Indigenous-white divide on behalf of Flatheads and others, as well as themselves.

Challenging a Fur Monopoly

Whereas most Iroquois heading west with the fur trade accommodated themselves to its imperatives, others did not. The impetus for a cluster's decision to challenge a fur monopoly was the dispatch west in December 1818 of seventeen Iroquois who were to be paid on a piecework basis for pelts they acquired. Likely unaware of the economics, the men almost certainly thought that hard work would have its just rewards, only to be disabused.

In a sequence of events reminiscent of the daring and self-determination of their predecessors over a century earlier respecting the Albany trade, Iroquois responded both to specific circumstances and to their more general realization of how easily they could be victimized based on others' assumption that they were inferiors. Alongside grievances, leadership was essential to effect change, and this too came into play.

Iroquois's complaints, accompanied by actions, would cause the Hudson's Bay Company, in charge of the fur trade across much of North America, to rewrite its financial structure. That Indigenous peoples could be the impetus for the HBC to do so is remarkable. Although the end result is important, so too is the testimony that events offer of Iroquois's persistence in making known their disagreements face-to-face on a rational basis. Evidence that they did so remarkably survives both in broad strokes and in fine detail. By their words and, when rebuffed, by their actions, Iroquois unsettled the superiority that those in charge took for granted. That the account of their doing so originates with those in charge makes the Iroquois perspective the more credible and persuasive.

The upenders did not thereafter disappear. They traversed the American West, where their self-confidence contributed to perceptions of Iroquois as animating the course of events. Iroquois's independence of character

transformed them into sometimes larger than life personages whose recollections continue to construct some historical understandings of Iroquois.

HIRING TRAPPERS

On 15 December 1818 the North West Company, which in the aftermath of
the War of 1812 had taken over in the Pacific Northwest from the Ameri-
can-controlled Pacific Fur Company, hired seventeen Iroquois on identical
four-year contracts to trap on the far side of the Rocky Mountains. They
each received an advance of 300 livres but, as was usual with the contracts
of chasseurs, or hunters and trappers, no salary and no employment. They
were individually advanced items necessary for trapping, not for free but
at the same price that was charged Indigenous peoples trading pelts,
against which they would be credited for pelts delivered to a central point,
with differential prices depending on the animal.

Possibly responding to Iroquois sensibilities, the seventeen Iroquois
were, as spelled out in their contracts, bound into "a body or partnership
of hunters."[1] They were to hand over everything they caught under the direction of two of their members, Meaquin Martin and Pierre Tevanitagon,
whose surnames were written on their contracts as Isini a quoin and Teané
Torens.[2] Half of the men had paddling trips on record, and four of them
had previously paddled with one of the others, being in this sense already
bound together.

These bonds were strengthened by the seventeen Iroquois heading west
together. A NWC officer reported from Cumberland House in eastern
Saskatchewan on 26 August 1819 the departure of "three light Canoes of
Iroquois and Canadian free-men for the Rocky Mountains by the way of
Fort des Prairies," another name for Fort Edmonton.[3] That post's head
recorded a month later, "All the N.W. Canoes arrived about 4 P.M. as well
as three Canoes of Iroquois who are going across the Rocky Mountains as
trappers for the NWC°."[4]

IROQUOIS'S UTILITY

The North West Company west of the Rocky Mountains was already engaged in trapping in the Snake Country, which was named after the river
of that name and extended from eastern Oregon to wherever streams were

rich in beaver. Led by NWC officers, self-sustaining trapping expeditions interspersed travel with time in one place. Expeditions relied for personnel on a handful of employees and on larger numbers of freemen, comprised of former employees and of nonemployees, such as the new Iroquois arrivals. During stops, men headed off early in the morning to set their traps in beaver streams, to be checked in the evening. The women partnered with them, who went along on trapping expeditions as a matter of course, were expected to manage the children and do most everything else.

Trapping in Snake Country was already perceived by those in charge as problematic, as evidenced by the arrival in 1816 of an Iroquois named Nicholas Oskononton, a veteran of a dozen years of paddling, who became a victim of the course of events: "A man by the name of Oskononton, an Iroquois, belonging to the Snake expedition suddenly arrived at the fort ... reduced to a skeleton." Along with a fellow Iroquois, he had persuaded the officer in charge to allow them to trap on their own, whereupon they "fell in with a small band of Snakes" who persuaded them "to exchange their horses, guns, and their traps with these people for women [to] such an extent that they had scarcely any article left." Having survived that encounter, Oskononton would be killed shortly thereafter on a subsequent expedition. Such stories heightened officers' concern over Iroquois "distracting, as they did, the natives, destroying the trade, and disgracing the Whites."[5]

Initially, the 1819 arrivals went along with what was expected of them. The two men put in charge of the contingent – Pierre Tevanitagon, whom we met in chapter 2, and Meaquin Martin – each formed his own band of Iroquois trappers comprised principally but not wholly of fellow arrivals.[6] The two thereupon entered into formal agreements with the NWC to trap and to trade pelts for goods as single entities. In August 1820 the Tevanitagon band, comprised of himself, his two grown sons, who either came with or followed him west, and one other 1819 arrival, purchased eight pack horses, to be followed over the next while by traps, scalping knives, guns, balls and powder, and horses, as well as by personal items ranging from tobacco, kettles, and soap to blankets and clothing. Against these purchases, the band delivered 720 beaver pelts over the next year. The much larger Martin band, comprising all but one of the other 1819 arrivals along with some others, acted similarly on a larger scale. Two years later, the Tevanitagon band delivered 575 beaver pelts and the Martin band 1,304.[7]

It soon became clear to the Iroquois that their hard work and large numbers of pelts did not equate to economic success. Rather, as the men's running accounts indicate, their efforts had left the two bands in debt. Not surprisingly, then, in 1822 six members of Meaquin Martin's band withdrew from the agreement in order to return east. The band's standing account was thereupon closed in the interest of "those leaving Canada," the assumption that the Pacific Northwest was part of Canada being of note given its actual lack of political status. Dispatched with each of the departing men was his share of the band's very considerable debt, which he was still obligated to pay. Whether or not the men did so appears not to have been recorded.

During this same period, the newly arrived HBC, which took over from the NWC in 1821, was pondering whether to continue its longstanding practice of relying on local Indigenous people to bring pelts to fixed posts or to fall in line with the NWC's reliance on large trapping expeditions. Once the HBC decided to continue the NWC's practice, it similarly advanced supplies, including trapping paraphernalia, whose cost was to be repaid in beaver pelts at the rate it set for them, all in the name of maximizing company profit. Those in charge were very aware that they were using the men to the company's economic advantage, comforted in doing so by the assumption that the men would not figure it out and that, even if they did, they had no recourse. Indicative of this general understanding, Fort Vancouver's head, John McLoughlin, reported to his superior in charge of the HBC across North America, George Simpson, respecting an early annual trapping expedition, that beaver skins valued by the HBC at 10 shillings and 2.5 pence were remunerated to trappers in goods worth only 2 shillings, or one-fifth of what they were worth.[8]

The HBC's Snake Country expeditions were uneasy affairs from the start. The earliest, dispatched in the summer of 1822, was poorly documented, but it did not go unnoticed that fourteen of its members, half of them Iroquois, abandoned it along the way, together with their families.[9] Among those who "did not come out of the Snake Country,"[10] to use the language of the day, were Pierre Kassawesa and Ignace Takakenrat, who had arrived in 1817, François Xavier Tenetoresere, who had come in 1819, and recent arrivals Lazard Teyecaleyeeaoeye and Thomas Narkaraketa. They each had had enough.

These Iroquois's departures did not prevent a second expedition consisting of up to fifty men of diverse backgrounds, along with five HBC employees, from setting out in the spring of 1823, in part to rescue the pelts that its predecessor had cached, or stored, along the way. The heads of the two independent trapping bands, Pierre Tevanitagon and Meaquin Martin, went along, as did some of their former band members. Most importantly from the HBC's perspective, the expedition returned in the fall of 1823 with a very profitable 4,339 beaver pelts.[11]

TWO CRITICAL EXPEDITIONS

It was during the next two expeditions, extending from February to November 1824 and from then to November 1825, that the Pacific Northwest's fur economy was challenged and upended. Because the two expeditions were, unlike their predecessors, closely documented, it is possible to track not only their members but also Iroquois's own words in ongoing and escalating interactions with those in charge.

Heading out from the usual departure point of Fort Flathead west of the continental divide in today's western Montana, the first of the two was led by Alexander Ross, whose time in the Pacific Northwest went back to the Pacific Fur Company. Eleven Iroquois were among its more than forty freemen and ten HBC employees. The second, headed by Anglo-Quebecker Peter Skene Ogden, included almost all the same Iroquois among over fifty freemen and twelve employees. Both also contained wives and children, up to eighty with Ross and thirty women and thirty-five children with Ogden.[12]

The continuity between the Ross and Ogden expeditions extended to personnel. Almost all the same Iroquois were on both expeditions, relying as they did on the already cohered 1819 contingent. By now five of that group had gone back east, two had not returned from the 1822 expedition, and three had opted for paid HBC employment. The others were on at least one of the two expeditions. Ignace Dehodionwassere, Ignace Hatchiorauquasha, usually known as John Grey, Ignace Kanetagon, Louis Kanetagon, Laurent Karatohon, Lazard Kayenquaretcha, Meaquin Martin, Jean Baptiste Saurenrego, and Pierre Tevanitagon were joined on both trips by Jacques Ostiserico, who had come in 1813, and by François Xavier

Sassanare, who had come in 1819. On the first expedition but not the second were Jacques Tehotarachten, who had arrived in 1822, and Tevanitagon's two sons Charles and Ignace. On only the second expedition was Jean Baptiste Tyeguariche, a twenty-five-year-old with ten years' experience in the fur trade, mostly in the Pacific Northwest, who was known familiarly as Norwest.

The 1824 expedition made visible the inherent contradictions in a one-sided economy intended solely to benefit those in charge. Unlike the more docile Canadiens, Iroquois were determined not just to trap but also to wrest benefits from the company for themselves, which Alexander Ross interpreted as misbehaviour. The worst of the Iroquois was in his view François Xavier Sassanare, with fifteen or more years' experience in the fur trade. Sassanare and some others soon had had enough of the extremes of weather and the lack of provisions for their starving families. Rather than tending to the situation as he might have, Ross grumbled that "Francis Sassanare a leading character among the black squad should be sent to some distant post."[13] It was on the next expedition, led by Ross's successor, that an increasingly desperate Sassanare decided that he had had enough: "Another scamp left us on the road, it is not surprising he being an Iroquois by the Name of Fras. Sassanare. He took nothing with him but his riding horse. Left wife and furs behind."[14] Empathy was not a strong suit among those in charge.

It is through a close reading of the journals kept by the heads of these two expeditions, which ran almost continuously over the two years 1824 and 1825, that the upending's rationale and process emerge. The tone of the accounts reflects the prejudices of the men in charge, which were not inconsiderable when it came to Iroquois, but the daily entries were written so close to the ground and at such great speed that it is possible to read through their biases. Not only that, but the expedition's heads, first Alexander Ross[15] and then Peter Skene Ogden,[16] were accountable on paper to their superiors, which gives their narratives a certain honesty.

The message that comes through loud and clear is that Iroquois were ambitious. They had crossed a continent in search of better lives, only to be thwarted not by a lack of hard work but by a system rigged against them. Once they realized what was happening, they did not sit on their hands but determined to rectify the situation. They did so first with words and, when their challenge failed, with actions. The upending would reorder the

HBC's finances to the advantage of Iroquois successors, even as it dispersed the protagonists across the western United States to become the Iroquois of the Wild West of the imagination.

LEADERSHIP

For Iroquois disquiet to translate into action as it did, leadership was critical. The sequence of events initiated during the 1824 expedition and culminating in the 1825 upending depended not only on a perception of legitimate grievances but also on effective action, which the two Iroquois from among the 1819 arrivals provided. A generation apart in age, they are upon first consideration an unlikely pair.

Pierre Tevanitagon's time in the fur trade went back to 1805 when "the chief," as he was termed, was among five Iroquois who signed three-year contracts to head to the Northwest as chasseurs. Listed from 1812 to 1818 as a hunter employed at unnamed locations, he sent funds to his wife back home in Caughnawaga each year. Tevanitagon's maturity is indicated by his nickname of Old Pierre.

The complement to Tevanitagon was young and cocky Jesuit-educated John Grey, who in the Pacific Northwest rarely used his Iroquois name of Ignace Hatchiorauquasha but considered himself, and was considered by others, to be Iroquois. He was born about 1795 on or near St Régis to a Scot named William L. Grey, who had settled there after serving in the American Revolutionary War. Siding with the Americans in the War of 1812, he was captured and died in prison.[17] According to one account, John Grey's mother was half Iroquois and half French.[18] By 1816 young John Grey and his sixteen-year-old Iroquois wife, Marianne Neketichou, also spelled "Nakatiehou," who was sometimes named as Mary Ann Charles, had a base camp in Idaho near the Wyoming border.[19] One of the few or possibly only Iroquois to do so, Grey not only brought his family along with him to the Pacific Northwest but also travelled with them as a matter of course.[20] The second officer in charge of Ogden's expedition described how, as they were about to depart, "John Grey returned to the Fort [Flathead] for his wife and Children, he came with them in the evening."[21] In the Pacific Northwest, Grey had been initially "of Tev's band," but by 1822 he had associated himself with Meaquin Martin's band.[22]

Figure 4.1
"Jean Grey Iroquois," by Nicolas Point, 1840

SETTING OUT IN 1824

From the perspective of the head of the 1824 expedition, Alexander Ross, whose antipathy stretched back in time to the North West Company, Iroquois were out for trouble. He was convinced of that virtually as soon as the expedition departed on 10 February.

The third morning out, Ross, in his words, "found the Iroquois in a body, with old Pierre [Tevanitagon] and John Grey at their head, standing at my tent-door." Ross should not have been surprised given that, he acknowledged plaintively, the Iroquois had earlier been promised they could see their individual financial records as soon as they were ready.

"What now Pierre?"
"Oh nothing. The Iroquois merely wish to see their accounts."

Ross acquiesced, explained the accounts, and queried the reason for the request.

"Our debts are heavy, and we are never able to reduce them in a large party; allow us to go off by ourselves, and we shall do much better."

In response, Ross sought to placate the Iroquois:

"The Company place great confidence in your exertions and I shall do everything in my power to make your undertaking comfortable and profitable."[23]

Words were not what the Iroquois wanted. Except for Meaquin Martin, they responded by staying put instead of setting out to trap, as was the usual morning practice. When Ross queried why they did so, Tevanitagon explained the situation as they saw it:

"The price the Company allowed for our furs is so small in proportion to the exorbitant advance on goods sold us, that we are never able to pay our debts ... much less make money. Consequently we will not risk our lives any more in the Snake Country. We are promised last fall that there would be no more N.W. currency [i.e., an internal medium of exchange not able to be used elsewhere] or doubling the costs of goods in settling our accounts."[24]

The Iroquois, who knew precisely what was happening to their disadvantage, achieved a minor victory when Ross promised to change the currency to sterling or some other generally used medium of exchange. In return, they all agreed to keep going, except for Jacques Tehotarachten, who departed on his own.

The lead taken by Pierre Tevanitagon persuaded Ross to put him in charge of the Iroquois contingent, and Nicholas Montour, a member of the similarly restless Canadien freemen who had arrived from east of the Rocky Mountains, was given parallel responsibility. Ross also decided to play tough, two weeks later going after and forcibly returning Laurent Karatohon and Lazard Kayenquaretcha, who had decided to follow Tehotarachten's example. Ross expressed relief that in this circumstance "Old Pierre behaved well."[25]

A POINTED EXCHANGE

The next recorded moment of contention came three weeks later in mid-March 1824, amid deep snow and freezing temperatures in southwestern Montana, after the men in a general council agreed to build a road to cross the mountains to the next potentially best trapping location. Pierre

Tevanitagon had initially been the only Iroquois who favoured the idea, but some others had followed his lead. John Grey, however, was opposed, and he confronted Ross late in the evening in what was a pointed exchange:

> "Ten other men and I have resolved to abandon the party and turn back."
>
> "Why?"
>
> "By remaining here, we will lose the spring [beaver] hunt. Besides, we are tired of the large band. We did not come to this country to be digging in snow nor passing our time in making roads."
>
> "I'm surprised at hearing a good, quiet, honest fellow like you utter such language, a person on whom I so much depend for your tact and activity in case of emergency."[26]

Ross added as an aside in his journal, "God forgive me for saying so." In the event, he continued to make his case:

> "By returning, you will not only miss the summer hunt but the whole year's hunt: here a subtle change in the weather will soon put us in a way to begin our spring hunt. As well, the nature of the country is such as to require us keeping together for the sake of safety & with regard to the snow. The same difficulties will present themselves in other places as well as in this & if we do dig in snow & make a road we will perhaps have a more dangerous barrier to pass. In any case we must bend to circumstances & necessity & our present situation is such as to require fortitude & perseverance & not a division of the party & furthermore that the views of the concern & the interests of all depend on it."[27]

Grey was not persuaded, and a forceful argument ensued:

> "I am neither a soldier nor engagé, nor am I a slave; I am under the control of no man."
>
> "You are a freeman & a freeman of good character & to be careful not to stain it."
>
> "Fair words are very good but I am determined to turn back, & back I will go."

"You are no stronger than other men & stopped you will be, I will stop you."

"I would like to see the man who will stop me ..."

"You will be, I will stop you. [pause] John, what are your views by wishing to turn back?"

"My views are to work in some place alone, to pay my debt. In the larger band I never can."

"Granted, that by forking [out on your own] you might make a better hunt in proportion to your members than in the larger band, would that compensate for the loss the Company would sustain by a division of the party? After a division of that kind the party could not proceed, being too weak in numbers. Your party walks off & the expedition fails!"[28]

According to Ross's journal, it was at this point that the much older and still loyal Pierre Tevanitagon appeared. Indicative of the possible power dynamic between the two Iroquois, Grey left but not before "having cursed the larger band, the Snake Country & the day he came to it."[29]

The next day, "John [Grey] as he swore last night did not start this morning, nor any of his gang."[30] Ross thereupon effected a compromise by promising Grey that if he did head out, "his debts amounting to nearly 4000 livres should be reduced one tenth, or 400 livres, which at the rate he sells his furs would be a reduction of about 20 beaver – To this he readily agreed & all is quiet once more."[31] In John Phillip Reid's apt characterization of the exchange, "unable to command obedience, Ross purchased cooperation."[32]

The details of the exchange point up Grey's impossible financial situation by virtue of his large debt. Using Ross's calculation, Grey would have had to trap an additional 180 beaver to pay off the remainder. The trip averaged twenty beaver per trap, of which Grey had seven, leaving him with a likely debt at the expedition's end equivalent to forty beaver.[33] Doing the calculation must have increased Grey's dissatisfaction.

A SECOND POINTED EXCHANGE

The related issue, Ross acknowledged at the end of the first exchange, was that, despite Grey's acquiescing to Tevanitagon, his behaviour mattered.

Ross knew a lot about him: "This man, an Iroquois half-breed from Montreal and educated, had no small degree of influence over his countrymen."[34] A follow-up encounter in Ross's tent at sundown the next day made clear that Grey was not easily conciliated:

"I am deputed by the Iroquois and other freemen to let you know that they regret their promise made at the council and can not fulfill it. They are all resolved on abandoning the undertaking and turning back! If they remain, they will miss the spring hunt and, besides, are tired of remaining in the large party and wish to hunt apart. They did not come to this country to be making roads; they came to hunt beaver. Others may do what they please, but I shall turn back. I am a free man, and I suppose I can do as I please."

"Whatever you have got to say, John, on your own behalf, I am ready to hear; but not one word on behalf of any one else. The present savours very much of a combination to defraud the Company and disappoints me. You have taken a weary view of things. Every rose has its thorn, John: so has the hunting of beaver. You say that by remaining to make the road you will lose the spring hunt. You will do no such thing; but by turning back you will lose not only the spring but the fall hunt. The spring here is later by a month than in any other part of the country. Your plan is a bad one, even were it at your choice, which is not the case. You follow my advice, John, I alone am answerable for your hunts. Since you dislike large parties you should have remained at home and not have come to this country at all. Small parties cannot hunt here. And as to your digging in snow and making roads, it is of two evils perhaps the least. It is better for you to be making roads for a few days than to have had for as many weeks to contend with a more powerful and dangerous enemy: which would have been the case had we passed through Hell's Gate and had to fight our way among the Blackfeet. We have all embarked on a sea of troubles; great quantities of furs are not to be secured in these parts without fatigues, cares, hardships, and perils. My advice therefore to you and to all is to submit to circumstances, abandon the idea of turning back."

"Neither fair words nor anything else would alter my mind. Back I will go."

"You are a most unreasonable man. You gave your consent two nights ago and things are not worse now than they were then, and you now withdraw that consent. But I did wrong in asking your consent, I ought rather to have commanded, and for the future I am determined to ask no man's consent in such matters, and if you attempt to turn back I shall certainly try to stop you or any one else."

"Good night."[35]

The next morning, according to Ross, Grey "collected, saddled, and loaded his horses ready for a start," with everyone in the camp watching him do so. Ross thereupon went up to him with a "cocked pistol" and "ordered him either to pay his debt or to unsaddle his horses," as otherwise "he was a dead man." When no one came to his defence, Grey unsaddled his horses.[36] Force won the day in the short term.

NEUTRALIZING DISSENT

Seeking to neutralize Grey's dissent, Ross divided the Iroquois into two groups to prevent them from continuing to connive, doing so with the concurrence of Tevanitagon. He dispatched one group to cross the mountains in search of buffalo for food, and the other, which included Grey, was to remain in camp. It turned out, however, that most of the Iroquois preferred to hunt, and Ross acquiesced. They returned six days later, having killed thirty buffalo, and promptly half dried 140 pounds of meat and made 10 pounds of fat.

The same day that most of the Iroquois went buffalo hunting, the dissatisfied Laurent Karatohon again acted on his unhappiness. He and Lazard Kayenquaretcha had in late February abandoned the expedition, only to be forcibly returned. This time, amid the toing and froing, Ross described in his journal how "that sly, deep intriguing black dog Laurent, who has once already on this [expedition] deserted, left the camp to day & returned back." A week later, "Big Ignace Kanetagon wishes to skulk off with himself," leaving the next day. "Big Ignace returned, with a promise, however, that it is only for a few days time."[37] Iroquois were setting the agenda.

Another serious problem, from Ross's perspective, was that the freemen, not only the Iroquois and the men from east of the mountains but others as well, "think of nothing but to get with the Indians, mostly to live & pass their time in idleness" as opposed to the still unfinished road building. Among the nine errant men were Lazard Kayenquaretcha and Laurent Karatohon, who had earlier been returned on attempting to leave; François Xavier Sassanare, who was a veteran of one of the NWC's Snake Country expeditions; and Pierre Tevanitagon's sons Ignace and Charles. Amid the disruption, Ross continued to put his faith in "Vieux Pierre the Iroquois."[38]

ACKNOWLEDGING IROQUOIS CONCERNS

Ross acknowledged to himself in this journal entry of 1 April 1824 the fundamental issue that the Iroquois and also some of the other freemen had sought to get across to him by their combination of words and actions. He understood that they were "completely disheartened at the means in which the trapping system is carried on in this quarter." Conveniently forgetting that the Iroquois had made the point prior to the expedition's departure, Ross preferred to contend that he was only now caught out and asked rhetorically, "Why did not you say so while at the fort & why did you not start the objections there & then the Company would have acted accordingly."[39] Ross then conjectured that if the freemen had done so, they would have had to choose between heading out and their families starving:

> They say so while at the fort but it was objected to & we were then told, said they, that unless we did consent to go to the Snake Country we should have no advances given us. We therefore could not let our families starve. We, it's true, did consent, but it was necessity that compelled us to it. What could we have done? The Company took advantage of us & should we now take advantage of them & go our own way. We think ourselves justified in so doing. Our intentions are good, we intend paying our debts, whereas by the present mode of proceeding we never can.[40]

Ross imagined what the response would have been from the HBC perspective: "The Company will do you all manner of justice. Let us therefore persevere. Let us, as I said before, lay consequences aside & hope for the best."[41] In other words, Ross was aware at the beginning of April 1824 of the issue that would a year later challenge and upend the fur monopoly.

PARRYING BACK AND FORTH

A day later, 2 April, Ross received what appeared to be good news: "I was surprised by the return of Laurent [Karatohon] who left us on the 23rd. I went says he, as far back as Hell's Gate, but finding no beaver, continued he, I returned again. At that place I went with nine Piegans with whom I smoked & we parted good friends." The arrival three days later, much to the delight of the Iroquois and other men in the camp, of about fifty Nez Percés to trade on their way home from hunting buffalo told another story. Ross discovered that Karatohon's time away had not been, as he alleged, to hunt beaver but rather "to encourage these Indians to come & trade with us!"[42]

About the same time, the other Iroquois once again made clear to Ross that they were their own persons: "This morning 4 of the Iroquois followed the track of Ignace [Kanetagon, who had gone off on 31 March] & went back, but said they … would be here again, as soon as we begin to make the road. Laurent [Karatohon] … makes one of the number. Will they or will they not come is a question."[43] Others among the Iroquois, including John Grey, returned to road building, during which, according to Ross in his memoir, "many hints were given by the Iroquois that had I now and then a dram of rum to give them, my road would soon be made."[44]

The Iroquois could be accommodating. A week later, it was Tevanitagon and then Grey who kept the road building going. Come the morning, "none of the freemen would work on the road except old Pierre the Iroquois, who alone went and alone worked all day." That evening one of the men "made a drum & John Grey a fiddle, the people were entertained with a concert of music," whereupon, taking "advantage of the good humor, I got them all to consent to go to the road tomorrow."[45]

ON TO TRAPPING

Over the next month, Iroquois lived up to their reputation as trappers, acquiring 246 pelts compared to the other men's 319. Given that the expedition had headed off with ten HBC employees and more than forty freemen, of whom only a dozen, by now down to eleven, were Iroquois, they accounted per trapper for two or three times as many pelts, or more, as did the others. Ross's grudging recognition that the Iroquois were "in general good trappers" was borne out.[46]

The Iroquois's utility did not prevent Ross from demonstrating his authority, but ironically his doing so reminded them of the financial in-
equities that, even he acknowledged, underlay HBC policy. According to
his retrospective account, one morning during spring trapping, Ross found
two dozen of the Iroquois's horses turned out to feed outside of the
guarded camp, which was against HBC policy. Despite a warning, the next
morning six of Meaquin Martin's horses were ridden outside of the camp
to permit them to feed, whereupon Ross took them, he told Martin, as
credit against his large debt owed to the HBC. When the camp was raised
a day later, Meaquin Martin and his family were left "sitting by the fire," at
least until the other Iroquois loaned them horses.[47] That evening Pierre
Tevanitagon and two others interceded with Ross to get the horses returned. Although we have no way of knowing Iroquois's perspective, it
seems almost certain that they tucked such high-minded treatment away
in their minds.

Certainly, Tevanitagon did. At least Ross thought so. Up to now Old
Pierre, as Ross called him, had been the designated leader and dependable mainstay among the Iroquois. In late May 1824 a decision had to be
made about where to trap next, whereupon Tevanitagon and some others
observed,

> "We have already been through the country on our left, and have
> trapped in that quarter for two years in succession; there is nothing
> very inviting there; we therefore prefer trying the west quarter."

Ross did not take kindly to Tevanitagon's assertion of independence, which
even he realized was in part a consequence of his own actions: "During
our journey the Iroquois had been plotting to abandon the main party
and hunt apart by themselves; more especially once my quarrel with John
Grey in the Valley of Troubles [over road building], and with Martin for
disregarding the regulations of the camp and neglecting his horse on
Salmon River. At last, Old Pierre was drawn into the cabal." Eventually,
Ross acquiesced, and Tevanitagon and eleven others, including "most of
the Iroquois," set out on their own in mid-June with a promise to meet up
in late September.[48]

Meaquin Martin and John Grey were among those who decided to stay
with the main party, and shortly thereafter Grey and fellow Iroquois

Jacques Ostiserico proved their worth in Ross's view. His journal entry tells the tale:

> Today we had all a fright from the Piegans. This morning almost all hands went to their traps as usual, & while they were scattered by one's & two's & the camp left with only 10 men, the Blackfeet to the number of 40 all mounted on horseback descended at full speed on a few of them at their traps. The trappers being upwards of twenty men were so divided, they could render each other or the camp no assistance. So they took to their heels among the bushes throwing beaver one way, traps another … Two, Jacques Ostiserico & John Grey were pursued in the open plain. Seeing their horses could not save them, like two heroes they wheeled about & rode up to their enemies, who immediately surrounded them. The Piegan chief asked them to exchange guns, but this they refused. He then seized Jacques' rifle but Jacques held fast & after a little scuffle jerked it from them saying to the Piegans "if you wish to kill us, kill us at once, but our guns you shall never get while we are alive."[49]

All ended well, but briefly so from Ross's perspective: "Though I had got rid of most of the Iroquois, I had not got rid of troubles; for there remained John Grey and Martin, who were enough to poison the minds of the rest." One day in late June, upon reaching the evening encampment, Ross discovered that "John Grey, Martin, and ten others had lagged behind, with the intention of taking a different road to the one we had taken, and we were then too far apart to overtake them."[50] It was during the men's few days away that a Snake Indian duped Meaquin Martin out of both his horse and some ammunition.

Ross was not at all sympathetic when, at the beginning of August, Martin announced that he and six of the prairie freemen, along with four other Iroquois, being "Big Ignace [Kanetagon], François Xavier Sassanare, Lazard [Kayenquaretcha] & John Grey," were going off to get salmon to feed "their families starving with hunger." Given that Ross "had come this far not for salmon but for beaver," he used the threat of their being at the mercy of the Snake Indians to dissuade the men. When two weeks later the same men again made the request, Ross used a different tactic to keep them together: "I broke open my little block of tobacco today & gave each half a pound. This is an article of such high value among the freemen for some time past it sold among them at a large beaver skin per inch."[51] Family well-being was not high, if at all, on Ross's agenda.

ENTER AMERICAN TRAPPERS

By now it was late August 1824, and Ross decided to head homeward from his present location in today's western Idaho, a decision that turned his mind to the dozen men, headed by Pierre Tevanitagon, who in mid-June had gone off on their own to trap and had not returned. Being informed by some Indigenous passersby that the Iroquois had "got into a scrape with the Snakes," Ross fretted at not locating them at the agreed rendezvous point.[52] Thereupon, "I wrote Pierre a note," attesting to Tevanitagon's literacy, in which Ross described the subsequent locations where they might meet.[53]

With "men, women & children reduced to walk on foot," Tevanitagon and his band turned up on 12 October "pillaged and destitute," which concerned Ross far less than did their having thereby "neglected their hunt altogether."[54] The Snake Indians had, according to Tevanitagon, robbed them of "nine hundred beaver, fifty-four steel traps, and twenty-seven horses," along with five guns and nearly all their clothing.[55] Although the men had, by Ross's count, lost "40 horses, 40 traps etc.," they had cached 470 beaver, which were rescued.[56]

More significant for the HBC over the long run than Tevanitagon and his band would be the seven American trappers who escorted them back and whom Ross permitted to accompany them to its home post of Fort Flathead. Ross by this means got news from their leader, Jedediah Smith, respecting the fourteen freemen, half of them Iroquois, who had abandoned the earlier Snake Country expedition in 1822: "Having crossed the mountains, they were put upon by Crows and Cheyenne who killed several of the men, robbed others, and took women and children captive."[57] As Ross's interest was economic, he was concerned about the possible caches of pelts they might have left behind rather than about the fate of the men and their families.

The 1824 encounter caused Americans to realize how lucrative the area was, Ross being informed that "all this quarter is swarming with trappers who next season are to penetrate to the Snake Country."[58] The initiative ran counter to the HBC's seeking to keep its activity secret from the Americans. Jedediah Smith was under the command of St Louis fur trading magnate William Henry Ashley, who headed the Rocky Mountain Fur Company. Men associated with Ashley had been divided into two groups. The other, larger group, headed by William L. Sublette, was trapping in southern Idaho, whereas Smith had headed north and so encountered the Iroquois.[59]

It was when Ross and his men were almost back at Fort Flathead that the expedition came full circle with the unexpected return of Jacques Tehotarachten, who had much earlier abandoned it. Ross wrote in his daily journal, "We met the miscreant Jacob [Jacques] who deserted on the 13th February. As for apologizing for his faults & acknowledging his error, he satisfied us & there the matter ended. It now remains with the Company to punish or forgive him for his conduct. He is a vagabond of the first degree."[60] Tehotarachten would return home in 1825.

The expedition's consequences for the HBC were considerable, as Ross discovered upon attempting to acquire the Americans trappers' 900 beaver. Having "offered them the highest prices given to our trappers," he had been summarily refused, the lowest price they would accept being based on Americans' much higher terms of trade: "3 dollars the price of common beaver."[61] The Americans would spend the winter at Fort Flathead, thereby picking up additional information about the HBC to be relayed to Smith's American employer, William Henry Ashley.[62]

QUICK TURNAROUND

Away since February 1824, Ross and his men returned to Fort Flathead on 16 November with 5,000 beaver pelts plus other skins to find his Snake Country successor, Peter Skene Ogden, waiting there to head out on a second expedition. Ogden did so on 10 December on a trip that extended to early November 1825. There was, in other words, no time for the rancour among the Iroquois to die down before they once again departed. From the HBC's perspective, all was well, the 1824 expedition netting a profit of £3,700, or US$18,000.[63]

The two expeditions were in effect continuous over an almost two-year time period. They were also ongoing in the sense that not only personnel but also the seven American trappers who had returned with Ross headed off with Ogden and his second-in-command, William Kittson. Although not travelling and camping together, the two groups shadowed each other, with the Americans breaking off on their own only as the two groups approached the fabled Snake River at the end of March. Kittson was not sympathetic to the Americans, considering their head, Jedediah Smith, to be "a sly cunning Yankey,"[64] as would prove true.

THE SECOND EXPEDITION

Part of the reason for the haste in starting out as soon as Ogden did was to get across the mountains "ere the Snow falls," which would begin with a fury on 12 January 1825.[65] That same day, at an elevation of 2,000 metres, or 6,560 feet, the expedition crossed over the continental divide at Gibbons Pass, heading south to the Big Hole Basin of southwestern Montana, where the men would trap over the next month.[66] Not only was the expedition virtually identical in personnel to its predecessor, but it also in general followed the same route. The consequence was, journal entries make clear, that Ogden relied on men who knew the options better than he did for the best direction in which to head.

Whether or not Ogden was briefed by Ross, he was very knowledgeable of the tumult of the earlier expedition, noting in his daily journal how "Old Pierre [Tevanitagon] … lost everything he had last Summer nearly on the Same Spot" where they then were.[67] To the extent that Ross had given advice, his rancour toward the Iroquois would have been evident. Still at Fort Flathead, Ross was attempting on 12 February 1825 to decide how to get letters to Ogden and wrote in his post journal that the Flatheads would not arrive in time to take the letters and that "to send them by Iroquois is out of the question."[68]

PERSPECTIVES OF THOSE IN CHARGE

Ogden and Kittson, who each kept a daily journal, were more accommodating than their predecessor of freemen in all their peculiarities and diversity. One of their most annoying traits, they considered, was freemen using their free time, such as it was, for their own pleasure. From the moment of departure, Ogden fretted that they willingly traded their horses and ammunition with the Kootenays and Flatheads who joined the expedition along the way. "For a good race Horse, they will part with all their Supplies thoughtless wretches," Ogden wrote on 26 December 1824.[69] Kittson reported the same day, "Races have taken place between horses of the Freemen and those of a Nez Percés they came off equal."[70]

Even so, Ogden's spirit of compromise was evident. A month after starting out, he wrote, "Raised Camp Still keeping the Road to the right tho' apparently much against the inclination & wishes of the Freemen who would prefer Crossing over & following the left. Buffalo being far more abundant by this means they would have full Scope to waste their ammunition." Ten days later, Ogden appears to have acquiesced: "Raised Camp & to the great joy of all took the road to the left." The next day, he recorded, "Many off in pursuit of Buffalo."[71]

It was also the case that, for Ogden and Kittson, the Iroquois were integral to the expedition as opposed to the nuisance they had most often been for Ross. Louis Kanetagon, who had earlier been in Meaquin Martin's band, was killed by his Pend d'Oreille wife two months after setting out. Louis and his brother Ignace had been among the seventeen Iroquois who signed identical contracts in December 1818 to trap for four years in the Pacific Northwest. Likely from Lac des Deux Montagnes, they were probably recruited by virtue of Louis's having signed six previous paddling contracts going back to 1810 and Ignace two beginning in 1814.

As for Louis Kanetagon's killing, according to Ogden, "the Cause of this was owing to his wife who in a careless manner cocked his gun she attempted to half cock it, when it went off the deceased was opposite to her at the time, the Ball entered the breast he survived not more than two minutes & did not utter a word."[72] In order to learn precisely what occurred, "questions were put to a relation of the Deceased, who was present at the time, regarding the way it was done, and he having said it was accidental nothing more rested on us to do than getting him buried which soon was done and prayers were said over him by his tribe." The deceased's Pend d'Oreille wife having been absolved of blame through the testimony of Louis's younger brother "Big Ignace," more than one eyebrow must have been cocked given the rapidity with which she "changed the situation of the lodge and the relation immediately took her as his wife."[73] The full extent to which the two men in charge felt accountable for those under them is indicated by the second-in-command later recalling that they were near to "where we lost an Iroquois on the 5th February last," being Louis Kanetagon.

Overall, Ogden and Kittson were almost, if not quite, as antagonistic to the Iroquois's independent spirit as Ross had been: "The snakes numbering 4 lodges came up and pitched near us. Iroquois as usual commenced trade and bought a horse at an enormous price."[74] John Grey in particular came in for little jabs. Kittson noted that Grey, while in an advance party, "was lower down hunting and reported the snow was plenty," but "I immediately suspected him of having told us a lie." The next day, Kittson "visited the lower quarter of this river, found it quite the opposite of [what] Grey said."[75] In what was a backhanded compliment, Ogden wrote in reference to some Snake Indians, "I never have met with any Indians So difficult to trade with, the Iroquois have most completely initiated them in the art of trade."[76]

FIVE DAYS OF UPENDING

It was in April 1825, as Ogden's expedition and the Americans shadowing it reached the Snake River of southern Idaho with the goal of trapping beaver, that the HBC's upending, which had been brewing since the previous Snake expedition, began to materialize. As Ogden's expedition approached the border with today's Utah, it became clear that the American presence was far greater than had been thought. Ogden wrote that the Snake Indians "inform us that a party of 25 Americans wintered near this [place] & are gone in the same direction we had intended going; if this be true, which I have no reason to doubt, it will be a fatal blow to our expectations." The next day, Ogden learned that the small river where they were camped "has been Well trapped by the Americans this spring."[77] Just as the expedition approached today's Ogden, Utah, later named in Ogden's honour, and its fortunes appeared to be turning around, the drama commenced that would give Iroquois the opportunity to act on their longstanding grievances. It began when fifteen trappers, having headed off on 14 May on the understanding they would return four days later, did not do so.

Another four days later, on 22 May, one of the trappers who had been away came back, along with Lazard Teyecaleyeeaoeye and another freeman, both among the fourteen who had not come out of the Snake Country in 1822. In what would be day one of the upending, Ogden learned from them that, much as Jedediah Smith had earlier reported, "6 are dead & the remainder with the Spaniards, at St. Louis & Missouri." As for the returned pair, "they belong to a party of 30 men who were fitted out by the Spaniards & Traders on the Missouri & have Spent the winter in this quarter & have met with little success." Not only was the Ogden expedition only "15 days march from the Spanish village" of Taos, New Mexico, but he was informed that "the whole Country [is] overrun with Americans & [French] Canadians all in the pursuit of the Same object as we had."[78]

The situation escalated with the arrival the next morning, day two, of "15 men Canadians & Spaniards headed by one [Étienne] Provost & Francois [Xavier Tenetoresere], an 1819 arrival," who was another of the seven Iroquois to have slipped away in 1822. In the afternoon, there turned up together "with 14 of our absent men a party of 25 Americans with Colours flying the latter party headed by one [Johnson] Gardner," being an American trapper about whom little information survives.[79] Characterized as "a blustering mountaineer," Gardner was likely, as was Prevost, a free trader associated with the Rocky Mountain Fur Company, based in St Louis.[80] Jedediah Smith and the others who had shadowed the Snake Country expedition, being in Prevost's view "intelligent young men, of strict veracity," had reported to the Americans then camped 14 kilometres, or 9 miles, away that the British flag had been hoisted in the HBC camp. It was this "impertinence" that instigated Gardner's action.[81]

The Americans' arrival was only the beginning, so Ogden described in his journal: "They encamped within 100 yards of our encampment & lost no time in informing all hands in the Camp that they were in the United States Territories & were all free, indebted or engaged, & to add to this they would pay Cash for their Beaver 3 ½ dollars p. lb., & their goods cheap in proportion to our Freemen [who] in lieu of Seeking Beaver have been with the Americans no doubt plotting."[82] What was being offered to the freemen echoed the consideration that the Iroquois had sought from the NWC and then the HBC.

The next morning, on 14 May, or day three of the upending, Gardner pushed home his point to Ogden respecting the British-based HBC being in American territory, a claim that would turn out to be wrong.[83] Upon

Gardner leaving Ogden's tent, the once loyal Pierre Tevanitagon entered, together with Lazard Teyecaleyeeaoeye and François Xavier Tenetoresere, who had been among those to depart the expedition in 1822. Tevanitagon explained to Ogden, based on written notes he had made, that the two men's debts had been paid by virtue of Iroquois continuing to trap on inequitable terms. Kittson interjected by pointing out mistakes Tevanitagon had made in the calculations, which rendered them in error.

Upon seeing Gardner go into the tent of John Grey, whom Ogden in his journal entry interestingly described as "an American & half Iroquois," Ogden also did so, whereupon Grey turned to him and said,

> "I must now tell you that all the Iroquois as well as myself have long wished for an opportunity to join the Americans & if we did not Sooner it was entirely owing to our bad luck in not meeting with them, but now we go, & all you Can Say Cannot prevent us from going."

Gardner was silent except for a single remark to Ogden:

> "You have had these poor Men already too long in your Service & have most Shamefully imposed on them, selling them goods at most extravagant rates & giving them nothing for their Skins."

Gardner then left, whereupon Grey again addressed Ogden, this time respectfully so:

> "That is true. The gentlemen in the Columbia are the greatest Villains in the World & if they were here this day I would Shoot them. As for you, Sir, you have dealt fair with me & with us all, but go we will we are now in a free Country & have Friends here to Support us & if every man in the Camp does not leave you they do not Seek their own interest.[84]

Grey then, in Ogden's words, "gave orders to his Partners to raise Camp & immediately all the Iroquois were in motion, & made ready to Start"; their "example was Soon followed by others." In the interim, Ogden and

Kittson sought to acquire as many skins as possible belonging to the men. For their part, "the Americans headed by Gardner & accompanied by two of our Iroquois who had been with them the last two years advanced to Support & assist all who were inclined to desert." Lazard Teyecaleyeeaoeye then addressed the crowd:

"We are Superior in numbers to them & let us fire & pillage them."[85]

Teyecaleyeeaoeye advanced with his gun cocked and pointed at Ogden, who had already gotten into a scuffle with Pierre Tevanitagon over the Iroquois's two horses. Ogden was determined not to allow Teyecaleyeeaoeye and the others to take the horses, and with the backing of Kittson and three employees managed to hold onto them against the Americans and thirteen freemen. Three of the freemen were persuaded to pay off their debts, the others escaping without doing so, along with 700 beaver pelts, a good part of which they had conveyed the night before to the American camp. The list Kittson made of the twelve indebted freemen who had left included eight Iroquois. Along with John Grey and Pierre Tevanitagon were Ignace Dehodionwassere, Laurent Karatohon, Lazard Kayenquaretcha, Meaquin Martin, Jacques Ostiserico, and Jean Baptiste Saurenrego.

On 25 May, day four, the drama continued. The previous evening, Ogden and Kittson had received a report that "the Americans and Iroquois are coming tomorrow to pillage us," so they put the remaining freemen on a double watch over night. Nothing happened, but as the camp was being raised, Gardner and three of the Iroquois turned up, likely in the expectation that more men were about to abandon the HBC. This time the freemen from east of the Rocky Mountains acted, five of them informing Ogden that, being "free & not indebted," they were going to join the Americans.[86] Again, it was HBC policy that rankled. For them, the problem was that men received any outstanding balances only on their departure from the fur trade, the HBC holding onto their funds as a credit against possible future debts.

As the freemen were leaving, Ogden and Kittson forcibly held onto the men's beaver pelts and horses, which they considered to be HBC property. Ogden was fully aware that the drama in its entirety centred on economics, and he reflected realistically on the possibility that his remaining freemen would be tempted away by the Americans if the "offers made them independant the low price they Sell their goods are too great for them to resist."[87]

On 26 May, day five, François Xavier Sassanare and another of the five trappers absent since 14 May showed up with a story of having had their two horses, sixteen beaver, and fifteen traps confiscated by the Americans, to be returned only if they would join them, which they had refused to do before escaping during the night. Ogden suspected that they might have come back because "they have both Women & Horses" left behind.[88] Ogden anticipated that others were planning to leave as soon as they could hide their furs, which he had guarded.

It was only on 29 May, by then in extreme southeastern Idaho near present-day Preston, that Ogden's suspicions were realized: "Three men deserted leaving behind them Women, Children, Horses, Traps & Furs; so greatly are they prepossessed in favour of the Americans that they sacrificed all to join them."[89] One who left was the just returned Sassanare, who became the seventh Iroquois freemen to follow Pierre Tevanitagon's and John Grey's lead in heading off on their own.

BACK TO TRAPPING

The upending shadowed the rest of the trip, as with the news "that a party of Americans & Iroquois are not more than three days march from us."[90] Having lost a total of twenty-three men, fourteen of whom successfully made off with their furs, traps, and horses, the beleaguered Snake Country expedition all the same returned to the task at hand, which was trapping beaver.[91] Using the opportunity given by three freemen passing by in late June 1825 with a large band of Piegans and Bloods, Ogden sent a letter to HBC headquarters in London reporting on the dramatic happenings, despite which the expedition now had almost 3,000 beaver.[92]

The expedition returned on 2 July 1826 to the more convenient Fort Nez Percés, also known as Fort Walla Walla, in today's southeast Washington State. Despite arriving with 4,000 beaver for a profit of £3,100, or a healthy US$15,500, which would have been £600 greater if not for the losses occasioned by the debts of departing freemen, the HBC had been upended.[93] According to the head of the HBC in the Pacific Northwest, by virtue of the eight Iroquois's and other fifteen freemen's actions, "the Concern has lost between two and three thousand Skins in furs [to the value of £3,700] and their future services."[94] An American estimate originating with Gardner Johnson was far higher: "the furs thus obtained amounted to about 130 packs or 1300 lbs. worth at that time about $75000."[95]

THE HBC'S RESPONSE

Iroquois were thereafter mostly absent from trapping expeditions. Leaving again almost as soon he returned, Ogden took along few freemen, Iroquois or not. The only Iroquois from the previous expedition was Jean Baptiste Tyeguariche, whom Ogden described as having been "far more honest than I expected."[96]

Ogden was well aware of the upending's larger import. Even as he prepared once again to head out, Ogden alerted the HBC's North American head, George Simpson, that so long as Americans "offer and give as high as three to three and a half dollars p. lb. for the most indifferent Beaver and goods at a trifling value," the HBC would suffer.[97] Ogden followed up with HBC headquarters in London: "The exorbitant price the Trappers paid for their Goods and horses is solely to be attributed their desertion and former misconduct, indeed from the enormous prices they have been charged with, the difficulties they had to encounter and subject to so many losses, it was almost impossible however industrious a Man might be to clear his annual expenses." Ogden backed up his assessment with hard data respecting the typical freeman: "His four horses and traps alone cost him One hundred fifty large Beaver, nor could he depend on the latter for the years as they have been of late years of an inferior quality."[98] The indebted situation in which Iroquois and other freemen had found themselves was structural.

Pierre Tevanitagon, John Grey, and the others were not in Ogden's view the villains of the piece. While trapping in the spring of 1826 in southeastern Idaho, "a Party of Americans and some of our deserters of last Year 28 in all" arrived. Among their number were the two men whom Ogden had during the previous expedition optimistically designated as leaders of their respective groups in order to keep them under control: Nicholas Montour from east of the Rocky Mountains and Tevanitagon of the

Iroquois contingent. To Ogden's surprise, "we received 81½ Beavers in part payment of their debts due to the Company, also two notes of hand from Mr. Montour ... and Pierre Tevanigogans."[99]

Reflecting on the significance of Tevanitagon's payment of his debt, Ogden described how "in the Hudson's Bay Company's service with the strictest economy almost depriving himself of common necessaries, barring accidents, in the course of ten years he might collect that sum." He asked rhetorically, "Is it then surprising that men who consult their own interests, should give preference to the American service?" Most remarkable from Ogden's perspective was that some men had stuck with him and the HBC: "Considerable credit is due to my party for their behaviour, so far it is to be observed they are under a written contract, but if inclined to go, would lay little stress on it and still less in regard to their debts."[100] Ogden effectively acknowledged the astuteness of Pierre Tevanitagon, John Grey, and the others in upending the fur monopoly that was the Hudson's Bay Company. Ogden would later learn to his regret that "Old Pierre the Iroquois Chief who deserted from me four years ago was killed, and before they could rescue his body, it was cut into pieces."[101] The Idaho site where Tevanitagon died in 1827 was, and is, memorialized as Pierre's Hole, encouraging the perception that Iroquois were integral, as they were, to a West in the making.[102]

Others more senior in the HBC also confronted the systemic inequity responsible for the upending. Writing to the HBC's London headquarters in the summer of 1827, John McLoughlin, the HBC head in the Pacific Northwest, laid the blame for the upending not on the Iroquois or on the Americans, who gave "no assistance to our Deserters except countenancing and receiving them in their party," but on "the Discontented state in which the whole party was, including even those who remained." McLoughlin had no doubt whatsoever that "the High price charged for the Supplies has been the cause of the troubles that have attended the Snake Expedition since its first commencement."[103]

If no disagreement existed on the ground as to the reasons that the Iroquois, along with other freemen, had upended a fur monopoly, only the centre in London could effect change. As Ogden set out into Snake Country for the third time in September 1826, McLoughlin was still "at a Loss" for instructions and perforce acted on his own volition in promising the twenty freemen accompanying Ogden "10/- for Every Full Grown Beaver

– half this amount for a cub" and in allowing them to purchase supplies at the same prices charged HBC employees and equipment at cost.[104] The next May, London headquarters accepted the legitimacy of the upending, instructing its North American head, "We can afford to pay as good a price as the Americans and where there is risk of meeting their parties it is necessary to pay as much or something more."[105] The realistic George Simpson lamented in response that "we now when too late perceive that our former system of trade with those people was bad."[106]

The best acknowledgment of the legitimacy of the Iroquois's position belongs to the HBC's head in the Pacific Northwest, John McLoughlin, who observed that "it is more surprising in my opinion that any of them remained than that any ran away."[107] Although HBC trapping expeditions over the next two decades would, by chance or by the choice of one party or the other, each include only one or two Iroquois freemen or employees, their imprint was on them. These expeditions would continue due in good part to the policy shift instigated by the Iroquois's introduction of free enterprise into the Pacific Northwest.

INTEGRATING INTO THE AMERICAN WEST

The consequences of a handful of Iroquois upending a fur monopoly affected not only the HBC but also the protagonists. Departing Iroquois's pathways across the American West speak to another dimension of their lives, being their integration into the edges of a western United States in the making.

Iroquois were unafraid to use whatever resources they could muster in order to get on with their lives. A year after Pierre Kassawesa slipped away from the 1822 expedition, he successfully sought the assistance of American Indian agent Benjamin O'Fallon, who wrote to a prominent American fur trader on his behalf: "I have given two Iroquois Indians my permission … to join your expedition to the mountains, with a view of recovering a squaw and two children, whom the Crow nation of Ind[ns] took from them on their passage to this place, and I wish you to be so good as to use your influence in affecting that object."[108] The woman and her "several children" were subsequently located and about to be restored "to her husband (an Iroquois Ind[n] from Canada now at this place)" when they were once again captured, with O'Fallon again on their trail a year later.[109] With an "Irogoi [*sic*] Hunter," possibly the "husband," as part of the expedition, "Two Iriquois [*sic*] prisoners were demanded of the Crows" during treaty making, likely without success given that there is no subsequent reference to the request.[110]

Iroquois turn up time and again in written accounts from the American West. One of a group of trappers led by Joseph Robidoux of the American Fur Company told of encountering in late summer or early autumn 1831 "a party of Iroquois" who had split off from a larger group of "ten free Iroquois, with their wives and children which [had] departed to hunt on the waters of the Columbia."[111] Robidoux hired three of the Iroquois, who were among his group of twenty when later in the year he met up by chance with that year's HBC trapping expedition led by Ogden's successor, John Work. Work reported that, among the Americans' number, "Frizzon an Iroquoy who was formerly deserted from us came to our camp but little news was obtained from him as it was late when he arrived."[112] The nickname Frizzon, used to signal curly hair, could have applied to numerous of the Iroquois who had earlier abandoned the HBC and not been heard of since.[113]

Clearly, Frizzon was known to at least one of the Iroquois with Work, for when the two groups met up again the next spring, Jean Baptiste Tyeguariche, who had been part of HBC trapping expeditions since 1825, sought to join the trio of Iroquois who were with the Americans: "Baptiste declared his determination to accompany the Iroquois his relations, who deserted from Mr. Ogden some years ago, and who are now with the American party." Its head, Lucien Fontanelle, told Work that he could not refuse the request since Tyeguariche was a freeman but that he would not accept any furs or provide him with supplies until he settled his HBC account. The more contentious issue had to do with Tyeguariche's horses, which Work considered to be on loan to him from the HBC. Work did not want to let the animals go, whereas "the Iroquois are determined to take them by force and to play the game they had with Mr Ogden some years ago." Work was "prepared to defeat their purposes even at the expense of the loss of life on both sides."[114] The Iroquois's attempt the next day at compromise was insufficient to satisfy Work, as he described in detail:

> Baptiste [Tyeguariche] came to settle his a/c this morning and paid
> 15 beaver which is within 4 beaver of the amount of his debts, but he
> insisted on taking one of the Company's horses which was lent him

and giving one which he had left in the hands of the Indians in his place, this I objected to, he nevertheless loaded the horse and when I went to take him from him, I observed his Iroquois friends priming & preparing their arms. I nevertheless seized the horse and though none of them offered to lay a hand on me yet several of them at different times laid hold of the horse ... till we were all driven into the river, things appearing to become serious.[115]

When several men with Work drew their weapons, he realized the situation was getting out of hand and effectively acquiesced to the compromise offered by Tyeguariche:

> I would have prevented Baptiste from going off but he gave notice last year not to return to the plains, and being a disabled man from wounds, he would have been an encumbrance to any of the Company's establishments [and] I therefore consider getting clear of him a good riddance. He had two horses of his own which I allowed him to take off. I would have taken one of them for the balance of his debts which he owes but was apprehensive had I done so he would have left his family consisting of a wife & three children on my hands, which would have greatly embarrassed me to take them back to their friends at Walla Walla.[116]

A member of the American contingent told a similar story, except that it was not the Iroquois but the Americans who "cocked our rifles" in the face of a potential armed confrontation with Work's men.[117] Tyeguariche would return to HBC country and, with a Walla Walla woman named Judith who travelled with him, have six children. The family eventually settled, as described in chapter 5, in Oregon's Willamette Valley.

The Iroquois were still trapping as part of the American contingent in September 1832 when one of their number was killed by the much-feared Blackfeet. Considered "one of our best hunters," Frasier, as he was known by the Americans, "went out the day previous to set his trap" but did not return. A search found him "shot in the thigh and through the neck and twice stabbed in the breast," but to general relief all around, although stripped, he was "unscalped." Described by fellow trapper Warren Angus Ferris as "a comrade, who but yestermorn was among us in high health, gay, cheerful, thoughtless, and dreaming of nothing but pleasure and content in the midst of relations and friends," Frasier was for lack of a coffin covered "in a piece of red scarlet cloth, around which a blanket and several buffalo robes were wrapped and lashed firmly, ... carefully laid in the open grave, and a wooden cross in token of his catholic faith placed upon his breast." Frasier's "friends and comrades" conducted "the simple rite," whereupon "the little herd of mourners retired to their respective lodges, where more than one of our ordinarily daring and thoughtless hunters" reflected on "the uncertainty of life."[118]

What is most remarkable about this first-hand account, published in 1844–45 in installments in an American literary magazine, is how much the young American knew and cared about the deceased Iroquois, who cannot be otherwise identified:

> Frasier was an Iroquois from St. Regis, in Upper Canada. He left that country seventeen years before, having with many others engaged in the service of the Norwest [North West] Company, and came to the Rocky Mountains. Subsequently he joined the American hunters, married a squaw by whom he had several children, purchased horses and traps, and finally as one of the Freemen led an independent and roving life. He could read and write in his own language, was upright and fair in all his dealings, and very generously esteemed and respected by his companions.[119]

Ferris was so moved by the death that a year later, in 1833, he "visited the grave of Frasier, the Irroquois, who was killed and buried here last fall, being desirous to ascertain what was generally believed already, namely, that his body had been stolen from the grave, robbed of its covering, and thrown into the Jefferson [River] by the Black foot Indians" who had killed him.[120]

Also in 1833 "four Iroquois hunters, driven by the snow from their hunting grounds, made their appearance" at the winter encampment in southeastern Idaho of American Benjamin Bonneville, who was heading west, he hoped, to compete with the HBC. Popular writer Washington Irving, drawing on Bonneville's journals, described how the Iroquois "were kindly welcomed, and during their sojourn made themselves useful in a variety of ways, being excellent trappers, and first-rate woodsmen." As recounted by Irving, "they were the remnants of a party of Iroquois hunters, that came from Canada into these mountain regions many years ago ... led by a brave chieftain named Pierre," who "gave his name to the fated valley of Pierre's hole."[121]

Iroquois long continued to animate the West. In his diary, published in 1914, American trapper Osborne Russell recounted how, faced in June 1837 with taunts from a nearby party of Blackfeet, "an Old Iroquois trapper ... turned to the Whites about him and made a speech in imperfect English," whereupon "he stripped himself entirely naked throwing his powder horn and bullet pouch over his right shoulder and taking his rifle in his hand began to dance and utter the shrill war cry of his Nation." The battle turned when "our leader (the same old Iroquois) Sallied forth with a horrid yell and we followed; the Indians were so much surprised with such a sudden attack that they made no resistance whatever but wheeled and took [off] toward the village as fast as their horses could carry them."[122] And so it went.

TRACKING JOHN GREY

Of all of the trapping Iroquois, the literate John Grey leaves one of the most intriguing trails, partly in his own voice, as he did earlier during the fateful HBC trapping expedition.[123] Grey was working for the American Fur Company in 1832 when he and another trapper were ambushed in early March by Blackfeet near today's Logan, Utah. His companion was killed, whereas Grey escaped across the river, during which, he recounted, "one of their balls grazed my thigh and another cut out a lock of my hair," and I ran so far "my moccasins became worn out and left my naked feet to be cut and lacerated by the ice and stones." Finding "a quantity of bull rushes ... I cut as many as I could grasp in my arms twice, and bound into three separate bundles; these I fastened together with willows, launched it without difficulty, and embarked upon it, allowing it to be carried along by the force of the current." The next day, Grey went ashore only to discover "the torture from my feet was such, that I fell down, unable to proceed further," at which point, to his good fortune, he was found by two hunters on horseback, who carried him back to their camp. It took two months for Grey's "mangled frozen feet ... swollen to twice the natural size" and "quite black," to recover. A short time later, Grey and a small party separated off at Pierre's Hole to trap independently, making "good hunts."[124]

By now John Grey was becoming a legend among Rocky Mountain trappers, his exploits extending to tangling with grizzly bears: "John Grey, a herculean trapper, has fought several duels with them, in which he had thus far been victorious, though generally at the expense of a gun, which he usually manages to break in the conflict." A hunting ground adjoining Pierre's Hole on the south was "called Grey's Hole, after John Grey, a half breed Iroquois, who discovered it some years ago."[125] From the perspective of a young American who encountered him at the annual summer fur trade rendezvous in June 1834, "Mr Grey who has long been with and is almost of the red skins" passed muster by virtue of being in the company of some of the leading American mountain men of the day.[126] Like so many other Iroquois, Grey strode the Indigenous-white divide.

A year later, John Grey and his family were among a group of Canadiens and Iroquois migrating from the Rocky Mountains down the Missouri River to Westport, which would become part of today's Kansas City, Missouri, and which was by virtue of its location at the junction of the Missouri and Kansas Rivers a gateway to the West.[127] A Jesuit priest assigned there a few years later described optimistically how Iroquois and others headed there "with the intention ... of looking to the salvation of their souls."[128]

Two of the earliest recorded Catholic baptisms at Westport, on 23 February 1834, were of "Iroquois-Flatheads," being brothers Francis and Louis Sasson Essassinary. Their father, François Xavier Sassanare, had been among those who abandoned the HBC along with John Grey in 1825. Not only that, but one of the two earliest recorded Catholic marriages, on 18 July 1836, joined "Charlotte Grey, daughter of John and Marianne, both Iroquois," to Benjamin Lagautherie, son of Victor Lagautherie and a woman who was almost certainly Indigenous. Although it is impossible to know whether Grey had a hand in selecting his son-in-law, he was known to be protective of his family, having two years earlier almost killed a man because of an improper advance to one of his daughters.[129] John Grey must have found his son-in-law agreeable, both being recorded as among Westport's early settlers.[130] A year later, John and Marianne Grey's twelve-year-old daughter, Agnes, was baptized.[131]

Iroquois daughters' circumstances at a time when white women were few and far between could be problematic, as they themselves sometimes realized. An early priest recounted the situation of "an Iroquois girl of very attractive personal appearance" in respect to a Westport ball to which she had been invited: "She was not ignorant of the pleasures in prospect for her did she go to the ball; yet as soon as she knew that its pleasures would be attended with risk to her future she put all thought of being present at it from her mind. Furthermore, not to be without a reason for her refusal, she cut her hair very close, a sign of deep mourning among the savages." There was, however, a difficulty: "Her friends insisted, and her father even went so far as to threaten to imprison her in the cellar if she persisted in her refusal." The priest recounted his persuading "the poor old Iroquois … that it belonged to his own honor to help his child not to lose but to preserve a treasure that she knew how to esteem so well."[132] The incident speaks both to the nature of the times and to this young woman's full awareness of the situation faced by persons like herself.

Grey and his wife, Marianne Neketichou, were part of the entourage travelling with Jesuit priest Pierre-Jean De Smet on his spring 1841 return trip from St Louis to his Flathead charges of chapter 3, likely having joined up with De Smet on his passing by Westport.[133] It is intriguing that, for all of De Smet's enthusiasm for the Flatheads' Iroquois intermediaries, he did not so describe Grey in his one reference to him in his writings. Grey's identity, which crossed the Indigenous-white divide, was linked rather to his utility, which was considerable: "We had a hunter named John Grey, reputed one of the best marksmen of the mountains; he had frequently given proofs of extraordinary courage and dexterity, especially when on one occasion he dared to attack five bears at once. Wishing to give us another example of his valor, he drove an enormous buffalo he had wounded, into the midst of the caravan … At last the hunter took a decisive aim, and the buffalo fell to rise no more."[134] A New Yorker who travelled part way with the contingent recalled Grey as "an old Rocky Mountaineer" who had taught the other men how "to kill buffalo for food," focusing on "the tongues and the marrow bones."[135]

For all of his daring on the trail, John Grey would be killed in 1842 or thereabouts over a minor dispute with a Westport neighbour.[136] The much-travelled Marianne, who lived to 1862, was subsequently flooded out of their home, whereupon she moved into "a small apartment" next to the Catholic church, which she tended. A newly arrived priest evoked her sturdy character: "She spoke English imperfectly, but had a good command of French and her own dialect. She was strong and fearless and at the approach of strangers carried a large stick which she held hoisted in a threatening manner until she was sure of the good intentions of the invaders."[137]

Among the ways that John Grey would be remembered is an Idaho historical marker adjacent to Greys Lake honouring him as "an Iroquois leader."[138] In the view of leading *coureur de bois* historian Gilles Havard, "by birth Scottish and Iroquois, John Grey, also known as Ignace Hatchiorauquasha, best personifies the backwoods heroism of mountain men."[139]

TO SUM UP

Iroquois's ambition in the West had multiple entryways, one of which originated with a cluster of trappers directly confronting the HBC for using them for its own financial gain. Their upending of the fur trade was no small matter, being the impetus for the company's reorganization of its financial structure. As John Jackson reminds us, "the western Iroquois went over to the Americans for strictly business reasons."[140] That Iroquois acted as they did not only improved economic conditions for their successors in the fur trade but also contributed to Iroquois's distinctive positioning in accounts of the American West. In referencing "his dual role as an Iroquois – Ignace Hatchiorauquasha – and as a white man – John Grey," Merle Wells astutely sums up Iroquois in the West.[141]

PART THREE

Sticking with the Fur Trade

Among Iroquois "Sticking with the Fur Trade" as opposed to venturing out on their own was a large contingent doing so in the Pacific Northwest, being the location of the fur trade's farthest distance – 5,000 kilometres, or 3,000 miles – from Montreal. Despite the fact that, or perhaps because, the region long lacked external governance, a sizable proportion of those "Committing to the Pacific Northwest" never left. Some of them, as explained in chapter 5, eventually set down in future Oregon on the pattern of white employees who did the same. Iroquois's daring to cross the Indigenous-white divide would be undone by Americans unable to perceive Indigenous persons, as Iroquois were, as worthy of doing so.

Chapter 6 attends to Iroquois's sons and daughters "Disappearing into a Changing Pacific Northwest." Coming of age at a time when the vast region was being transformed into American and British possessions, sons had to scramble to make a living. Daughters were in contrast sought out by white men at a time when the gender ratio was enormously skewed. Lives went on but unevenly so.

Committing to the Pacific Northwest

During the first two decades of the nineteenth century, the fur trade raced west. As areas became trapped out, others were prospected. Hence in 1811, as described in chapter 2, David Thompson crossed the Rocky Mountains, beyond which lay a vast swath of territory unknown to outsiders, except for coastal traders in search of sea otter pelts much valued in China for trimming garments.

Iroquois were integral to the fur trade's expansion across the Rocky Mountains and into the Pacific Northwest, which extends north through present-day British Columbia, south through the American states of Washington and Oregon, and east into parts of Idaho, Montana, and Wyoming. Many of those there early on had worked elsewhere, bringing with them expertise alongside strong senses of self. Iroquois so proved themselves that they continued to be employed into the years of the fur trade's decline in the mid-nineteenth century. Among the last to arrive would be Louis Oteakorie, whose story prompted my interest in Iroquois in the West. As did a goodly number of Iroquois before him, he committed to the Pacific Northwest.

THE PACIFIC NORTHWEST'S DISTINCTIVENESS

The Pacific Northwest is as far west as it is possible to go without falling into the Pacific Ocean. To the north at the time that the first outsiders arrived over two centuries ago lay Russian America, today's Alaska, and to the south lay Spanish California, now an American state. The earliest trading post originated in sea travel around South America. Established by the Pacific Fur Company out of New York at the mouth of the Columbia River in 1810, Astoria proved to be short-lived, passing to the North West Company, based in Montreal, at the end of the War of 1812 between Britain and the young United States. In 1821 the NWC was folded into the Hudson's Bay Company, based in London.

The far west fur trade was long unencumbered by any nation caring enough to impinge politically. At the end of the War of 1812, Britain and the United States, neither of which had any interest in the remote region, agreed to joint oversight intended to prevent any other country from poking around. Growing numbers of land-hungry Americans heading west caused the United States to make a claim in the early 1840s for the entirety of the Pacific Northwest. Britain opposed the move, not because of any interest in this remote territory but due to the HBC's seeking to hold onto fur-rich New Caledonia, located in the heart of today's British Columbia. As a consequence, the Pacific Northwest was divided in 1846 between the two countries at the 49th parallel, with a jog south around the tip of Vancouver Island. The United States would quickly take charge of its newly gotten gains, with Britain doing so more slowly. Vancouver Island, to which the HBC relocated, was declared a British possession in 1849, with the mainland of today's British Columbia being so in 1858 consequent on a gold rush.

The 170 named Iroquois who can be tracked as in the Pacific Northwest at some point between 1811 and 1858 were enmeshed in a larger fur trade setting. They never comprised more than 1 in 10 of the regular employees. Most of the 200 to 450 men at work across the Pacific Northwest at any one time were Canadiens. A small minority, comparable in size to numbers of Iroquois, were of mixed Canadien and Indigenous descent.[1] Another handful, also similar in numbers to Iroquois, were Indigenous Hawaiians. They had initially been hired by the Pacific Fur Company, subsequently by the NWC, and then by the HBC during sailing ships' usual stops, due to the trade winds, on the Hawaiian Islands on their way from Britain or eastern North America to the Pacific Northwest.[2]

ARRIVING WITH THE NORTH WEST COMPANY

Up to 1821, when the Hudson's Bay Company took charge, the NWC dispatched seventy-five Iroquois, mostly veterans of the fur trade, to the Pacific Northwest. Numerous of them having already paddled together, they were familiar with each other not only from their childhoods in one of the three Iroquois villages but also from the intimate understandings that came from the workplace.

Initially, Iroquois were something of an oddity. At the time that David Thompson reached the American post of Fort Astoria in July 1811, Pacific Fur Company clerk Alexander Ross described with awe, in what was a numerical exaggeration, "Mr. Thompson, northwest-like, dashing down the Columbia in a light canoe, manned with eight Iroquois, and an interpreter, chiefly men from the vicinity of Montreal."[3] Although Thompson almost immediately turned around, other Iroquois were not far behind.

The earliest named Iroquois to arrive were seven members of the cross-country brigade that in 1813 brought the first NWC officers to newly acquired Astoria, renamed Fort George. Ignace Salioheni had since 1800 worked in various capacities, being by some accounts the Iroquois named as Ignace who helped to guide David Thompson across the Rocky Mountains.[4] Étienne Oniaze and Thomas Canasawarrette signed up together on 28 December 1810 to go to the Northwest for three years as milieux, each being provided in the usual fashion with "a 3-point blanket, a 2.5-point blanket, 6 yards of cotton, a pair of leather shoes, and a tumpline" for carrying heavy goods.[5] Jacques Shatackoani, who in 1810 had twice paddled to and fro, signed a similar contract a week later, likely to join the pair. Nicholas Monique had agreed to paddling contracts in 1808 and 1809. Jacques Ostiserico turns up in the NWC ledger in 1811 and George Tewhat-tohewnie in 1812–14.[6] These seven earliest Iroquois would commit to the Pacific Northwest for periods ranging from nine to thirty-seven years, for a remarkable total of 130 person-years of labour.

It was only in the aftermath of the War of 1812 that the NWC turned its attention to the Pacific Northwest's utility. As explained by long-time employee Alexander Ross, "connected with this new arrangement was the introduction of Iroquois from Montreal," who, "being expert hunters and trappers, might, by their example, teach others."[7] With this goal in mind, the NWC dispatched four annual contingents of Iroquois to the Pacific Northwest, comprised of sixteen arriving in 1816, ten in 1817, eleven in 1819, and twenty-one in 1820, including the seventeen chasseurs profiled in chapter 4. With this exception, Iroquois worked where and when needed. In the summer of 1818, thirty-eight unnamed Iroquois, along with twenty-five Canadiens and thirty-two Hawaiians, constructed the new NWC post of Fort Nez Percés on the Columbia River.[8] Given that forty some Iroquois were then in the Pacific Northwest, virtually every one must have been put to work.

The human dimension of Iroquois heading as far away from home as it was possible to go in order to secure a living for themselves and their families comes through in the arrangements that the sixteen experienced paddlers of the 1816 contingent made prior to heading west. With seventy recorded contracts from 1803 onward between them, they well realized that they were taking a chance on the unknown and honoured their obligations by designating prior to their departures that part of their earnings would go to sustaining their families. Eleven named their wife, twelve their mother, and one a sister. Marital status may have played into their actions over the longer term. Of the eleven who designated funds for their wife, just three stayed in the Pacific Northwest for ten or more years, whereas of the thirteen who had money sent to a mother or sister, likely because they were not married, seven did so. Family life back home mattered.

Iroquois variously fashioned lives for themselves in and out of the workplace. Among those who were not sent back east in the course of their employment or who who did not opt to return home at the end of a contract was 1813 arrival George Tewhattohewnie, who paddled back and forth to Montreal on cross-country brigades.[9] Describing Tewhattohewnie as "a powerful man about six feet high," NWC officer Ross Cox had no doubt, within the hierarchy that was the fur trade, of his authority over him. Cox recorded admonishing Tewhattohewnie for not responding to his request to manage the canoe differently than he was doing: "I was at length obliged to use peremptory and threatening language, which produced a forced and sulky obedience." A few days later, Tewhattohewnie was, according to Cox, drunk when he entered Cox's room determined to "have satisfaction" for the insult to his capacity. The consequence was a violent struggle at whose end Tewhattohewnie is said to have promised Cox "never again to drink to intoxication."[10]

Tewhattohewnie responded to his circumstances by, at the end of either his first or the next contract, not renewing but becoming a freeman and living on his own resources. In December 1824 he was invited to join an HBC expedition heading north when it came across him on the Olympic Peninsula at the northwestern tip of future Washington State: "The Iroquoy George had been stationary near this bay sometime past hunting sea otter." Persuaded to go along, "George an Iroquoy Freehunter and his slave accompany the party on account of his being acquainted with the coast part of the way."[11] Slaves were part of Indigenous culture on the West Coast, and this individual may have belonged to the local woman with whom Tewhattohewnie had partnered.

ENTER THE HUDSON'S BAY COMPANY

According to long-time NWC officer Alexander Ross in respect to the forty-some Iroquois at work when the Hudson's Bay Company took charge of the Pacific Northwest fur trade in 1821, "they form nearly a third of the number of men employed by the Company on the Columbia," this at a time when New Caledonia to the north was still a separate entity.

The HBC may have initially been conflicted respecting Iroquois's presence, given its long-lived preference for English speakers as regular employees. Very possibly for that reason, over half of the NWC's Iroquois employees were gone by 1826, replaced during the same five years by just over half that number of Iroquois, all but three of whom were also soon gone.[12]

The critical counterbalance to sidelining Iroquois was George Simpson, who had charge of the HBC across North America and was sympathetic to Iroquois based on his experience with them as his paddlers. The consequence was that the HBC held onto the remaining twenty-two NWC Iroquois, all old hands who had proven themselves. Between the NWC and the HBC, they were each employed a decade or more, a dozen for over two decades. Nine of them would almost certainly have worked longer if they had not died or been killed on the job. These twenty-two Iroquois contributed 460 person-years of labour to the Pacific Northwest fur trade.

NWC Iroquois provided a base for the ninety-five Iroquois the HBC hired in three waves between 1821 and 1858. The first wave would run from 1821 to 1830 and the second from 1831 to 1841. Hiring ceased until 1845, whereupon it continued modestly until 1858, by which time the HBC was in retreat. Twenty-nine of the HBC hires would, as with the NWC core, contribute a decade or more of their labour, totalling 540 person-years, to the Pacific Northwest fur trade.

Iroquois were an everyday presence in the Pacific Northwest fur trade, as at Fort Langley, which opened in 1828 in the Fraser Valley of today's southern British Columbia. In what was a typical mix of employees, eight of the thirteen there in 1830 were Canadiens, one was an Abenaki, two were Hawaiians, and two were Iroquois.[13] Thirty-eight-year-old Étienne Oniaze, who had come in 1813, was employed as a hunter. Forty-year-old Louis Satakarata, arrived in 1813, was one of four carpenters. The pair were variously at work across the Pacific Northwest until their deaths in 1852 and 1850 respectively.[14]

Satakarata's contract renewal at Fort Langley in 1841 quite remarkably survives in its French-language original as a lone document in the British Columbia Archives. The agreement testifies to Iroquois's response to the Pacific Northwest being virtually identical to what it had been across the West over the past four decades, including the element of respect that such documents denoted. Satakarata "voluntarily engaged himself" as a "milieu," an all-purpose term, for two years in exchange for a salary of "£17 sterling a year," a contract that he signed with his mark.[15]

RECRUITING PADDLERS

Water transport connected the Pacific Northwest with its distant sources of supply and men. Without paddlers' skills, the vast distances occasioned by its location in the far corner of North America would have made the pursuit of pelts virtually impossible. Complex water routes linked the various posts to Fort Vancouver, from which pelts and other products were dispatched to Britain each autumn on a ship that earlier in the season had brought trade goods and supplies. As well, by the mid-1830s the "annual express," as it was termed, headed east each March by water with letters and departing men and returned in the autumn with dispatches and new recruits.

Led by Simpson's firm belief that Iroquois were the best paddlers, the HBC relied on them, along with Canadiens. Of the thirty-two Iroquois who arrived between 1821 and 1830, thirteen had previously worked east of the Rocky Mountains as paddlers going back in time to 1807. Seven had recently done so in nearby Athabasca. Another three had served on the Far North expedition of the mid-1820s headed by English Royal Navy officer John Franklin, who went on to command the abortive mid-century successor expedition with which his name would be identified.[16] Among the sixteen paddlers on Franklin's inaugural trip of 1818–21 was bowsman Michael Teroahauté, who continued to hunt as starvation weakened bodies to the point of death. Teroahauté was with two others when one of them was likely accidentally shot or possibly killed himself. The expedition's surgeon, who was Franklin's second-in-command, blamed the death on Teroahauté's desire to eat the dead man's flesh, and fearful that he would be next, he killed Teroahauté.[17] This "execution," in the words of the editor of Franklin's journal, re-emerged on the second expedition of 1825–27, when one of the three Iroquois, all experienced with previous contracts going back into the first decade of the century, informed Franklin that he was Teroahauté's brother, whereupon the defensive Franklin paid off and dismissed all three at the first stop along the way.[18] The three Iroquois thereupon turned their sights on the Pacific Northwest, where Thomas Agonaiska and Teroahauté's brother, Charles Arahota, would make their careers, the third, Charles Kawenion, remaining there only briefly. As with Agonaiska and Arahota, at least half of the thirty-two Iroquois who arrived during the 1820s were already in their middle years and may have similarly sought somewhere reasonably safe to land. Their doing so explains why three-quarters of these Iroquois who did not die early on or were not sent back east in a year or two remained a decade or more.

Reflective of numerous Iroquois unable to decide in their own minds whether to stay or go was Joseph Monique. Contracting in 1816 for three years as a milieu, he was briefly in the Pacific Northwest prior to being employed as a "boute," or endman, in Athabasca. Returning home for part of the 1820s, he then recontracted. Arriving in the Pacific Northwest in 1829, he was employed at Fort Vancouver as a boute. Typical HBC journal entries about him ran, "Joseph Monique with one boat returned from conducting the Brigade up the [Columbia] River" and "Joseph Monique and three other Iroquois Boutes started this afternoon in a boat for the interior, to meet the Express from York [Factory]." There followed two melancholy entries on 18 and 19 March 1845: "Joseph Monique one of the River Boutes died to night" and "Buried Monique this morning."[19] Monique's memory survives in the homage paid to him by Scots HBC officer Angus McDonald, perhaps especially conscious of Monique's distinctive inheritance by virtue of having himself partnered with a daughter of long-time Iroquois employee Jean Baptiste Tyeguariche, who had arrived in 1817:

The voyageur Joseph Monique, an Iroquois steersman, was one of the best at running the Columbian rapids and whirlpools that ever ran that formidable river. And his personal appearance was as prepossessing as was his singular address in the prow of his canoe or barge. He made his last voyage with me and died. Of all the celebrated H.B.C. steersman, he was the most notoriously audacious in the most dangerous torrents of the Northwest. One glance of that fiery black eye of his read leagues of the turbulent stream at once.[20]

The HBC early on sent a dozen Iroquois paddlers to remote, fur-rich New Caledonia, some briefly and others for long periods of time. Among the latter were Thomas Tiegne, born in 1796 in Caughnawaga, and Rhene Selahoanay, born in 1791 in Lac des Deux Montagnes. Among the 1816 arrivals in the Pacific Northwest, Tiegne was one of those who designated part of their wages to their wives. Prior to being contracted in 1823 to cross the mountains, Sclahoanay had similarly done so. Neither man returned home, Tiegne being dispatched to New Caledonia in 1825 to spend the next two decades there and Selahoanay being a boute and guide there until his death in 1854. Bowsman Charles Arahota, who had been on the second Franklin expedition, was based there for fifteen years prior to returning home to Quebec. Fellow Franklin veteran Thomas Agonaiska, already entering his forties upon his arrival in 1830, was initially also posted there but soon transferred to Fort Vancouver. The daily journals of New Caledonia's principal post of Fort St James, which survive in their entirety from 1820 to 1856, testify to these and other Iroquois becoming an everyday presence after having earlier been suspect by virtue of fraternizing with local Indigenous peoples.[21]

The HBC's hiring priorities did not change over time. Ten Iroquois boutes and twenty-four middlemen were hired in the 1830s, along with a son of 1813 arrival Thomas Canasawarrette, killed in 1832, who was taken on as a trapper. Due possibly to the model of older Iroquois still comfortably at work, over half of the thirty-five who did not die early on, as did three of them, committed to the Pacific Northwest for a decade or more.

Several newly arrived boutes were dispatched to New Caledonia, possibly not to their disliking given that Iroquois were already there. Jean Baptiste Asanyenton, aged twenty-eight upon his crossing the mountains in 1831, had a decade earlier been among twenty-six Iroquois hired for twelve months to go to what was described as the "New York spectacular of July 1821."[22] Now at the other extreme of urban conviviality, Asanyenton spent a decade in New Caledonia, possibly on cross-country brigades that took pelts to market, prior to returning home. Louis Aurtaronquash, who had come in 1837, was two decades in New Caledonia before his transfer to Colville in present-day Washington State, where he likely settled down. A discontented HBC clerk stationed in New Caledonia from 1833 to 1847 described regular employees there, who were "apparently contented and happy," as "principally Iroquois and half-breeds," the latter term restricted to persons of mixed Indigenous and white descent.[23] It was because of New Caledonia's profitability that, when a boundary had to be decided, Britain secured British Columbia for future Canada as opposed to its being melded into the United States.

TARGETING IROQUOIS

The optimistic mood of the 1830s was shattered by a traumatic event that put Iroquois hires at a standstill. Its impetus was an agreement the HBC signed in 1842 with the Russian-American Company, which oversaw today's Alaska, that permitted the HBC to establish coastal trading posts in exchange for providing foodstuffs. Three Iroquois were among the twenty men dispatched to the new post of Fort Stikine, now Wrangell, Alaska. Simon Anaheurase arrived as a middleman in 1839 to find himself constructing the equally remote Fort Taku, now Juneau, before being assigned to Stikine along with newcomer Pierre Kanaguasse. Following his four years as a woodcutter on the coastal steamship *Beaver*, Kanaguasse's nephew Antoine Kawanessa joined them there in 1841.

The next year, Fort Stikine's head, John McLoughlin Jr, was killed by one or more of the twenty men under him, with Kanaguasse and Kawanessa accused of complicity. In the aftermath, the deceased's namesake father in his capacity as HBC head in the Pacific Northwest was determined, whatever the cost of doing so, to clear his son, who had a reputation as a bully. As young McLoughlin described in the post journal, his favourite victim had been one of the three Iroquois: "In going round the men's houses I found in Peter Kanaguasse's room a barrel of salt salmon," which, given that "I am not starving the men under my care," must be for some nefarious purpose.[24] The head's assistant would later testify that he had "frequently seen the deceased punishing Peter Kananguasse very severely (when [McLoughlin was] in a state of intoxication) to such a degree as to disable the man from duty for weeks together."[25] Kanaguasse and his nephew would, following time in detention along with others similarly suspect, be returned east in 1844 along with Anaheurase. News almost certainly followed them there respecting Iroquois's maltreatment in the Pacific Northwest.

After a hiatus until the mid-1840s, Iroquois hires continued modestly, with twenty-two more arriving up to 1858, by which time the fur trade was in decline. The longest employed, at eighteen years, would be middleman Louis Oteakorie, who worked from 1849 to 1867, whereupon he set down on Vancouver Island.

Contributing to the relatively small numbers of Iroquois hired during these years was the changing character of Quebec, from which the men came. George Simpson observed in 1841 that "voyaging seems to be getting into disuse."[26] A long-time officer in the Pacific Northwest lamented in 1844 that "we get no Iroquois up now and all the old ones are either gone or [off] on their own."[27]

THE EVERYDAY CONDUCT OF THE FUR TRADE

The 1842 killing and its aftermath did not override the reciprocity that had long characterized the everyday conduct of the Pacific Northwest fur trade. The common denominator was hard physical labour with strategic breaks in the routine to keep up morale. On a trapping expedition's arrival at Fort Vancouver with pelts, "the men composing the crews, principally Canadians, Iroquois and Half-breeds, were indulged, after their long abstinence, with an allowance of liquor, pork and flour, as a *regale*."[28]

Just as with the deaths of Canadiens, Hawaiians, and others, Iroquois were mourned and, as appropriate, revenged. In October 1830 McLoughlin alerted fellow officers that "Poor Gros [Big] Pierre Karaganyate is dead."[29] Arrived in 1816, the sometime paddler on the cross-country express had fallen victim to malaria, to be respectfully buried in Fort Vancouver's graveyard. The killings not long after of 1813 and 1818 arrivals were taken seriously indeed, with McLoughlin commanding a fellow officer in the spring of 1832, "You will proceed with the party under your command to the Killimook country for the purpose of punishing the atrocious murder of Pierre Kakaraquiron and Thomas Canasawarrette who were savagely murdered by the above tribe [Tillamooks] twenty days since."[30] Within a month, not only were "6 of the Murderers of the late Pierre and Thomas" killed, but the two Iroquois's horses were recovered.[31]

Iroquois who died after long service were remembered in post journals, as at Fort Vancouver, where the entries of 19 and 21 November 1845 read, "Old Louis Jironquay is no more!" and "Old Louis buried." A boute, he had been sixteen years in the Pacific Northwest. Two and a half years later, the entry of 16 February 1848 ran, "Thomas Agoniasta was buried evening. He died two days ago. He was one of the oldest hands at this place." A week later, the journal recorded, "Joe Tayentas died of inflammation of the lungs, after an illness of only four days. He was guide to York Factory for eight years running, and was one of the most efficient men in the Columbia. His loss will be much felt." The entry of the next day added, "Joe Tayentus was buried this morning before breakfast."[32] The three were among the boutes recruited at the end of the 1820s and had done the jobs for which they were hired, excepting that Agonaiska had not been able to resist the California gold rush of 1848. He returned north to die in a measles epidemic three days before the Grand Dalles woman, named Susan, with whom he was partnered. They were buried together.

Not just in respect to their physicality, Iroquois variously revealed their distinctiveness. The typical "Iroquois Frenchman," so a granddaughter characterized Jean Baptiste Tyeguariche, was more likely than his Canadien counterpart to have arrived earlier in time.[33] Almost half had come prior to 1821, as opposed to one in five Canadiens, and so were more experienced in the ways of the fur trade. The mean age of Iroquois crossing the Rocky Mountains whose birth year survives was twenty-two compared to twenty for Canadiens.[34]

Music and dance were key aspects of how Iroquois displayed themselves. Long immersed in Catholicism, they had their own take on music; according to a Scots officer, they sang "hymns oftener than paddling songs."[35] The latter, however, become so engrained as to be hummed during their everyday activities as a matter of course.[36] Dance vied with music as a means of sociability. On New Year's Day in 1835 at Fort McLoughlin on the North Coast, officers and men danced, Canadiens "sung several paddling accounts," and the two Iroquois "danced the war dance with the great spirit of their tribe."[37] Another time, on the eve of tracking down Indigenous peoples to revenge five killings, "the men received a regale and the Iroquois went through a war dance, in character."[38]

CENTRALITY OF FAMILY LIFE

So long as we accept that there is no reason for the surviving slivers of stories from the shadows of the past to differ substantially from those that do not survive, we get some sense of what ensued in respect to that critical dimension of human activity that is family life. It is impossible to know how long men kept the trust of the women they initially sustained while away, but it seems likely that most relationships faltered.

Iroquois engaging in family life in the fur trade did so with Indigenous women likely local to where they were then stationed. That Iroquois acted thus even as they were from time to time in direct confrontation with local peoples speaks to the complexities of everyday life. Women were almost certainly a stabilizing force that encouraged men to stay, both generally and at specific posts. At the same time, there were potential hindrances to unions' stability. Although arrangements were routinely made for women partnered with officers to be moved as part of men's transfer between posts, regular employees, including Iroquois, might well be on their own in impossible situations.[39]

Drawing on post journals and church records, Bruce McIntyre Watson has tracked three dozen Iroquois unions across the Pacific Northwest, and there were clearly many more that did not make it into the public domain.[40] Ledgers attest to Iroquois who took care of their families by purchasing against their wages not only household items such as tin kettles but also niceties, including tartan and cashmere shawls and in at least one instance a "Scotch bonnet."[41]

Although Iroquois were not the point of interest for most passersby, they sometimes remarked on family life. At Fort Vancouver around the time of the boundary settlement, Toronto painter Paul Kane heard at its employee village "quite a Babel of languages, as the inhabitants are a mixture of English, French, Iroquois, Sandwich Islanders, Crees and Chinooks."[42] Ethnographers Franz Boas and James Teit concluded two-thirds of a century later based on what they were told, observed, and inferred that the Okanogan, Colville, Spokane, Flathead, Pend d'Oreille, and nearby Indigenous peoples had significant levels of "intercourse and intermarriage," which was "chiefly with Iroquois and French."[43]

One of the most revealing vignettes referencing family life goes back in time to one of the earliest Iroquois in the Pacific Northwest. In March 1814, not long after the newly acquired Astoria was renamed Fort George, "two canoes with freemen arrived Bellaire & Ignace L'Iroquois and their families."[44] Registre Bellaire was a Canadien who worked variously for the NWC, and Ignace Salioheni was an Iroquois steersman who had come the previous year.

It took only a month for the presence of Salioheni and his family at Fort George to be contested by the local Chinook chief's daughter, Ilchee, who lived with Duncan McDougall, a Scot at the very top of the fur trade hierarchy. The post journal tells the story: "Battle between Mrs McDougall and Ignace's woman regarding the children of the latter, who were playing with some trifling things, when the former lady who is of a haughty and imperious character thought proper to take the play things from them and set them a bawling." The children's mother slapped Ilchee for doing so, which did not go down well. The next day, the post head described in the journal how "Mr McD thought proper to revenge the insult offered to his lady yesterday, and gave a slap and a kick to Ignace's Boy which I conceive was very improper, for what business had she to go into Ignace's woman's tent to interfere or wish to deprive the children of their play thing."[45]

Nevertheless, a week later, the journal recorded, "Removed Ignace's family out side the fort, to make place for storing under the shed; placed her in the house with Nipassengues," then employed at Fort George.[46] Even though Ignace Salioheni was currently taking a brigade up the Columbia River, his status was no match for that of Ilchee, the NWC officer in her life, and her chiefly father, a frequent post visitor. Ignace Salioheni would ply his skills for another decade in the Pacific Northwest before disappearing from view.[47]

A second account highlights the everyday circumstances of Iroquois family life. As did other employees, Iroquois partnering with local women very often acquired in-laws. Two years after joining the HBC in 1831, middleman Louis Sagoshaneuchta was posted to help construct Fort Nisqually, which was intended to produce foodstuffs for Russian America. There, he partnered with a local Nisqually woman known as Marie Anne, with whom he had Catherine in 1834 and Ignace three years later.

Not only was Marie Anne's brother soon working at the post, but its head also became actively involved in family affairs when illness struck the extended Sagoshaneuchta family. The compassionate account in the fulsome Fort Nisqually post journal merits reproducing in its entirety:

4 March 1836. No less than 5 Indians of one family unwell. I paid them a visit & found them all suffering with sore throat.

5 March. During the night a young woman about eighteen years of age belonging to the number above died. She was a fine Girl, a sister to Louis the Iroquois' wife. Her brother is also not expected to live.

6 March. The Indians are still gathering about the sick, but without success in their singing and blowing, the poor people are getting worse daily.

9 March. During the night another girl died from want of care, she was a sister to the other that died on the 5th instant during the night. The remainder of the family consisting of the Father, Mother, two sons both men and a young boy have come near us, where the process of blaming has commenced with a vengeance.

10 March. I paid a visit to the sick, the eldest is very low, the next getting bad, the latter came [to] put himself under my care. The complaint is an inflammation of the throat. I have given him a doze of Dover's Powder [for cold and fever], put his feet into warm water and blistered his neck, then into bed well covered over.

11 March. The Indian Doctors succeeded in killing the oldest son by improper application of cold water to the belly ... The mother of the late sick family is not expected to live ... The Indian Doctor has given out that it was my Tobacco that made the Indians sick. I suppose this is done to cover their sin of murdering them as they have done.

19 March. Louis wife finds the mother is now very well and a young daughter.

20 March. The young sick Indian under our care is off to his friends against my will, but expect that if he takes care of himself he may recover. The Father and Louis's wife were the cause of his going.[48]

A year later, the complexities occasioned by Louis Sagoshaneuchta's in-laws again made it into Fort Nisqually's journal:

22 February 1837. Louis' family coming.

25 February. Louis' wife's Father and Mother are now again near us, poor people, still feel the loss of their Children, given number died last spring.

17 March. Louis' Brother-in-law like a coward shot Sou-cat's brother-in-law in course of the night then took to his heels. This morning I proceeded to his lodge but he was absent. Gave a severe reprimand to his Father, Mother, and his only sister, saying that should the Indian die I would immediately pay 2 blankets for the murderer's head. Today news was received from the wounded man who appeared to be doing well.[49]

Surprisingly, the journal did not record Sagoshaneuchta's death by drowning the next day in the Cascades Rapids on the Columbia River until over a year later and then only indirectly: "16 May 1838. Several Indian women sick among them is the Widow Louis."[50]

The post journal has unfortunately not survived for the rest of the month. Nor are there subsequent entries respecting Sagoshaneuchta's family. What does survive is a record, following the first priests' arrival, of the baptism on 28 April 1839 of Ignace, son of the "late Louis Sagoshaneuchta, Irouqois," and of "Mary-Anne, Nisqually."[51] As with so much of Iroquois families' lives, what survives are more slivers than whole stories.

An important signifier of the importance accorded family life was Iroquois's minding their sons' wellbeing. Growing up in the fur trade, numerous sons edged into the workplace almost as a matter of course. Killed by local Indigenous peoples in 1832, Thomas Canasawarrette left behind fourteen-year-old Ignace, taken on by the HBC in 1838. Fellow Iroquois Étienne Oniaze fathered Baptiste around 1828, who at age seventeen was hired as an apprentice carpenter and within the decade was so well placed that he outfitted himself with corduroy trousers, a regatta shirt, and a "Suchong silk scarf."[52] Having arrived in 1813 and been employed to his death in 1852, Louis Satakarata fathered François, who in 1845 at age fourteen was similarly taken on as an apprentice.[53] Having arrived in 1816,

Michel Ouamtany almost certainly fathered Thomas, born about 1824, who upon his father's death was sent to Red River, possibly to be schooled, before returning in 1843 as an HBC interpreter and carpenter.

Serving to solidify families was the first priests' arrival in the Pacific Northwest in late 1838. The Catholicism integral to Iroquois men's upbringing was evident in the speed with which the priests legitimized relationships and thereby offspring. The earliest Iroquois to formalize their unions were those able to do so by virtue of proximity to Fort Vancouver, which was near the priests' base in the Willamette Valley, whereas Iroquois at a distance had longer to wait. It was likely not his first union when in 1850 St Régis native Thomas Sagoyawatha, in the Pacific Northwest since 1836 and a sometime woodcutter and stoker on the coastal steamship *Beaver*, wed a woman named Josephine, with whom he had Joseph, Thomas, and Mariam. Late arrival Thomas Atrareiachta spent five years in remote New Caledonia prior to being moved to Fort Langley, where in 1856, as a prerequisite to their Catholic marriage, a local Indigenous woman was baptized as Marie. And so it went.

BUILDING NANAIMO

As some Iroquois settled down into family life, others were only then arriving. Among the latest was Louis Oteakorie, who came in 1849 largely on his own resources, as described in the introduction. By then times were changing. Vancouver Island became in the same year, in the aftermath of the 1846 boundary settlement, a British Crown colony centred on the HBC post of Fort Victoria, which had been established three years earlier. To the extent that the HBC foresaw a future in the Pacific Northwest, its preferred base of operations was Vancouver Island, consequent on the discovery there in 1852 of coal needed to fuel British Royal Navy ships travelling up and down the coast. Oteakorie was initially dispatched to an unsuccessful mining venture at the island's northern tip, then to its successor of Fort Rupert, and in 1852 to Fort Nanaimo, 100 kilometres, or 60 miles, north of Victoria.[54]

Indicative of Iroquois's workplace skills, half a dozen Iroquois and Iroquois sons, along with a handful of others, constructed Nanaimo on a heady schedule in anticipation of forty coal miners and their families arriving from England in the fall of 1853. Lazard Onearste, Ignace Karo-

Figure 5.1
Early Nanaimo, largely constructed by Iroquois, by Edward D. Panter-Downes, 1859

huhana, and Thomas Sagoyawatha, all in the Pacific Northwest since the 1830s, headed there from Victoria by canoe on 24 August 1852, two days before the arrival of twenty-three-year-old Joseph McKay, who had charge of the project. Entering their forties, the three Iroquois had lengthy work experience as carpenters and woodcutters on the North Coast, followed by time together at Fort Victoria.

Speed was of the essence, and the trio obliged. McKay recorded in the post journal on 30 August that they had "removed to the log hut which they roofed on a temporary manner with cedar bark and floored with gravel."[55] On 9 September they "commenced building miners house," and a week later "Carpenters are now roofing the miners' house."[56] Work continued day after day, week after week, month after month. More help was needed, hence McKay's note in the journal on 3 April 1853 that "Louis Oteakorie arrived."[57] The next year saw the arrival of Iroquois sons François Satakarata, whose sister Theresa was married to Onearste, and Thomas Ouamtany, known as Tomo. They had earlier been employed at

Fort Victoria as, respectively, a woodcutter for the *Beaver* and an axeman, skills needed in Nanaimo.[58]

McKay's journal entries detailed the men's work over the next several years on every aspect of Nanaimo's construction. In May and June 1853, week after week, he recorded, "Lazard, Thomas, Ignace and Louis building Bastion," which was intended for defence and which still stands in a different location as a Nanaimo landmark. Other days, he wrote, "Lazard and gang as before," testifying to their routinely working together.[59] The two Iroquois generations were largely responsible for constructing, along with buildings, the handmade parts of the coal mining equipment.

Nanaimo Iroquois astutely used the openings that came their way by virtue of their hard work. In August 1853 Ignace Karohuhana, whose family was settled in Victoria, explained his circumstances to McKay, who passed the information on to the HBC head on Vancouver Island, James Douglas: "Ignace has sent his children to Victoria to school. He says that he was promised rations for his family at the time of his engagement with the Company, and desires that such extra rations may be furnished his family in Victoria."[60] Given that Karohuhana was one of the mainstays who saw construction to completion, the matter must have been resolved to his satisfaction. Other men took their families to Nanaimo with them, which could be cause for concern, as with the report of January 1856 that "Lazar's child fractured his arm in a fall."[61]

Still at work in Nanaimo upon the arrival of young Englishman Mark Bate in January 1857 were, to use his spellings of how he heard the names pronounced, "Lazaar Oreasta, Tomo Saklowatti and Louis Oteekorie [who] lived in the next house." Bate was especially generous respecting Oteakorie, whom he may have remembered as older than he was: "Louis Oteekorie was an elderly man of a quiet, tractable, disposition, though of bulky, strong frame. He was a woodman, and a famous hunter – one of the sharpest, of sharpshooters. It was made part of his duty, in the services of the Hudson's Bay Company, to go deer-stalking when venison was needed at the store."[62]

As is so often the case respecting Iroquois, they are absent in histories of Nanaimo, with the exception of Bate's account. Even where a principal primary source is McKay's daily entries in the post journal, with its numerous references to Iroquois, they are left out of the story.[63] The bastion's construction is attributed to others.[64] It is as though Iroquois never existed, which from the perspective of those doing the writing was the case.

SETTLING DOWN ON THEIR OWN RESOURCES

South of the international border established in 1846, nothing more signifies Iroquois's commitment to the Pacific Northwest than a dozen, and perhaps others, settling down on their own resources. Their initiative followed on Canadiens doing the same on the aptly named French Prairie in the fertile Willamette Valley south of Fort Vancouver.[65] Men farmed even as some of them continued to work part time for the HBC, with which they traded grain and other commodities for supplies. The aspects of their lives that survive testify to men's hard work and self-determination alongside that of the women with whom they partnered.

According to local historian Harriet Munnick, three Iroquois – Thomas Tewatcon, Jean Baptiste Tyeguariche, and Charles Tchigt, who arrived in 1816, 1817, and 1819 respectively – settled "in a little cluster of their friends and countrymen" on the north side of the Yamhill River a mile north of today's Dayton, Oregon, and a few miles west of French Prairie.[66] Nearby were Laurent Karonhitchego, Louis Shaegoskatsta, and Louis Shanagraté, who all came in 1816; Pierre Satakarass, who arrived in 1821; and Joseph Tehongagarate, who followed the next year. Two later arrivals were Louis Onskanha, known as Monique, who came in 1830, and boute Jacques Tahetsaronsari, who arrived in 1831. Historian and fur trade descendant John Jackson adds to this list Étienne Oniaze, who arrived in 1813, and Michel Kaonassé, who came in 1834.[67] The dozen men's stories reveal much about how Iroquois, the Indigenous women with whom they partnered, and then their children made their lives in the Pacific Northwest.

That the workplace served to bind Iroquois together is evidenced by Thomas Tewatcon, Jean Baptiste Tyeguariche, and Louis Onskanha all marrying the Indigenous women in their lives at Fort Vancouver on the same day, 8 July 1839, before the same witnesses.[68] In 1814, as a twenty-year-old, Tewatcon had agreed to paddle back and forth to Michilimackinac. Two years and another three paddles later, he was contracted to head to the Pacific Northwest, with all or part of his wages being paid to his mother. Tewatcon partnered with a Chinook woman named Catherine, with whom he had Thomas, Catherine, and Susanne in the early 1820s. Whatever happened in the interim, in the 1839 joint wedding, Tewatcon wed a Walla Walla woman named Françoise, which legitimized both of their children together, two-year-old Louise and three-month-old Pierre, as well as Tewatcon's three older children. Indicative of Iroquois's ongoing ties with their birth places despite being so long away, Tewatcon described himself at his marriage as "formerly of Sault St. Louis," the Catholic name for Caughnawaga.[69] The couple also had Andrè and Philomene prior to Tewatcon's death in 1846, two years after the family had headed to the Willamette Valley.

Tewatcon's death left Françoise, as with so many other Indigenous women in similar situations, no option but to rebound, and here the everyday relationships that existed as a matter of course between Iroquois and Canadiens come into play. Françoise wed Tewatcon's long-time friend Paul Guilbeau, whose first Walla Walla partner, on her death in 1848, had left him with half a dozen children to raise. Within the year, Guilbeau was dead, possibly in the California gold rush, then at its height, and once again Françoise acted decisively in her family's interest. The third time around, she wed Canadien Laurent Sauvé, who worked principally at Fort Vancouver as a cowherd and was the father of two daughters by a Clallam woman. As of 1880 Françoise was living with her youngest Tewatcon daughter, Philomene, her Tennessee-born son-in-law, and their four children, who were farming in the Walla Walla country of eastern Oregon. In the pattern of her mother and also of her Iroquois father, Philomene was determined to do the best she could by her family, and by the end of the century she had claimed her maternal inheritance and resettled the family on the Umatilla Indian Reservation, which had become the home of the Walla Walla people.

That Tewatcon had settled in the Willamette Valley contributed to his daughters' appeal. In 1854 Philomene's older sister Louise wed Montrealer Jean Baptiste Goyé, who appears to have been a relative newcomer to the Pacific Northwest.[70] Of Tewatcon's two daughters by his first union, Catherine married André St Martin from Sorel, who was ten years her senior, and Susanne wed Amable Petit from Berthier, who was eighteen years older than her. Catherine's Catholic union of April 1839 legitimized her two-year-old daughter Catherine Davis, whose father was almost certainly English seaman Thomas Davis, briefly on the coast.[71] St Martin and Petit had been so eager to be properly wed to these Iroquois daughters that they first did so in Anglican ceremonies overseen by Rev. Herbert Beaver, briefly at Fort Vancouver in the mid-1830s, followed by Catholic marriages as soon as priests arrived.[72] Like numerous of the Iroquois, Petit had left a wife, and in his case also two sons, back home in Quebec. Both Petit sons would in young adulthood follow their father and his half-Iroquois wife west to farm on their own in the Willamette Valley.

Unlike Thomas Tewatcon, who mostly trapped, the versatile Jean Baptiste Tyeguariche, an 1817 arrival known as Norwest with earlier paddling contracts going back to 1811, worked as a middleman and cook. By the time he set down in the Willamette Valley, he had a stable union of over two decades and six recorded children with a Walla Walla woman named Judith, whom he had married on the same day as Tewatcon's wedding.[73] On her death, Tyeguariche wed a Pend d'Oreille woman named Henriette, who died in 1852, three years before he did.[74] Tyeguariche's daughter Catherine married Angus McDonald. Tyeguariche's son Thomas Norwest farmed north of the Yamhill River, with other Tyeguariche offspring scattering across the Pacific Northwest, including Oregon's large Grand Ronde Reservation, created with the intention of getting a number of tribes out of the way.[75]

The third Iroquois to wed on the same day in 1839 before the same witnesses was considerably younger than the others. Louis Onskanha was twenty-one upon his arrival in the Pacific Northwest in 1830. Nine years later, "Louis Onskanha, Iroquois, dit Monique, formerly of Sault Saint Louis, in Canada," wed "Charlotte Tchinouk by nation," meaning she was Chinook by inheritance. Charlotte had earlier partnered with Canadien Antoine Plante, by whom she had an eight-year-old son, also named Antoine, who was born about the time his father drowned. By 1939 Onskanha and Charlotte already had Catherine and Marie Anne, who were legitimized as a consequence of their parents' marriage.[76] A continent away from home, not only was the thirty-year-old doubly surnamed Louis Onskanha Monique still so identified, but also, as revealed at a later baptism in which he was a witness, he "alone has known how to sign in Iroquois." Reflecting his literacy, Onskanha used the opportunity offered by a Catholic girls' boarding school established in the Willamette Valley in

Figure 5.2
Jean Baptiste Tyeguariche's daughter Catherine,
who married Angus McDonald, ca. 1875

1844 to secure the admission of his daughter Catherine, who would sadly die before she could wed.[77] Fellow Willamette settler Jacques Tahetsaronsari, who arrived as a twenty-eight-year-old boute in 1831, a year after Onskanha, may have headed to the Willamette Valley due to their acquaintance. Stationed principally at Fort Colvile, he partnered with an Okanogan woman named Suzanne, by whom he had a daughter in 1837 and a son two years later.[78]

Also securing French-language literacy for his daughters was Laurent Karonhitchego, who had come in 1816 at age twenty-two as a paddler. That he had had part of his wages paid to his wife upon leaving home may explain his partnering much later than was usual in the Pacific Northwest, perhaps consequent on his finally deciding to make it his new home. When he formalized his union with a Chinook woman named Therese on 28 March 1840, their only child was just two years old, to be followed over time by four siblings. Indicative of his religiosity, Karonhitchego acted as the personal servant and boatman of the two Catholic priests, who arrived in late 1838, and in that capacity he repeatedly witnessed baptisms.[79]

Also among 1816 arrivals opting for the Willamette Valley were Louis Shanagraté and Louis Shaegoskatsta. Like Karonhitchego, Shanagraté had had part of his wages paid to his wife upon his departure, and over the course of time he would turn to a local Kalapuyan woman. He was likely the earliest, and the shortest termed, of the Iroquois to settle in the Willamette Valley, dying shortly after he did so in 1835.[80] Arriving in the Pacific Northwest at the age of twenty, sometime steersman Louis Shaegoskatsta in the summer of 1839 wed a twenty-five-year-old Kalapuyan woman known as Churathea, whom the priest named Louise.[81] Their daughter Marianne also attended the Catholic sisters' school in the Willamette Valley.[82] Iroquois were ambitious for their daughters' as well as for their sons' wellbeing.

Much more is known about Charles Tchigt, also known as Charles Tsetse and Carlo Chata, who was distinctive among Iroquois for his active participation in public affairs. Canadiens who settled in the Willamette Valley were determined to acquire a priest, whose absence troubled them as much as it did their Iroquois counterparts. Tchigt was among eighteen men who signed petitions for a priest in 1836 and again in 1837, each doing so with an X.[83] When in January 1837 two American arrivals decided to construct a distillery, thereby challenging the HBC policy of restricting access to liquor, Tchigt along with fifteen Canadiens signed a letter of protest in the name of temperance.[84] Over time, Tchigt repeatedly crossed the Indigenous-white divide, likely on invitation.

Tchigt partnered thrice in succession. Following the death of a Pend d'Oreille woman named Charlotte, by whom he had Agathe in 1835, he opted for a daughter of fellow Iroquois Thomas Canasawarrette, who had been killed by the Tillamooks in 1832. Tchigt had been among those dispatched to exact revenge, which likely explains how he encountered Canasawarrette's daughter. On her death, Tchigt wed a Kalapuyan woman named Therese in 1847, by whom he had a son, Laurent, born the previous year. According to Munnick, in 1848 the aging Tchigt sold his fenced and mostly cultivated Willamette Valley claim of 100 acres to a white newcomer.[85]

Also heading to the Willamette Valley was Pierre Satakarass, born in 1788, who arrived in New Caledonia as a boute around the time that the HBC took charge. He comes into view consequent on the Okanagan woman in his life slipping away from an HBC trapping expedition to California in the spring of 1833 on which Satakarass was a boute. Great consternation was expressed when "P. Satakarass' wife deserted" along with one other, to be found "at one of the [Catholic] mission farms where they had just arrived naked having been stripped by the Indians into whose hands they fell."[86] Whether the couples reconciled appears not to have been recorded.

The three other of the dozen Iroquois to settle in the Willamette Valley were Étienne Oniaze, who came in 1813 as a twenty-four-year-old middleman with three years of employment east of the Rocky Mountains, Joseph Tehongagarate, who followed in 1822, and Michel Kaonassé, who arrived in 1834 as a nineteen-year-old boute and guide. Oniaze's first partner was Catherine Kanatawose, said also to have been from Caughnawaga; his second was a Kwoithe woman by whom he had Baptiste and Ignace; and his third was a Chinook woman named Jany, whom he wed in 1842. Whether Kaonassé, whose wife died in New Caledonia in 1843, remarried is not known. Oniaze and Kaonassé are said to have settled near present-day Brooks, Oregon, as early as 1838, where the families were still living as of 1860.[87]

DREAMS DASHED

These dozen Iroquois, and likely numerous others whose lives are lost from view, signalled by virtue of setting down in the Willamette Valley their commitment to the Pacific Northwest.[88] They moved beyond a job to an everyday life on their own resources. Iroquois were, however, able to do so only so long as the Pacific Northwest lacked external governance. In settling in the Willamette Valley, they considered themselves to be as capable of doing so as the Canadiens and others alongside whom they worked, which indeed they were by virtue of their similar employment in the fur trade.

Iroquois's dreams were not to be. Successfully engaging the Indigenous-white divide in no way equated to their finding acceptance for doing so. Their daring was for naught. Following the Pacific Northwest's division in 1846, these dozen enterprising Iroquois, along with other persons perceived as Indian, came under American jurisdiction. Legislation enacted in 1850 that made it possible for individuals to claim their holdings was limited "to every white settler or occupant of the public lands, American half-breed Indians included."[89] Iroquois were disqualified out of hand, their hopes dashed.

HEADING IN DIFFERENT DIRECTIONS

Attitudes and actions toward Iroquois who dared to live in the Willamette Valley as though they belonged point up the considerable extent to which hard work did not amount to white newcomers perceiving Iroquois by virtue of their actions as being on a par with themselves. Newcomers, almost all from within the United States, took for granted the Indigenous-white divide as indicative of the way things were and ought to remain.

Iroquois were not inert. Along with the dozen who settled in the Willamette Valley, another twenty retirees opted for other Pacific Northwest locations. That nine of these were employed at Fort Colvile in eastern Washington State helps to explain a boundary surveyor in the early 1860s coming across "a curious medley ... of old servants of the Hudson's Bay Company, the old trapper, the voyageur, Canadian, French, Iroquois & half-breeds ... now settled quietly in the valley with their wives & families round them." Indicative of Iroquois's growing comfort with outsiders in their midst, even if the reverse was not the case, on New Year's Day 1862, the surveyor recorded, "we were visited by a delegation of half-breeds, Iroquois Indians, who fired a *feu de joie* [i.e., volley of rifle shots] in our honour."[90] Other Iroquois set down in future British Columbia, where, unlike in the United States, their property rights were respected. One in five Pacific Northwest Iroquois overall sought to transition from the fur trade to economic independence.

Other Iroquois tracked by name as employed in the Pacific Northwest fur trade between 1813 and 1858 went in three different directions. One in five died while still at work. Two in five did not find the fur trade to their liking or vice versa. With just under half of these men, it was the company who found them unsatisfactory, and they were sent back east either during or at the end of their first three-year contract. The others variously abandoned the Pacific Northwest fur trade.

The remaining one in five almost certainly, or very likely, returned home. Indicative are Henric Tasitaharie, who did so possibly as early as 1821 after six paddling trips, which were followed by five years of mostly trapping, and Jacques Shatackoani, who did so by 1831 after ten years of paddling to and fro elsewhere, which were followed by a decade and a half of doing the same work within the Pacific Northwest. Among others likely heading back east were ten men whose names or that of someone else with the same name turn up on the 1825 or 1831 census lists of their home village, as well as another fifteen men who probably did so, as suggested by surviving bits of information.[91] What is clear is that the life from which Iroquois came did not tug them back in large numbers. Time played a role in their decisions to remain in the Pacific Northwest, but another factor must have been the stories shared by new arrivals or those employed on cross-country brigades of hard times back home.

When these factors are combined, and after the initial sorting out, the numbers of Iroquois who committed to the Pacific Northwest are considerable. The principal time for the dismissal of unwanted or unneeded arrivals or for contracted men to decide that the Pacific Northwest, or perhaps the fur trade in general, was not for them was during the first three years. This was the usual time period for contracts, at the end of which one could either sign a new contract or take up the standing offer to be returned home so long as debts owed to the company were paid. A third of the Iroquois employed in the Pacific Northwest between 1813 and 1858 were gone or had died by the end of their third year. Thereafter, departures slowed. As of year ten, half of the men at work at the end of their first contract were still employed. As of year twenty, four in ten of the men at work after ten years were still in the fur trade.

As to the reasons why so many men with a choice to make stayed so long, Iroquois in the Pacific Northwest might from time to time offend those in charge, who were as a matter of course superior-minded, but, except for those involved in the traumatic 1842 events at Fort Stikine, Iroquois were needed and tolerated. Iroquois's satisfaction may have stemmed in part from the fur trade's relatively smooth operation and in part from their being clustered together between the major posts with considerable responsibility for water travel, which facilitated ongoing or intermittent communication with each other. For all of New Caledonia's remoteness, at least half of the eighteen Iroquois stationed there for a period of time stuck with this most remote edge of North America.

Apart from relatively brief forays into trapping, the principal way that Iroquois stood out, and coalesced, was as paddlers, most notably as boutes. Of the 240 men of all backgrounds identifiable by name as employed as boutes in the Pacific Northwest through 1858, 4 in 10 at any one time were Iroquois, another 4 in 10 were Canadiens, and the remainder were of mixed descent or otherwise Indigenous.[92] Iroquois were the most persistent, comprising two-thirds of those spending over a dozen years as boutes. A British military officer in the Pacific Northwest in 1845 was so impressed by his Iroquois bowsman, Baptiste, that he both sketched and described him at length: "The Bows man is the responsible Guide. He is constantly on the look out for sunken rocks; or dangerous 'snags' (sunken trees); invisible to the Steersman, whose duty is to follow exactly the motions of the Bowsman, and to assist in navigating the frail bark, through the numerous dangers, arising from Falls & Rapids – Sunken Trees or Rocks – Sands & Shoals."[93] Iroquois in the Pacific Northwest knew who they were and what they were capable of in the workplace, and they lived accordingly.

TO SUM UP

Iroquois engaged the Pacific Northwest fur trade on their own terms. They not only worked there, but almost half of those who did not soon die or who were not sent back east stayed for the middle term, if not longer.

Figure 5.3
"Baptiste, Iroquois Bowman, Our Canoe,"
by Henry James Warre, 1845

Rather than necessarily deciding whether or not to leave, they may have stayed for a time, then longer, and thus maybe forever. Among their reasons for doing so, a large proportion there for any period of time bound themselves to one another in and out of the workplace, and to local Indigenous women, with respect to their goals and aspirations. Sharing lives of hard work and determination, they committed to the Pacific Northwest.

6

Disappearing into a Changing Pacific Northwest

Following the 1846 agreement to halve the Pacific Northwest between Britain and the United States, the fur trade wound down, except for its northern reaches. A handful of Iroquois continued to be employed at the margins of the white ways of life coming into being, but that was about it, both for the first generation and for their offspring, who knew no other home than the Pacific Northwest. That sons and daughters navigated the changing times as well as they did does credit to their upbringing.

OFFSPRING ON THEIR OWN

The Pacific Northwest that Iroquois knew as their own had been altered beyond recognition by the time all but the earliest of their offspring came of age. Among factors causing Iroquois to disappear from view, even as descendants got on with their lives, was the economic imperative. The fur trade had been a way of life as much as it had been a job. Iroquois at work had been shielded from a monetary economy by virtue of their jobs being all inclusive. No more.

Once the fur trade went into decline, Iroquois and their offspring had to provide for themselves and their families by means of their own resources. The ways for sons to do so were not only limited but increasingly in the control of others whose assumptions and ways of life were very different from their own. Daughters almost certainly wed, with the economic imperative, at least to some extent, thereby passing out of their control. Be it sons or daughters, there was a certain irony to their circumstances. Whereas outsiders most often viewed Iroquois as solely Indigenous, offspring had a broader inheritance on which to draw, including knowledge of languages, experience of Catholicism, and, very importantly, senses of self acquired by virtue of their heritage and upbringing in the fur trade.

Other factors were also at play. The white newcomers arriving in growing numbers, especially south of the border, had no interest in the Pacific Northwest's human history. From their perspectives, Indigenous peoples were all the same. They were nuisances to be got out of the way as expeditiously as possible, if necessary ruthlessly so. At the same time, the small number of Iroquois spread across a vast territory that extended 1,500 kilometres, or 930 miles, from north to south and 1,000 kilometres, or 620 miles, inland from the Pacific Ocean had the advantage of being for the most part invisible.

That Iroquois and their descendants largely disappeared from view does not mean that no information about their lives survives. Total numbers are impossible to know, just as broad generalizations cannot be made, but stories, some of them shared by descendants, have broken free of the past.[1] If it is impossible to know how representative surviving accounts are, they do give us some sense of how Iroquois disappearing into a changing Pacific Northwest enacted their lives.

NARROWING OPTIONS SOUTH OF THE BORDER

South of the border, more so than to the north, Iroquois's indigeneity was their undoing. From the perspective of those in charge once the border was put in place in 1846, Iroquois's origins trumped their sometimes lengthy work experience alongside whites. The 1850 legislation excluding Iroquois settlers from legally acquiring the properties on which they had set down in the Willamette Valley, described in chapter 5, was emblematic of attitudes more generally. Alternatives grew fewer, and whereas some Iroquois and their descendants persisted at the edges, others turned to the single option meant for Indigenous peoples, which was to settle on one of the reservations intended to get them out of the way.[2]

Given that the American government limited reservations to specific Indigenous peoples, they were closed to Iroquois as such. For them, gaining admittance to a reservation required either appropriate maternal descent or some manoeuvring in the form of "adoption" into one of the eligible Indigenous groups. Once this feat had been accomplished, an advantage was to be had in the form of a land allotment possibly large enough not only to sustain a family but also to produce a surplus of food items for sale. Accessing a reservation was a strategic undertaking. As explained to me by a descendant, "it was a step up."

Three accounts narrate Iroquois offspring settling on the massive Grand Ronde Reservation, established in 1855 in western Oregon to house a broad swathe of disparate Indigenous peoples.[3] In finding a place among a reservation population of 350 to 400, Joseph Sanagratti, Frank Norwest, and Marianne Vautrin drew on their maternal inheritances.

In September 1835 Jason Lee, the recently arrived Methodist missionary in the Willamette Valley, was called to assist at the behest of Fort Vancouver's head when Louis Shanagraté, who had arrived in 1816, "burst a blood vessel in the lungs and died almost immediately." He left behind "three orphan children" along with his Willamette property, all of which Lee co-opted.[4] Shanagraté's thirteen-year-old daughter, Isabel, had been married off to an incoming white settler a few months earlier, to die two years later, his son Nicholas also soon died, and his twelve-year-old son, Joseph, attended the mission school.[5] He was possibly permitted to do so because, as a fellow missionary put it, his father was "a civilized Indian formerly from the vicinity of Montreal."[6]

Joseph Sanagratti, as his surname became spelled, early on committed himself to his mother's Kalapuyan people. Subsequent to serving in the local militia formed to avenge the murders of Methodist missionaries Marcus and Narcissa Whitman by the Cayuse in 1848, Sanagratti was a signatory to the treaty made by the Kalapuyans in 1855. In the mid-1860s, by which time he was living at Grand Ronde, he became chief of the St Mary's band of Kalapuyans. His knowledge of Chinook jargon, which emerged during the fur trade out of a combination of newcomer and Indigenous words, propelled him into a leadership role among disparate peoples with mutually unintelligible languages forced together in this quasi-confined space.[7] In 1876 Sanagratti was elected president of the Grand Ronde Indian Legislature, in which capacity, and later as a judge, he promoted community and individual wellbeing.[8] By one account, he was chief for forty years; by another, he was "one of the prominent men of the Grand Ronde Reservation community."[9] An allotment assisted family life.[10] The 1886 reservation census, one of the very few to include such information, admired his "good small house, small barn," and "good garden."[11]

Figure 6.1
Grande Ronde leader Joseph Sanagratti, ca. 1900

The second account begins in the Willamette Valley, where Jean Baptiste Tyeguariche set down with his family by Judith, a Walla Walla. Their youngest son, Frank Norwest, born in 1847, is said to have made his own way to Grand Ronde at such a young age that the resident Indian agent dispatched him to the local day school. Finding acceptability by marrying within the community, Frank acquired an allotment to support his family, as well as working as a sometimes carpenter.[12] He was described almost admiringly in the 1886 census as having a "good house & barn" with 29 acres "fenced" and 7 acres "in cultivation," extensive farming equipment, horses, cattle, hogs, and chickens.[13]

Reflecting narrowing options for Iroquois offspring, Frank's older brother Thomas Norwest, who had settled in the Willamette Valley, eventually joined his brother at Grand Ronde, as did their sister Mary, who wed a Canadien's son by a Chinook woman.[14] Indicative of Iroquois's commitment to Catholicism, just as with Louis Sanagratti, the Norwest brothers and their spouses repeatedly acted as witnesses to religious and civil events.[15] Reflecting the gender divide, the Norwest siblings' older sister Catherine wed, as noted in chapter 5, Scots HBC officer Angus McDonald.

The third, more complex account of migrating to Grand Ronde has two Iroquois progenitors. In 1831 an Iroquois remembered only as "Jacques Iroquois" fathered a son named Joseph with a woman named Marguerite of the Sooke people of southern Vancouver Island. Seven years later, in 1838, Marguerite wed Canadien Jean Baptiste Brulé, whom she may have met while he was working on the coastal steamship *Beaver*. Brulé bequeathed Marguerite's half-Iroquois son, Joseph, his surname.

A decade later, in 1848, in the Willamette Valley, where the Brulé family had settled, young Joseph Brulé wed sixteen-year-old Marianne, who like him had an Iroquois father, likely 1816 arrival Louis Shaegoskatsta, who had partnered with a Kalapuyan woman and also settled there, as explained in chapter 5.[16] Marianne's words having survived, which is unusual for the time, she tells us that "when I was small I was taken to French Prairie and was sent to the sisters' school in St. Paul [in the Willamette Valley] until I was fifteen."[17]

Joseph Brulé and Marianne's son Jean Baptiste, by descent half Iroquois through a combination of paternal and maternal descent, was born in the Willamette Valley in 1849.[18] Relocation north followed consequent on a combination of unease over remaining in American territory after the boundary settlement and the longing of Joseph's mother, Marguerite, to return home to the territory of the Sooke people. In 1849 the two generations, including Joseph and Marianne Brulé with their infant son Jean Baptiste, headed north to Vancouver Island. There, the couple had several more children together, prior to Brulé's death in 1860, whereupon Marianne wed Canadien François Xavier Vautrin, recently retired from the fur trade. In 1869 Marianne's son Jean Baptiste Brulé pre-empted land in the Sooke area, which he would not have been allowed to do south of the border, and settled down into married life.[19]

Marianne's strength of character comes through shortly after her Vancouver Island marriage to François Xavier Vautrin. Travelling home to Sooke from Victoria, she and an Indigenous friend were set upon and raped by two white men, whereupon they had the courage to bring charges. The newspaper account of the police court hearing makes clear that this Iroquois daughter was not about to be intimidated: "Mary Vautriere, when questioned as to her knowledge of the obligations of an Oath, replied through an interpreter, that she believed in the truths of Christianity; she had been baptized by a priest who gave her her first name; and she knew that if she did right she would go to heaven; if not, that she would go to hell." The account described how both women "seemed to stand cross examination very well." They were both "legally married" but were all the same "Indian women," and the magistrate concluded that their evidence was not strong enough to bring the case to trial.[20] Challenging the Indigenous-white divide was no easy matter, especially for women.

After having eight or nine children over the next two decades, the sturdy Marianne Vautrin, whose father was Iroquois and mother was Kalapuyan, had the same longing as her mother-in-law had experienced a generation earlier to return to her maternal territory. Due to the passage of time, doing so meant heading south to Oregon's Grand Ronde Reservation, to which Kalapuyans had been dispatched. There, according to a government account, a returning Marianne and her family were "welcomed by the people," including "a number of near relatives, notwithstanding her long absence."[21]

The Iroquois connection was soon in play. Through the intercession of Joseph Sanagratti, who was like Marianne half Iroquois by descent, she got permission for her and her husband, François Xavier Vautrin, and for each

Figure 6.2
Marianne Shaegoskatsta Brulé Vautrin at Grande Ronde, ca. 1917

of the five children who had come south with them to acquire an allotment.[22] Not unexpectedly given their recent arrival, the 1886 census described Marianne and her husband as having a "good garden" and "3 hogs"
but being "very poor."[23] Vautrin offspring became integrated by marriage
with Grand Ronde's Iroquois contingent when in 1895 Marianne's daughter
Olive wed Thomas Norwest's namesake son.[24]

Despite the small number of Iroquois at Grand Ronde among a total population that had grown to between 500 and 750, they were visible.[25] A federal government inspector reported to the United States secretary of the interior in 1880 that Grand Ronde was "the first Indian agency yet visited where all the Indians live in houses, understand the English language and engage with reasonable diligence in civilized pursuits" and "where all are able to support themselves and want to become citizens."[26] To this way of life, Iroquois and their descendants contributed their hard work and strong senses of self. A federal government report of 1933, which listed two Iroquois living at Grande Ronde, could not understand why they were there at all, yet another indication of their distinctiveness.[27] As explained by Joseph Sanagratti's descendant Bobby Mercier, who also has Jean Baptiste Tyeguariche in his lineage, "people always said Joseph looked different from everyone else and you could tell he was not from around here because he had such a long face."[28]

The Iroquois presence on American reservations endures. Two decades ago, Edgar Des Autel described for me at his home on the Colville Reservation that his mother's "great-great-grandfather was a full blood Scotchman, from Scotland, and came to New York and married an Iroquois woman." As to the union's meaning for him, as well as being Okanogan, Rogue River, Puyallup, Sioux, and Shasta, "I'm an Iroquois," he explained proudly.[29] The Grande Ronde museum displays a variety of objects described as Iroquois.

DAUGHTERS IN DEMAND

Whichever side of the 1846 border they found themselves on, Iroquois daughters were, unlike sons, in demand. That they were sought not only by Iroquois of the first and second generations but also by others speaks to Iroquois's intermediate status. Whereas daughters' indigeneity was likely reflected in their persons, their fathers had been employed in the fur trade on a par with Canadiens and others. It was taken for granted by non-Indigenous men during these years that women's identities would in any case be subsumed into their own.

Much as with the daughters of Willamette Valley settler Thomas Tewatcon, introduced in chapter 5, who divided themselves between white newcomers and Canadiens employed in the fur trade, young women, or their families on their behalves, had choices almost wholly denied their brothers. The daughters of Canadiens and Indigenous women might be preferable, but Iroquois daughters would do.[30] Three Iroquois daughters' and granddaughters' encounters speak to what occurred generally.

Within a year of arriving in the Pacific Northwest in 1837 as a Hudson's Bay Company tinsmith, well-educated Montrealer Adolphe Chamberland married Iroquois daughter Julienne Watièce. The union's acceptability is attested by its being among the very first performed at Fort Vancouver following the priests' arrival. Julienne was described at their wedding on 27 December 1838 as "the natural daughter of George Watièce and of a woman of the country," the latter a common phrase used for Indigenous women marrying out.[31] Immediately prior to the ceremony, she was baptized Catholic, the fundamental prerequisite to a church marriage.[32] In line with the practice of Iroquois surnames being shortened between generations, Julienne's father was George Tewhattohewnie of chapter 5, who arrived in 1813 on the cross-country brigade, had very much a personality of his own, and was by the 1820s a freeman living on the Olympic Peninsula. It was likely there, as deduced from Harriet Munnick's transcriptions, that he fathered Julienne in 1819 and Thomas in 1821. The Chamberlain union thrived in the Willamette Valley through six children as well as his involvement in public affairs as a member of the inaugural Oregon legislative assembly of 1847.

The second encounter of an Iroquois daughter reflects changing times following the 1846 boundary settlement. Daughters' desirability was enhanced by the scarcity of white women compared to the large numbers of white men who had arrived in the fur trade as well as the many thousands who had been attracted by the gold rush that broke out in British Columbia in 1858 alongside a lesser counterpart in the American Pacific Northwest.

So it was for Charlotte, the middle daughter of Ignace Karohuhana, an Iroquois who arrived in 1832 as a paddler and was based at the North Coast post of Fort Simpson. Transferred to Fort Victoria in 1850, Karohuhana had been among the half a dozen Iroquois who constructed Nanaimo, as described in chapter 5. Daughters Charlotte and Marie Josephine had accompanied him south, as indicated by their baptisms as the "fille[s] leg[itimates] de Ignace Arohiwois de la tribe des Iroquois" on 28 April 1850 at St Andrew's Catholic Church in Victoria, testifying to their parents' earlier

Catholic marriage.[33] Whereas Marie Josephine subsequently disappears from view, Charlotte and her sister Cecile, baptized a year later, became valuable commodities in the marriage market.

Cecile was the first daughter to wed. On 13 February 1855, in St Andrew's Catholic Churh in Victoria, eighteen-year-old Cecile, given as born in British Columbia to Iroquois Ignace Aronhiowan and a Nass woman, married thirty-two-year-old George Boucher. His father, Jean Baptiste Boucher, of mixed Canadien and Cree descent, had been a stalwart of the New Caledonia fur trade since his arrival in 1806 with NWC officer Simon Fraser, and his mother was the daughter of an HBC officer and a local Indigenous woman.[34] George had joined the HBC in New Caledonia in 1850, being transferred three years later to Fort Victoria. Indicative of her father's comfort with a union that was safely within the nexus of the fur trade, Aronhiowan was one of the two witnesses to the ceremony. The young Bouchers had four children together over the next decade, during which they migrated between Victoria and nearby San Juan Island. Family ties were important. Cecile's sister Charlotte witnessed the baptism of Cecile's son William in late 1857 and, along with "Antoine Iroquois," was present at the infant's burial two months later. Cecile's father, whose name was this time written as "Ignace Aaronkiwana," witnessed the baptism a year later of the couple's next son, also named William.[35]

Whereas her sister Cecile married someone with whom she shared Indigenous descent, Charlotte wed a white man. On 8 June 1860 in the same church as had her sister, eighteen-year-old Charlotte Aaroniaton wed thirty-seven-year-old Englishman John Witty.[36] Perhaps indicative of the union's acceptability, one of the two witnesses was Gideon Thibadeau, a Catholic Brother who had two years earlier accompanied the Sisters of St Ann west from Montreal to establish a Catholic girls' school in Victoria and who repeatedly witnessed weddings.[37] By now, in the common pattern for Iroquois surnames being written according to how they were heard, Karohuhana had variously become Arohiwois, Aronhiowan, Aaronkiwana, and Aaroniaton.

Initially also living on San Juan Island, Witty grew concerned that it might become American, which it would in 1872. Learning in 1867 of a 385-acre farm operated by the HBC that was for sale in Metchosin southwest of Victoria, Witty purchased the property.[38] To encourage the establishment of a community nearby, in 1871 Witty donated land for a public school that their children would attend and for an Anglican Church and cemetery.[39] Then disaster struck. Following the birth of John, William, Margaret, and Robert, Charlotte was pregnant with their fifth child when in October 1873 Witty died from a kick received while shoeing a horse, becoming the first person buried in the new cemetery.[40]

Iroquois daughter Charlotte Aaroniaton Witty regrouped. Indicative of Iroquois and their offspring sustaining each other, among the witnesses testifying on Charlotte's behalf in the legal proceeding settling the Witty estate was Agnes Antoine, a fellow Iroquois daughter who had earlier witnessed the baptism of the Wittys' daughter Margaret in 1866.[41] Nine years earlier, when George and Cecile Boucher's son William died in Victoria, one of those acting as a witness at the burial had been "Antoine (Iroquois)."[42]

By inference, Antoine was Antoine Anewscatcha, who upon his arrival in 1837 as a twenty-year-old had been, like Charlotte and Cecile's father, dispatched to Fort Simpson, hence their acquaintance. Over the next three decades, Anewscatcha cut wood for the HBC's coastal streamship *Beaver*, likely getting him to Fort Victoria from time to time. Three years after the baptism in Victoria in 1851 of Henriette, described as "the daughter of Antoine Iroquois in the service of the Hudson's Bay Company," Anewscatcha was accompanied south by a "native woman of the North" so they could be married.[43] During the same visit of October 1854, Michel Nassiat, who would die a month later in Victoria as the son of "Antoine (Iroquois)," was baptized as the son of Antoine Nassiat, a witness being his older sister Agnes, who would befriend Charlotte and Cecile.[44]

As for the widowed Charlotte Witty, this Iroquois daughter carried on their Metchosin farm sustained by fellow Iroquois. As well, as explained in a lengthy profile of the family published over a century later, "other settlers helped to keep the farm going," as did "the kindness of the native Indians who camped at the beach."[45] John and Charlotte Witty's sons, John, William, and Robert, born in 1862, 1863, and 1869, and their daughters, Margaret and Mary, born in 1865 and 1872, also sustained their mother and in doing so created community. Given the Witty family's large landholding and Metchosin's relative isolation, it is not surprising that children married close to home. Almost certainly facilitated by the family's prominence, they turned to a combination of early settlers' offspring and new arrivals. John opted for an English family's widowed daughter, one of whose daughters by her prior union subsequently married John's younger brother Robert. Middle brother William wed a woman born in Saxony who had come to Vancouver Island as an infant. Margaret opted for a Swedish immigrant and Mary for an Englishman. Prior to her death on 5 August 1900, a quarter of a century after that of her husband, Charlotte Witty made out a will that divided her Metchosin farm, house, and buildings, as well as a horse, cattle, sheep, geese, ducks, and chickens, between her children.[46]

The submerging over time of Charlotte Witty's Iroquois descent may have been cumulative rather than deliberate.[47] In the 1891 census, she was described as born in "N.W.T.," being the Northwest Territories, not that different from the British Columbia North Coast.[48] Despite having died in December 1900, Charlotte was included in the 1901 census, possibly taken earlier. In this record, the single Canadian census enumerating everyone by colour, she described herself as "R" for "Red," or Indigenous, as being of Scotch origin, as able to read and write, and as a farmer by occupation.[49] Although on her death certificate Charlotte was described as a Catholic in line with Iroquois sensibilities, she was buried, as had been her husband, in the churchyard of St Mary's Anglican Church on land her husband had much earlier bequeathed for religious purposes. The information provided either then or subsequently for her headstone named her as "Charlotte, nee Thibault."[50] The surname, which also appeared as "Tebo" in church records, may have been a mistaken reference to Gideon Thibadeau, who had witnessed Charlotte and John Witty's wedding.[51] The death certificates of Witty sons John and William in 1945 and 1950 also gave their mother's maiden surname as "Tibeault." Both brothers were described as English by origin, which completed the family's erasure as Iroquois and more generally as Indigenous.

The third account of an Iroquois daughter takes us to the British Columbia interior. Thérèse Toccatone's story begins with the arrival in the Pacific Northwest in 1825 of her father, Michel Tokatani, aged twenty-four, as a middleman on the way to becoming a boute. Dispatched to remote New Caledonia, he worked there until his death in 1855. By a process of elimination, it can be surmised that Thérèse Toccatone, born in 1842 almost certainly to a local Chilcotin woman, was his daughter.[52]

The closest first-person descriptions of what ensued come from censuses where heads of households responded to questions asked by a visiting enumerator. In the earliest census for the Cariboo region of central British Columbia, taken in 1881, farmer William Laing Meason described himself as a Catholic, born in Scotland, a farmer, and living with Thérèse Toccatone, an "Iroquois" born in British Columbia who was also a Catholic. Their seven children were aged between one and seventeen, meaning the union went back in time at least to 1863.[53] For the 1901 census, which demanded colours, Laing Meason gave himself as "White" and Thérèse and their children as "Red." The 1901 census also asked for precise birthdates, being 28 December 1822 for himself and 15 January 1842 for Thérèse.[54]

The man sharing Thérèse Toccatone's life was no ordinary catch. Born in Scotland's Orkney Islands, William Laing Meason was a classically educated British army officer enticed by the British Columbia gold rush. His subsequent land acquisitions made him one of the most prominent ranchers in the former New Caledonia, whose main part was, and is, known as the Cariboo.[55] They were married in the early 1870s.[56] Also serving as the local Indian agent, Laing Meason took pride in how, he confided to a fellow rancher in 1884, the local Chilcotin "are awfully fond of me – partly by reason of my children & wife having Chilcotin blood in them."[57]

To what extent Thérèse Toccatone's Iroquois and Chilcotin descent affected the Laing Meason offsprings' adulthoods is impossible to know but interesting to speculate about given their life courses. As indicated by the 1891 and 1901 censuses, the Laing Meason children remained at home longer than their contemporaries, which for the daughters was particularly unusual given the preponderance of newcomer men over women.[58] The sole exception was the namesake eldest daughter, who at age seventeen, in what may have been a family arrangement, wed Henry Otto Bowe, the nineteen-year-old mixed-descent son of a Cariboo rancher even more successful than her father.[59] All four of her brothers and one of her sisters never married, the other three sisters doing so only in their thirties.

Julienne Tewhattohewnie Chamberland, Charlotte Aaroniaton Witty, and Thérèse Toccatone Laing Meason melded into their husbands' lives and more generally into the everyday ways of the Pacific Northwest. The three women's paternal Iroquois and maternal Indigenous descent did not thereby disappear and may have affected their life courses, but it was likely not a principal determinant.

SONS NORTH OF THE BORDER

The fur trade wound down more slowly north of the border, including at Fort Victoria, to which the London-based HBC had moved its headquarters. Among members of the second generation cohering an Iroquois presence were Nanaimo builders François Satakarata and Thomas Ouamtany, who upon returning to Victoria volunteered for the British territory's defence corps, which was known as the Victoria Voltigeurs and repeatedly in action until the formation of the British colony of British Columbia in 1858. Indicative of discrimination similar to what was occurring south of the border, whereas the twenty-five Canadiens who also joined up were rewarded for their service with 20-acre lots on which to settle, that was not the case for the two Iroquois sons or the six Hawaiians who also took part. They were unwanted as permanent residents in what was a largely British enclave.[60]

The subsequent lives of the six Nanaimo builders are indicative of changing times. Their task over, in 1861 Ignace Karohuhana, Thomas Sagoyawatha, and Louis Oteakorie were dispatched north to Fort Simpson alongside fellow Iroquois Pierre Turcot, who had earlier been employed there. For Karohuhana and Sagoyawatha, it was a return to familiar territory, as they had earlier worked there for two decades and for a decade and a half respectively. It is possible their wives' northern origins prompted their return, or perhaps they had no choice. It could also have been that the three sought fellow Iroquois with whom to congregate. Among those then working at Fort Simpson were middleman Alexis Tasitayerie, there from 1856 until his death in 1862, and woodcutter Antoine Anewscatcha, there from 1838 to 1869. Fort Simpson was not a distant alien place, especially given the coastal access provided by the streamship *Beaver*, which some of them serviced, but rather an Iroquois enclave not unlike the Willamette Valley a decade and a half earlier.

Emerging out of this Fort Simpson cluster would be the Pacific Northwest's most recognized Iroquois son in the person of artist Frederick Alexcee, who was born in 1853 in Fort Simpson and died there in 1939.[61] As explained to Canadian ethnographer Marius Barbeau by his long-time interpreter, William Beynon, based on conversations with Alexcee, "His father was of Iroquoian stock, having come to Port Simpson with the Hudson's Bay when they first came overland from the interior. Many of

Figure 6.3
Artist Frederick Alexcee with his wife, Angelina, and child, ca. 1900. The painting
in the lower right is Alexcee's "Pole Raising at Fort Simpson" (ca. 1900),
auctioned by Heffels in 2013, to disappear from view.

these inter-married with the Tsimshian."[62] Given the frequent practice of Iroquois's first names becoming their offspring's surnames, Alexcee's almost certain father was Alexis Tasitayerie, whose reasons for staying in Port Simpson were his family with a local Tsimshian woman and his association with early Anglican missionary William Duncan, the construction of whose house he superintended in 1858.[63]

It was another missionary presence, that of the Methodists, that nourished Alexcee's artistry. Beynon described to Barbeau how "Alexcee, while a young man became a crew member on the missionary boat, 'Glad Tidings,' first as a stoker and then he became an engineer and was with the steamer until she became a wreck."[64] Constructed in 1884 under the aegis of Methodist missionary Thomas Crosby, who was based in Port Simpson, the *Glad Tidings* plied the coast doing good works until 1903.[65] Entry into the cash economy made it possible for Alexcee to apprentice with Tsimshian maternal relatives as a carver and then to paint and carve what he knew. To do so, he employed various means of supporting his family, including fishing and picking hops.[66]

William Beynon, who was born in 1888 in Victoria of a Welsh father and a Tsimshian mother and made his life at Port Simpson, was among those to take pride in Alexcee's growing success: "As a boy, I remember his first painting which was of Port Simpson and this was exhibited in Victoria. I would say about forty-five years ago [ca. 1900]."[67] Barbeau encountered Beynon while doing fieldwork at Port Simpson in 1915, and he met Alexcee upon watching his coloured lantern slides illustrating Tsimshian stories and legends. Returning to Port Simpson in 1926 with celebrated Canadian painter A.Y. Jackson, Barbeau "brought some of Alexie's work to the attention of this well-known artist," who thereupon "bought a water colour sketch showing a few Tsimsyan houses with totem poles." The next year saw two of Alexcee's paintings in an exhibition of Northwest Coast art organized jointly by the National Gallery and National Museum of Ottawa that travelled to Toronto and Montreal. The paintings' style was described in the tenor of the times as "Indian primitive."[68]

Alexcee was modest about his success. Upon Beynon informing him that one of his paintings was on display in the National Gallery in Ottawa, Canada's capital, and showing him the catalogue, he responded, "Oh! well. You tell them that I will paint another for them if they want it. It will cost them $30.00."[69] Alexcee knew who he was, and it was not his aim to be a celebrity but rather to be true to himself and his craft. Shortly before Alexcee's death in 1939, Barbeau described how "he still lives, an old man in his 80's, entirely out of the art world, fishing salmon in the neighbourhood of Prince Rupert."[70] As Barbeau astutely summed up based on his long association with Beynon and repeated conversations with Alexcee, "His Iroquois blood, plus prolonged experience on a mission boat, were not enough to make him into an artist. For his craftsmanship he was indebted to the Tsimsyan relatives on his mother's side."[71] In that combination of attributes, as shared with me by Frederick Alexcee's grandson, Iroquois descent mattered in all of its complexity: "In the family, when someone misbehaved, we would tell them, 'you're an Iroquois,' or 'you're acting like an Iroquois.'"[72]

Nanaimo builder and Iroquois son Thomas Ouamtany, known as Tomo, whose father was introduced in chapters 2 and 5, went in a different direction.[73] When not at work as a carpenter, he lived in the Cowichan Valley, where a dispute over a local woman resulted in her Indigenous suitor so wounding Ouamtany that his arm had to be amputated.[74] Henceforth known as "One Arm Tomo," he compensated for being unable to paddle a canoe or fire a rifle by honing his expertise with small arms and as an interpreter and guide.[75]

Among those drawing on Ouamtany's repertoire of skills was twenty-one-year-old Scotsman Robert Brown, who arrived in 1864 under the auspices of the Edinburgh Botanical Association to head what he termed the Vancouver Island Exploring Expedition.[76] The expedition's success depended on its having the best possible support, which meant hiring Ouamtany despite stories circulating about his behaviour. Heading to the Cowichan Valley, Brown searched out "one-armed Tomo an Iroquois."[77]

News having travelled, Ouamtany turned up at the expedition's overnight stop to offer "his services as hunter to *M'sieur le Capitaine*." As a portrait of an Iroquois son making his way as best he could at the edge of the monetary economy and of the rapidly changing social structure coming into being, Brown's very lengthy profile of Outamtany, written after the trip for an English travel magazine, is unrivalled:

As he sat apart on a log, his solitary hand in his pocket, a more unpromising looking character could not be imagined. He was no less a man than "One-armed Tomo," or Thomas, famous among hunters and trappers all the way from Vancouver Island to Rupert's Land [i.e., HBC territory], and of late years not unknown to Her Majesty's courts of justice in a rather uncompromising light. His father was an Iroquois *voyageur* from Canada, his mother a Chinook from the Columbia River. He had for forty years moved about over the country among Hudson Bay forts and hunting stations – voyageur, farmer, hunter, trapper – possibly worse; speaking every Indian language and most European ones so far as he had met with anybody to teach him; very often "wanted," but rarely to be found. Under more favourable circumstances he would have been an Admirable Crichton [i.e., learned person crossing social boundaries]. As it was, One-armed

Tomo was only a roving vagabond, to whom an expedition of this sort was just a windfall; and though I had been particularly warned to give a wide berth to this same north-western genius, yet, at that time being very much in want of his accomplishments, I risked the engaging of him on trial for a few weeks. Among our motley crew Tomo was not long in finding an old acquaintance who promised to become guarantee for him, and before evening was over he delighted us all by the versatility of his accomplishments. Story after story dropped from his ready tongue; jokes in English, *jeux d'esprit* in French, and slow, sonorous proverbs in Spanish, were rattled off in quick succession; while he kept up a by-talk with the Indians, who appeared to half fear, half admire him. Tomo's outfit was not extensive. He stood five feet odd in his ragged trousers and woolen shirt; a grey cap was set jauntily on his head, and a pair of wooden soled boots, made by himself, on his feet. More than that he had not. He borrowed a blanket from his friend the chief, and we supplied him with a rifle; so he declares with a very big oath, as he squints along the barrel, that "he is a man once more," and in two minutes is asleep under a tree, with the gun between his legs. During all our long conversations none of us had ever reason to regret the day when he joined our party, and to this hour One-armed Tomo, the swarthy vagabond of the western forests, is only remembered as a hearty fellow – a prince of hunters and doctor of all wood rafts – whose single arm was worth more than most men's two, and without whose help the map of Vancouver [Island] would have been but a sorry blank yet, and the first Exploring Expedition a sorry affair.[78]

Ouamtany was hired as "hunter, guide, and canoe man, at $1.50 per day – for such time as I might choose to take him."[79] He signed the formal agreement as "Thomas Anthony."[80]

The expedition of four and a half months in the summer and fall of 1864 was a resounding success. Brown's misgiving were not borne out but rather the reverse. Not only did Ouamtany hunt deer for food and otherwise assist, but in his "English without an accent" he also elucidated "Indian astronomy" around the evening campfire and on request located mineral specimens.[81] For Brown, one of the most intriguing insights respecting Ouamtany related to his inner self as expressed in circumstances where he was respected: "Sat round the fire till late telling me stories of Indian life & warfare. Fine Moon-light."[82] As the trip was nearing conclusion, Brown wrote, "Miserable wet stormy day. Spent it as I spend most stormy days, in drawing on Tomo's extensive store of Indian lore and tradition and committing them to paper. A Savage's Indian lore and tradition are his history; his superstitions, his Metaphysics."[83] Some of the stories almost certainly found their way into Brown's four-volume *Races of Mankind*, published in London four years later, where without acknowledging Ouamtany by name, he echoed what he had earlier written respecting him: "'Tell me the songs of a nation, and I will tell you their history,' is an old truism. It is equally true regarding a savage race, that their traditions are their songs, their history, their metaphysics."[84]

Following the expedition's return, the Vancouver Island House of Assembly voted to grant all of its members, with the exception of Ouamtany, a cash gratuity for their services ranging from $50 to $400. A newspaper account described how "discontent" ensued "that Tomo the hunter of the expedition whose services were unanimously vouched to by the men received no portion of the reward, notwithstanding the fact that his skill was of the utmost use to the expedition on more than one occasion, and that without this individual their exertions would have met with an indifferent reward." Brown along with others "waited upon the Governor [James Douglas] with a view of a redress," only to be informed that nothing could be done.[85] From the perspective of those in charge, Ouamtany did not matter.

While continuing to make his home in the Cowichan, Ouamtany spent enough time in Victoria for him to be tracked, as is the case with Indigenous people generally, as an intruder into a white settler enclave.[86] Within the year, Anthony Thomas, as he was known in court records, was jailed for three months for "selling spirits to Indians," which was illegal, at which time he was described as "dark and sallow," illiterate, and with "right arm off by ... shoulder."[87] Two years later, on 11 May 1867, a "drunk and disorderly" Thomas Anthony was imprisoned for six hours.[88] Death was not long in coming. By one account, Ouamtany was killed in 1868 when he was ambushed not far from his Cowichan home.[89] For a good quarter of a century, he had determinedly strode the Indigenous-white divide on his own terms.

The sons of two other Nanaimo builders, Lazard Onearste and Louis Oteakorie, went in wholly other directions. Their trajectories demonstrate

Figure 6.4
Sooke chief Louis Lazare, ca. 1890

the authority exercised by Indigenous women over offsprings' lives. Working at Nanaimo through at least January 1857, Lazard Onearste is said to have been killed shortly thereafter.[90] His legacy was his son Louis Lazare, who in the common pattern took his father's first name as his surname. Louis Lazare was doubly Iroquois by inheritance, his mother being Therese Rabesca, whose father was early arrival Louis Satakarata and whose maternal uncle was François Satakarata, who had been briefly in Nanaimo alongside Onearste. On 29 July 1849 Louis was baptized in Victoria as, to quote from the church register, "fils legitimé de Lazare Ognioroghette de la nation des Iroquois."[91] The double Iroquois inheritance of Louis Lazare was reinforced by his parents' association with the Brulé contingent, which had arrived in Sooke from Oregon in 1849, with its own double Iroquois inheritance. With Therese's death not long after, it seems possible that young Louis's care was taken on by the Brulés.[92]

Louis Lazare would be presented in young adulthood with two choices as to his life course. He was almost certainly the "Lazar an Indian" jailed in October 1863 for shooting and killing a Sooke chief while drunk, to be discharged within two months.[93] Two years later, he was again arrested, this time for shooting and wounding an Indigenous woman at Sooke while drunk, to be convicted and released only in September 1867.[94] A newspaper account explained how "his civilized name is Lazar la Buiscay; his father was Iroquois in the service of the Hudson's Bay Co.'s service," upon whose death he "lived with the tribe."[95]

The second possible life course, and the one young Louis Lazare took, was to accept an invitation by Sooke chief Jack Kwakayuk to be adopted by virtue of Louis marrying his niece.[96] On 10 November 1873 in Victoria, "Ludovicum dictum Lazare (Louis called Lazare)" wed Tiamteno, who was known as Susan. Indicative of Louis's ongoing ties to his Sooke Iroquois compatriots, the two witnesses were Jean Baptiste and Marguerite Brulé.[97]

Louis Lazare became the Sooke chief in about 1890 at the behest of his father-in-law, to be succeeded on his death in 1925 by his eldest son, Andrew, who would be the last hereditary chief of the T'sou-ke people.[98] Their paths were anything but easy, given the lowly, powerless status of Indigenous peoples in Canada. One of the two Sooke reserves was, as recorded in meetings in June 1913 with a Royal Commission on Indian Affairs, too small and had only a few patches of land of poor quality. Testifying on behalf of his father, Andrew Lazare explained that the soil "is gravel and not fit for cultivation." The other Sooke reserve was so small that, "if a Whiteman took it, it would be only be big enough for one person."[99]

That the reserves overseen by Lazare's descendants were ineffectual did not prevent them from being caught out by virtue of their descent. As explained to me by a proud Sooke, "Louis Lazare is Iroquois and French. He was working for the Hudson's Bay Company years ago ... He married her and became a Sooke. He's not really a Sooke though."[100] Disrupting the Indigenous-white divide as it was intended to be configured was, and is, to invite criticism.

The remaining Iroquois builder was Louis Oteakorie, whose life story precipitated my interest in Iroquois in the West. Arriving at Fort Vancouver, he had been, as explained in the introduction, taken on by the HBC and variously dispatched. Returning in 1864 to his original posting of Fort Rupert, he met a Kwakiutl chief's sister, Mellas or M-las, also called Mary,

Figure 6.5
Kwakuitl chief Alexis Oteakorie, ca. 1920

with whom he had half a dozen children. When ethnographer Marius Barbeau visited Fort Rupert in 1947, the couple were remembered by a woman whose mother had been Tlingit and whose father had been the fort's early HBC employee Robert Hunt: "There was an Iroquois here at the Fort, named Louis. He married a Fort Rupert chief's sister M-las, they had a big family ... Their type was very different from the others. They were very dark copper color."[101] In this description, to be Iroquois was to be an outlier. On Mellas's death, since she was the Kwakiutl chief's oldest sister, the chieftainship passed to the couple's oldest son, Alexis.

The trajectory of Louis Oteakorie's descendants echoes that of many others across the Pacific Northwest. His great-great-grandson Carey Myers, whom I knew well over a number of years, was no different in his person and everyday life from most British Columbians and Canadians, except for his consciousness of, and growing pride in, his Iroquois inheritance.[102]

TO SUM UP

Iroquois who disappeared into a changing Pacific Northwest had no reason not to do so, given the antipathies in the larger society and their knowing in any case who they were. Each of these stories of Iroquois sons and daughters getting on with their lives has counterparts that survive in parts and glimmers. Whether or not lives were well lived had little to do with outside knowledge of how they did or did not manage the feat but depended instead on how persons valued themselves and those around them across time. Proudly to be Iroquois was, and is, no mean feat.

PART FOUR

Banding Together

Much more information survives respecting a fourth group of Iroquois in the West than about any of the others introduced in parts 2 and 3. In the mid-nineteenth century, the area where this cluster banded together became a favoured destination of adventurous outsiders who described them in the course of recording their travels.

Chapter 7 follows across the nineteenth century three Iroquois progenitors who slipped away from the organized fur trade to set down in today's western Alberta. "Becoming Jasper Iroquois," they and their families navigated the Indigenous-white divide so effectively as to be chronicled almost as a matter of course by visitors to whom they gave assistance.

Chapter 8 turns to offspring "Persisting in Jasper's Shadow." No less than their parents, they were Iroquois, they were Catholic, they valued family life, and they were committed to place. Twice displaced over the course of the twentieth century, descendants pushed back. They countered and to some extent withstood white newcomers' perception that Indigenous peoples, Iroquois or not, wanted to be confined and forgotten. Determined descendants were assisted in doing so by their strong Iroquois senses of self, including an ongoing commitment to Catholicism.

Becoming Jasper Iroquois

The ways that Iroquois minded themselves in the West related both to their places of origin and to their new settings. Nowhere was this more the case than with the cluster whose members, starting in the early 1800s, centred their yearly round on the fur trade post of Jasper House, sited on the Upper Athabasca River in the foothills of the Rocky Mountains. Iroquois of the first and subsequent generations pursued their preferred ways of life, so far as was possible, on their own terms, trading pelts and sometimes their labour for what they could not produce themselves. Men's partnering with Indigenous women facilitated their relationships generally with local people.

Despite all of the difficulties of following individual Iroquois across time and place, a trio of Jasper progenitors comes into view. Just as Ignace La Mousse of chapter 3, Pierre Tevanitagon and John Grey of chapter 4, and others left traces, so too did Louis Karakontie, Joachim Tonatunhun, whose first name became his descendants' surname, and Ignace Nowanionté, whose surname became Waniyandie.[1]

To follow these three Iroquois and their families across the nineteenth century is to glimpse the ways that markers of identity long survived in the West. They were Iroquois by inheritance, Catholic by religion, and Jasper people by association. When a choice had to be made, Jasper Iroquois were determined not to become "Indians" dependent on the government for their wellbeing. Just as they had long been doing, Karakonties, Waniyandies, and Joachims opted to continue to live as they would as best they could on their own resources.

ENTER LOUIS KARAKONTIE

Iroquois's lives in the Rocky Mountain foothills and valleys are best introduced by progenitor Louis Karakontie, who quite remarkably left a first-person account. In April 1846 he shared his story as he wanted others to know it with passing Jesuit priest Pierre-Jean De Smet, whom we encountered in chapters 3 and 4. On his way west over the Rocky Mountains in search of new objects of conversion, De Smet wintered at Fort Edmonton, during which he visited the newly established Catholic mission of Lac Ste Anne about 75 kilometres, or 45 miles, to the west. Hearing from Iroquois whom he baptized there about family members around the Hudson's Bay Company post of Jasper House, De Smet was on the lookout.

At the time that Karakontie and De Smet met, the latter had been involved off and on for half a dozen years with the Flatheads and their Iroquois mentors in Montana, which explains his knowledge of the Iroquois language, in which they may have conversed. De Smet was both a good listener and a fairly accurate conveyor of accounts, particularly when they reflected well on him or when he made them do so. As narrated by De Smet in a letter of 16 April 1846,

> On the banks of Lake Jasper, we met an Iroquois called Louis Kwaragkwanté, or Walking Sun, accompanied by his family, thirty-six in number. He has been forty years absent from his country, during which he has never seen a priest – has dwelt for the last thirty-four years in the forests of the Athabasca and on Peace River and subsisted by hunting and fishing. The good old man was overwhelmed with joy, and the children experienced a similar feeling with their father. I will give the old man's words in English, on learning that I was a priest:
>
> > "How glad I am to have come here, for I have not seen a priest for many years. To-day I behold a priest, as I did in my own country – my heart rejoices – wherever you go I shall follow you with my children – all will hear the word of prayer – all will have the happiness to receive baptism. Therefore my heart rejoices and is happy."[2]

Lake Jasper, where De Smet met Karakontie, is a broad portion of the Athabasca River, which runs northeast across Alberta.

The information that Louis Karakontie shared makes it possible to know quite a lot about him. By his recollection, he had been away from home for forty years, or since about 1806. The date puts his departure in the midst of the fur trade's height of accessibility to Iroquois like himself. The Voyageur Contracts Database attests to Karakontie's account. On 4 April 1805, as described in chapter 2, two Iroquois named as Louis Karakontie and Ignace Kayenthoway, both from Lac des Deux Montagnes, contracted with the North West Company to go to "Indian country known as the Northwest" for three years as hunters. In the usual pattern, they were not paid a salary and so were not employees as such but were given "a small assortment of merchandize" at Montreal prices and obliged to deliver all pelts acquired to the NWC at one of its sites for specified prices against which they could acquire goods. Any credit balance owed them would be paid upon their returning to Montreal at the end of their contracts. Perhaps a partial explanation for his future activity, Louis Karakontie was described by the notary as having "signed" his contract as opposed to putting his X on it, signifying that he was literate.

Following the expiry of their contracts in 1808, the two Iroquois continued to rely on the NWC. "Ignace Kayenthoway (& associates)" – the term "associates" indicating that he led a band of trappers, which possibly included Karakontie – maintained an account from the beginning of the NWC ledger in 1811. Notations in 1815 and 1816 show that Kayenthoway had money sent to his wife back home, to whom he may have returned.[3] As of 1818–20, Louis Karakontie was on his own, trading pelts for goods at the NWC's Dunvegan post on the Peace River about 400 kilometres, or 250 miles, north of Jasper. By 1821, when the Hudson's Bay Company took over, Karakontie had amassed considerable debt, which he appears to have offset by a combination of working it off and trading yet more pelts.[4]

One of the intriguing aspects of Karakontie's life course as a freeman is the impression he made a quarter of a century later on De Smet, who honoured the aging Iroquois as Walking Sun, either on his own volition or because the name was shared with him. De Smet depicted the Iroquois contingent, which included the other two Jasper progenitors, as a picture of contentment. In a letter written three years later, in 1849, to the head of his religious order in France about "the present condition of the Indians of the upper Missouri and among the Rocky Mountains," De Smet had little good to say, with three exceptions. Among them was "an old Iroquois with his children and grandchildren, numbering about thirty-seven."[5] Louis Karakontie took pride of place.

THE FORCE OF CATHOLICISM

The force of Catholicism explains the encounter. It was because of their religious conviction that Karakontie and the others accompanied De Smet to Jasper House, which the priest knew by its earlier name of Fort Jasper. De Smet's letter of 16 April 1846 described what ensued, to his pleasure:

> The little Iroquois camp immediately set out to follow me to Fort Jasper. Most of them knew their prayers in Iroquois. I remained fifteen days at the fort, instructing them in the duties of religion – after mass, on Easter Sunday, all were regenerated in the waters of baptism, and seven marriages renewed and blessed. The number of baptisms amounted to forty-four; among whom was the lady of Mr. Fraser (superintendent of the fort) and four of his children and two servants.[6]

In a second letter written a few weeks later, De Smet described how "the large Iroquois family being encamped round about resolved to remain until my departure." The family's determination to do so prompted the post's head to propose, due to a scarcity of provisions at the post, that De Smet and his followers, in total "fifty-four persons and twenty dogs," gather at a nearby site "where we could subsist partly on fish." De Smet and his "new children in Christ" fared so well together that he was saluted on his departure by a volley of musket charges.[7]

De Smet explained in a third letter that he had earlier paid with some gold he kept for contingencies to have three persons from Lac Ste Anne accompany him on his travels. It was they who taught "the prayers to the poor Iroquois and to the family of Mr Colin Fraser" during their "stay of 26 days."[8] Given that "most" of the Iroquois already "knew their prayers in Iroquois," the instruction might now have been limited to those who did not, or it may have been in Latin.

Figure 7.1
"Jasper's House, Athabasca River," by Henry James Warre, 1846

The willingness of the "little Iroquois camp" to accompany De Smet to Jasper House indicates it was familiar territory. The trading post went back in time almost as long as did Karakontie in the area. Founded by the NWC in 1813 as Rocky Mountain House, it was renamed Jasper House by its first head, Jasper Hawes, to avoid confusion with another post of the same name. As of June 1817, Hawes's employees at what a passing NWC clerk described as "a miserable concern of rough logs" were two unnamed Iroquois alongside two Canadiens.[9] Moved upriver a decade later in the aftermath of the HBC's taking charge in 1821, Jasper House functioned as a stopping place for exchanging furs for goods and also, as with De Smet, for travellers heading to or from the Athabasca Pass through the Rocky Mountains.[10]

DISENTANGLING JASPER IROQUOIS

Disentangling Jasper Iroquois is neither easy nor certain. In a postscript to his third letter, De Smet begged excuses for including a "filthy" piece of paper listing the baptisms and marriages he had performed at Lac

Ste Anne and Jasper, which he had "not had time to copy" into a clean version, and he likely never did so.[11] It is this list, virtually identical in number with respect to the "seven marriages" and "forty-four" baptisms noted in De Smet's earlier letter of 16 April 1846, that makes it possible to sort out, to some extent, the families of the three Iroquois progenitors. The list also includes the family of Jasper House's head from 1835 to 1850, Colin Fraser, and those of his two servants, one of whom, Geneviève Mondion, De Smet described in his third letter as the daughter of an un-named "métif Iroquois."

As was commonplace among white outsiders, De Smet reduced Iroquois names, including that of Louis Karakontie, which he had earlier written in full, to their first names, with "l'Iroquois" or possibly "Iroquois métif" appended. That members of the first generation had come west is attested by their not being baptized alongside the others. De Smet accepted what individuals told him, likely in Iroquois, about their already being baptized in "my own country," to use Karakontie's words. It is also the case that De Smet may have misheard relationships and that some family members were away.

The first of the three progenitors was Louis Karakontie. In De Smet's tattered list of baptisms and marriages, he was identified as "Vieux Louis" or "Vieux Louis l'Iroquois." As for his children, thirty-year-old Thomas, who gave his mother as Marie, had been baptized at Lac Ste Anne in February along with Thomas's two children, Joseph, aged two years, and Angelique, aged two months, and the children's mother, Angelique Finley. Louis Karakontie's younger children, Marianne, Suzanne, Marie, Ignace, and Michel, aged twenty-four, twenty-two, twenty, seventeen, and fifteen respectively, were baptized at Jasper. There, De Smet married Thomas to Angelique Finley, described as the daughter of Augustin Finley and Marguerite Cardinal, both from Canadien families active in the fur trade.

The progenitor of the family whose surname became Waniyandie was almost certainly De Smet's "Vieux Ignace" or "Vieux Ignace l'Iroquois." Going back in time, "Ignace Nowaniouter, un Iroquois," was employed by the NWC as a steersman in Athabasca in 1804–06.[12] The NWC ledger includes Ignace Nowanionté in 1814–17 and 1819–20, with part of his earnings paid to his wife back home in 1816 and 1817, the only two years such notations were made.[13] Under the name of Ignace Waniante, he was described in the 1818–19 journal of the HBC post of St Mary's, located at the confluence of the Smoky and Peace Rivers, as trapping, possibly along the Smoky, which runs north from the Jasper area.[14]

De Smet named Vieux Ignace as the father of Isabelle, Jean Baptiste, and Pierre, aged twenty-six, twenty-two, and fifteen respectively, who had all been baptized at Lac Ste Anne in February, along with Isabelle's children, Marie, aged nine, and Pierrish, aged five, both fathered by Augustin Lorme, likely Delorme, of another early Canadien family in the area. At Jasper, De Smet baptized an infant son of Isabelle Iroquoise, almost certainly the same person, and of Jean Baptiste Oniaze, and he married Isabelle, described as the daughter of Vieux Ignace, to Jean Baptiste Iroquois, clearly the same person. De Smet also married twenty-four-year-old Ignace, described as the son of Ignace l'Iroquois, to Lisette Court-Oreille.[15] And he baptized Louise, aged four, as the child of Waniandjay, which would become Waniyandie, and Isabelle.

The third Iroquois progenitor, whom De Smet named as "Joaquim Iroquois" and identified as having a baptized daughter, Ance, aged sixteen, was almost certainly Joachim Tonatunhun, recorded in the NWC ledger in 1819–21. Following a stop at Lac la Pluie, he had been dispatched to Athabasca, where in 1821 he purchased goods.[16] It was this family that became the Joaquims.

Also baptized were two children of Louis Iroquois, William and Therese. In addition, Therese's four children, aged two to eleven years, by François Berland, another of the Canadiens in the area, were baptized, and the couple were married. Louis Iroquois was Louis Calihoo, become Calliou, who had been contracted in Caughnawaga in 1800 to head to the North for two years. He would have a large family, not based at Jasper, which over time spread out across Athabasca.[17]

De Smet's visit attests to Iroquois valuing their selves. De Smet's characterization of those travelling with Louis Karakontie as a "family" speaks to the sense of community that had grown up between Karakontie, Joachim, and Waniyandie and their families. That it is possible, at least in part, to affix identities speaks to the critical role played by the Catholic Church, with its life-course markers of baptism, marriage, and death. Although it is very difficult to follow female descendants through time, those in the male line have left traces in some instances into the present day.

JASPER HOUSE AND THE SMOKY RIVER
AS PIVOT POINTS

By the time of the 1846 encounter, free Iroquois had for a generation made Jasper House and the Smoky River pivot points of their yearly round. Jasper House was where pelts were traded for supplies; the Smoky River, flowing from west of Jasper House north into the mighty Peace River 500 kilometres, or 310 miles, distant, was where beaver and other animals were trapped. An HBC officer writing in 1820 took for granted that "the sources of the Smokey River" were where beaver could be had, particularly by "Iroquois," to use his spelling.[18] The Smoky's ease of transport is attested by a NWC employee recommending to his superior that he "send a light Canoe" up the river with needed supplies.[19] Among favoured sites was where the Smoky passes today's Grande Cache, named for a cache of pelts once stored nearby.[20] Ignace, Charles, and especially Thomas, on whose knowledge and expertise David Thompson relied to cross Athabasca Pass in the winter of 1810–11, may have had families in the area.

Attesting to Iroquois's long-time presence, the NWC's 1817 eastward spring brigade stopped three days out from Jasper House at "a hunting-lodge of free Iroquois" that was being used as a post office. The head anticipated a letter addressed "To the gentlemen from the Columbia," which was eagerly received. It was not only letters that were to be had there but also the latest news, with the head ascertaining in this case "from the Iroquois" that another brigade laden with pelts from central Alberta was "not more than four days ahead."[21] Iroquois's utility was wide-ranging.

THE YEARLY ROUND

Two very different early accounts give entryways into Jasper Iroquois's everyday life and their yearly round. Scots botanist Thomas Drummond, who had earlier been on John Franklin's second expedition, passed the winter of 1835–36 "alone with Indians," gathering plants between Jasper House and "the Smoking River." Amid lengthy descriptions of flowers, Drummond now and then diverted his attention to his Indigenous companions:

> The hunter whom I had engaged was accompanied by his brother-in-law, an Iroquois Indian, whose wife was taken in labour. According

to the custom of these tribes, the women quitted the tent to in which she had lodged, until she should be delivered, and owing to the extreme severity of the weather, the ground being covered in snow, and the mercury indicating 38 degrees below zero, both the mother and the infant perished. The despondency which this event excited in the minds of the survivors, was so deep, that ten or fifteen days elapsed before they could be induced to quit the spot.[22]

Not only was it taken for granted that a woman accompanied the man in her life, but the relationship also mattered to all involved. Drummond's reference to an "Iroquois Indian," compared to his more usual "Indian," may indicate their differing imprints on him.[23]

Iroquois's economy and yearly round, along with those of other freemen, comes through in the Jasper House journals. The post operated seasonally, with surviving journals covering 1 October 1827 to 26 May 1828, 18 October 1829 to 10 May 1830, and 15 September 1830 to 9 May 1831. On Monday, 1 October 1827, Quebec-born Michel Klyne, who had charge, recorded – with his usual idiosyncratic spelling – his arrival at the post, whereupon "I found all they Freemen and Iroquois at the place waiting for the canoes; a month ago they bought their furs and provisions. I gave them each a dram with a half of tobacco." The long wait may explain the gifting. The next day, "I received they Iroquois Beavers say 280 small and large. I gave them each a few drams with each one quart rum for there good hunt of Beavers. If they Iroquois live [leave] this place the return will be very little and I hope they will make another hunt. This winter for the first time they promist to make one." A day later, Klyne "received the freemen Beaver say 160 very poor hunt for them; some of them would do, but some all most nothing."[24] Klyne's comments speak to Iroquois's freedom of action.

Jasper House's wellbeing depended on Iroquois goodwill. Thus not surprisingly, on 4 October 1827, in Klyne's words, "They Iroquois sober. I gave them some debt [i.e., credit against their accounts] and as sune don as sune drunk, I do not stop them as yet. I which [wish] to please them well to give them some ambition to work well the winter." The next day, "they Iroquois are geting ready to be off, in the afternoon I gave them some more rum upon debt to take way with them and they went off very well pleased." Although other freemen were not as courted as were the Iroquois with the currency of alcohol, they also mattered, as indicated by Klyne's agreeing to trade with freemen and Iroquois but not with local Indians: "I told them to be off that I had no goods for them; what goods I brought was for the free men and Iroquois of this place."[25]

Come the next spring, 1828, "they Iroquois arrived" along with three freemen, whereupon Klyne observed that "ther hunt is not very great but still more ever they dit at this place." A day later, "I received they Iroquois and free men furs 360 martens afew foxes afew wolverines afew cats and afew beaver skins." And two days later, "they Iroquois and freemen went off to kill Beavers and not to come bi fore the arrival of the canoes in the fall."[26]

The first entry in the second surviving journal, on 24 October 1829, is a likely reference to Louis Karakontie: "I exchange four mares for four horses for the winter with Louis the Iroquois. I know he will take good care of them; as June he will be at Smokey river [and] the mares will be quit for the winter and a very good place for them."[27] It is unclear whether Karakontie, if it was him, remained at the post for any length of time.

In respect to pelts arriving a week or so later, Klyne wrote, "I sent for the free men and Iroquois to give them each a few drams with a piece to-bacco." The next day, "they Iroquois took debt, with each a few pints of rum; in the evening they went off for ther winter quarter." Given that a day later "they freemen went all off for their winter quarter," the two groups appear not to have travelled together.[28] Following on the fleeting fall stay, the Iroquois's spring arrival, if in fact it took place, was not recorded by Klyne, who closed up the post on 10 May 1830.

Whether due to Iroquois being less present or to Klyne now taking their comings and goings for granted, the third and final surviving Jasper House journal, for 1830–31, is even sparser in its references. Klyne noted in passing on 19 October 1830, "2 freemen and one Iroquois left."[29] The next Iroquois surfaced on 14 December, when Klyne recorded, "in the af-ternoon Ignace the Iroquois and François Berland arrives from the Smokey river; the[y] brought a part of their furs say 200 Beavers small and large and left apart of this lodge for they others to bring as sune as they will be back." As indicated by De Smet's 1846 baptisms, Ignace Karakontie's daughter Therese would partner with Berland at about this time or soon after. Two days later, "Those two days cole weather I equipet the Iroquois and the freemen for one year. I told them to till others not to come with the furs for the month of April; they will have more furs to bring with them in the spring."[30]

The next spring, on 21 April 1831, Klyne recorded, "In the afternoon two Iroquois and Dick Couhin a free man arrived from the Smoky River, the starvagen [starvation] oblige them to leave the furs in cach at Batist [Athabasca] river." The next day, "I equiped those two Iroquois [and] the[y] went off to work beavers; the[y] are not to come be fore the month December with ther hunts." A day later, two weeks before the post would close for the summer, Klyne sought to locate any remaining pelts, and so "I sent off Loyer for these Iroquois furs at Batiste river with two horses."[31] These entries are interesting for indicating that not only Iroquois but also at least some of the freemen wintered along the Smoky River and, more generally, that at this time Iroquois were using Jasper House, or perhaps permitted to do so, only for the briefest of periods. No further Jasper House journals survive. Nor do other sources of information for these years during which Jasper Iroquois got on with their lives principally, it seems, along the Smoky River and largely on their own terms.

JASPER IROQUOIS AT MID-CENTURY

Iroquois again come into view at mid-century with the arrival of Oblate priest Albert Lacombe, based at Lac Ste Anne about 300 kilometres, or 185 miles, to the east of Jasper. The eagerness of "the Jasper hunters," Lacombe's phrase, to be baptized and married heightened his awareness of how, alongside Catholicism, they were bound together by language, places of origin, and commitment to family life. When interviewed around 1890 respecting his first impressions, Lacombe echoed De Smet:

> In 1852, after sending word to the Iroquois of the mountains for a guide and three horses, in the month of June I left our then only mission, Lac Ste. Anne, to go and visit the Jasper hunters. After nine days of incredible difficulties, through the swamp, the thick forest, rivers and creeks overflowing, I arrived exhausted, but soon forgot my difficulties by the warm welcome given me by the whole population who had been waiting for the priest. I passed fifteen days with them,

teaching day and night, and baptizing, marrying, and giving the sacraments to the happy people of the mountain. In my life as a missionary I never felt more spiritual consolation than with that population, whom I found so well disposed to receive the Gospel.[32]

Lacombe recalled having "met some of the old Iroquois, the founders of the colony," including "the last who survived, and died not long ago, [who] was named Joachim," almost certainly Joachim Tonatunhun. The priest described Iroquois's life courses as he understood them. Most young men, hired for their "energy, strength, good conduct, and skill in hunting," served out a single contract. "After two or three years, having piled for the company a great quantity of furs, the Iroquois were free and asked to be paid what was promised to them. Then they bought a large outfit of ammunition, traps, knives, axes, blankets, etc., and left Edmonton to go and hunt for themselves in the direction of the Rocky Mountains, at the head of the Athabasca River, where was established afterwards Jasper House." That these now freemen did so was accommodated by the setting: "There were plenty of moose, beaver, mountain sheep, deer, bears, etc. It was a glorious time for hunting when that part of the Rockies was the home of these wild animals."[33] Trudy Nicks puts the number of Jasper Iroquois of the first and subsequent generation at 150 about this time.[34]

Despite the fact that Lacombe was a generation younger than De Smet and only met him once in passing, his description of Iroquois's lifeways was remarkably similar:[35]

These Iroquois were living together like brothers, sharing their good and bad luck. Being Catholics, they were determined, though far from church and priest, not to neglect their religious duties. In that country at the time the Sikanais and Shouswab [Shushwap] Indians were camping and hunting, and they made acquaintance with them. Not having been married in their own country, the young Iroquois took the Indian maidens for their wives, intending to marry them before the Church as soon as they met a minister of their faith.[36]

As for family life, "In a little while large families came from these unions. The women and children spoke their own dialect, and learned the language of their husbands and fathers. They were taught to say prayers in Iroquois."[37] Iroquois and local languages were spoken side by side.

ENTER HENRY JOHN MOBERLY

The languishing Jasper House was revived as a trading post upon the arrival in 1855 of twenty-year-old Henry John Moberly. The son of English migrants to Ontario, Moberly had recently been hired by the HBC as a clerk with orders to inspect Jasper House. The post was in disrepair consequent on Colin Fraser's departure five years earlier: "The buildings, so long untenanted, badly needed repairing, the chinks between the logs re-mudding, the chimneys patching and windows fitted with new parchment – glass in those days being unknown."[38]

Moberly quickly became aware that "Jasper House was headquarters for a band of Iroquois from Eastern Canada, married to Cree women and settled there."[39] Cree were relative latecomers to the area, arriving in the 1700s at a time when other Indigenous peoples may have been losing numbers or heading elsewhere.[40] As explained by Trudy Nicks, "Cree had displaced the Beaver tribe from the Athabasca River before 1760."[41]

The seasonal round held. Thus, after various tasks were performed, Moberly "paid off four of the Iroquois and sent them to join their families, who were pitching along the Lac Ste. Ann," indicative of the long distances Iroquois travelled on their yearly round. Moberly was convinced that "the Iroquois would return to that post if it were re-established," and he proposed to the HBC that it be revived over the winter on a seasonal basis to acquire beaver pelts.[42]

Mobery's offer to take charge of Jasper House may have been sparked by his everyday comfort with Iroquois. He described in his memoir how on his way west in the canoe belonging to HBC head George Simpson, he had struck up an acquaintance with his "Iroquois cook," which "gained me the friendship of all the Iroquois," including members of Simpson's usual "picked crew of Iroquois crewmen from Caughnawaga, near Montreal, than which there is no better in the world."[43] His proposal accepted, Moberly was back at Jasper House in 1858, whereupon "I communicated with the Iroquois, advising them to 'pitch up' hunting in different directions, and when short of ammunition or other supplies to come to Jasper

House."[44] To "pitch up" was to camp. A visitor described a freezing February visit to Iroquois freemen hunters on the side of a river "in huts built of the branches of pine trees."[45]

Indicative of Moberly's trust in, and reliance on, Iroquois and their continuing primacy at Jasper House, he described in his memoir being accompanied by "six young Iroquois," sending horses to the winter range with "two Iroquois," and leaving "an Iroquois to put the place in order" while he went hunting "with three other Iroquois."[46] With buffalo, elk, and grizzly bears all in decline, big-horn sheep were a principal target for food and easiest to kill when they were descending the mountains in the morning for the salt licks.[47] Pelts and other items acquired at Jasper House were dispatched in the spring to Fort Edmonton, from which, along with such goods from other posts, they were sent by water to Hudson Bay.[48]

Moberly's relationship to Jasper House soon took another turn. It is uncertain precisely when he came into contact with Louis Karakontie's daughter, Suzanne, a decade his senior, but it was likely in the ordinary course of events, and they were soon starting a family, with their first child born in 1860. Whatever ensued in the interim, Moberly left behind the ragtag post of Jasper House just a year later and with it a pregnant Suzanne. On the eve of doing so, he wed her in a Catholic ceremony at Lac Ste Anne, thereby bestowing his surname on their son and the unborn child she was carrying. Suzanne, who prior to meeting Moberly had given birth to a daughter, would later partner with Moberly's successor at Jasper House, John McCauley, there in 1863–64, by whom she had a fourth child.[49]

Moberly's reason for leaving can be variously interpreted. Although he did not in his later memoir mention his relationship with Suzanne Karakontie, much less by name any of the other Iroquois he encountered at Jasper House, he hinted at the reason:

> At this time the country of the Northwest was considered a vast desert, and with the exception of a small tract round Red River Settlement [in today's Manitoba], good only for buffalo and Indians ... From Red River Settlement to the Rockies – all open prairie – not a single settler dwelt outside the Company's posts, the sole exceptions being a few halfbreeds around the [Catholic] missions at Lac la Biche [500 kilometres, or 310 miles, to the northeast] and Lac Ste. Anne.[50]

It is possible Moberly had dared in the moment to consider otherwise: "Had any employee of the Hudson's Bay Company ventured to express an opinion that the territory was fitted for settlement he would have found himself transported to the Arctic region."[51] For a well-educated white man in his mid-twenties, as was Moberly, staying around on an independent basis was not feasible. Moberly's great-grandson by Suzanne Karakontie, Ron Pelletier, has reflected on the sequence of events:

> Henry did leave after the marriage but I believe he tried to persuade her to go with him. In his book [published in 1929] he talks of getting two pack horses loaded at Fort Edmonton and camping a few miles away from the Fort. He then says he proceeded to Lac Ste. Anne where he spent the night at the Roman Catholic Mission. It is my belief this was his last attempt to persuade Suzanne to go with him … When Henry left that day he never saw his oldest son ever again, the sad thing is he never saw his unborn son John.[52]

Whatever the couple's motivations, the sequence of events would shape descendants' lives. A hundred and twenty years later, a Moberly grandson remained utterly convinced that "my Grandmother … refused to go with him when he left so he left alone."[53]

CHANGING TIMES

Moberly's arrival and departure presaged changing times. Up to then, the area around Jasper House was almost wholly unknown to outsiders, except for Catholic priests. Now growing numbers of travellers began to pass by, it being the fashion among men of means to undertake genteel exploration that they would subsequently recount in print. Their doing so had two important outcomes. First, by virtue of visitors needing guides, Iroquois and others were given opportunities for short-term employment. Second, visitors' accounts provide the earliest nonpriestly, non-fur-trade windows into Jasper Iroquois. The intimacy of these accounts testifies to Iroquois's comfort with the way of being they had created for themselves, which involved living on natural resources generated through their hard work and persistence.

In 1859 James Hector, a young naturalist attached to a British exploring expedition headed by geographer John Palliser, sought out Iroquois, already familiar to him by virtue of George Simpson having arranged for mostly Iroquois paddlers to take them as far west as Red River. Even though Hector's observations and those of the expedition's youthful interpreter, Peter Erasmus, were influenced by subsequent contact with Moberly, they attest in their essence to what the pair observed.

The Palliser expedition's initial encounter with Iroquois occurred while ascending the Athabasca River "in sight of the mountains" on the way to Jasper House. As described by Hector,

> As we were preparing to encamp, we observed a smoke rising out of the woods, and ascending the bank found a camp, four tents of Iroquois half-breeds. We brought our dogs up the bank, and encamped beside them. They were badly off for provisions, and living altogether on the little hare, but which they said is very scarce this year in the woods. These Iroquois were originally trappers in the service of the N.W. Company ... and have since been tented about like Indians, trading the skins and furs they procure at Jasper House. There are only about 30 tents of them, and they all talk the Cree language besides their own, and have latterly intermarried a good deal with the Cree half-breeds of Lac St. Ann's.[54]

Half a century after the earliest Iroquois had left home, those of the second generation still held onto their language alongside Cree.

Born and educated at Red River, where he had been a schoolmaster, Peter Erasmus observed that "Iroquois Indians" stood out from their Indigenous counterparts by virtue of their ambition and determination:

> They all appeared better dressed, healthier, and better equipped than the Assiniboines [encountered a day or two earlier]. Possibly they had acquired a knowledge and experience in their travels that fitted them better to their new environment. Perhaps Company largesse allowed them more privileges than the other less-energetic tribes. They were all good trappers and hunters, physically well-built men, and a great deal more active in their movements, around camp than their indifferent slow neighbours, the Assinboines.[55]

Arriving at Jasper House, Hector took note of "two or three Iroquois hunters attached to the trading post, and they are sent off every morning before daybreak [to hunt big-horn sheep for food], and seldom return till late in the afternoon." He admired "the perfection to which the Iroquois carry [on] moose-hunting."[56]

Hector recounted the Smoky River's utilty as explained to him from an Iroquois perspective:[57] "Smoking River is about two days journey to the N.W., and along its valley there are extensive prairies, of which the Iroquois hunters speak in high terms as the finest land in the country. They say that the winter there is very open, and the pasture is always good. In autumn wild fruit is plentiful … The Iroquois have several times grown turnips, potatoes, and barley there with great success, but only as an experiment."[58] From Hector's perspective, there was no question that the Smoky River was fundamental to the Iroquois's yearly round.

Another 1859 visitor similarly glimpsed Iroquois group dynamics. On a hunting trip through the Rocky Mountains, the Earl of Southesk was already disposed toward Iroquois by virtue of HBC head George Simpson having lent him two of his trusty Iroquois canoe men, described by the English aristocrat as resembling "commonplace Europeans, southerners in aspect," and "picturesque with their green or scarlet blankets and their long, streaming, coal-black hair." Southesk considered one of the pair, Thomas Ariwakenha, whom he knew as Toma, to be "the trustiest and best of fellows," whether "driving the wagon, cooking my meals," or "acting as my special attendant" to the extent of carrying him bodily across a river.[59]

Southesk's decision to head to "the neighbourhood of Jasper's House, a fort in the mountains," was precipitated on his leaving Fort Edmonton by a chance acquaintance's having commended it as "a good country for game." Along the way at "about 5 P.M. we found a Jasper's House Iroquois camping with his family, consisting of his wife, two children, and a servant girl." The Iroquois, whom Southesk later identified as Pierre, might have been Ignace Waniyandie's son, thirty-year-old Pierre Waniyandie, who was married to Canadien descendant Olive Gauthier. Given the time of day, "we pitched our tents not far from the place chosen by our new friends."[60]

The consequence was a travelling relationship engendering a fine-grained description that may have been precipitated by the fact that Southesk, only in his early thirties, had an eye for the ladies:

> The Iroquois and his family are travelling with us. His wife is a good-looking, clear-skinned, black-haired French half-breed, too flat in her proportions like all her race. Her dress is of dark blue cloth. She and the [servant] girl ride astride, of course, but quite modestly, wrapping up their legs in the shawls in which they carry the little children. The wife rides a very pretty grey-and-white pied mare, with two bells round its neck, which makes a pleasant rural sound; these are not mere ornaments but are meant to scare away wolves, and very generally do so.[61]

The two groups travelled together. Hence a few days later, when "the baby of our fellow traveler Pierre, the Iroquois, was taken ill at night," his father was comfortable requesting that Southesk "come and give it medicine," which he did successfully.[62]

Southesk next encountered, among other Iroquois, Ignace Waniyandie, whose name Southesk spelled "Eneas Oneanti," as "Ignacc" and "Eneas" were routinely interchanged at this time.[63] Pierre and Ignace Waniyandie were almost certainly brothers or possibly half-brothers. While on the way to Jasper, "three or four Iroquois and half-breed hunters were encamped with their families, and there we halted, in the hope of getting horses and other things that were required." A day later, perhaps at Southesk's request, "the wife of one of the hunters has made me a gun-cover of moose-leather, ornamented with fringes and narrow braidings of red and black cloth, after the picturesque fashion of the country."[64] The gun case's quality was such that Southesk held onto it, as did his family for the next century and a half.[65] Southesk's crediting the artistry of Ignace Waniyandie's wife, Lisette Court-Oreille, so identified by textiles scholar Susan Berry, extended by inference to the men themselves:[66] "These hunters are fine-looking men; dressed either in the usual fringed leather hunting-shirts, or in blue cloth capots. Their caps are of blue cloth, small, with a leather shade, and covered with streamers of ribbon, chiefly black, blue, and red." It was not only the adults who impressed Southesk: "One pretty brown pony passed us, carrying a little girl five or six years old, who was riding quite alone. Near one of the tents I saw two girls, of much the same age, cleaning a beaver-skin with a bone, while two others were cutting up fat with great knives."[67]

Southesk was so impressed with Iroquois's horses that from Ignace Waniyandie he acquired a pony, which he named Jasper, "as he belonged to the Jasper's House district."[68] Waniyandie, a sharp bargainer, upon discovering that the horse for which he had traded the pony did not ride well, demanded and got a replacement. A month later, he turned up at Fort Edmonton some 350 kilometres, or 215 miles, to the east to exchange for goods a £12 note of credit he had received from Southesk. The wide selection Waniyandie acquired, ranging from fine fabrics to blankets to clothing, showed that he had Lisette and their children as well as himself in mind.[69] The encounter speaks to the complexities and sophistication of the lives of women who were aligned with second-generation Iroquois.

As these visitors attest, times were changing despite, by Michael Payne's calculation, reasonable numbers of beaver and also marten pelts being traded annually into the 1870s.[70] Much as James Hector encountered Iroquois short of provisions on his way to Jasper House, Southesk was told there was "no game in the neighbourhood; the people starving, and making haste to leave the desolated place."[71] A pair of visitors the next year heard a similar story. Viscount Milton, accompanied by English physician Walter Cheadle, reached Jasper House at the end of June 1863 to find everyone away foraging for food. Returned from hunting, Moberly's successor as post head, John McCauley, explained that "a winter rarely passed now without a great scarcity of provisions at Jasper House."[72]

The most significant indicator of changing times comes from Henry John Moberly's older brother Walter, who passed through in the fall of 1872 in the course of his employment as a surveyor for a proposed transcontinental rail line to cross south of Jasper House. Visiting "that remarkable point of the mountains," he described how "the glory of Jasper House" had departed, its "picturesque buildings" being replaced by "two wretched little log cabins." Walter Moberly's encounter gives yet another entryway into the area's ethos: "I passed the night in Jasper House, where there was only one single room, and I had therefore some dozen Iroquois half-breeds, men, women, and children to keep me company. They were very quiet, extremely civil; and the men fine, handsome, athletic fellows. They presented me with some Rocky Mountain sheep meat, which was a great treat." Reflective of the isolation that still held, his hosts were "rather puzzled to make out what kind of a drink coffee was," upon its being offered to them by their grateful visitor.[73]

Walter Moberly depended on local labour, and there being no snow to permit his sleds to get up a hill, "Louis, one of the Iroquois hunters, sent back for his two daughters to pack the loads to the top of the ridge." One of them, whom Moberly described as "a tall and very powerful young woman," also intended to "pack me over the ice." Moberly protested but to no avail: "She insisted, saying I was much lighter than the load she had just packed over, and if she did not take me her father would be very angry; so I resigned myself to my fate, and was ignominiously packed over." The story had a postscript:

> Louis was very proud of the girl's strength, and that evening, as we were smoking a pipe, he pointed out the great advantages in having such a powerful girl, and, as he wished to get a horse I had, he made me an offer to make an exchange – I to give him the horse and a few other things, and take the girl instead, to which she did not object; but as I had no idea of becoming a permanent resident of that country, and hardly liked the idea of presenting her in the civilized world, I was obliged to decline.[74]

There is no information to indicate Louis's identity or to know whether the offer made to Walter Moberly was linked to his younger brother Henry's earlier penchant for a Jasper Iroquois daughter.

A parallel account comes from Walter Moberly's contemporary George Grant, a Presbyterian minister and public intellectual from the Maritimes who passed by Jasper at virtually the same time in 1872. Grant was already aware of, and kindly disposed toward, Iroquois, having as with the others been introduced to their utility by George Simpson. Grant and the men with him had been paddled west by "Iroquois from Caughnawaga near Montreal," whom he described in his journal as "sinewy, active, good looking men ... above the medium size, broad shouldered, with straight features, intelligent faces, and graceful," and with "good head[s] of hair, thick, well cropped and, though always black, quite like the hair of a civilized man instead of a savage." If this were not praise enough, albeit rendered in the language of the day, "the Iroquois dressed as simply and neatly as blue jackets," being the term for British sailors.

In line with common practice, Grant confined Iroquois's identities to their first names and utility, thus referring to steersmen "Louis, who had been cook to Sir George [Simpson] on his expeditions," and Baptiste and Toma, who were in charge of two smaller canoes and sometimes sang "Iroquois boat songs." The farther west Grant travelled, the more he contrasted "our noble Iroquois" with "Indians" encountered along the way, whom he characterized as "vain, lazy, dirty and improvident." At no time was Grant more taken with the Iroquois in his midst than at a Sunday religious service. "Although the Iroquois understood but few words of English, they listened most devoutly" and sang the traditional hymn "Veni Creator" in Iroquois.[75] Once again, Iroquois were perceived as navigating, if not also in the moment crossing, the Indigenous-white divide.

Nearing Jasper House from Fort Edmonton, Grant passed by "Indians [with] straighter features and a manlier cast of countenance than the ordinary Wood-Indians," who turned out to be "Iroquois from Smoking River, to the north of Jasper's." Respecting Jasper House itself, Grant's pessimism was similar to that of Walter Moberly: "Now there are only two log houses, the largest propped up before and behind with rough shakes, as if to prevent it being blown away into the river or back into the mountain gorges. The houses are untenanted, locked and shuttered. Twice a year an agent comes from Edmonton to trade with the Indians of the surrounding country and carry back the furs."[76]

Times were changing. Two years after these 1872 visits, Jasper House was reduced to an adjunct of an HBC post located at Lac Ste Anne and in 1884 was closed entirely. It was now necessary to travel to Lac Ste Anne to exchange pelts for supplies, to catch up on baptisms and marriages, and from 1889 to participate in its annual Catholic pilgrimage.[77] A passerby a quarter of a century later described Lac Ste Anne as a "quaint little village, with the pretty Whitewashed buildings of the Hudson's Bay Company against a background of still yellow poplars and the grey Roman Catholic church, toward which gaily-dressed half-breeds were sauntering."[78] Physical deterioration did not result in Iroquois wholly abandoning the setting with which their families had for so long identified. A Hudson's Bay Company count of 1879 found six families of Iroquois at Jasper House, a total upped three years later to thirteen families.[79]

In his interview of about 1890, long time Oblate priest Albert Lacombe reflected on the consequences of the passage of time for Jasper Iroquois. Language had been a principal casualty: "The Iroquois dialect is nearly extinct among them, except the old people, and the French and the Cree are predominant. They are so scattered and mixed that it is difficult to recognize much trace of the Iroquois [language], but I do not think their numbers are decreasing."[80] It is within this context that Suzanne Karikonti Moberly would be revered on her death in May 1905, while gathering plants for healing, for staying true to her inheritance.[81]

VALUING MARKERS OF IDENTITY

However much the times might have been changing around them and for them, Jasper Iroquois continued to value their markers of identity. Karakontie, Joachim, and Waniyandie descendants were Iroquois and to an increasing extent also Cree by inheritance and language, Catholic by religion, and Jasper people by association.

Iroquois descendants' markers of identity come through loud and clear in applications for scrip.[82] Parallel to Indigenous peoples signing away in treaties the lands guaranteed them in the Royal Proclamation of 1763, Canadian legislation was passed in 1879 and implemented in 1885 "to satisfy any claims existing in connection with the extinguishment of the Indian title, preferred by half-breeds resident in the North-West Territories [i.e., Saskatchewan and Alberta] … by granting lands to such persons."[83] In exchange for ceasing legally to be an Indian with consequent land rights, eligible persons resident prior to 15 July 1870 and children born between then and 31 December 1885 were given their choice of land scrip entitling them to 160 acres of surveyed land or money scrip worth $160 toward such a purchase. The latter was in practice easily sold to speculators in exchange for ready cash.[84]

As to who qualified, absent in the legislation but legally described earlier in time, "half-breeds" comprised "all those of mixed blood, partly white and partly Indian."[85] The assumption that they would be the offspring of white men arrived with the fur trade and the Indigenous women in their lives did not deter Iroquois descendants from applying in large numbers, almost always for money scrip. Nor did it deter the visiting officials who wrote the information down and read it back for verification from accommodating Iroquois's distinctive circumstances so long as some white ancestry could be demonstrated.[86] Among exceptions to Iroquois descendants taking advantage of this opportunity was a Calliou son who in 1878 signed a treaty, only to have the 25,000 acres allotted to the band so reduced in size that in 1958 its members would opt out.[87]

Figure 7.2
Money scrip issued to Baptiste Waniyande, 6 June 1898

What becomes clear from an examination of scrip applications held in Library and Archives Canada containing one or more of the key surnames of Joachim, Waniyandie, and Karakontie, the latter sometimes becoming Moberly, is that, although Jasper descendants might no longer be Iroquois speakers – indeed, numerous scrip applications were read back for verification in Cree – they were Iroquois by self-identification, Catholic by religion, and Jasper people by geography.[88] Unlike many applicants who were said "not to know their parents' names," much less their other markers of identity, Iroquois descendants knew who they were.[89]

Members of all three core families retained awareness of their Iroquois inheritance, with the Joachims being the most determined to give it priority, possibly due to their later arrival.[90] Members of the second and third generations described their progenitors or themselves on scrip applications by their Iroquois surname, written down variously, according to how it was heard, as Tewanatanahow, Tenawatanshow, Tenanatanaham, Tenanatanahow, and Tawanatahan. Despite Joseph Joachim's being almost certainly the son of an earlier Iroquois and a local Indigenous woman, his sons Louis and Patrick and daughter Madeline, born between 1874 and 1883, all described him on their scrip applications of 1900 as solely an "Iroquois Indian."[91] The information was so emphasized as to be underlined

on the form by the official to whom they orally submitted it. The same occurred with Joseph Joachim's brother Alexis, whose sons Martin and Adam
and daughter Marie each initially described themselves as an "Iroquois Indian."[92] Attempting to clarify that these descendants were eligible for scrip,
an official wrote on the side of Louis Joachim's application, "Joachim's father was Iroquois Indian, i.e. One of the halfbreed Iroquois B^d [Band] of
Jasper. They are mixed blood."[93] The distinction made between generations
for the purposes of scrip did not accord with family members' perceptions
of who they were. Descendants' pride in their identities could be their undoing, as with a Waniyandie born in 1838 at Jasper House proudly describing both of his parents as "Iroquois Indian," to be thereby "Disallowed and
to be classed Indian," making him ineligible for scrip.[94] From time to time,
either during the oral submission or as the application travelled up the
line of authority, an official changed one of the responses to the two key
questions regarding whether the applicant's father or mother was "a Half-
breed or an Indian" from "Indian" to "Halfbreed" in order to make for an
acceptable application.

Catholicism also shadowed scrip applications, just as it did everyday
lives. Baptismal records gave the means for individuals to prove who they
were in applying for scrip and more generally to attest to their senses of
self. Exemplary is Suzanne Joachim, who was born about 1850 to Joachim
Tonatunhun and Marie Waniyandie and had at least seven children born
between 1869 and 1878 at Jasper House with Pierre Delorme, who had two
older sons with Isabelle Karakontie.[95] Despite five of her oldest children
dying young, four by drowning, Suzanne explained proudly that each had
been baptized in a river near where a priest encountered the family on their
yearly round.[96]

Descendants took pride in Jasper as their place of being. Suzanne
Joachim's scrip application stated, "I was born and have lived all my life in
the Jasper House country."[97] Louis Karakontie's great-grandson Simon explained in applying for scrip that "our family has lived in the Jasper House
country as long as I can remember."[98] As put by a Waniyandie great-grandson, "my father lived in the neighbourhood of Jasper House all his life."[99]
A local trader acting as a witness for a Karakontie descendant made the
point on his behalf: "He always lived between Jasper House and Smokey
River. He is a hunter."[100] Whether or not it was literally so, Jasper House
was where most individuals considered they were born.

Iroquois's attachment to Jasper House was not to diminish the yearly round. In 1872 a son of Karakontie daughter Isabelle and of Waniyandie son Jean Baptiste wed a daughter of "halfbreeds," to use the term on the scrip application, and over the next two decades they had eight children together. Indicative of how families moved about, each of their offspring, apart from twins, was born in a different location from the next child in age. As recalled by their mother on her scrip application of 1900 in her first language of Cree, the sequence ran: Smoky River, the British Columbia side of the Rocky Mountains, between the Rocky Mountains and Grand Prairie northwest of Edmonton, Burnt River near Dunvegan, between Grand Prairie and Spirit River, again the British Columbia side of the mountains, and Grand Prairie.[101] As an outsider explained in attesting to the birth of a fourth-generation Joachim in 1873, his parents "were at Smokey River at the time he was born," but their "home was at Jasper House."[102] Iroquois's mobility is attested by the statement written across an outside expert's map drawn in the early 1880s that "A Band of Iroquois Immigrants Now Hunt Between Jasper House & Dunvegan," located 450 kilometres, or 280 miles, apart.[103] A 1900 map has "Iroquois" written "in the immediate vicinity of Jasper House."[104]

Markers of identity were solidified through generations of intermarriage, which was, on the one hand, a matter of practicality given proximity and, on the other, an assertion of their Iroquois, Catholic, and Jasper identities. Scrip applications from descendants of the three core families testify to Karakonties, Joachims, and Waniyandies partnering with each other across the generations. Two-thirds of the applications located with one of the three surnames contain at least two of the three, if not all three.[105] Where families did not intermarry, sons looked to Indigenous women, and daughters turned to men of mixed descent or white newcomers.[106]

ANOTHER IROQUOIS MARITAL OPTION

Another marital possibility for Jasper Iroquois was to partner with an Iroquois descendant living at a distance. In 1899 a Waniyandie great-granddaughter whose maternal grandmother was a Karakontie married Modeste Testawich, whose family was said to have originated with Iroquois paddler François Tustavits, who had arrived in northwestern Alberta with George Simpson in 1828.[107] Visiting a branch of the family in 1889, young English adventurer Warburton Pike was so impressed by its members' inheritance that he referred to his host admiringly as "the Iroquois."[108] As explained by Randy Bouchard and Dorothy Kennedy, Testawich grandson Duncan, as "headman" at the forks of the Peace and Smoky Rivers, acceded to Treaty 8, which covers northern Alberta and parts of British Columbia, Saskatchewan, and the Northwest Territories. His consequent acquisition of farm land would prove to be short-lived. In a pattern happening more generally with Indigenous peoples, land pressures from whites resulted in eight of the ten reserves allocated to Duncan's Band, as it was called, being stripped away within two decades.[109]

Indicative of Iroquois descendants preferring each other, three decades earlier, in 1869, while in his early twenties, Duncan Testawich had wed Sophie Thomas of similar Iroquois descent. The Thomas family, which would in the 1890s again intermarry with the Testawiches, was headed by Sophie's brother Napoleon, well known in northeastern British Columbia as a hunter and guide.[110] A Northwest Mounted Police inspector who hired him in 1897 for a four-month winter stint described him as "a Half-breed Iroquois" and, despite himself, was impressed by how Thomas negotiated his salary upward from the proffered $75 to $90 a month.[111]

Unlike Duncan Testawich, Napoleon Thomas saw his future in the white world and applied to homestead the land on which he had lived since 1891 as soon as it was possible to do so in 1911–12. His decision would be for naught. Through a combination of government requirements and minutiae, others' determination to have the land, and Thomas's attention sometimes being elsewhere, all carefully explained by Dorothea Calverley, the issue was still unresolved on his death in 1920 or 1921.[112] His son Jack, to whom the land was willed, was finally granted a patent in January 1922 without being told about the necessity to pay taxes on it or how to reclaim the land if sold in arrears. A hundred plus official letters, documents, and maps detail how the Thomas family's title to the land slipped away.[113] Being Iroquois across changing times was not necessarily an easy matter.

TO SUM UP

No westward Iroquois were more ambitious and more determined to live as they would as best they could than were those who set down at Jasper and along the Smoky River starting in the early 1800s. They arrived as outsiders but as Indigenous outsiders who accommodated themselves to the locality, most visibly through their hard work and in men's unions with local women. For a century, these outsiders persisted in a way of life uniquely their own, as indicated by descendants being referred to by visiting whites as "Iroquois" and "Iroquois half breeds," as opposed to just plain Indians.

With the exception of Louis Karakontie, the voices of Jasper Iroquois survive through the voices of others. Despite white outsiders telling their stories in bits and scraps intended to reflect well on themselves, Iroquois's presence is there. Race was ever visible, inevitably so, but there was also from time to time respect and even a touch of envy. That they were stereotyped without being rendered inert speaks to Jasper Iroquois's determination across a century to engage the Indigenous-white divide pragmatically on their own terms.

8

Persisting in Jasper's Shadow

As the nineteenth century became the twentieth, descendants of the trio of Iroquois progenitors in chapter 7 were seemingly fixed in place at Jasper. They were living as they would without offending those around them. The future they anticipated was not to be. They would be twice cast out, first from their homeland and then from the place where some of them resettled in Jasper's shadow.

Iroquois's forced removal from newly established Jasper Park in 1910 would break a century-old link to their place of being, but in no way did it render Iroquois inert. It is a measure of their strong senses of self, solidified by several lifetimes together, that Joachims, Waniyandies, and Karakonties, some become Moberlys, regrouped. Descendants were assisted in doing so by their longstanding markers of identity. They were Iroquois by inheritance and Catholic by religion, and they shared a homeland reinforced through intermarriage. By virtue of men having families mostly with local women, they were also Cree, which became an everyday language and a fourth marker.[1] Unlike their counterparts of chapter 6 who seemingly disappeared into a changing Pacific Northwest, Iroquois descendants persisting in Jasper's shadow have continued to be visible into the present day.

JASPER IROQUOIS AT THE TURN OF THE TWENTIETH CENTURY

Jasper Iroquois at the turn of the twentieth century retained their attachment to each other, to their ways of being, and to making up their own minds about where and how they lived. An American report of 1879 attests to the latter characteristic in its observation that "the settlement of a band of Iroquois in the Rocky Mountains is a striking illustration of the roaming propensity of savages."[2] In a 1903 description of "Iroquois Indians of Eastern Canada," the Indian agent at Edmonton wiped his hands of them, explaining that "the majority appear to have gone up to the Jasper Pass country, and though I hear of them occasionally, they are outside my field of enquiry."[3]

Oblate priest Albert Lacombe, based at Lac Ste Anne, was understandably keen on Jasper Iroquois heading there, even more so on the closure of Jasper House in 1884. Six years later, he described approvingly how some descendants had "abandoned their hunting grounds, where they had no church and no school, and came to join with their fellow half-breeds of Lac Ste. Anne."[4] In line with such a movement, in about 1895 Waniyandie brothers Adam and Pierre built a large new cross for Lac Ste Anne's cemetery.[5] A decade later, in 1905, fifty-eight-year-old Adam Waniyandie applied to homestead an already fenced river lot with a log cabin, two stables, six head of cattle, and eight horses on which he had been living for the past eleven years with his wife and family.[6]

Lacombe was well aware that Jasper Iroquois were in practice "scattered everywhere," including "the Athabasca and Peace rivers and mountains."[7] A Moberly descendant told much the same story: "When they closed down Jasper House, there's no more store there – they move away. Some of them moved to Lac Ste. Anne, some of them moved to Grand Prairie or farther north where the trapping is good – where they still could go to the store."[8]

JASPER HOUSE'S CONTINUING APPEAL

Jasper House also continued to exercise appeal, as shown by scrip applications and by Augustine Waniyandie's application in 1901 to homestead 140 acres there.[9] According to University of Toronto geology professor Arthur Coleman, who visited in 1907, there were at Jasper "about a hundred in all" in what he described as "a colony of Iroquois half-breeds, many of them named Moberly from a White ancestor," who "are fairly civilized, and some of them are well off."[10]

Coleman was referring to the two Moberly sons living just south of Jasper House. Ewan Moberly, whose first name was pronounced "Ayvon" or "Evan,"[11] and Madeleine Finlay, of the large Canadien fur trade family of that name, lived with their children on the west side of the Athabasca River near where the brothers' mother, Suzanne, by birth a Karakontie, was buried. John Moberly and Marie Joachim, descended from the large Iroquois family of that name and also from Jasper's head Colin Fraser, had settled on the east side of the river with their family. Alberta historian James MacGregor describes the brothers as "two of the leading men in the valley."[12]

The brothers were not alone. Ewan Moberly's father-in-law, Isadore Findlay, lived nearby, as did Ewan's son Adolphus, born in 1878.[13] So did Ewan's daughter Fresnine, married to Adam Joachim, born in 1875 and descended both from the Joachims and from Jasper House's onetime head Colin Fraser. Lacombe had intended that Adam should become a priest on the pattern of his paternal grandfather, Joachim Tonatunhun, who on his death, the priest wrote, "had yet with him, as precious relics, his prayer-book in Iroquois, and other articles of piety he brought with him from Montreal."[14] Lacombe arranged for Adam to be educated at an Alberta Catholic residential school and then to study for the priesthood in Montreal, from which he returned home three years later in 1896. By one account, it was due to a family emergency, and by another, which may have originated with Adam, he quite simply "got extremely lonesome."[15] All his life, Adam Joachim would be admired by outsiders for speaking French and English "along with his Native Cree language" and for knowing Latin, all of which, in the words of a visiting priest, "conferred on him a superiority and an authority which nobody could deny."[16]

To the south of Ewan Moberly's homestead on the same side of the Athabasca River lay the property of Lewis Swift, an American who had come in 1894 and a few years later wed a woman he liked to introduce, as he did to Coleman, as "an Iroquois half-breed."[17] Swift's being, in the parlance of the day, a white man – and the only white man – gave him a credibility denied to the others. Swift was a known source of supplies and had for that reason been Coleman's first point of call on his 1907 visit, ensuring he knew in advance that the others were "half-breeds." It was Swift's shortage of items that sent Coleman to the Moberly brothers, who provided similar services to passersby.

Coleman headed "a few miles down the valley" to Ewan Moberly, whom he described as "a shrewd-looking, swarthy man who came out of a well-built house a little off from the river to see us." Soon realizing that his host

Figure 8.1
Adam Joachim with his wife, Fresnine Moberly, and her brother Lactap *(left)*,
early 1900s

and family did not accord with his stereotypical preconceptions, Coleman found the visit revealing: "Moberly took us into his house, where the women were at work, one a very pretty girl, and we were rather surprised to see a sewing-machine and a battered phonograph in the room, the latter singing a ragtime song in a very brazen voice."[18] Ewan Moberly moved easily between languages and was self-sufficient and enterprising:

> At first Iwan answered our questions in Cree, the *lingua franca* of the plains, *nemoya* (no) being a very prominent word; but presently he melted into a very fair English, and admitted that he had nearly everything humanity could want except bacon, which he was short of; but flour, beans, rice, raisins, even some canned stuff, he could supply. Taking us into his smoke-house, we saw rows of Whitefish hanging from the roof; seven big ones for a dollar, also a bony side of bear-meat, very dirty-looking; which he did not recommend because the animal was old and tough. We then went into his store, where flour and other things were measured out to us in a free-and-easy way without using the huge pair of steelyards hanging on the wall.[19]

Ewan Moberly was well positioned to participate in the paid economy, Coleman explained: "Our money had quickly vanished at Swift's and Moberly's, where prices were very high because all except fish and bear-meat and potatoes had to come in 250 miles [400 kilometres] on the backs of ponies," this from Lac Ste Anne.[20]

Coleman was not the only visitor. An American naturalist and explorer arrived in 1908 with similar assumptions and preconceptions. Mary Schäffer had read in a government report that Swift was the "true pioneer of the country" and so sought him out. Swift was "courtesy itself," if without space to host Schäffer and her party in his one-room log house amid his wife, who demonstrated for the visitor her proficiency at buck-skin needle work, and their six children; and so the visitors camped, as was their usual practice.[21]

Schäffer and the others with her had earlier come across, a mile or so away from Swift, "a second bunch of shacks surrounded by wheat-fields and a small garden of cabbages, potatoes, and turnips." She was not without her prejudices: "Peeping in the windows quite free of curtains, it looked just as lonesome and free of comfort as the average shack which the breed inhabits." She described how "over the door of the log-cabin hung sheep, goat, and deer horns," and on the other side of the Athabasca River lay "two dugout canoes lashed together." Schäffer realized that "this must be John Moberly's, a half breed of whom we had heard," but he was not at home.[22] Made from popular trees, the dugout canoes were the means of water transportation.[23]

Back from hunting, John Moberly and his wife, Marie Joaquim, along with their children crossed paths with Mary Schäffer prior to her departure:

> Though there were several horses loaded with hides and meat, it looked far more like the moving of an orphanage than the return from a month's hunting expedition. John, with a small child in front of him, headed the band, two grinning kids on one horse followed, and so on till Mrs. Moberly brought up the rear in a dignified manner, carrying a small infant under one arm. In all, they counted eight, and I wondered how many White mothers would go on such a trip and look so placid on their return. She smiled a pleasant smile at our greeting, and we each passed on our way.[24]

The much-travelled Mary Schäffer succumbed at least in the moment to their common humanity.

Coleman and his group returned in 1909, this time camping by invitation on the property of Ewan Moberly's brother John, depicted as "enjoying an ancient and well-ordered civilization." Coleman was taken by how John Moberly's "fields of oats were ripening, well fenced in, and cows and horses were quietly feeding or lining up behind smudges to escape the flies." It was not only John who impressed but also his wife, Marie Joaquim, who, much as with Swift's wife, "makes embroidered buckskin suits, fringed and tasseled and margined with otter fur, worth $60 each, but far too magnificent for ordinary life."[25] Women were integral to family economies.

Again, Coleman was short of supplies: "John Moberly is not only rancher and ferryman, but, like his brother Iwan on the other side of the river, keeps a store where most backwoods necessaries can be purchased at high prices. We bought mainly dried and pounded goat-meat, cheap because manufactured in this country, though some of us invested in grizzly bear claws and other frontier trifles." As well as being a part-time merchant, the enterprising John Moberly used what Coleman described as "his cranky canoe, hollowed out of a log of balsam poplar," to ferry persons like him and his entourage across the broad Athabasca River.[26] John Moberly, whose family also spoke Cree at home, was multilingual like his older brother Ewan.[27]

Prior to arriving, Coleman had an unexpected encounter with Ewan Moberly's son Adolphus, he explained in his journal: "On our way to Moberly's two young halfbreed swells passed us in the same direction on fine horses with showy trappings, and later we made the closer acquaintance with one of them, Dolphus, as he was known, [who] was resplendent in one of the silk-embroidered buckskin suits ... and with a mirror flashing on the brow of his sleek black pony. We engaged him as guide."[28]

That Coleman hired the thirty-year-old Adolphus speaks to how the Moberly family and others made a living and also to the dynamics of family life:

Adolphus Moberly and his family, with some relations, joined us, being rather tardy at the start; and henceforth our cavalcade was most picturesque; the stylish Adolphus riding ahead and a party of Indians, including men, women, children, and dogs, with a mob of ponies, following at their leisure behind. We camped at the South of Moose River, whose valley we were to follow into the mountains, Adolphus going off alone to select and blaze out the little traveled and poorly marked trail.[29]

The entourage soon had the company of Adolphus Moberly's brother-in-law Adam Joachim and his family, whom Coleman specifically designated as Iroquois:

We had just got our camp set when the Iroquois came cantering up in joyous confusion, the women carrying their young children in their arms instead of in the blanket on their back as the Stony women do. Beside the Moberlys there was a related family of Adams in the party, Adam himself being rather a curious compound of civilisation and savagery, who had been educated for the priesthood in an eastern college and spoke English and French as well as his native tongue. He talked intelligently and looked somewhat delicate and refined, yet here he was living meagerly by the hunt, not more than supporting his small family, and far less efficient than brawny Adolphus, who was ignorant but a mighty hunter and a born leader.[30]

To cross the Indigenous-white divide, as Adam Joachim had attempted for a time, was to invite scorn.

Coleman showcased gender and racial stereotypes as a matter of course: "I was putting up the teepee and asked him [Adolphus Moberly] to show me how to do it properly, but he smiled contemptuously and said, 'Don't know.' It was woman's work, quite beneath the dignity of a man who could shoot caribou and goat." The next day, Adolphus announced his family needed meat and so gathered up the caribou and goat and departed, which Coleman considered "was probably only an excuse to leave us, for an Indian alone is uncomfortable with White men." Despite Coleman being an academic, or perhaps for that reason, he was bound by the stereotypes of the day, as evidenced by his ambivalent reflection on the very useful Adolphus Moberly:

> He was the most typical and efficient savage I ever encountered, a striking figure, of powerful physique and tireless muscles, and thoroughly master of everything necessary for the hunter in the mountains ... Mounted erect on his horse, with gay clothing and trappings, Adolphus was the ideal centaur, at home in the wilderness, and quite naturally dominated the little party of Indians who had been travelling with us, though he was not more than twenty-one, while Adam must have been thirty-five.[31]

Coleman was so taken by Adolphus that he named the body of water in which the Smoky River originates in his honour, and Adolphus Lake it remains today.

Upon his departure, Coleman waxed nostalgic respecting that "pretty settlement of Iroquois halfbreeds and the one White man," being Lewis Swift.[32] The Indigenous-white divide was ever present during these years as part of the way things ought to be, just as it would be long thereafter and has been to some extent into the present day.

The outsider perspectives of Arthur Coleman and Mary Schäffer are complemented by an insider view from about the same time. Born in 1901,

Figure 8.2
Edward Moberly, Jasper Park guide, early 1920s

John Moberly and Marie Joachim's son Edward never forgot the world of his childhood: "Times was tough – hard to make a go of things ... sometimes you have to go far away for things, but everybody was happy – because everybody helped one another, all the time ... so I think the system was alright." Reflecting in old age, he was ambivalent: "Sometime I think about that way of life. I probably don't miss it – but once you went through it, it's not easy to forget – though it's tough – but I guess we didn't know nothing else but to face the hard problems. Had to make it!"[33]

In his reminiscence, Edward Moberly emphasized families' self-sufficiency, enterprise, and ingenuity. Various crops were grown, each with its own utility. As Edward explained, oats were used to feed horses, barley was used in soup, and wheat was ground into flour, for which "My uncle Ewan had a little hand grinder." They "had cattle – all of us – you know, to make living a little bit easier – milk for children – milk and cream, butter – that was a great help." The hay needed to feed cattle over the winter was cut in the fall, to be brought down on packhorses, with fields burned in the spring to ready them for that year's growth. Whitefish netted in a creek between two nearby lakes were dried and taken to Lac Ste Anne, the nearest supply centre, for sale. The Moberlys were strategic in another way as well: "See, what they do – they get down at Lac Ste. Anne – my father and my uncle Ewan they hire a team of horse and a wagon – and haul their fur [from animals trapped over the winter] to Edmonton where they'd get more – and buy stuff there where it's a bit cheaper too."[34]

FUNDAMENTAL CHANGE

Even as visiting University of Toronto academic Arthur Coleman departed Jasper in late summer 1909, a future premised on Iroquois's ambition and determination disappeared from view. The change agent beyond their control was a new rail line, which brought, along with short-term employment, outsiders who arrived not in transitory events, as with visitors over the past half-century, but rather in a whoosh.

The earlier transcontinental rail line, the Canadian Pacific Railway, had gone farther south, bypassing Jasper. Not so the Grand Trunk Pacific, constructed in the early twentieth century to run from Winnipeg to the British Columbia coast, whose surveyors made their presence known by tearing down Jasper House's last structures to get wood for building rafts. Over the short term, families took advantage of rail construction. As recalled by Edward Moberly, "My uncle Ewan and his two boys, Adam [Joachim, who was Ewan's son-in-law], [Isadore] Findlay [who was Ewan's father-in-law,] and my Dad" combined their slim financial resources to buy a sleigh and sets of harnesses in Edmonton. "And they went on that freighting deal, freighting supplies ahead of the construction – for surveyors, and one thing or another." Edward's mother, Marie Joaquim, got a job cleaning house for a railway official stationed nearby.[35]

A much more fundamental shift was in the offing, as Mary Schäffer had foreseen in 1908: "As we crossed the Athabaska, we realised that next time we came that way our horses would not have to swim for it, all would be made easy with trains and bridges; that the hideous march of progress, so awful to those who love the real wilderness, was sweeping rapidly over the land."[36] Coleman had been ambivalent upon having similarly "discovered that civilisation had made a long march towards the mountains" in the form of "a railway construction camp" that "occupied a once lovely river valley, up which a long scar was being cut."[37]

BECOMING A NATIONAL PARK

Schäffer's march of progress and Coleman's civilization resulted not so much from the trains themselves as from the utility of the sites they passed by and made accessible. The establishment of national parks premised on facilitating widespread access to natural beauty and grandeur was by now well accepted across North America as a public good, as with the creation of Yellowstone in 1872, nearby Banff in 1885, and Yosemite in 1890. The highly fashionable conservation movement saw national parks as a principal means of protecting pristine wilderness from development, and business-minded counterparts saw them as a vehicle for tourism, but either way, they were valued. Parks were the fashion of the day.[38]

Early in the new century, the idea was floated of creating a national park in the region of the Upper Athabasca River, soon to be accessible by rail. The area had long charmed visitors, some of whom wrote about their experiences, as with those who had encountered Iroquois over the years. The principal instigator of Jasper Park, established in 1907, two years after Alberta became a province of Canada, may have been the Grand Trunk Pacific Railway itself, which could see the economic advantage of a tourist destination along the way, much as the Canadian Pacific Railway was profiting from Banff Park to the south. Grand Trunk Pacific's president, Samuel Hays, had a reputation as imaginative and dynamic.[39]

A land base for the new park was easily resolvable. Crown lands in Alberta were at this time administered by the federal government, which made it a major player in the course of events. The federal minister of the interior, Frank Oliver, was an Albertan from Edmonton who had influenced that city's selection as provincial capital and was a railway booster.[40] An order-in-council of September 1907 reserved land for what would become Jasper Park on the completion of railway construction.[41]

There followed harbingers of change. As explained by a then young Edward Moberly, "When ... they were going to take this area for Jasper National Park – they put the notes all over – 'everybody to watch fire' – 'no fire' – 'watch your campfire, always put it out' – 'watch your smoke' – all this – they put the notices out. How do we know? Because Adam Joachim can read – he read them out for us – for the people – what it says."[42]

EVICTION

Attention soon turned to persons living within the projected park's boundaries, particularly to the self-reliant Moberlys who had effectively homesteaded there. Making their living from a combination of farming, trading, and trapping, as well as being "squatters" in the view of the federal minister of the interior, they were targeted. Whereas logging and mining would continue to be permitted in Canada's national parks to 1930, hunting was prohibited in line with what Ted Binnema and Melanie Niemi characterize in respect to the earlier Banff Park as conservationists' larger goal of ensuring a "sustained yield for sportsmen outside the park."[43] I.S. MacLaren goes one step further in pointing out how the "distinction symbolized nothing less than the gulf between uncivilized and civilized humans that newcomers were anxious to mark."[44] The distinction was another rendering of the Indigenous-white divide.

In late summer 1909, government officials presented eviction notices to six of the seven families living in what was now a national park. According to well-educated contemporary James Shand-Harvey, who was present at the proceedings, "Swift told them to get the hell out," and they obligingly did so. These six families did not have the insurmountable advantage of being white and thus, through their intermediary, Adam Joachim, who interpreted for the others, acceded to the promise made to the head of each household that he could stake a corresponding claim "anywhere you like outside of Jasper Park." As recalled by Shand-Harvey, the government official in charge "did not tell them where to go, outside of the fact that they could settle anywhere they liked outside of the Park," beyond whose boundaries land had not yet been surveyed.[45]

The six families, being the Moberly brothers John and Ewan, along with Ewan's sons Adolphus and William, son-in-law Adam Joachim, and father-in-law, Isadore Findlay, agreed to accept a cash payment for the value of "improvements" to their holdings, including buildings, fences, and ditches, "and to move out" by a March 1910 deadline.[46] They did so cognizant, as explained by John's son Edward, that "the Government had promised they can move wherever they want to move – and they will not be bothered by the Government no more."[47] The amounts received ranged from $1,670 to Ewan Moberly, $1,200 to Adam Joachim, and $1,000 to John Moberly down to $175 to the former's son William.[48] Following a trip to Edmonton to buy farming equipment, they began their new lives.

Recalling the forced removals, Edward Moberly emphasized families' agency as opposed to their being victims: "We knew we won't exist there no longer because the hunting and trapping – we won't be able to do so. So we moved." What particularly irked Edward about his family's experience was that, "after they have sold out – they have to spend the winter there, and they put two policemen" in charge, and "the rifles were all sealed – no more fresh meat."[49]

It must have been especially grating to have the seventh family, headed by long-time neighbour Lewis Swift, treated wholly differently. Not only were the Swifts allowed to stay, but in his new capacity as acting game warden of Jasper Park as of January 1910, Swift was also given charge of sealing the others' guns and padlocking their homesteads.[50] Swift would be permitted both to stay on his property and, according to Jasper historian C.J. Taylor, to "have it transferred freehold into his name."[51] Whiteness had its advantages.

Waniyandies, Joachims, Karakonties, and especially the others fared less well. As explained by a descendant, "the rest, about 100 who lived in teepees, were escorted out of the park by police."[52] As well as being expelled, families could no longer rely on the new park's natural resources, from trapping, hunting, and fishing to picking berries. They did not matter in the new order of things brought into being by the rail line and accepted the necessity to move out of the way.

OPTING FOR THE HINTON AREA

In heading somewhere else, the Moberly sons, joined over time by other Iroquois descendants, divided themselves between two locations. Younger brother John settled his family of seven children by Marie Joachim about 30 kilometres, or 20 miles, northeast of Jasper National Park toward the new rail station of Hinton on the Athabasca River. There, the family farmed and raised cattle.[53]

Reflecting the changing times, sons David and Edward were in 1912 sent away to the Catholic residential school at St Albert near Edmonton, earlier attended by Adam Joachim, who was their uncle by virtue of their mother, Marie, being his sister.[54] According to Edward, "My father decided at least two of us should go to school someplace – to learn the language, to learn a new way of life of people – that we will have to follow." The outbreak of the First World War two years later returned the brothers home, "but we had our books – the two of us – we studied at home."[55] Descendants have made their home in the area into the present day.

Among those living nearby was a Waniyandie grandson born near Jasper House in the middle of the nineteenth century whose mother and wife were Karakonties. James MacGregor recalled a visit: "Vincent Waniyandie was camped some thirty miles [50 kilometres] north of Prairie Creek [and 5 kilometres, or 3 miles, east of Hinton] ... where they had ample pasture for their horses, he and a small group of neighbours and relatives tended their trap lines, which radiated out for miles north and west ... There rich and succulent grasses sprang up – grasses that through the long winters nourished their pack ponies."[56] Life went on for this Jasper grandson much as it long had for his extended family.

SETTING DOWN ALONG THE SMOKY RIVER

Because, according to one account, the Hinton area preferred by John Moberly "was too crowded," his older brother Ewan went in a different direction, along with his wife, Madeleine Finlay, their ten children, including sons William and Adolphus, and their son-in-law Adam Joachim. Travelling with over 200 head of stock, they cut a trail in the summer of 1910 that went northwest from their former home about 150 kilometres, or 95 miles, to the Smoky River near Grande Cache, where Iroquois had long trapped. What James Shand-Harvey described as the "rich soil in the valley of the Smoky at Grande Cache" was very possibly the draw.[57] There, the extended family raised livestock and bought and sold furs.[58]

A thirty-year-old Bostonian passing by in the summer of 1914, in the pattern of curious outsiders going long back in time, attested to the second cluster's wellbeing on the pattern of earlier Jasper Iroquois. Samuel Elliott Fay described "what is known as the Grande Cache settlement, where three families of Moberlys and some other Cree half-breeds have settled and built log shacks" plastered with mud and "have a number of horses and cattle, and live here all the year." Their two diversions were going to Hinton annually for goods and "into the mountains to get a supply of meat, as there are moose and sheep around." Fay came to buy flour and baking powder since, in his spelling based on how the name sounded, "Ivan keeps a few things for trading with the Indians that pass through here." Ewan Moberly periodically packed in goods from Hinton, by virtue of which he charged $5 for a sack of flour purchased there for $3. Fay explained that the Moberlys "came here four years ago, being driven out of the valley of the Athabasca when Jasper Park was planned."[59]

Fay found Ewan Moberly in a meadow "cutting hay (mostly weeds) to feed his cattle during the winter" with the assistance of "squaws, children and all." To Fay's "surprise," Moberly used "a mowing machine, big hay rake and wagon," which had been among items purchased in Edmonton and packed in on horses. Recording "an altitude of 3500 feet [1,065 metres]," Fay was impressed by how "no one could have chosen a more ideal spot" for their horses, being "a big, green, grassy hill looking ... up the valley of the Smoky, with green steep hills on one side and snow mountains on the other." Fay was especially taken with how he "talked quite freely and although his English was rather broken it was intelligible." At afternoon's end, "we left him carrying his axe with his rifle done up in a buckskin case slung over his back."[60]

Fay returned the next day. To cross the rain-soaked Smoky River with his men, horses, and supplies, he sought the use of Ewan Moberly's "eighteen-foot dugout, capable of carrying a thousand pounds," for which he was charged "seven dollars." Trip accomplished, "we offered Ivan some of the powerful Hudson Bay rum, but he said, 'me no touch,' which impressed us greatly." Reflective of the Indigenous-white gap in understanding, Fay summed up Ewan Moberly, who was half white by descent, as "one of the nicest and most willing Indians I ever saw."[61]

As indicated by Fay's passing reference to "other Cree half-breeds," it was not only the Moberly contingent who opted for the Grande Cache area. The Smoky River watershed had long been integral to Iroquois's yearly round and was home to numerous families setting down on the long-familiar banks of the Smoky River and on suitably named Wanyandie Flats, as well as along Wanyandie Creek and along the Muskeg River, both flowing into the Smoky River.[62] By oral accounts, as attested by an archeological dig, it was "the community of Wanyandie Flats where the early Iroquois first settled."[63] Among those now doing so were Waniyandies who had not been compensated upon leaving the park by virtue of being perceived as having made no "improvements."[64] Numerous families lived much as before.[65]

Other Waniyandies made other decisions. In 1913 nineteen-year-old Modeste Waniyandie applied to homestead a quarter section of land at Lac Ste Anne. That same year, Louis and Christopher Waniyandie applied for land at Spirit River 450 kilometres, or 280 miles, northwest of Lac Ste Anne. The pair were followed there a year later by sixty-year-old Isabelle Waniyandie, a self-described housewife who applied for a river lot in her own name.[66]

RESISTING A SECOND REMOVAL

Jasper families' accommodation of outsiders' intrusions was insufficient to satisfy those in charge. Almost as soon as the Moberly cluster was dealt with in 1909–10, officials in the Forestry Branch of the federal Department of the Interior turned to creating what would become in 1915 a large forest reserve extending northward from the new Jasper Park. Its establishment followed the passage in 1906 of a federal Forest Reserve Act intended to conserve forested lands across the country.

Thanks to the primary research of Moberly descendant Richard Ouellet and to the work of fellow historians Trudy Nicks and I.S. MacLaren, it is possible to follow the sequence of events by which Jasper families resisted outsiders' determination to cleanse the Athabasca Forestry Reserve on the pattern of Jasper Park. Ewan Moberly, his son Adolphus, his son-in-law Adam Joachim, and two others who had settled along the Smoky River were targeted, even though their places of residence were not within the forestry reserve as it had been established in 1910 at the time they had moved to the Grande Cache area but within it consequent on a boundary expansion enacted in 1913 subsequent to their settling there. As explained by MacLaren, the reserve's "original boundary did not include the area occupied by Moberly and others."[67]

In 1912, in anticipation of the expansion, the federal Forestry Branch asked James Shand-Harvey, who had been appointed a forest ranger, to determine who lived in the larger reserve. His detailed response testifies to the Moberly family's resourcefulness in having regrouped after, in Shand-Harvey's astute language, "a sum of money and a verbal permission was given to them to settle anywhere outside of the said Jasper Park's limits." Shand-Harvey pointed out how "at the time Moberly and the others moved to Grande Cache (1911) there was no posters, boundary markers or other marks to show the Reserve lines and no Fire Rangers to my knowledge." As for the location that they selected, "'Grande Cache' is mostly open prairie with clumps of small poplars and willows" with "no timber of commercial value."[68]

In his report, Shand-Harvey characterized Ewan Moberly, by now not much over a year there, as a "rancher, hunter, and trader" possessing "50 head of cayuses, one black draught stallion and about 14 head of cattle." His son Adolphus and son-in-law Adam Joachim "both have bunches of cayuses and some cattle."[69] The fourth and fifth persons enumerated were Phillip Delorme, whose mother was a Joachim and grandmother a Waniyandie, and a woman named only as Paulette, who may have been Paulette Joachim, married into the Karakonties.[70] "Both have small bunches of cayuses."[71] Referring to the last four or possibly only to the last two, Shand-Harvey added, "like most half-breeds they live principally by hunting, trapping, and packing."[72]

Shand-Harvey had been asked to value the five families' structures, as occurred with the earlier removals. The senior Moberly had erected a dwelling house with a ruberoid waterproof roof and sawed-lumber flooring, a cattle and horse barn, and large and small storehouses on 8 acres of fenced-in land, from which he had a crop in 1912. Adolphus had a dwelling house and small storehouse, Adam Joachim a dwelling house, Phillip Delorme a house, and Paulette two houses. Shand-Harvey valued the structures at $1,200, $700, $800, $300, and $700 respectively.

The sympathetic Shand-Harvey concluded his report with his case for permitting the five families to stay: "I do not consider their presence any detriment to this Forest Reserve whatever, rather an advantage as in their own interest the safe-guarding of fires ... and I strongly recommend that permission should be given them to remain." In preparation for the reserve's expansion to include their properties, Shand-Harvey applied for a permit on behalf of the Moberly contingent "for residential and pasture for stock non-commercial," which would be "renewable annually and subject to strict observation."[73] In response, Shand-Harvey was to "instruct Adam Joachim, the only one on the settlement who can read and write English, to make the application in writing to this office for permit to remain at Grande Cache," which the forest supervisor in charge recommended be granted.[74]

This seemingly smooth course of events was undone. Indicative of attitudes at this time toward persons not white like the government officials themselves were the observations by a forestry reserve surveyor in a report published in 1915:

> Five families were found living in one of the proposed reserves. They are Indians or half-breeds. One has squatted on Smoky flat, about 15 miles [25 kilometres] above Sheep creek entrance [to the park]; while the other four are on Smoky flat immediately below the entrance of Sheep creek. They have built themselves shacks, but they have made no other improvements whatever on the land. During the summer months these people spend a good deal of the time on these flats, – leaving only at intervals for hunting tours. During the winter months they scatter through the territory for their different trapping grounds.[75]

The description is at odds with another report of the same year describing Ewan Moberly's log house as containing a four-poster bed, rough-hewn chairs, a sewing machine, a trunk, bearskin rugs, and curtains. Outside were a vegetable patch, thirty head of cattle, including a black bull, and a canoe of more than 10 metres, or 33 feet, that was being rented out. Not only that, but he had for the past five years been running a trading post on nearby Victor Lake where he bought and sold furs and, it seems from the report, where he or family members led "hunting tours."[76]

Attitudes similar to those of the 1915 report underpinned the letter written in January 1916 by the forest supervisor asked to make recommendations "relative to the breed settlement on the [Forest] Reserve." As with the surveyor, he gave his prejudices free rein:

> For fear of any misconception I should say that these people while called 'half breeds' are, except in the eyes of the law, to all intents and purposes Indians. There is in all of them a little White blood but just enough to have them inherit the White man's vices and none of his virtues. These people are living an isolated nomadic life and the children growing up in absolute ignorance and as shiftless and irresponsible as their parents.[77]

If the children had schools to attend, "I can see no reason why they should not become as independent and thrifty as anyone," but only so long as "they afterwards are continually associating with the White man."[78] The force of the Indigenous-white divide could not be more visible.

These observations were not, however, the forestry supervisor's principal argument for removing the five families: "These people for the most part derive a very comfortable income from the sale of furs; in fact make more money than the average white man residing in this district," thereby impinging on revenues better had by others killing animals in "what is probably the finest big game country in the Dominion."[79] By one account, the letter was instigated by one of the area's principal white hunting guides, who was seeking to dispose of competition; by another, it was written on behalf of a friend seeking grazing land.[80] In his letter, the forestry supervisor proposed to give each family "a quarter section of agricultural land in the Grande Prairie or Pouce Coupe districts," both northwest of Edmonton, which could not be sold, a plan that would, by sending them off to this remote area, keep them out of the way.[81]

Matters came to a head in the spring of 1916. James Shand-Harvey was requested to accompany, as an interpreter into Cree, a Northwest Mounted Police officer dispatched to evict the numerous families, including that of Ewan Moberly, who were living on the expanded Athabasca Forest Reserve.

Told "they're trespassers and will have to get off," Shand-Harvey responded that he had been at the meeting with the Moberly cluster when they had been informed that they could head anywhere outside the new park.[82] In his version of the story, it was because of his obtaining statements from many persons also aware of what had been said that this particular initiative was eventually dropped.

Not to be thwarted, in the fall of 1916 the secretary of the federal Department of the Interior sent out letters ordering everyone in the Forestry Reserve out by 1 March 1917.[83] The Moberly contingent responded in two ways. Adam Joachim opted for the legal route by contacting an Edmonton law firm. In a letter of 30 December 1916, representing him "and the other members of the small colony in question," the firm reminded the secretary of the interior in Ottawa that "by a show of force supplemented by corollary and wheedling, these people were driven out of the land which they and their predecessors had held" on the promise that "they might go to their present location freed from all fear of any future removal," and now they were being so threatened. If there was no remedy, "we shall have no hesitation in opposing publicly and privately the callous brutality such as was handed to these people."[84]

Ewan Moberly took a direct approach. On 8 March 1917 he dispatched a long letter to the deputy minister of the Department of the Interior on behalf of thirty-two named families, as well as his own, who "have lived all our lives in this section of Alberta, and quite a few of us had settled in what is now the Jasper Park." The names on the list made clear that it was no longer only the five Iroquois-descended families enumerated by Shand-Harvey four years earlier who had set down on or near the new forestry reserve. Half of the thirty-two families, numbering seventy-five persons, were headed by a descendant in the male line of the Joachims, Karakonties, or Waniyandies, whereas the others were not so, although they might well have been descendants through the female line.[85] The list almost certainly included families earlier set down on Wanyandie Flats or along the Muskeg River.

Ewan Moberly's letter of 8 March countered the argument being used to dispossess the families, namely that they were destroying "the finest big game country in the Dominion."[86] The letter made the reverse argument as to who was conserving and who was wasting resources: "We wish to state that we never kill anything except forced to do so by necessity and that we utilize every thing, head, hides, bone and flesh, but that we see White men come in our country: some kill game and take only the heads leaving the balance for the coyotes, while others shoot moose and cariboo, and only utilize part of the meat, the balance being left to rot." The letter detailed how "we are law abiding citizens; crime is unknown amongst us … we are all making an honest living interfering with no one … We only ask for justice which we are not getting from the Forestry people."[87]

The two interventions may have sidelined direct action against the families. Matters were unresolved by the time of Ewan Moberly's death during the influenza epidemic of 1918 and by the fall of 1920 when his son Adolphus requested from the secretary of the interior a "grant of the land at Grande Cache."[88] He was directed to a regional supervisor who, disdainful of descendants seeking to make their way in Jasper's shadow, informed the federal director of forest services,

> Dolphus Moberly is an illiterate and unable to read or write even his own name and consequently some other person translated it and deliberately misinformed him as to the true contents of the letter also wrote the letter in reply with a view to blocking the movement on foot to get the breeds located on land outside the reserve and as a result the Moberly family have taken out more agricultural machinery to Grande Cache with a view to staying there, every effort on the part of the Forestry Branch to get rid of the Grande Cache trespass … has been secretly and systematically blocked and successfully.[89]

The supervisor urged twin remedies. The first was the passage of appropriate federal legislation. The second was, in respect to "breeds" located there, "issuing instructions to the Athabasca Forest officials to seize them by the necks and land them outside the reserve and let them shift for themselves."[90] Men were during these years routinely described as "breeds" and their wives as "squaws," both being by definition unwanted and disposable.[91]

The same attitude of moral superiority informed a follow-up letter on 28 March 1921 from the Alberta district forest inspector also to the federal director of forest services. Having been asked "the status of the Moberly case," he reported no recent development given that "the half-breeds have been advised not to move unless paid to do so," which in his view "is out

of the question." As with the earlier letter, he proposed two possible remedies: "We can either forcibly remove the halfbreeds from the Reserve or we
can refrain from direct action but crowd them so badly that they will
choose to move," by which he meant to "make life so unpleasant for them
that they will be glad to move out."[92] During these years, as the two letters
attest, an Indigenous-white divide with power and authority resting solely
on one side was a given.

The final letter in this remarkable sequence was written ten months later,
on 26 January 1922, to the Calgary district forest inspector by a fire ranger
seeking to persuade Catholic authorities to intervene against the families
on the grounds that, if moved, they would have access to schools and religious teachings. Catholic officials from the archbishop down were unwill-
ing to do so without the agreement of prominent provincial politician
Charles Cross, who had "pledged himself to support them (the Moberly
family) if they don't want to move." He "contends they are doing no harm,"
"thinks they will get title to land there," and had knowledge of a letter from
Sir George Foster, the acting prime minister, "saying that their rights would
be protected."[93]

Information on what thereby ensued, or not so, is hazy. Even though, as
recalled by Shand-Harvey, "in the end, after long and voluminous correspondence with Ottawa, the matter was dropped, … there was some fear
even then that some action still might be taken."[94] It would be only in the
1960s, after their ownership was again called into question, that the families
would receive title to their properties.[95]

The attempt to remove the Moberlys and whichever other Iroquois descendants had set themselves down on the Athabasca Forest Reserve prior
to its expansion speaks clearly to attitudes of the time.[96] Although those
targeted were not named as Iroquois, the force of such identity is evident
in the fact that half of those attaching themselves to the 1917 letter had
descended in the male line from one of the three Jasper progenitors. The
unsuccessful attempt to suborn descendants through the mechanism of
the Catholic Church testifies to officials' understanding of Iroquois's
senses of self.

That the campaign for relocation fell apart, or appears to have done so,
was not due to efforts from within the locality but from afar, whereas attitudes closer to home did not much change, if at all. Indicative is the perspective expressed toward "the Indian settlement of Grande Cache" in the

published memoir of a forest ranger on the Athabasca Forest Reserve from 1920–40: "Nearly all those living in the Athabasca Reserve originally roamed what is now Jasper Park. When the Dominion Parks Board decided to create the Park they paid the Indians a sum of money to vacate. This they did, but they did not go far, just squatting on the choicest spots they could find in the Forest Reserve and there they remained despite all efforts of the provincial government to move them."[97]

To the extent that the author approved of the campaign's failure, if condescendingly so, it was in respect to how "the native women of Grande Cache were very skilled in needle- and bead-work," so much so that he "bought a lovely whistler or marmot robe from Mrs. Ewan Moberly who guides the destiny of the tribe."[98] The now elderly Madeleine Moberly's father was Isadore Findlay, who had resettled from Jasper with the Moberlys, her mother likely being Iroquois-descended. With that utilitarian exception, from this forest ranger's perspective, Jasper families did not belong.

RETURNING TO JASPER

During these same fraught years, several Jasper descendants went a different route, symbolically and literally returning to their long-time homeland of what was now Jasper Park. They did so as packers and guides for visitors, who were in effect superseding their families there. By virtue of doing so, they were de facto complicit in the phenomenon of trophy hunting, which had been part of the impetus for exiling descendants.

Rail access made Jasper Park a favoured site for wealthy Canadians, Americans, and Europeans seeking an outdoor adventure. To the earlier Grand Trunk Pacific Railway was added the Canadian Northern Railway in 1913, whose lines would merge into the Canadian National Railway in 1923.[99] The consequence, as explained by I.S. MacLaren, was that "although the establishment of a park curtailed hunting in the valley, the well-heeled began to make Jasper the departure point for their hunts farther up the eastern slopes."[100] Very much like the earlier half-century of visitors to the Jasper area, they came for the adventure.

Not only were Iroquois descendants familiar with the area, but the attributes necessary for facilitating visitors' three- to four-week hunting trips in the surrounding area were also precisely those they possessed by virtue of their upbringing and physicality. By one insider account in respect to the Moberlys in particular, "many of them stand over six feet, broad-shouldered and erect, big men with aquiline noses and strong features."[101]

John Moberly's son Edward, proficient in English by virtue of having been sent away to school with his brother David on the model of their uncle Adam Joachim, may have been the earliest to be so employed. He explained, "I went back to Jasper in 1920 – worked as a guide out of Jasper … for 52 years."[102] Edward's brothers Dave and Frank were recruited along with Adam Joachim, now also their cousin upon marrying Ewan Moberly's daughter Fresnine. The Moberlys' brother-in-law Felix Plante, born at Lac Ste Anne and married to their sister Caroline, was also a long-time guide, as was Adam Joachim's son-in-law Louis Delorme, notable for guiding singer Bing Crosby and appearing in a movie filmed at Jasper featuring actress Marilyn Monroe.[103] Whether or not descendants considered themselves or were perceived by others to be Iroquois, they were joined by sets of relationships originating in their distinctive inheritance.

That members of the contingent were apparently successful as guides and packers did not amount to their acceptance by their white counterparts, who comprised almost all of the others. Of twenty white guides interviewed in the early 1980s who had worked in Jasper Park prior to 1950, just eight, despite being specifically so queried, mentioned any of the contingent as having been among their number.[104] The most dismissive of the eight, upon being asked whether he had ever guided "with some of the Indians from around Grande Cache," mentioned "The two Moberly boys, Frank and Ed … There was more of them, but I never got to know them. I worked two trips with Ed and one trip with Frank. They were … Well, I don't know, I don't think they stood up to the so-called White guys at all. It was a job for them, you know, but it was … They tended to be lazy, both of them. It was just a job sort of … Nice enough guys in their way, but they …"[105] Another interviewee, upon being asked about "some of the Indians that guided," responded that he knew Edward Moberly "the best," that "he told me he was born in 1896," and that "they took them out of the park in 1910."[106]

Two of the white packers referred to Adam Joachim. An early Jasper outfitter described him as "the senior packer" on a 1927 expedition that had climbed thirty-eight mountains in thirty-four days, but then he added, in almost the next sentence, that shortly thereafter he himself had become the head guide in charge of "half-breeds, who resented that." To his credit, he stated later in the interview, in reference to "the breeds," whom he identified as Dave, Frank, and Edward Moberly, that "most of them were pretty dependable, had guide licences … [The] fact that I accepted them made a difference."[107] The wife of a long-time white packer described Adam Joachim as "one of the ones that was in the park when they moved them out in 1911," to which her husband added, "He was an Iroquois. The old-time, the old-time Indians that are half-breeds here are principally Iroquois."[108] Adam's superior status, such as it was, is evidenced by the fact that he and his son Henry, who also guided, are the only persons of Iroquois or other Indigenous descent included in a 360-page history of Grande Cache published in 1999.[109]

To what extent the familiarity gained through packers' everyday conversations overcame at least some of the easy prejudice is impossible to know. The Moberly sons Edward, Dave, and Frank were one-fourth white through their paternal grandfather, Henry Moberly; and Adam Joachim was three-eighths white through his maternal grandparents, Colin and Nancy Fraser. Their being so did not, it seems, counter the taint of indigeneity in whatever form it was perceived. What is admirable is the Moberly family's persistence and also their sharing of some of themselves with others to the extent that, for at least one fellow guide, their Iroquois descent endured over a century and a half after their families had arrived at Jasper.

CONTINUING TO MIND THEMSELVES

Unlike the livelihoods earned by the handful of principally Moberlys who returned to Jasper seasonally as guides and packers, most descendants' economies were premised not on employment at others' behest but on trapping and then selling pelts or products made from them to obtain needed supplies. Even guides had little reason to shift away from this satisfying way of being. Along with some others, Adam Joachim, whose wife was a Moberly daughter, lived about 30 kilometres, or 20 miles, east of Grande Cache between Victor Lake and Muskeg on the river of that name.[110] By setting down there, he was affirming, if not necessarily replicating, a long-held seasonal round premised on "the extensive use of large tracts of land for hunting, trapping, guiding, etc., and the intensive use of river valley meadows" as "home areas."[111]

For Iroquois descendants, continuing to live as they would did not amount to deprivation. As explained by Shand-Harvey,

They had comfortable log houses in which they lived in winter, with cookstoves, furniture, and many modern accessories, such as gramophones and sewing machines. They also had many necessary farm implements to cultivate the land where suitable. Nevertheless they preferred to live by the chase instead of by agriculture, especially since the climate was rather too severe for extensive cultivation. In summer they lived in their teepees, moving about as their fancy dictated, always camping where there was good feed and water for their considerable herds of horses.[112]

DISADVANTAGING JASPER DESCENDANTS

Jasper descendants were increasingly disadvantaged in relationship to other Canadians not only by their longstanding resourcefulness outside of

Figure 8.3
Adam Joachim smoking caribou meat on a hunting trip, 1935

the larger society that was coming into being around them but also by the law. As historian James MacGregor reminds us, "all the people of the Smoky River country, the Waniyandies, Caracontés, Joachims, and so on, are technically White men."[113] By earlier opting for scrip, they had affirmed a legal status that did not correspond to the changing times, which tended toward an ever firmer division between whites and their lesser counterparts, who were conveniently shunted aside and out of the way as "Indians." Iroquois descendants were in practice neither.

The consequence was that Jasper descendants were twice disadvantaged during the 1930s. The first instance was due to provincial legislation limiting where they and others who were not party to a treaty legally designating them as "Indians" could trap.[114] The situation became fraught as Indigenous groups from elsewhere that were subject to treaties "invaded the Smoky River country" to trap, thereby challenging the principal means by which Jasper Iroquois and their descendants, women as well as men, had for generations made their living. Long-time trappers now also faced "White men who went in with large outfits of grub and traps, with the sole object of making a 'stake' and getting out again after two or three years," by which time they had "cleaned out a district."[115] As opposed to a way of life, trapping was for them a short-term proposition.

The second means by which Jasper Iroquois were disadvantaged related to settlement generally. The spaces that descendants and others with an Indigenous inheritance had long considered to be their own by virtue of sustained use were increasingly coveted by outsiders. The transfer in 1930 of responsibility for natural resources from the federal government to provincial governments did away with the earlier concept of squatter's rights, whereby persons living unimpeded on property for a specific period of time could claim ownership.[116] As more and more land was surveyed and opened up for settlement, the long-established ways of life of Iroquois descendants and others were increasingly challenged.

The situation became fraught to the extent that there was discussion of setting aside land for those who, having earlier taken scrip, were not legally Indians and were thus without access to reserves. Spurred on by local groups, eight Métis settlements, each with its own land base, were established across Alberta, uniquely so in Canada, but none in the area of Smoky River and Grande Cache. Adam Joachim was part of the new Métis Association of Alberta, which was formed in the 1930s with a broad membership base that encompassed "all British subjects with Indian an-cestry" and so included him along with other Iroquois descendants.[117] The association strongly recommended Grande Cache–Muskeg River for one such settlement, but nothing ensued despite the fact that, or perhaps be-cause, the provincial government was negotiating in 1939 to sell the land, with purchasers being given an option to lease adjacent property that had long been settled by a dozen families, including Waniyandies, Joachims, and Moberlys. An offer for compensation and relocation was rejected by descendants on the grounds that the proposed new site was unsuitable for grazing their cattle and horses. However the issue was resolved, and it is not clear what ensued, the families stayed where and as they were.[118] Once again, for the third time over two decades, Jasper descendants were deemed expendable.

RESPONDING TO CHANGING TIMES

Despite Jasper descendants being disadvantaged seemingly at every turn, they in no way gave up but rather did the reverse. Canada voters' lists for Athabasca and Peace River from 1935 and 1940 include a plethora of Waniyandis and Waniandis, so the surname was variously spelled, describ-ing themselves as farmers, trappers, river pilots, ship's carpenters, married women, and housekeepers. The Jasper-Edson lists for 1945 and 1957 are filled with Karakonties, or Caracontes, Joachims, Moberlys, and Waniyan-dis who described themselves as trappers and who, by the time of the 1960s lists, had been reduced to being labourers, many residing at Muskeg.[119] Very importantly, whatever the time period, the fifty or more descendants through the male line on any one voters' list were there because they chose to be there despite the racial or other boundaries that those around them might seek to impose. In their own minds, they belonged.

Even as descendants responded on a political level, greater change was on the way. Economic development across Canada during the interwar years, more so in the aftermath of the Second World War, fundamentally altered Jasper descendants' ways of life. Areas that up to then had been in their natural state were increasingly being transformed into new sites of settlement for a growing newcomer population.

Some families retreated. As early as 1947 a number of Karakonties who had set down on the Smoky River headed about 100 kilometres, or 60 miles, north to the remote Kakwa Valley in the Rocky Mountain foothills so as to be able to continue to trap. Some did so seasonally, whereas others lived there all year round. Moose, big-horn sheep, and other animals were still abundant, and no roads invited newcomers to join them.[120]

Other Karakonties, along with some Waniyandies and Joachims, opted in the 1950s and 1960s for Nose Creek to the northwest of the Kakwa Valley on the way to a long-time Iroquois trapping and hunting area that would in the 1950s become the new settlement of Grande Prairie. According to a local history, "they trapped there and lived off the land," as well as inter-marrying.[121] The daughter of a Moberly and a Joaquim recalled that her grandmother and mother had tanned hides for "jackets, vests, mittens, all the bead work not too complicated but takes a lot of work."[122] At least for a time, life went on much as before.

OVERLAID BY GRANDE CACHE

New challenges were most difficult for Jasper Iroquois descendants settled along the Smoky River at Grande Cache, which was quite literally overlaid in the 1960s by a new town of the same name. Families living at Wanyandie Flats along Wanyandie Creek and along the Muskeg River, both flowing into the Smoky River, were similarly disrupted.

Coal finds along the Smoky River were the impetus for the creation in 1966 of the new town of Grande Cache. Indicative of the ways that the presence of Iroquois descendants shadowed events, the initial proposal of siting it at Muskeg was disallowed upon someone's realization that Indigenous people living there would have to be moved. As determined by R. Bruce Morrison, who did primary research in the area at about this time, apart from that brief respite, "the government of Alberta failed to take into account the needs and rights" of persons already living in the area. "Not only were they deprived of the opportunity to decide whether or not the development should take place at all, but once the construction took place, they were denied the resources to develop adaptive strategies which would be consistent with their desires and cultural values."[123] The disregard by those in charge was breathtaking. A long and detailed provincial government report of August 1966 recommending and costing out every aspect of the creation of Grande Cache mentioned "local Indians" only in respect to their possible knowledge respecting the climate.[124]

The everyday life of this "Cree-Iroquois Metis community," in the language of Morrison and fellow ethnographer C. Rodrick Wilson writing in the mid-1970s, was swept aside. They described how "the Grande Cache native community presently numbers some 215 persons who are largely the descendants of Iroquois men who came to the area with the fur trade and married local woman," to be subsequently "dispossessed of their ranch and farming operations when Jasper National Park was created in 1910." As perceptively evoked by the two ethnographers, almost certainly based on what descendants told them, the community had thereupon regrouped:

As one might surmise, the community was structured rather loosely. Settlements were widely scattered, but concentrated in the occasional broad meadows of river valleys. In winter the settlements broke up into mobile family units for trapping and hunting activities. Springtime saw people coming out to sell furs, buy new supplies, and establish larger camps, culminating in the annual pilgrimage to Lac Ste. Anne in late July. The annual cycle of periodic concentration and dispersion was accentuated by considerable family and individual mobility, as families or other kinds of groups took advantage of perceived economic or social opportunities. It should also be mentioned that one of the primary mechanisms of social control was the avoidance of conflict situations by physically removing oneself. Relations with the White community were largely mediated by trusted individuals, such as traders or priests, functioning in typical patron-client fashion.[125]

This long-lived, satisfying way of life was now cast aside due to the actions of outsiders without, almost wholly, any realization on their part that it had existed in the first place.

New roads took no notice of persons living in the way. An airstrip and railway ran through grazing meadows, a coal mine sat on horses' wintering site, coal dust blanketed vegetable gardens, affluence made Smoky River water unfit for drinking, and soil removal for landscaping and quarrying destroyed pastures and drainage routes.[126] Workers' housing and community amenities were constructed amid families' homes, across registered and thereby legitimate trap lines, and through a favourite fall site for elk hunting around Victor Lake.[127]

The consequence was, not unlike Grande Prairie to the north, an instant town of several thousand newcomers. Some of them had been recruited as skilled miners, and virtually all of them were understandably concerned with their own wellbeing in this alien setting located 160 kilometres, or 100 miles, away from the next nearest town of Hinton.[128] From picnics and pickup trucks to recreational shooting at whichever targets caught their attention, newcomers took no notice of who else but themselves might be living there.[129]

Overlaying one way of being with another extended beyond the town itself. About 20 kilometres, or 12 miles, from shiny new Grande Cache languished, as put by a white outsider, the "native settlement of Winniandy," which consisted of "six houses, a log cabin under construction, and a tent," its Cree-speaking "small band of metis known as the Winniandies" being headed by a hard-of-hearing seventy-five-year-old.[130] As dismissed by another visitor of these years, "they had lived there as long as they could remember."[131] A young Ontarian hitchhiking through in 1970 recalled his initial amazement "at the people living down there – horses all over the place and game abundant – living forty years behind everyone else – no running water – I was taken back – I just fell in love with the style … they were living off the land." It was, even so, "getting harder and harder on them."[132]

The more outsiders arrived, the more Jasper Iroquois descendants, knowing "Cree as their first language," were sidelined.[133] Their "limited familiarity with the English language," as explained by one of them, impeded everyday communication.[134] More generally, as described by Morrison, "they rapidly discovered that their cultural knowledge was not appropriate to the new setting."[135] To the extent that change came in this respect, a school had been opened at Muskeg on a part-time basis in 1958, becoming full-time from 1961, and then a school had been opened in Grande Cache itself.[136]

Despite their language difficulties, according to Morrison, who conducted numerous interviews, Iroquois descendants were very aware of their circumstances, which they viewed within the historical context by which they defined themselves: "Along with their reactions to the industrialization of the area were their fears of being resettled by the government as they had earlier been from Jasper." It was not only that "many of the

Metis were descendants of those who had been removed from Jasper National Park at the turn of the century and the memory of that dislocation was still fresh in their minds," but also that "some of the original folk who had experienced that resettlement still lived in the area." Within this context, "the construction of a new town, the myriads of roads and the coal mine in their midst caused considerable alarm," which was "heightened by the lack of preparation they received prior to the onset of construction."[137]

TOWARD A RESOLUTION OF SORTS

As tracked by Joe Sawchuk in collaboration with others, Jasper descendants were not inert in response to their ways of life being once again overturned.[138] In 1969 they began negotiations with the provincial government over land and hunting rights. The government's hard-headed, self-interested approach was modified, allowing for a compromise land settlement, upon two members of the Joachim family along with two others stepping into leadership positions.[139] Morrison, who was himself involved with events, described how the resulting committee "worked with great resolve and courage ... enlisting local White support for their land tenure proposal."[140] In 1972 an agreement was reached that minimally satisfied both parties.

The reality of an agreement comes across as almost miraculous, following as it did on two-thirds of a century of dispossession and threats thereof. For all of its faults, the arrangement acknowledged a direct line of descent comparable to the concept of adverse possession. Under English common law, occupants of land acquired ownership rights over title holders if those occupants were not removed within specified periods of time. The concept of adverse possession, also termed "squatters' rights," put the onus on owners to have kept others off their property. With Jasper Park descendants, rather than the usual requirement of sixty years, the time period was extended back to when the government had accepted the validity of holdings in future Jasper Park by virtue of promising land elsewhere and back to when the subsequent decision had been made not to forcibly dispossess them from the Athabasca Forest Reserve.[141]

In fashioning the agreements, Jasper descendants took the lead. The names of two of the six resulting entities – Wanyandie Flats and Joachim

Enterprises, parts of a total land grant of 4,150 acres – testified to a line of descent going back in time to the first Iroquois's arrival over a century and a half earlier. The signatories to the six agreements included six adult and six minor Joachims, five adult and three minor Moberlys, two adult Waniyandies, and one adult Karakontie, for a total of fourteen adult and nine minor descendants alongside eleven adults and fourteen minors with other surnames, the families of which for the most part had long since been intermarried with Iroquois descendants.[142] By one outside assessment, part of the success, such as it was, was due to "the oft-repeated statement" by white newcomers that "these Indians are different," by which "was meant that they were hard working, clean, sober, and proud of it."[143] The shadow of the Indigenous-white divide was still, as it continues to be, ever present.

Despite being the best possible agreements under the circumstances, the aftermath was bittersweet. Awarded in the form of leases unable to be sold, the land grant to a total of 260 persons amounted to 6.5 acres each, which was intended to be used for residences, gardens, grazing, and business enterprises. It was an ongoing matter of contention, according to a local source, that "they basically received a lease for the land on which they had been living" for up to half a century, whereas they "feel that they should have received clear title and more land, so that they could support themselves via their traditional lifestyles."[144] In effect, descendants were still lesser than, not equal to, others in the community. As assessed by Trudy Nicks, "the land granted amounted to only the river flats which were traditional living sites but did not encompass the range of resources necessary if a hunting and trapping lifestyle were to continue as a viable option."[145] A local history says it best in its observation that "the old days are gone and never will be again."[146]

The consequence was that menfolk of the just over 200 descendants Nicks has traced to the three Iroquois patriarchs – Karakontie, Joachim, and Waniyandie – and tracked as living in the Grande Cache area were soon being employed in wage labour.[147] As explained by Morrison, cognizant "that a return to their traditional hunting and trapping economy was impossible, many felt that involvement in the wage economy was their only alternative."[148] Once again, life went on but not as it might otherwise have done.

SUSTAINED BY CATHOLICISM

To the extent that Jasper descendants were sustained through these difficult times, Catholicism still mattered a century and more after Jesuit priest Pierre-Jean De Smet's visit in 1846, discussed in the opening of chapter 7. Two Oblate priests testify to Karakonties, Joachims, and Waniyandies still identifying themselves as Iroquois and also as Cree by descent and language, as Jasper people by their history, as Catholic by religion, and as a "family" in the sense that De Smet used the word long ago.[149]

Access to the life-course rituals marking births, marriages, and deaths, which had been so valued during De Smet's visit, continued to be sporadic. The necessity for trips to Lac Ste Anne by those living in the vicinity of Grande Cache had been eased by the construction in 1935 of a Catholic church at Victor Lake, for which Adolphus Moberly and Louis Delorme, who was Adam Joaquim's son-in-law, furnished sawn lumber and which subsequently fell into disrepair.[150]

In another initiative, Oblate priest Marcel Landry held services in the devout Adam Joachim's house prior to the Oblates constructing a church at Muskeg in 1958 and then in the church for a decade thereafter. Adam looked after the new church and also the cabin intended for the priest, briefed him on the latest happenings, assisted as a teacher and catechist in his absence, and served mass until his death in 1959, whereupon his widow took on the first responsibility. Landry, whose other parish was seven hours distant, spent one week per month at Muskeg, during which, in a tradition by then over a century old, families "used to come and live around the church for that period of time." Each day of their doing so was given over, all in Cree, to morning mass, children's catechism in the early afternoon, the rosary along with prayer, and an evening sermon with hymns. Landry recalled that in his absence families prayed together on Sunday evenings and that "in every home there was a long evening prayer."[151]

In a third instance, from 1974 to 1986 fellow Oblate priest Nicolas Roué ministered as often as he could to families at Nose Creek descended from the Joaquims, Karakonties, and Moberlys. He professed, "I got attached to them ... and would have liked to go there more often," but as with Landry he had other obligations. Roué recalled that there was no church, making the services a matter of improvisation:

It was at the Moberly house we would pray because it was the most spacious house in the place. In the meantime, someone went to the school to tell the people that the priest had arrived and to please let the students out for the remainder of the afternoon. In the meantime, there were many handshakes and the joy of having mass and of praying was expressed. Soon, everyone would be ready for confession. I set up my portable altar on the table ... I admired the boys and girls who knew their prayers and who confessed like adults. It is clear that they were accustomed to praying by their families. Then the mass began. There was a hymn in Cree that everyone sang as well as the *Kyrie* in Cree ... The prayers of the mass as well as the Eucharist prayer were in Cree ... Everyone felt at home and the tongues unwound.[152]

The yearly round might include a summer pilgrimage to Lac Ste Anne.[153]

As summed up by a fellow Oblate reflecting back in time, "One thing is absolutely certain, these Iroquois men had received a deeply Christian formation, that is to say that the Jesuit fathers had a wonderful way of instructing their people; they married to Cree women and their own families were brought up in an exemplary Christian manner."[154]

TAKING BACK THE PAST

A distinctive inheritance continues to bind Jasper families together. In 2005 a self-organized Council of Elders of Descendants of Jasper Park initiated a process of identifying graves and familial sites located within the park's boundaries and elsewhere through a combination of oral recollections, archeological expertise, and technology.[155] As explained by a Moberly granddaughter, "It means a lot to me. It's like coming home. We were being ignored, but now we're not. We were the forgotten people."[156] Three local historians writing at the turn of the twenty-first century concluded almost as a matter of course that "most of the Aboriginal people in the Grande Cache area are descended from the Iroquois, either directly or through marriage."[157]

Indicative of growing recognition is a young woman proficient in Cree and English who in 2014, after spending time with her grandmother who was born a Moberly and married a Waniyandie and after visiting her great-great-great grandfather Ewan Moberly's homestead, was "hoping to learn the Iroquois language." As to the reason, Edna Doire proudly explained, "My grandfather was Daniel Wanyandie. He spoke Cree but was of Iroquois descent. I found out that the Wanyandies were among the first families in the Rockies along with the Karakunties, Findlays ... Joaquims, and others."[158] If today in their everyday lives most descendants speak a combination of Cree and English, they are no less, consciously so, Iroquois by inheritance.

The past is now.

TO SUM UP

In navigating the changing times, Jasper Iroquois and their descendants were pressured and harassed by others seeking to dispossess them of their ways of life. The assumption of an Indigenous-white divide justified newcomers' attitudes and actions toward whoever stood in the way of the future they marked out for themselves.

Jasper Iroquois and their counterparts across the West repeatedly engaged this divide, which was intended to set them apart and to render them inert. Their responses across time and place reflect the self-confident dispositions Iroquois took west with them. Not only at Jasper but wherever Iroquois and their descendants have set themselves down and however diverse their life courses and outcomes, they have valued their autonomy and that of the bands or clusters into which they have formed themselves. They have respected themselves, their ways of life, and each other, just as the generations before them did. Iroquois in the West were, and are, independent-minded both by inheritance and by disposition.

What is distinctive about the life courses of Jasper Iroquois and their counterparts across the West is that, although Indigenous by descent, they were not rounded up, which was the easy alternative for pushing Indigenous peoples out of the way. Even when whites sought to distance themselves, such as by describing Jasper Iroquois as "Indian people" and as "kind of roaming," there was a grudging respect.[159]

For over two centuries, Iroquois in the West have navigated, and sometimes crossed, the Indigenous-white divide. In doing so, they have continued to be their own selves, their presence across time and place sufficiently noticed by others to make it possible, drawing on slivers of stories from the shadows of the past, to tell their story.

Research Note

One of the first tasks I set for myself in telling the story of Iroquois in the West was to approximate how many there might have been in the first generation. This research note describes that process.

THE COMPLEXITIES OF NAMING

The term "Iroquois" was almost always used by Iroquois in the West to describe themselves, which is consistent with its long history of usage by others. General agreement exists that "Iroquois" was the name given to the language spoken by five, later six, Indigenous peoples living south of Lake Ontario who came together in the mid-1400s, prior to contact with white outsiders, into a confederacy to protect their common interests.

The name accorded this grouping varied between the three European powers that from the early 1600s coveted its territory. The French routinely referred to speakers of "the Iroquois tongue" as the "Iroquois Nations" or simply "Iroquois."[1] The word "Iroquois" was also used by the French to identify residents of the Jesuit mission of Sault St Louis, known as Caughnawaga, and of splinter groups setting themselves down not that far away at St Régis and Lac des Deux Montagnes.[2] Almost all Iroquois in the West came from these three communities located not that far from present-day Montreal.

The English and Dutch had their own terminology. Possibly because the Mohawk people were the easternmost member of the Iroquois-speaking confederacy and thereby closest to white settlements, documents originating in the two countries used the word "Mohawk" or a variant both specifically and also, it seems, generally.[3] Although the terminology adopted by the English, being the British after the Acts of Union of 1707, shifted over time to "Five Nations" and then to "Six Nations" with the adhesion of the Iroquois-speaking Tuscaroras in 1722, French usage of the term "Iroquois" held.[4]

Contemporaries were well aware of the varied namings and sometimes offered clarification. A Jesuit writing in 1693 to a Protestant missionary based in New York referenced "the Iroquis [sic] Indians (being the five Nations)."[5] An English official writing in 1698 to a French counterpart described "our Five Nations of Indians, whom you call Iroquois."[6] A 1747 history differentiated in a glossary between the term "Iroquois" as "used by the French" and the term "The Five Nations" as used by "the English."[7] In reporting to his superior in London in 1773, the governor of New York referred to "the Five Nations or Iroquois," a usage that he justified by Lake Champlain's having been called "Mere des Iroquois."[8]

North America's Indigenous peoples came under central government control in the United States in 1824 and in Canada in 1867. The US Office of Indian Affairs, whose annual reports go back to 1826, has not used the term "Iroquois," except rarely in reference to very small numbers living in Oregon, New York, or elsewhere and in reference to Canada. Until 1955, when all mention of specific Indigenous groupings was removed, Canada's Department of Indian Affairs routinely referred in its annual reports to Iroquois in relationship to earlier religious missions, hence "Iroquois at Caughnawaga, Lake of Two Mountains [Lac des Deux Montagnes], and St. Regis" and "Hurons of Lorette, also of Iroquois stock."[9] When the word "Iroquois" is spoken, it is pronounced "Irokwa" in Canada and "Irokoi" in the United States.

A recent shift has Caughnawaga, Lac des Deux Montagnes, and St Régis known respectively as Kahnawà:ke, Oka, and Akwesasne, with residents most often self-identifying as Mohawk.[10] Another shift replaces "Iroquois" with "Haudenosaunee," or "People of the Longhouse."[11]

The term "Iroquois" is preferred here for two reasons. As well as being most appropriate to the subject and time period at hand, it was and is the term by which Iroquois in the West describe themselves. The same reason applies to my preference in the text for the names Caughnawaga, Lac des Deux Montagnes, and St Régis.

IN SEARCH OF IROQUOIS IN THE WEST

In seeking to determine how many Iroquois were in the West, I was enormously assisted by fellow historians Nicole St-Onge and Bruce McIntyre Watson, who early on generously shared their databases with me. Both then privately held, St-Onge's database is now accessible on the website of the Société historique de Saint-Boniface and Watson's database has been published and is also available online as *Lives Lived West of the Divide*.[12] These two sets of data reveal the past differently.

Nicole St-Onge's Voyageur Contracts Database, constructed with Robert Englebert and others, comprises 35,000 contracts signed in or near Montreal by men of all backgrounds between 1714 and 1830, who were hired principally to engage in a westward expanding fur trade. Montreal notaries oversaw this final stage of a process initiated by recruiters for some twenty fur trading and other entities.[13] Contracts for the same positions at around the same time were usually identical in form and substance between named Iroquois and others. The fullest entries contain the name, hometown or parish, date of the agreement, employment position and conditions, destination, company with whom one contracted, salary with advances on signing or departing if any, and notary's name.[14] Contracts can be searched by name and date, as well as by other variables.

From the Voyageur Contracts Database, I extracted 1,100 contracts signed between 1800 and 1821 by named Iroquois of Caughnawaga, Lac des Deux Montagnes, or St Régis. My chronological beginning point was when likely or certain Iroquois started signing contracts that have found their way into the database, and the end point was when the Hudson's Bay Company, headquartered in England, took over the North West Company, based in Montreal, ending the heady competition that had encouraged the hiring of Iroquois.

Based on a systematic and thorough reading of fur trade journals and other primary sources for the Pacific Northwest, which extended from British Columbia, Washington, and Oregon east into parts of Montana, Idaho, and Wyoming, Bruce McIntyre Watson constructed capsule biographies of roughly 4,000 persons of all backgrounds active in the Pacific Northwest fur trade up to 1858, by which time it was in fast decline. Watson located 170 Iroquois by name as working there through 1858.

My own research centred on, but was not exclusive to, published primary accounts and fur trade records originating with the North West Company and Hudson's Bay Company, available on microfilm from the HBC Archives in the Manitoba Archives. St-Onge's and Watson's databases familiarized me with Iroquois surnames, and I extracted records from these sources relating to likely, along with certain, Iroquois.

Surviving NWC and HBC records are partial. Unlike an earlier counterpart that has disappeared, the NWC ledger of employees survives for 1811–21. Included among its many hundreds of employee accounts are 175 that possibly or certainly belonged to Iroquois.[15] NWC general accounts and miscellaneous documents for 1805 and for 1819–21, included in the bibliography, contain 700 possible Iroquois surnames.[16] NWC and then HBC accounts for 1821–24 include 130 possible Iroquois surnames.[17] In respect to Iroquois employed in the fur trade who transferred in 1821 from the NWC to the HBC, I interrogated the account book for 1820–25 of its then headquarters at Fort George, formerly the American trading post of Astoria.[18] I also selectively surveyed surviving records for individual posts that likely had Iroquois contingents.[19] In each case, I looked both for the presence of Iroquois and for whatever I could locate respecting their everyday lives. In sum, I turned up 1,200 possibly Iroquois names.

TURNING NAMES INTO IROQUOIS PERSONS

The next task I set for myself was to turn the certain or probable Iroquois names I had located in the various sources respecting the early-nineteenth-century fur trade into Iroquois persons. Iroquois names, it must be said, pose a challenge.[20] Catholic first names acquired through baptism almost always held through the life span, whereas surnames were written down variously as they were heard by others. Differences in spelling and pronunciation more often reflected haste or the recorder's bad hearing than they did surnames themselves changing over time. Not only are original records sometimes very difficult to read, but whoever recopied the names into other records, including into present-day sources, also had to cope with earlier handwriting that was sometimes blurred or otherwise impossible to read by virtue of the passage of time.

A four-prong process was used to turn into discrete Iroquois persons the 170 certain Iroquois names as determined by Watson, the 1,100 almost certain Iroquois names on contracts in the Voyageur Contracts Database, and the 1,200 possibly Iroquois names located in primary data originating with the fur trade, which include some contracts signed away from home.

The first and very significant prong attended to Iroquois first names, which were bestowed at Catholic baptism and almost always remained stable through the life span. The second prong involved phonetically sounding out for their similarities Iroquois's surnames, written down in contemporary documents as they were heard. It was almost always less a matter of identical spellings than it was a matter of a similar mix of consonant and vowel sounds.[21] The third prong was matching up dates associated with names to determine the chronological feasibility of their being associated with the same person. Given imponderables at every stage, I was 90 per cent certain that potential matches referred to the same individual as opposed to two or more persons with the same or a very similar surname. The fourth and critical prong was to determine from the various pieces of information whether the individual was almost certainly, as opposed to only likely, Iroquois. I made a match to my satisfaction only so long as I located at least one such indication in a primary source describing the individual as Iroquois.

As demonstrated in the following example, spellings were as likely to be irregular as the same. Here, I matched eight entries from four different sources to a single person. The five entries located in the Voyageur Contracts Database were, if different in spelling and appearance, sufficiently compatible in timing, destination, employment, and sound when spoken to be comfortably joined together:

Name	Contract date	Destination	Employment
Te-hy-ka-we-he, Lazard	18110122	Temiskaming	Milieu
Tékykawyhy, Lazare	18130227	Ft William, etc	Gouvernail
Tehykawetti, Lazard	18140413	Ft William, etc	Gouvernail
Thehikawehe, Lazare	18160920	Fort William	Gouvernail
Teyica Teyé Caoueyé, Lazare	18181215	Pays sauvage 4 yrs	Devant

With each of the first four paddling trips, contracted in Caughnawaga over a five-year period, this individual returned home at the trip's end. It was a seasonal adventure. The fifth time was very different, both as to the specified length of the commitment to the "pays sauvages," or wild country, and because he signed up along with other mostly experienced fellow Iroquois, recruited on the same day to the same destination, as I learned through searching the online Voyageur Contracts Database by contract date. His circumstances upon agreeing to the four-year contract are attested by a brief entry in the North West Company ledger:

Tehyoiwehé, Lasard   1819–20   Hunter

A third primary source, HBC accounts of Pacific Northwest employees, refers to his membership in one of the two bands, or clusters, of trappers led by fellow Iroquois:

Tayecawehe, Lazard   1820–22   In Meaquin Martin's band

Bruce McIntyre Watson's database, grounded in years of primary research, rounds out the story:

Teyecaleyeeaoeye, Lazard   1818–25   Trapper
                            when he deserted

As for the certainty of this person having been Iroquois, he was so described in his contract of 27 February 1813. In his brief biography of this individual in *Lives Lived West of the Divide*, Watson explains that the last sighting able to be tracked was at the edge of Mexican California, at which point he disappears from view.

Teyecaleyeeaoeye's story is recounted in chapter 4. Eight spellings of his surname do not make for a complete biography, but along with other bits and pieces of information, they give a sense of just this one Iroquois life across a decade and a half. The process I employed with each potential match was similar.

RESULTS

The matching process turned up 615 named Iroquois. Of these, 175 were matched between two or more sources, at least one of which described the individual as Iroquois. The other 440 signed only a single contract describing them as Iroquois.

Another 200 possible but not certain Iroquois signed single contracts identifying them as being from one of the three communities but not specifically an Iroquois. I excluded them from consideration for two reasons. Some may have only been living in one of the three largely Iroquois communities of Caughnawaga, Lac des Deux Montagnes, and St Régis, or they might have come from elsewhere explicitly to join the fur trade, knowing that employees were repeatedly recruited in the three communities. Numerous other named and unnamed Iroquois also found their way west, as explained in chapters 2, 3, 4, 5, and 7.

SPELLING OF SURNAMES

The spelling of surnames presented its own challenge. While holding onto variants in my research files, I decided in the interests of making individuals visible across time so far as was practical to use a single spelling to refer to a single individual. In doing so, I sought out the version closest to the ways that the variants were sounded out, which included those in Watson's biographies, grounded as they are in the multiple surnames he consulted, the versions used in the NWC ledger, and the variants in the Voyageur Contracts Database. I also attended to the spellings in the census enumerations of 1825 and 1831 for Caughnawaga and of 1831 for Lac des Deux Montagnes and St Régis, which survive in the original and which I used to search for persons returning home.[22] Where relevant, I included in the text more than a single surname spelling for an individual.

Notes

INTRODUCTION

1 Simpson, *Mohawk Interruptus*, ix.
2 See the bibliography for monographs by Daniel Barr, José António Brandâo, William J. Campbell, William Engelbrecht, Laurence Hauptman, Gilles Havard, Kelly Hopkins, Gail MacLeitch, Michael Leroy Oberg, Jon Parmenter, David L. Preston, Timothy J. Shannon, and earlier in time, Richard Aquila, Matthew Dennis, William Fenton, Barbara Graymont Francis Jennings, D. Peter MacLeod, Daniel K. Richter, and Dean Snow.
3 See Lounsbury, "Iroquoian Languages."
4 On the various names by which Caughnawaga was known, see Jennings et al., eds, *History and Culture*, 217. On St Régis's origins, see Reid, *Khañawà:ke*, 12; and Bonaparte, "History of Akwesasne."
5 Iroquois's date of departure from Caughnawaga to Lac des Deux Montagnes is taken from chiefs' testimony of 20 June 1855 in United States, *Journal of the Senate, 1852–55*, 260. Among scholars who attend to these Iroquois, each of whom is included in the bibliography, are Gerald Taiaiake Alfred, David Blanchard, John Demos, Jack Frisch, Gretchen Lynn Green, Allan Greer, Jean-François Lozier, Gerald F. Reid, Daniel Rueck, Audra Simpson, and Matthieu Sossoyan.
6 Pierce, *Making the White Man's West*, xvi, xxv.
7 Simpson, *Mohawk Interruptus*, 2.
8 Wicks, "Louie Otoihkori." The conversation, recalled by Thomas Wicks in 1939, was between Wicks, early settler Neil Fregonne, Oteakorie, Mellas, also called Mary, and their son Alex. Elements giving every impression of having been added for effect are omitted.
9 Ibid.
10 Ibid.
11 Peterson and Peers, *Sacred Encounters*.

CHAPTER ONE

1 Thwaites, ed., *Jesuit Relations*, vol., 1, 11.
2 See Blanchard, "Patterns of Tradition," 2–3, for a listing of Indigenous peoples speaking an Iroquoian language. Tuscaroras joined the Iroquois Confederacy in 1722.

3 Marquis de Denonville to M. Dougan, 22 August 1687, in Brodhead, ed., *Documents*, vol. 3, 469.

4 John Megapolensis, "A Full Account of the Maquaas Indians," 1644, in Hazard, *Historical Collections*, vol. 1, 523. For a summary, see Green, "New People," 22.

5 "Treaty of Peace between the Iroquois and Governor de Tracy," 25 May 1666, in Brodhead, ed., *Documents*, vol. 3, 123. On the complexities of Catholicism's arrival among the Iroquois generally, see Richter, *Ordeal of the Longhouse*, 105–30.

6 The Jesuit mission's moves and their impetuses are well described in Green, "New People," ix, 25–9, 39–47, 53–4. Also useful is Mohawk Council of Kahnawake, *Seigneury of Sault St Louis*.

7 "Mission of St. François Xavier de Prés, near Montreal, during the Years 1672 and 1673," in Thwaites, ed., *Jesuit Relations*, vol. 58, 77; "Narrative for Each Year from the Foundation of the Mission of the Sault until 1685," in Thwaites, ed., *Jesuit Relations*, vol. 65, 167. The religious obligation was to abstain from "the idolatry of dreams," as recorded in Thwaites, ed., *Jesuit Relations*, vol. 58, 77; on the nature of religious observances, see 79, 81, 171. The total number is inferred from the statements respecting 1673–74 that since the mission began in 1668 the number "has increased considerably, and still increases every day" and that during the past "fifteen months, over one hundred and eighty new Savages have settled here." "Mission to the Iroquois of St. François Xavier, at la Prairie de la Magdeleine, during the years 1673 and 1674," in Thwaites, ed., *Jesuit Relations*, vol. 58, 249, 251. The "Letter of Father Claude Cauchetiere Respecting the Iroquois Mission of Sault St.-Francois Xavier, near Montreal," October 1682, in Thwaites, ed., *Jesuit Relations*, vol. 62, 173, described "sixty Cabins – that is to say, from one hundred and twenty to 150 families, as there are at least two in each Cabin." The mission's growth in numbers is detailed in "Narrative for Each Year from the Foundation of the Mission of the Sault until 1685," in Thwaites, ed., *Jesuit Relations*, vol. 65, 145–243. On the utility of the Jesuits' records, see Richter, "Iroquois versus Iroquois"; and Greer, ed., *Jesuit Relations*.

8 Greer, *Mohawk Saint*. See also Béchard, *Original Caughnawaga Indians*.

9 "Mission to the Iroquois of St. François Xavier, at la Prairie de la Magdeleine, during the years 1673 and 1674," in Thwaites, ed., *Jesuit Relations*, vol. 58, 249.

10 Green, "New People," 32, also 19, 42–3. Among those arriving were Hurons from north of Lake Ontario whose numbers had been decimated by warfare and who would over time gravitate to the Jesuit mission of Lorette, whose origin near the French capital of Quebec City up the St Lawrence River from Montreal went back to 1651.

11 Simpson, *Mohawk Interruptus*, 46.

12 Green, "New People," 43n36, 186. Lozier, "In Each Other's Arms," 206–8, describes relatively unsuccessful recruitment efforts of the late 1600s, as well as providing population totals at 155–6, 169, and 208.

13 McLean, *John McLean's Notes*, 11. See also Mackenzie, *Voyages from Montreal*, vol. 1, xxix; and entry of 19 September 1817, in Cox, *Adventures on the Columbia River*, vol. 2, 329.

14 Green, "New People," 212–13. My use of the names Lac des Deux Montagnes and St Régis responds to terminology in fifty related biographies by scholars in the field in *Dictionary of Canadian Biography* (online). See also Frisch, "Iroquois in the West"; and Tooker, "Iroquois since 1820."

15 Hopkins, "New Landscape," 23.

16 Blanchard, "Patterns of Tradition," 155.

17 Alfred, *Heeding the Voices*, 42. See also Reid, *Khanawà:ke*, 7–9.

18 Blanchard, "Patterns of Tradition," 141. Surtees, "Iroquois in Canada," 68–70, describes the history of the three Iroquois villages from newcomers' perspectives.

19 Hopkins, "New Landscape," 25. See also Blanchard, "Patterns of Tradition," 171.

20 Simpson, *Mohawk Interruptus*, 15. See also Fenton, *Great Law*.

21 See Blanchard, "Patterns of Tradition," 139–40, 170n1; and Hopkins, "New Landscape," 26–7, 42.

22 "Of the Mission of St. François Xavier du Sault Near Montreal," in Thwaites, ed., *Jesuit Relations*, vol. 60, 279.

23 "Lettre au R.P. Bonin," 2 October 1735, in Thwaites, ed., *Jesuit Relations*, vol. 68, 275.

24 Lozier, "In Each Other's Arms," 164. See also Greer, "Conversion and Identity," 183–5.

25 "Of the Mission of St. François Xavier du Sault Near Montreal," in Thwaites, ed., *Jesuit Relations*, vol. 60, 293.

26 Green, "New People," 57–8. The liturgy was in the Huron language due to the Jesuits' earlier mission to the Hurons.

27 Lozier, "In Each Other's Arms," 164. Respecting the mission's self-governance as early as 1677, see "Of the Mission of St. François Xavier du Sault Near Montreal," in Thwaites, ed., *Jesuit Relations*, vol. 60, 277. As one of the Jesuits who was in charge early on put it, "The iroquois [*sic*] have their government like all the rest of the peoples of the earth," those in positions of authority receiving the "majority of votes" cast by "the elders of their village." "Narrative for Each Year from the Foundation of the Mission of the Sault until 1685," in Thwaites, ed., *Jesuit Relations*, vol. 65, 163.

28 Richter, "Iroquois versus Iroquois," 10. For detail on the course of the sometimes fraught manoeuvrings between Caughnawaga and the Five Nations in the shadow of relations between the French and the English, see Green, "New People," 61–227.

29 Grabowski, "Searching for the Common Ground," 60, 72.

30 Green, "New People," 72.

31 Lozier, "In Each Other's Arms," 214. See also Alfred, *Heeding the Voices*, 48–9.

32 Havard, *Great Peace*, 17, 125–6, 253n43. See also Havard, *Empire et métissages*, 226.

33 For early references to "praying Indians," see "Answer of the Six Nations to Governor Dongan," 13 February 1688; Robert Livingston to the Government of Connecticut, 9 May 1690; "Propositions of the Christian Mohawks to Governor Slaughter," 26 May 1691, and related documents; and "The Council of New York

to Mr. Blathwayt," 30 May 1692, all in Brodhead, ed., *Documents*, vol. 3, 534, 729, 771–86, 836. For the definition of "praying Indians," see Brodhead, ed., *Documents*, vol. 4, 689. On the term's use in reference to English territory, see "Extracts from Edward Randolph's Report to the Council of Trade (September 1676)," in Brodhead, ed., *Documents*, vol. 3, 243.

34 Unidentified Oneida, quoted in "Journal of Major Dirck Wessel's Embassy to Onondaga," August 1693, in Brodhead, ed., *Documents*, vol. 4, 60. See also "Propositions of the Five Nations at Albany," 2 February 1693; and "Message from the Governor of Canada to the Five Nations and Their Answer," 31 January 1694, both in Brodhead, ed., *Documents*, vol. 4, 85, 120.

35 Edward Randolph to Lords of Trade, 29 May 1689, in Brodhead, ed., *Documents*, vol. 3, 580, with added punctuation.

36 On precontact vegetables, see Engelbrecht, *Iroquoia*, 22–7. See also Fenton, *Great Law*.

37 "Letter of Father Claude Cauchetiere Respecting the Iroquois Mission of Sault St.-Francois Xavier, near Montreal," October 1682, in Thwaites, ed., *Jesuit Relations*, vol. 62, 169. In reference to 1669, see also "Narrative for Each Year from the Foundation of the Mission of the Sault until 1685," in Thwaites, ed., *Jesuit Relations*, vol. 65, 157.

38 "Lettre au R.P. Bonin," 2 October 1735, in Thwaites, ed., *Jesuit Relations*, vol. 68, 275.

39 Hopkins, "New Landscape," effectively makes this point. See also Campbell, *Speculators in Empire*, 21.

40 On beavers' uses, see "Memoir of M. De Denonville [governor general of New France] on the State of Canada," 12 November 1685, in Brodhead, ed., *Documents*, vol. 9, 287. In the decade between 1675 and 1685, 780,000 pounds of beaver were dispatched from New France.

41 Trudel, "Samuel de Champlain."

42 Six Nations to Governor Dongan, 16 February 1688, in Brodhead, ed., *Documents*, vol. 3, 536. Francis and Morantz, *Partners in Furs*, 20–2, record Iroquois as far north in the late seventeenth century as James Bay.

43 On the significance of the trade with the Dutch, see Richter, *Ordeal of the Longhouse*, 76–96; and Parmenter, *Edge of the Woods*, 162–3.

44 "Capt. Mason to [Mr Secretary Cole?]," 2 April 1632, in Brodhead, ed., *Documents*, vol. 3, 17.

45 Armour, "Merchants of Albany," 3–4, 64, 64n7; Willmott, "From Stroud to Strouds," esp. 204–5.

46 Lunn, "Illegal Fur Trade," 65.

47 "Report of Messrs. Schuyler and Dellius' Negotiations in Canada," 2 July 1698, in Brodhead, ed., *Documents*, vol. 4, 347.

48 Ibid., 351.

49 Green, "New People," 233, 240; for a detailed overview, see 228–89.

50 Sagronwadie to Commissioners of the Indian Affairs in Albany, 20 June 1700, in Brodhead, ed., *Documents*, vol. 4, 692. See also Shannon, *Iroquois Diplomacy*, 118–20; and Parmenter, *Edge of the Woods*, 155.

51 Lunn, "Illegal Fur Trade," 72. See also Blanchard, "Patterns of Tradition," 160–3, which draws on Lunn.

52 The specific cases are recounted in Lunn, "Illegal Fur Trade," 73, 73nn80–4.

53 See Norton, *Fur Trade*, 83, 121–51; and Blanchard, "Patterns of Tradition," 153.

54 Lunn, "Illegal Fur Trade," 73–5, among numerous sources recounting the Desauniers sisters' exploits.

55 Ibid., 61–2. The merchant was Robert Saunders, and the letter book used was for 1752–55.

56 Interview before the Indian Act Review Committee in Ottawa in 1947, in Blanchard, "Patterns of Tradition," 159.

57 Ibid., 160.

58 Richter, *Ordeal of the Longhouse*, 270–1.

59 On the importance accorded captives, see ibid., 32–8, 60–74; Parmenter, *Edge of the Woods*, 102–3; Thwaites, ed., *Jesuit Relations*; and more generally Barman, *Abenaki Daring*. For a case study of a captive taken in 1704 who opted to make her life at Caughhnawaga, see Demos, *Unredeemed Captive*.

60 "Lettre au R.P. Bonin," 2 October 1735, in Thwaites, ed., *Jesuit Relations*, vol. 68, 277, 279. On this phenomenon, see also Barman, *Abenaki Daring*.

61 See Blanchard, "Patterns of Tradition," 172.

62 Peter Wraxell, "Some Thoughts upon the British Indian Interest in North America, More Particularly as It Relates to … the Six Nations," 1755, in Brodhead, ed., *Documents*, vol. 7, 15–31.

63 William Johnson to Edmond Matthews, 21 June 1755, in Johnson, *Papers of Sir William Johnson*, vol. 1, 643, also 595–6, 639–40, 644, 646–7.

64 William Johnson to Thomas Pownall, 24 and 25 August 1755, in ibid., vol. 1, 886, 883. For detail, see Green, "New People," 214–25. The hostilities extending from 1756 to 1763, known as the Seven Years' War, are tracked from the perspective of Caughnawaga in MacLeod, *Canadian Iroquois*.

65 Green, "New People," vi. See also Sawaya, "Les Sept Nations"; and Alfred, *Heeding the Voices*, 44–8.

66 "Proceedings of Sir William Johnson with the Indians," 7 September 1763," in Brodhead, ed., *Documents*, vol. 7, 553. The meeting was held at German Flatts, New York. Ibid., 559.

67 "Enumeration of Indians within the North Department," 18 November 1763," in Brodhead, ed., *Documents*, vol. 7, 582.

68 "Proceedings of Sir William Johnson with the Indians," 7 September 1763," in Brodhead, ed., *Documents*, vol. 7, 558, italics in original.

69 See Blanchard, "Patterns of Tradition," 180.

70 Mohawk Council of Kahnawake, *Seigneury of Sault St Louis*; Sossoyan, "Kahnawake Iroquois," 23.

71 See Alfred, *Heeding the Voices*, 49–50.

72 Campbell, *Speculators in Empire*, 4.

73 See Graymont, *Iroquois in the American Revolution*, esp. 67–8, 87, 101.

74 Among other sources on this shift, see Campbell, *Speculators in Empire*, 211–12.

75 Long, *Voyages and Travels*, 6, also 20.

76 Blanchard, "Patterns of Tradition," 238.

77 Long, *Voyages and Travels*, 6, also 20. For a broad scholarly perspective, see Rueck, "Enclosing the Mohawk Commons," 42–53.

78 Long, *Voyages and Travels*, 25; Blanchard, "Patterns of Tradition," 238.

79 Mackenzie, *Voyages from Montreal*, vol. 1, xxix–xxx.

80 Long, *Voyages and Travels*, 5–7.

81 "Lettre au R.P. Bonin," 2 October 1735, in Thwaites, ed., *Jesuit Relations*, vol. 68, 263, 265.

82 Devine, *Historic Caughnawaga*, 10.

83 Long, *Voyages and Travels*, 6–7.

CHAPTER TWO

1 Gates, ed., *Five Fur Traders*, 4.

2 Moodie, "Trading Post Settlement," 363. See also "General Return of the Departments and Posts Occupied by the North West Company in the Indian Country," 23 October 1802, in "Courts of Justice," 142. Gordon, *Laird of Fort William*, is useful on this time period from a North West Company perspective.

3 For contending approaches to the use of "Métis," see Andersen, "*Métis*"; and Ens and Sawchuk, *From New Peoples*, esp. 1–9, 42–69, 380–418.

4 For a critique, see Andersen, "*Métis*."

5 Podruchny, *Making the Voyageur World*, 4–5.

6 This argument is made more fully in Barman, *French Canadians*.

7 Entry of 5 December 1794, in M'Gillivray, *Journal of Duncan M'Gillivray*, 48; Peter Fidler, entries of 8 and 14 February, 17 March, and 15 May 1797, in MacGregor, *Peter Fidler*, 105. See also William Tomison to George Sutherland, 25 February 1798, in Johnson, ed., *Saskatchewan Journals*, 130. On this possibly being the earliest reference to migrating Iroquois, see editor Sean T. Peake, in Thompson, *Travels of David Thompson*, vol. 2, 424.

8 Mackenzie, *Voyages from Montreal*, vol. 2, 298.

9 Entry of 22 July 1800, in Harmon, *Sixteen Years*, 25; entry of 19 October 1800, in "Chesterfield House Journal," in Johnson, ed., *Saskatchewan Journals*, 272; Archibald McLeod, entry of 17 December 1800, in "Alexandria Journal," in Gates, ed., *Five Fur Traders*, 141.

10 Mackenzie, *Account of the Athabasca Indians*, 21–2.

11 William Tomison, entry possibly of 19 January 1802, in "Cumberland House Journal," in Johnson, ed., *Saskatchewan Journals*, xci, also ci–xcii. See also running entry of 24 January to 4 February 1804, in Selkirk, *Lord Selkirk's Diary*, 207.

12 Concerning the Voyageur Contracts Database, see St-Onge, "Early Forefathers"; St-Onge, "'He Was Neither'"; Grabowski and St-Onge, "Montreal Iroquois *Engagés*"; and Voyageur Contracts Database. Contracts can be individually searched in the database under the person's name and also by the date they were signed.

13 Most totals have been rounded off to the nearest 0 or 5 to account for possible small errors in calculation.

14 North West Company, HBCA, *Ledger (Account Books), 1811–1821.*

15 As an example, see Masiewicz, *Gervase Macomber,* being the biography of a non-Iroquois fur trade employee living in Caughnawaga.

16 Long, *Voyages and Travels,* 6, also 20; Blanchard, "Patterns of Tradition," 238.

17 Courville, *Entre ville et campagne,* 284.

18 Caughnawaga, *Census, 1825;* Caughnawaga, *Census, 1831;* Oka, *Census, 1825;* Oka, *Census, 1831;* St Régis, *Census, 1825.*

19 Butler, *Great Lone Land,* 167.

20 The following section draws on Gates, ed., *Five Fur Traders,* 5–8; Morse, *Fur Trade Canoe Routes;* and Huck, *Exploring the Fur Trade Routes.*

21 Mitchell, *Fort Timiskaming,* 33–5, 62, 65–6.

22 "Moose Port Journals," cited in Francis and Morantz, *Partners in Furs,* 109.

23 Berton, *Pierre Berton's War,* 686.

24 Ibid., 697, 698.

25 Entry of 26 July 1817, in Cox, *Adventures on the Columbia River,* vol. 2, 266.

26 For a description, see Moberly, *When Fur Was King,* 11–12.

27 Morrison, *Superior Rendezvous-Place,* 43.

28 One source of such information is the NWC ledgers and account books. See all of the items in the bibliography under North West Company, Hudson's Bay Company Archives (HBCA), Archives of Manitoba.

29 North West Company, HBCA, *Account Books, 1819–1821,* Athabasca; North West Company, HBCA, *Ledger (Account Books), 1819–1821.*

30 Pierre Ounaratier, "Contract Notes," in Voyageur Contracts Database, my translation of the French original, http://archivesshsb.mb.ca/en/permalink/voyageurs59835.

31 Entry of 22 October 1803, in Harmon, *Sixteen Years,* 70–1.

32 Mackenzie, *Account of the Athabasca Indians,* 1–2.

33 For closer descriptions, see Victor, *River of the West,* 64–5; and Thompson, *David Thompson's Narrative,* 204–5.

34 North West Company, HBCA, *Servants' Contracts, 1811–1822.* See also Nicks, "Iroquois and the Fur Trade," 87; and St-Onge, "Early Forefathers," which describes this group of Iroquois within the larger context of their Canadien counterparts.

35 Entry of 2 October 1808, in Harmon, *Sixteen Years,* 117.

36 "Edmonton District Report, 1815," in Binnema and Ens, eds, *Edmonton House Journals,* 427.

37 Colin Robertson to Ignace Giasson, 18 December 1819, in Robertson, *Colin Robertson's Correspondence Book,* 261.

38 Ignace Giasson to Colin Robertson, 29 March 1820, in ibid., 274.

39 George Simpson to Ignace Giasson, 18 May 1820, in Simpson, *Journal of Occurrences,* 56.

40 Entry of November 1820, in Simpson, *Journal of Occurrences*, 176.
41 George Simpson to Duncan Finlayson, 7 December 1820, in Simpson, *Journal of Occurrences*, 196.
42 Entry of 22 November 1800, in Thompson, *Travels of David Thompson*, vol. 2, 317, 423.
43 Thompson, *David Thompson's Narrative*, 317.
44 Charles Simonet, "Contract Notes," in Voyageur Contracts Database, my translation of the French original, http://archivesshsb.mb.ca/en/permalink/voyageurs62950.
45 Ibid.
46 Ignace Caiatonie, "Contract Notes," in Voyageur Contracts Database, my translation of the French original, http://archivesshsb.mb.ca/en/permalink/voyageurs62953.
47 Ibid., my translation of the French original.
48 North West Company, HBCA, *Ledger (Account Books), 1811–1821*.
49 "Minutes of an Inquiry Held at the Office of the Indian Department at Montreal," 22 December 1828, in Canada, Indian Department, *Pre-Confederation Records*, C-13,377, vol. 590. A survey of the unorganized Iroquois correspondence on microfilm in Library and Archives Canada turned up a wealth of materials in Iroquois, English, and French wanting to be interrogated to understand what occurred subsequent to Iroquois returning home. With this exception, it proved impossible, as was the intention, to track specific persons forward in time.
50 Canada, "Report of the Special Commissioners," 20.
51 Gates, ed., *Five Fur Traders*, 204–5; Voyageur Contracts Database.
52 Entry of 2 October 1804, in "Rainy Lake Journal," in Gates, ed., *Five Fur Traders*, 213, also entries at 210–33.
53 Gates, ed., *Five Fur Traders*, 204–5. The credit balances, in the currency of the day, were 278.10 and 819.10 respectively.
54 North West Company, HBCA, *Ledger (Account Books), 1811–1821*.
55 Entry of 29 September 1819, in Binnema and Ens, eds, *Edmonton House Journals*, 359.
56 North West Company, HBCA, *Ledger (Account Books), 1811–1821*; HBCA, *Fort Chipewyan, Alberta: Account Books, 1821–1822*, Iroquois and Freemen's Book. See also North West Company, HBCA, *Ledger (Account Books), 1819–1821*.
57 Entry of 8 March 1802, in "Chesterfield House Journal," in Johnson, ed., *Saskatchewan Journals*, 317.
58 Entry of 21 February 1802, in "Chesterfield House Journal," in Johnson, ed., *Saskatchewan Journals*, 312.
59 Entry of 22 February 1802, in ibid., 312n3.
60 Entry of 25 February 1802, in ibid., 313.
61 Entry of 3 March 1802, in ibid., 314, 314n3.
62 Entry of 5 March 1802, in ibid., 314–15.
63 Entry of 8 March 1802, in ibid., 315–16.

64 For the extremes of David Thompson's ambivalence toward Iroquois, see Thompson, *David Thompson's Narrative*, 311–17. See also Thompson, *Writings of David Thompson*, vol. 2, 280; and Nicks, "David Thompson."

65 Nisbet, *Mapmaker's Eye*, 67.

66 Entry of February 1810, in Thompson, *David Thompson's Narrative*, 418–19.

67 Alexander Henry, entry of 8 July 1810, in Coues, ed., *New Light*, vol. 2, 610, also 610n7, 626.

68 Entry of February 1810, in Thompson, *David Thompson's Narrative*, 438.

69 Entry of October 1810, in ibid., 441.

70 Entry of 29 December 1810, in ibid., 443n1.

71 Entry of 10 January 1811, in ibid., 446.

72 Entry of 11 January 1811, in ibid., 448.

73 Nisbet, *Mapmaker's Eye*, 90.

74 Entry of 3 May 1811, in Thompson, *David Thompson's Narrative*, 457. For somewhat different wording respecting what occurred, see Thompson, *Writings of David Thompson*, vol. 2, 274; and Nisbet, *Mapmaker's Eye*, 96,.

75 Entry of 11 May 1811, in Thompson, *David Thompson's Narrative*, 460.

76 Thompson, *Travels of David Thompson*, vol. 2, 485.

77 Entry of July 1811, in Thompson, *David Thompson's Narrative*, 472. See also Nisbet, *Mapmaker's Eye*, 103.

78 Entry of 22 July 1811, in Thompson, *David Thompson's Narrative*, 511.

79 Entry of 18 September 1811, in ibid., 534–5.

80 Ferris, *Life in the Rocky Mountains*, 185.

81 Thompson, *David Thompson's Narrative*, 311.

82 Irving, *Astoria*, 120–1.

83 Entry of 2 June 1817, in Cox, *Adventures on the Columbia River*, vol. 2, 193, 195, 199.

84 Ibid., 353–4. On Cox, see Holmgren, "Ross Cox."

85 Ross, *Fur Hunters*, ed. Quaife, vol. 1, 295.

86 Devine, *Historic Caughnawaga*, 327.

87 Caughnawaga, *Census, 1825*; Caughnawaga, *Census, 1831*; Oka, *Census, 1825*; St Régis, *Census, 1825*. No 1831 census survives, or one was not taken, for St Régis (Akwesasne).

88 For such agreements, see North West Company, HBCA, *Servants' Accounts, 1820–1821*.

89 See Reid, *Khanawà:ke*, 24–36; Sossoyan, "Note de recherché"; Sossoyan, "Kahnawake Iroquois," 18–32; and Tooker, "Iroquois since 1820."

90 De Kay, *Zoology of New York*, 73.

91 For diverse accounts, see Benn, *Mohawks on the Nile*; Blanchard, "Entertainment, Dance"; Blanchard, "High Steel"; Blanchard, "Patterns of Tradition," 216–37; Bruemmer, "Caughnawagas," 10–11; Gass, "Proud Tradition"; Hind, *Narrative of the Canadian Red River*; and Reid, *Khanawà:ke*, 19–20.

92 Devine, *Caughnawaga*, 327.

CHAPTER THREE

1 See Brown, "History of the Flathead Indians," 8–9, for a good description of natural foodstuffs.
2 Fahey, *Flathead Indians*, 15–17.
3 William Clark and John Ordway, entries of 4 and 5 September 1805, in Lewis and Clark, *Journals of the Lewis and Clark Expedition*.
4 Thompson, *Writings of David Thompson*, vol. 2, 246. See also Thompson, *David Thompson's Narrative*, lxxxvii, xc–xci, 410–11; and Dempsey, "David Thompson's Journeys in Idaho," 102.
5 De Smet, *Life, Letters and Travels*; Mengarini, "Recollections of the Flathead Mission"; Point, *Wilderness Kingdom*; Buckley, *Nicolas Point*.
6 Palladino, *Indian and White*. For an elaborate origin story that does not correspond with other information about the same individuals, see Mellis, "Coyote People"; and Mellis, "Ignace Portui."
7 Joseph Rosati to Father General of the Society of Jesus at Rome, St Louis, 20 October 1839, quoted in Palladino, *Indian and White*, 8, 29. Going further back in time, a descendant who grew up on the Flathead Reservation recalls her grandfather explaining how their ancestor Ignace La Mouse was the same Ignace whom David Thompson encountered among the Kootenay people, as described in chapter 2, and hired as a steersman to get him to Astoria in the summer of 1811. See Helen Julian, cited in Steigmeyer, "Entiat woman."
8 Ronan, *History of the Flathead Indians*, 23.
9 Michel Revais, quoted in Boas and Teit, *Coeur d'Alene, Flathead and Okanogan Indians*, 288.
10 Palladino, *Indian and White*, 7–9.
11 Jean Baptiste Gervais, quoted in Mengarini, "Recollections of the Flathead Mission," 228.
12 Palladino, *Indian and White*, 9.
13 Ronan, *History of the Flathead Indians*, 43–4.
14 Fahey, *Flathead Indians*, 65–6.
15 Palladino, *Indian and White*, 9–10.
16 Joseph Rosati, 31 December 1831, quoted in Palladino, *Indian and White*, 11.
17 Ibid.
18 Joseph Rosati to Father General of the Society of Jesus at Rome, St Louis, 20 October 1839, quoted in Palladino, *Indian and White*, 28.
19 Joseph Rosati, 31 December 1831, quoted in Palladino, *Indian and White*, 11.
20 Catlin, *Letters and Notes*, vol. 2, 561–2. According to Palladino, it is likely, but not certain, that they were the two men from Flathead country. Palladino, *Indian and White*, 13–19.
21 Catlin, *Letters and Notes*, vol. 2, 562.
22 Palladino, *Indian and White*, 10.
23 Carriker, *Father Peter John De Smet*, 18.
24 Brosnan, *Jason Lee*, 2n8, 2–16.
25 Lee and Frost, *Ten Years in Oregon*, 109–11.

26 Palladino, *Indian and White*, 21.

27 John McLoughlin, quoted in Brosnan, *Jason Lee*, 71. See also Lee and Frost, *Ten Years in Oregon*, 127–8.

28 Palladino, *Indian and White*, 25; Pierre-Jean De Smet to Father Provincial, 15 August 1842, in De Smet, *Life, Letters and Travels*, vol. 1, 28–9.

29 Joseph Rosati to Father General of the Society of Jesus at Rome, St Louis, 20 October 1839, quoted in Palladino, *Indian and White*, 28.

30 Parker, *Journal of an Exploring Tour*, 275–6.

31 Palladino, *Indian and White*, 27.

32 Ronan, *History of the Flathead Indians*, 25–6.

33 Palladino, *Indian and White*, 27, 29.

34 Palladino, *Indian and White*, 27.

35 De Smet, *Life, Letters and Travels*, vol. 1, 29–30. No details are given in the text as to letter specifics.

36 Letter, Fort Hall, 15 August 1841, in ibid., vol. 1, 290.

37 Joseph Rosati to Father General of the Society of Jesus at Rome, St Louis, 20 October 1839, quoted in Palladino, *Indian and White*, 29.

38 Ibid.

39 Ibid.

40 Ibid.

41 Ibid.

42 De Smet, *Life, Letters and Travels*, vol. 1, 263, also on the trip, 31, 98n2, 216, 220.

43 Ibid., 230–1, also 263 for the total number of persons. The ethos is captured in Peterson and Peers, *Sacred Encounters*.

44 Ronan, *History of the Flathead Indians*, 29.

45 Palladino, *Indian and White*, 33–7.

46 Hiram Martin Chittenden and Alfred Talbot Richardson, "Introduction," in De Smet, *Life, Letters and Travels*, vol. 1, 39.

47 Palladino, *Indian and White*, 38–9.

48 Pierre-Jean De Smet to Father Provincial, Fort Hall, 16 August 1841, in De Smet, *Life, Letters and Travels*, vol. 1, 303.

49 Ibid., 289–90.

50 Ibid., 292.

51 Palladino, *Indian and White*, 41.

52 Point, *Wilderness Kingdom*, 20.

53 Pierre-Jean De Smet to Father Provincial, Fort Hall, 16 August 1841, in De Smet, *Life, Letters and Travels*, vol. 1, 293.

54 Pierre-Jean De Smet to Father Provincial, [spring 1841], in ibid., 286. See also Pierre-Jean De Smet to Father Provincial, St Mary's, 26 October 1841, in ibid., 327.

55 Ronan, *History of the Flathead Indians*, 30.

56 De Smet, *Life, Letters and Travels*, vol. 1, 51. Ewers, *Gustavus Sohon's Portraits*, 22–3, puts the onus for deteriorating relations on the Flatheads, whereas Garraghan, *Jesuits of the Middle United States*, vol. 2, 379–92, offers a more nuanced interpretation.

57 Bigart and Woodcock, eds, *In the Name*, 112. See also Weisel, ed., *Men and Trade*. The estimate is for 1853.

58 Malone, Roeder, and Lang, *Montana*, 121–2.

59 Ewers, *Gustavus Sohon's Portraits*, 4.

60 Gustavus Sohon, plate 19, in ibid., 58.

61 Weisel, ed., *Men and Trade*, 31.

62 Entry of 14 October 1854, in Owen, *Journals and Letters*, 87.

63 Proceedings of 10 July 1855, in "Official Proceedings at the Council Held by Governor Isaac Stevens, Supt. Indian Affairs, W.T., with the Flathead, Pend Oreilles and Kootenay Tribes of Indians at Hell Gate in the Bitter Root Valley, Washington Territory, Commencing on the Seventh Day of July, 1855," quoted in Bigart and Woodcock, eds, *In the Name*, 39, 39n34, 40–2.

64 Entry of 27 May 1856, in Owen, *Journals and Letters*, 129, with added punctuation.

65 Letter of Adrian Hocken, Mission of the Flatheads, 15 April 1857, in De Smet, *Life, Letters and Travels*, vol. 4, 1246–7.

66 Bigart and Woodcock, eds, *In the Name*, 113–14. On the use of the name Aeneas, see Bigart and Woodcock, eds, *In the Name*, 113–14; and Weisel, ed., *Men and Trade*, 28–9.

67 Joset ad Roothaan, 8 September 1845, quoted in Garraghan, *Jesuits of the Middle United States*, vol. 2, 294.

68 Weisel, ed., *Men and Trade*, 30.

69 Gustavus Solon, plate 20, in Ewers, *Gustavus Solon's Portraits*, 60.

70 Mullan, *Report on the Construction*, 5.

71 Bigart and Woodcock, eds, *In the Name*, 113–14.

72 Ibid., 116.

73 Weisel, ed., *Men and Trade*, 27, 27n1.

74 Gustavus Solon, plate 21, in Ewers, *Gustavus Solon's Portraits*, 61.

75 John Owen, cited in Weisel, ed., *Men and Trade*, 64.

76 Weisel, ed., *Men and Trade*, 27–8.

77 Entry of 19 April 1851, in Owen, *Journals and Letters*, 29, with added punctuation.

78 Entry of 27 April 1851, in ibid., 32.

79 Entry of 28 April 1851, in ibid., 34. For other references to Francis Lamoose, see entry of 13 November 1854, in ibid., 88; and entries of 6 and 9 June 1856, in ibid., 124–5.

80 Weisel, ed., *Men and Trade*, 64–5.

81 Entry of 2 June 1865, in Owen, *Journals, and Letters*, 331. John Owen's wife repeatedly enters his journal.

82 Palladino, *Indian and White*, 149.

83 Weisel, ed., *Men and Trade*, 36–7.

84 Entries of 15 and 17 June 1856, in Owen, *Journals and Letters*, 127.

85 Letter of Pierre-Jean De Smet, St Louis, 10 November 1859, in De Smet, *Life, Letters and Travels*, vol. 2, 766.

86 Ronan, *History of the Flathead Indians*, 24.

87 "Census of Salish Montana, 1886," in United States, Bureau of Indian Affairs, *Indian Census Rolls, 1885–1940*.

88 Palladino, *Indian and White*, 38.

89 De Smet, *Life, Letters and Travels*, vol. 1, 292n3.

90 Palladino, *Indian and White*, 15, 26.

91 Jerome D'Aste to L.B. Palladino, St Ignatius, 28 October 1910, quoted in Palladino, *Indian and White*, 479.

92 Bigart and Woodcock, eds, *In the Name*, 116.

CHAPTER FOUR

1 Martin Isini a quoin [Meaquin Martin], "Contract Notes," in Voyageur Contracts Database, my translation of the French original, http://archivesshsb.mb.ca/en/permalink/voyageurs51179.

2 Contracts are accessible online by name and date on the Voyageur Contracts Database.

3 Colin Robertson to William Williams, 26 August 1819, in Robertson, *Colin Robertson's Correspondence Book*, 257.

4 Entry of 27 September 1819, in Binnema and Ens, eds, *Edmonton House Journals*, 367.

5 Ross, *Fur Hunters*, ed. Quaife, vol. 1, 187, 196, also for McKenzie's account, 199–212.

6 For detailed information on Iroquois and others on trapping expeditions taken from a close reading of expeditions' journals, see Simpson, "Snake Country Freemen."

7 Agreements and running accounts are in HBCA, *Fort George, Oregon: Account Books, 1820–1822*.

8 John McLoughlin to George Simpson, 20 March 1827, in McLoughlin, *Letters of John McLoughlin, 1825–38*, lxv.

9 Alexander Kennedy, "Spokane House Report 1822/23," cited in Ogden, *Peter Skene Ogden's Snake Country Journals, 1824–25 and 1825–26*, 49. See also the entry of 12 September 1822, in "Spokane House Post Journal," cited in Morgan, *Jedediah Smith*, 121. For a useful complementary perspective on the time period through 1824, see Reid, *Forging a Fur Empire*.

10 Alexander Kennedy, "Spokane House Report 1822/23," quoted in Ogden, *Peter Skene Ogden's Snake Country Journals, 1824–25 and 1825–26*, 49.

11 Morgan, *Jedediah Smith*, 125.

12 Numbers of participants are deduced from entries in Ross, *Fur Hunters*; and Ogden, *Peter Skene Ogden's Snake Country Journals 1824–25 and 1825–26*, which includes William Kittson's "Snake Journal, 1824–25."

13 Entry of 27 September 1824, in Ross, *Snake Country*.

14 Entry of 29 May 1825, in William Kittson, "Snake Journal, 1824–25," in Ogden, *Peter Skene Ogden's Snake Country Journals 1824–25 and 1825–26*, 236.

15 See Ross, *Fur Hunters*, ed. Quaife; Ross, *Fur Hunters*, ed. Spaulding; Ross, "Journal of Alexander Ross," 367; and Ross, *Snake Country*. The copy of the latter source in the Hudson's Bay Company Archives is written in the same script and ink day after day, indicating that it is a copy of an original.

16 See Ogden, *Peter Skene Ogden's Snake Country Journals, 1824–25 and 1825–26*, which includes the journals of both Peter Skene Ogden and the expedition's second-in-command, William Kittson.

17 Hough, *History of St Lawrence*, 198–200; Mathis, "Timeline."

18 Wells, "Igance Hatchiorauquasha," 161n2.

19 On the "Nakatiehou" spelling, see Garraghan, *Catholic Beginnings*, 122.

20 Anderson, *Rocky Mountain Journals*, 322.

21 Entry of 26 August 1825, in William Kittson, "Snake Journal, 1824–25," in Ogden, *Peter Skene Ogden's Snake Country Journals, 1824–25 and 1825–26*, 250.

22 The 1819 reference to Tevanitagon is under Meaquin Martin's entry in North West Company, HBCA, *Ledger (Account Books), 1811–1821*, and the 1822 reference to Tevanitagon is in "Names of Iroquois Comprising Martin's Band," in HBCA, *Fort George, Oregon: Account Books, 1820–1822*. For biographies of the two leaders, accurate in most respects, see Wells, "Pierre Tevanitagon"; and Wells, "Ignace Hatchiorauquasha."

23 Ross, *Fur Hunters*, ed. Quaife, vol. 2, 9–11. Conversations either replicate the original text or are reconstructed as a series of complete, first-person sentences drawing on one or more of the three texts that recount the expedition.

24 Entry of 13 February 1824, in Ross, *Snake Country*.

25 Entry of 25 February 1824, in ibid.

26 Entry of 19 March 1824, in Ibid.

27 Ibid.

28 Ibid.

29 Ibid.

30 Entry of 20 March 1824, in ibid.

31 Entry of 21 March 1824, in ibid.

32 Reid, *Forging a Fur Empire*, 170.

33 See Wells, "Ignace Hatchiorauquasha," 163.

34 Ross, *Fur Hunters*, ed. Quaife, vol. 2, 36.

35 Ross, *Fur Hunters*, ed. Spaulding, 229–30.

36 Ibid., 230.

37 Entries of 23, 30, and 31 March 1824, in Ross, *Snake Country*.

38 Entries of 30 March and 1 April 1824, in ibid.

39 Entry of 1 April 1824, in ibid.

40 Ibid.

41 Ibid.

42 Entries of 2 and 5 April 1824, in ibid.

43 Entry of 3 April 1824, in ibid.

44 Ross, *Fur Hunters*, ed. Quaife, vol. 2, 42.

45 Entry of 10 April 1824, in Ross, *Snake Country*.

46 Entry of 10 February 1824, in ibid.

47 Ross, *Fur Hunters*, ed. Quaife, vol. 2, 61.

48 Ibid., 64, 73–4, 88.

49 Entry of 19 June 1824, in Ross, *Snake Country*.

50 Ross, *Fur Hunters*, ed. Quaife, vol. 2, 88, 99.

51 Entries of 4, 20, and 21 August 1824, in Ross, *Snake Country*.

52 Ross, *Fur Hunters*, ed. Quaife, vol. 2, 99.

53 Entry of 9 October 1824, in Ross, *Snake Country*.

54 Entries of 12 and 13 October 1824, in ibid.

55 Ross, *Fur Hunters*, ed. Quaife, vol. 2, 128.

56 Entry of 13 October 1824, in Ross, *Snake Country*.

57 Ibid.; Morgan, *Jedediah Smith*, 120–1.

58 Entry of 13 October 1824, in Ross, *Snake Country*.

59 Burt Brown Barker, "Introduction," in Ogden, *Peter Skene Ogden's Snake Country Journals, 1824–25 and 1825–26*, li(n2).

60 Entry of 25 November 1824, in Ross, *Snake Country*.

61 Entry of 13 October 1824, in ibid.; Morgan, *Jedediah Smith*, 120–1.

62 Burt Brown Barker, "Introduction," in Ogden, *Peter Skene Ogden's Snake Country Journals, 1824–25 and 1825–26*, xlviii.

63 Simpson, *Part of Dispatch*, 53.

64 Entry of 19 March 1825, in William Kittson, "Snake Journal, 1824–25," in Ogden, *Peter Skene Ogden's Snake Country Journals, 1824–25 and 1825–26*, 221.

65 Entry of 31 December 1824, in Ogden, *Peter Skene Ogden's Snake Country Journals, 1824–25 and 1825–26*, 10.

66 Ibid., 14n2, 15n1.

67 Entry of 23 April 1825, in ibid., 39.

68 Alexander Ross, entry of 12 February 1825, in "Flathead Journal," quoted in ibid., 251.

69 Entry of 5 January 1825, in ibid., 11.

70 Entry of 26 December 1824, in William Kittson, "Snake Journal, 1824–25," in ibid., 210.

71 Entries of 19, 26, and 27 January 1825, in ibid., 16, 18.

72 Entry of 5 February 1825, in ibid., 20.

73 Entry of 6 February 1825, in William Kittson, "Snake Journal, 1824–25," in ibid., 216–17.

74 Entry of 8 May 1825, in ibid., 231.

75 Entries of 8 July and 28 and 29 March 1825, in William Kittson, "Snake Journal, 1824–25," in ibid., 242, 224.

76 Entry of 18 October 1825, in ibid., 89.

77 Entries of 4 and 5 May 1825, in ibid., 43–4, with added punctuation.

78 Entry of 22 May 1825, in ibid., 49.

79 Entry of 23 May 1825, in ibid., 51.

80 Utley, *After Lewis and Clark*, 76.

81 William Henry Ashley, quoted in *Missouri Observer and St. Louis Advertiser*, 31 October 1827, cited in Morgan, *Jedediah Smith*, 40.

82 This account is recreated by combining the entry of 23 May 1825, in Ogden, *Peter Skene Ogden's Snake Country Journals, 1824–25 and 1825–26*, 51–3, with the entry of 23 [*sic* 24] May 1825, in William Kittson, "Snake Journal, 1824–25," in ibid., 234–5.

83 Ogden's location near present-day Ogden, Utah, lay west of the continental

divide, which was the eastern border of British claims and also south of the 42nd parallel, which the United States, but not Britain, had set as its southern boundary. In other words, Johnson Gardner, not Ogden, was by his country's international arrangements out of bounds. See John McLoughlin to Governor and Committee, HBC, 6 October 1825, in McLoughlin, *Letters of John McLoughlin, 1825–38*, 9; Committee and Governors, HBC, to George Simpson, 2 June 1826, in ibid., lxiv; and Governor and Committee, HBC, to John McLoughlin, 20 September 1826, in ibid., 9n2.

84 Entry of 24 May 1825, in Ogden, *Peter Skene Ogden's Snake Country Journals, 1824–25 and 1825–26*, 51–3; P.S. Ogden to Governor and Traders, Northern District, 27 June 1825, in McLoughlin, *Letters of John McLoughlin, 1825–38*, 297.

85 Engry of 24 May 1825 in Ogden, *Peter Skene Ogden's Snake Country Journals, 1824–25 and 1825–26*, 51–3.

86 Entry of 23 [*sic* 24] May 1825, in William Kittson, "Snake Journal, 1824–25," in ibid., 235.

87 Entry of 25 May 1825, in Ogden, *Peter Skene Ogden's Snake Country Journals, 1824–25 and 1825–26*, 53–5.

88 Entry of 26 May 1825, in ibid., 55.

89 Entry of 29 May 1825, in ibid., 56, with added punctuation.

90 Entry of 20 March 1826, in ibid., 143.

91 John McLoughlin to Governor and Committee, HBC, 6 October 1825, in McLoughlin, *Letters of John McLoughlin, 1825–38*, 8.

92 Entry of 19 October 1825, in "Edmonton House Journal," quoted in Ogden, *Peter Skene Ogden's Snake Country Journals, 1824–25 and 1825–26*, 64–5, 64n1, 64–6n2; P.S. Ogden to Governor and Traders, 27 June 1825, in McLoughlin, *Letters of John McLoughlin, 1825–38*, 296–9.

93 Simpson, *Part of Dispatch*, 52–3, 70.

94 John McLoughlin to Governor and Committee, HBC, 6 October 1825, in McLoughlin, *Letters of John McLoughlin, 1825–38*, 10; entry of 10 August 1825, in ibid., 253–4.

95 Nathaniel J. Wyeth to Henry Hall and others, 8 November 1833, in Wyeth, *Correspondence and Journals*, 74.

96 Peter Skene Ogden to Governor, Chief Factors, and Chief Traders, Northern Department, HBC, 2 February 1826, in Ogden, *Peter Skene Ogden's Snake Country Journals, 1824–25 and 1825–26*, 261.

97 Peter Skene Ogden to George Simpson, 12 November 1825, in ibid., 256.

98 Peter Skene Ogden to Governor, Chief Factors, and Chief Traders, 10 October 1826, in Simpson, *Fur Trade and Empire*, 283–4.

99 Entries of 9 and 10 April 1826, in Ogden, *Peter Skene Ogden's Snake Country Journals, 1824–25 and 1825–26*, 154; entry of 20 March 1826, in ibid., 143.

100 Entry of 18 February 1828, in Ogden, *Peter Skene Ogden's Snake Country Journals, 1827–28 and 1828–29*, 64.

101 Entry of 17 February 1828, in ibid., 63. Tevanitagon's killing is described in Campbell, "Narrative," n.p. According to popular American writer Washington Irving, "this branch of the Iroquois tribe has since remained among these

mountains, at mortal enmity with the Blackfeet, and have lost many of their prime hunters in their feuds with that ferocious race." Irving, *Adventures of Captain Bonneville*, 107.

102 For an example, see Ferris, *Life in the Rocky Mountains*, 81.

103 John McLoughlin to Governor and Committee, HBC, 6 July 1827, in McLoughlin, *Letters of John McLoughlin, 1825–38*, 40. See also Utley, *After Lewis and Clark*, 76.

104 John McLoughlin to Governor and Committee, HBC, 1 September 1826, in McLoughlin, *Letters of John McLoughlin, 1825–38*, 32.

105 Governor and Committee, HBC, to George Simpson, 12 March 1827, in Simpson, *Fur Trade and Empire*, 286.

106 George Simpson to Governor and Committee, HBC, 25 July 1827, quoted in Burt Brown Barker, "Introduction," in Ogden, *Peter Skene Ogden's Snake Country Journals, 1824–25 and 1825–26*, lvi.

107 John McLoughlin to George Simpson, 20 March 1827, in McLoughlin, *Letters of John McLoughlin, 1825–38*, 290–1.

108 Benjamin O'Fallon to Joshua Pilcher, 1 August 1823, in Morgan, *Jedediah Smith*, 400n17.

109 Ibid., 401.

110 Entry of 4 August 1825, in Reid and Gannon, eds, "Journal of the Atkinson-O'Fallon Expedition," 36.

111 J.H. Stevens, quoted in Ferris, *Life in the Rocky Mountains*, 33.

112 Entry of 10 October 1830, in Work, *Snake Country Expedition*, 31.

113 For confirmation that the enigmatic Frizzon was part of this group, see the entry of 16 April 1831, in Work, *Snake Country Expedition*, 95.

114 Entry of 16 April 1831, in ibid., 95.

115 Entry of 17 April 1831, in ibid., 95.

116 Entry of 17 April 1831, in ibid., 96.

117 Ferris, *Life in the Rocky Mountains*, 43.

118 Ibid., 62. The burial practice was virtually identical to that described for a Canadien killed accidentally in the summer of 1834 while trapping. He was "wrapped in a piece of coarse linen, over which was sewed a buffalo robe." See entry of 28 July 1834, in Townsend, *Narrative of a Journey*, 108.

119 Ferris, *Life in the Rocky Mountains*, 62, 105. This book was originally published as a serial in *Western Literary Messenger* (Buffalo), 13 July 1842 to 4 May 1844.

120 Ibid.

121 Irving, *Adventures of Captain Bonneville*, 126–7.

122 Russell, *Journal of a Trapper*, 87–8, with added punctuation. The first edition was published in 1914 from the original manuscript as *Journal of a Trapper: Or, Nine Years in the Rocky Mountains, 1834–1843*.

123 For various sightings of Grey, see Anderson, *Rocky Mountain Journals*, 322–5.

124 John Grey, recounted in Ferris, *Life in the Rocky Mountains*, 62, 72–4, 118.

125 Ibid., 78, 189.

126 Entry of 15 June 1834, in Anderson, *Rocky Mountain Journals*, 130.

127 The first Catholic priest there used the term. See Point, *Wilderness Kingdom*, 20.

128 Garraghan, *Catholic Beginnings*, 93. See also Point, *Wilderness Kingdom*, 20.

Point was not sympathetic to the Westport Iroquois, terming them "drunkards, [who] emerged from their wretchedness, only to fall back in to it." Ibid., 22.

129 Anderson, *Rocky Mountain Journals*, 365.
130 Garraghan, *Catholic Beginnings*, 15–16n11, 110–11 (map), 122 (on Marianne's surname).
131 Marriage record, in ibid., 67n58, 92–3, also 122–3.
132 Nicolas Point, unpublished memoir, entries of 1 November 1840 to 10 May 1841, in ibid., 108.
133 Ronan, *History of the Flathead Indians*, 27. See also Buckley, *Nicolas Point*, 194, 200–1.
134 Pierre-Jean De Smet to Father Provincial M. Rollier, 10 September 1841, in De Smet, *Life, Letters and Travels*, vol. 4, 1398.
135 Bidwell, "First Emigrant Train," 113, 117.
136 Anderson, *Rocky Mountain Journals*, 325; Wells, "Ignace Hatchioauquasha," 173–4; Mathis, "Timeline."
137 Quoted in *Kansas City Journal*, 1 January 1876, cited in Wells, "Ignace Hatchioauquasha," 174.
138 "John Grey – #362," in "Idaho Historical Markers," http://www.waymarking.com/waymarks/WM29W0_John_Grey_362.
139 Havard, *Histoire des coureurs de bois*, 541, my translation of the French original.
140 Jackson, *Children of the Fur Trade*, 26.
141 Wells, "Ignace Hatchiorauquasha," 174.

CHAPTER FIVE

1 For specifics by year, see Barman, *French Canadians*, chart 4.1, 77.
2 On Hawaiians, see Barman and Watson, *Leaving Paradise*.
3 Ross, *Adventures of the First Settlers*, 85.
4 The spellings of surnames of Iroquois in the Pacific Northwest, which sometimes had numerous variations based on what those writing them down heard, are principally taken from Watson, *Lives Lived*.
5 Etienne Onayaissa [Étienne Oniaze], "Contract Notes," in Voyageur Contracts Database, my translation of the French original, http://archivesshsb.mb.ca/en/permalink/voyageurs64550.
6 North West Company, HBCA, *Ledger (Account Books), 1811–1821*.
7 Entry of June 1816, in Ross, *Fur Hunters*, ed. Quaife, vol. 1, 73–4.
8 Ibid., 178. See also Hines, "Erection of Fort Nez Perce."
9 Jones, *Annals of Astoria*, 236.
10 Cox, *Adventures on the Columbia River*, vol. 2, 354–5, 357.
11 Entries of November and 26 December 1824, in Work, "Journal of John Work," 200.
12 Ross, *Fur Hunters*, ed. Quaife, vol. 1, 295.
13 The list is taken principally from Archibald McDonald, "Report to the HBC Governor and Council," 25 February 1830, in HBC, *Fort Langley Journals*, 221–2. The Abenaki's life is examined in Barman, *Abenaki Daring*.

14 Munnick, ed., *Catholic Church Records: St Paul*, A45. On Satakarata being known as Rabesca, see the entry of 5 July 1845, in HBC, *Journal of Occurrences at Fort Nisqually*.

15 Satakarata, "Contract with Hudson's Bay Company." I am grateful to Chris Hanna for turning up this document.

16 For a succinct summary, see Holland, "Sir John Franklin."

17 This version of events is taken from Officer and Page, *Fabulous Kingdom*, 75.

18 Entries of 2 May and 23 July 1825, in Franklin, *Sir John Franklin's Journals*, 32, 32n119, 76–7.

19 Entries of 31 July 1843, 31 August 1844, and 18 and 19 March 1845, in Lowe, *Private Journal*. See also entry of 2 September 1843, in ibid.

20 McDonald, "Dying Voyageur of Columbia," n.p. On McDonald's wife, see Williams, "Daughter of Angus MacDonald," 107.

21 HBCA, *Fort St James, British Columbia: Post Journals, 1820–1856*. For earlier references to Iroquois trading on their own with local Indigenous people, see the entries of 10 and 11 June, 5 August, and 1 September 1820, 21 April 1821, 16 October 1823, and 11 May 1824, in ibid.

22 Entry of 7 July 1821, in North West Company, HBCA, *Account Books, 1820–1821*, F.4/43. No further information has been located respecting what this event entailed.

23 McLean, *John McLean's Notes*, 186.

24 Entry of 17 March 1841, in HBCA, *Stikine, Alaska: Post Journals, 1840–1842*.

25 Philip Smith, quoted in John McLoughlin to HBC Governor and Committee, 19 August 1842, in McLoughlin, *Letters of John McLoughlin, 1839–44*, 65.

26 George Simpson to the HBC Governor, Deputy Governor, and Committee in London, 20 June 1841 in Simpson, *London Correspondence*, 43.

27 Archibald MacDonald to Edward Ermatinger, 22 May 1844, in Phillips, "Family Letters," 38.

28 Allan, "Reminiscences of Fort Vancouver," 78, italics in original.

29 John McLoughlin to Francis Heron, 14 October 1830, in McLoughlin, *Letters of Dr John McLoughlin, 1829–1832*, 150. See also John McLoughlin to Donald Manson, 15 November 1830, in ibid., 153.

30 John McLoughlin to Michel Laframboise, April 1832, in ibid., 269.

31 John McLoughlin to P.C. Pambrun, 8 May 1832, in ibid., 271; John McLoughlin to Michel Laframboise, 18 May 1832, in ibid., 274.

32 Entries of 19 and 21 November 1845 and 16, 23, and 24 February 1848, in Lowe, *Private Journal*.

33 Williams, "Daughter of Angus MacDonald," 107.

34 Data taken from Watson, *Lives Lived*.

35 Ross, *Fur Hunters*, ed. Spaulding, 195.

36 See Walkem, *Stories of Early British Columbia*, 80.

37 Entry of 1 January 1835, in Tolmie, *Journals of William Fraser Tolmie*, 300.

38 Francis Ermatinger to Edward Ermatinger, running entry, [1828], in Ermatinger, *Fur Trade Letters*, 98.

39 This point is emphasized in Barman, *French Canadians*.

40 Watson, *Lives Lived*.

41 HBC, *Fort Nisqually: Servants' Accounts*, vol. 10, esp. entries of 8 and 24 July 1855 for Narcisse Kanatasse, Michel Tayarouyokarari, and Louis Aurtanonquash.

42 Kane, *Wanderings of an Artist*, 171–2.

43 Boas and Teit, *Coeur d'Alene, Flathead and Okanogan Indians*, esp. 4, 162, 179–81, 259, 286–7.

44 Entry of 25 March 1804, in Henry, *Journal of Alexander Henry*, vol. 2, 704.

45 Entries of 19 and 20 April 1814, in ibid., 723.

46 Entry of 6 May 1814 in ibid., 737. Henry's journal entries would be cut short by his accidental death later in May.

47 Grabowski and St-Onge, "Montreal Iroquois *Engagés*," 56n89.

48 Entries in HBC, *Journal of Occurrences at Fort Nisqually*.

49 Entries in ibid.

50 Entry in ibid.

51 Munnick, ed., *Catholic Church Records: Vancouver*, 40pB137.

52 Entry of 24 February 1855, in HBC, *Fort Nisqually: Servants' Accounts*, vol. 10.

53 Louis and François Satakarata's work lives are tracked in HBCA, *Fort Victoria, British Columbia: Post Journals, 1846–1850*.

54 Joseph McKay to James Douglas, 9 April 1853, in HBC, Nanaimo Archives, *Nanaimo Correspondence*.

55 Entry of 30 August 1852, in HBC, Nanaimo Archives, *Nanaimo Journal*.

56 Joseph McKay to James Douglas, 9 and 16 September 1852, in HBC, Nanaimo Archives, *Nanaimo Correspondence*.

57 Entry of 3 April 1852, in HBC, Nanaimo Archives, *Nanaimo Journal*.

58 The Nanaimo builders' earlier Fort Victoria years are chronicled in HBCA, *Fort Victoria, British Columbia: Post Journals, 1846–1850*.

59 Entries of 9, 16, 23, and 30 May and 4, 20, and 27 June 1853, in HBC, Nanaimo Archives, *Nanaimo Journal*.

60 Joseph McKay to James Douglas, 2 August 1853, in HBC, Nanaimo Archives, *Nanaimo Correspondence*.

61 Entry of 31 January 1856, in HBC, Nanaimo Archives, *Nanaimo Journal*.

62 Bate, "Men Who Helped."

63 Peterson, *Black Diamond City*, 40–3.

64 Norcross, *Nanaimo Retrospective*, 22; Peterson, *Black Diamond City*, 47.

65 This phenomenon is traced in Barman, *French Canadians*.

66 Munnick, ed., *Catholic Church Records: Vancouver*, A40; Jameson, "Iroquois of the Pacific Northwest," 90. See also Olson, *Living in the Great Circle*, 304, who states that the claim was not far from that of Joseph McLoughlin, whose father had charge of Fort Vancouver.

67 Jackson, *Children of the Fur Trade*, 31; Watson, *Lives Lived*, 740.

68 Munnick, ed., *Catholic Church Records: Vancouver*, A40–1.

69 Ibid., 45pB172, 45pB173, 47pM56. See also Munnick, ed., *Catholic Church Records: St Paul*, A90–1.

70 Munnick, ed., *Catholic Church Records: St Paul*, 65pM3.

71 Munnick, ed., *Catholic Church Records: Vancouver*, 38pM43, 42pB141. Two

biographies in Watson, *Lives Lived*, have an English seamen named Thomas Davis on the coast in 1836.

72 Munnick, ed., *Catholic Church Records: Vancouver*, 20pM17, 37pB108, 38pM43.

73 See ibid., 49pB194–6, B198–9, in which Tyeguariche's surname was spelled "Téykwachii" or "Tyekwariche"; and Munnick, ed., *Catholic Church Records: St Paul*, A72.

74 Munnick, ed., *Catholic Church Records: St Paul*, A-72.

75 Williams, "Daughter of Angus MacDonald," 107–8; Jameson, "Iroquois of the Pacific Northwest," 91–2; Olson, *Living in the Great Circle*, 342.

76 Munnick, ed., *Catholic Church Records: Vancouver*, 45pB178, 47pM54. On the almost certain father, Michel Plante, see Watson, *Lives Lived*.

77 Gandy, "Fur Trade Daughters," 211, 213, 218–19.

78 Munnick, ed., *Catholic Church Records: Vancouver*, 12pB153.

79 Ibid., 59pM3, A40; Gandy, "Fur Trade Daughters," 218.

80 Lee and Frost, *Ten Years in Oregon*, 132.

81 Munnick, ed., *Catholic Church Records: Vancouver*, 45pB176, 50pM65.

82 Testimony of Mary Ann Voutrin, in Berreman, "Field Notes," n.p.; Gandy, "Fur Trade Daughters," 211.

83 Gervais, *Letters, 1836–1837*.

84 The letter is reproduced in Slacum, "Slacum's Report on Oregon," 211–13. On HBC policy, see John McLoughlin to HBC Governor and Committee, 20 November 1844, in McLoughlin, *Letters of John McLoughlin, 1844–46*, 33.

85 Munnick, ed., *Catholic Church Records: St Paul*, 153pM4, A92.

86 John Work, 27 June and 13 July 1833, quoted in in Maloney, "Fur Brigade," 38, 126.

87 Jackson, *Children of the Fur Trade*, 31.

88 Jameson, "Iroquois of the Pacific Northwest," 93, is suggestive.

89 *Donation Land Claim Act (1850)*. See also Barman, *French Canadians*, 233–7.

90 Charles Wilson, entries of 29 June 1860 and 1 January 1862, in Stanley, *Mapping the Frontier*, 110, 168, italics in original.

91 Caughnawaga, *Census, 1825*; Caughnawaga, *Census, 1831*; Oka, *Census, 1825*; St Régis, *Census, 1825*. No 1831 census survives, or one was not taken, for St Régis (Akwesasne).

92 These data are derived from the biographies in Watson, *Lives Lived*.

93 Warre, *Overland to Oregon*, 16.

CHAPTER SIX

1 As with chapter 5, Harriet Munnick's transcription of Catholic records of baptisms, marriages, and deaths from the time of the first priests' arrival in late 1838 gives an entryway, along with Bruce McIntyre Watson's biographies of individual Iroquois drawn from a wide range of primary sources, including post journals. Munnick's *Catholic Church Records* for Grand Ronde, St Paul, and Vancouver include biographical information at the back of each volume, and Watson's *Lives Lived* integrates such information into each biographical entry.

2 I am grateful to Ann Cameron for this insight based on her family's experience.

3 "Eight distinct tribes of Indians and in all twenty-eight bands," forced off their lands by seven separate treaties, were in some cases literally herded there. Oliver C. Applegate to Commissioner of Indian Affairs, 14 August 1905, in United States, Bureau of Indian Affairs, *Correspondence Respecting Funds*.

4 Lee and Frost, *Ten Years in Oregon*, 132.

5 Carey, "Mission Record Book," 238–40, 258, 263.

6 Missionary letter from Cyrus Shepard, 28 September 1835, reproduced in Hulbert and Hulbert, eds, *Oregon Crusade*, 194, also 194n80.

7 Olson, *Living in the Great Circle*. See also Zenk, "Chinook Jargon," esp. 157–9. Zenk talked with grandchildren of Sanagratti who had childhood memories of speaking Chinook jargon with him (ibid., 36), which is today the official language at Grand Ronde.

8 Jameson, "Iroquois of the Pacific Northwest," 94; Olson, *Living in the Great Circle*, 401, also for examples of Sanagratti's community service at Grand Ronde, 44, 53.

9 Jameson, "Iroquois of the Pacific Northwest," 94; Zenk, "Chinook Jargon," 37; Olson, *Living in the Great Circle*, 401–10.

10 Olson, *Living in the Great Circle*, 401.

11 United States, Bureau of Indian Affairs, *Grand Ronde Reservation Census, 1886*.

12 See Olson, *Living in the Great Circle*, 4, 270, 276, 300.

13 United States, Bureau of Indian Affairs, *Grand Ronde Reservation Census, 1886*.

14 Olson, *Living in the Great Circle*, 339, 342; Munnick, ed., *Catholic Church Records: Grand Ronde*, 51pB116. Mary's father-in-law was Amable Arquette.

15 Olson, *Living in the Great Circle*, makes this point time and again.

16 Testimony of David Leno, in Berreman, "Field Notes," n.p.; Peers, "Grandmother of the West."

17 Testimony of Mary Ann Voutrin, in Berreman, "Field Notes," n.p.; Gandy, "Fur Trade Daughters," 211.

18 Munnick, *Catholic Church Records: St Paul*, 21.

19 British Columbia, Department of Lands and Works, *Pre-emption Records*, box 9.

20 "Alleged Rape," *Victoria Colonist*, 28 October 1862.

21 Oliver C. Applegate to Commissioner of Indian Affairs, 14 August 1905, in United States, Bureau of Indian Affairs, *Correspondence Respecting Funds*.

22 Ibid. See also Pederson, "Identity Politics," 59–60; and testimony of Peter Menard and Joseph Corner, in Berreman, "Field Notes," n.p.

23 United States, Bureau of Indian Affairs, *Grand Ronde Reservation Census, 1886*.

24 Munnick, ed., *Catholic Church Records: Grand Ronde*, 47pM6.

25 United States, Bureau of Indian Affairs, *Grand Ronde Reservation Census, 1886–1901*.

26 J. Pollock to Secretary of the Interior, 26 November 1880, quoted in Leavelle, "'We Will Make It,'" 442.

27 Jameson, "Iroquois of the Pacific Northwest," 96.

28 Bobby Mercier, quoted in ibid., 94.

29 Edgar Des Autel, conversation with author, 20 August 1997.

30 On the appeal of Canadiens' daughters, see Barman, *French Canadians*.

31 Munnick, ed., *Catholic Church Records: Vancouver*, 20pM13.

32 Ibid., 20pB206. I am endebted to Ann Cameron for sharing her family's story.

33 St Andrew's Catholic Church, Victoria, *Baptismal, Marriage, and Death Records, 1849–1934*. Baptized at the same time was "Louise, wife of Ignace Iroquois," who shortly thereafter died in child birth.

34 On the Boucher family, see Evans et al., "Métis Networks."

35 St Andrew's Catholic Church, Victoria, *Baptismal, Marriage, and Death Records, 1849–1934*.

36 Ibid. I am grateful to Chis Hanna for searching down the Witty family history.

37 Greene et al., *French Presence*, 49, 57, 64.

38 Evelyn Bligh, "The Witty Family," in Helgesen, ed., *Footprints*, 274–5. Reminiscing in old age, a Witty son put the cost at $6,000 paid in cash, which if so must have been money acquired in the recent gold rush. See Fulford, "Spell of Metchosin."

39 Evelyn Bligh, "The Witty Family," in Helgesen, ed., *Footprints*, 186–7, 275.

40 "Death at the Hospital," *Victoria Colonist*, 24 October 1873; "Witty in St Mary's Churchyard."

41 Agnes Antoine, "Witness Statement," 25 October 1873, in British Columbia, Supreme Court, *Probate Files*; Margaret Witty, "Baptism," 3 August 1866, in St Andrew's Catholic Church, Victoria, *Baptismal, Marriage, and Death Records, 1849–1934*.

42 William Boucher, "Death," 19 February 1858, in St Andrew's Catholic Church, Victoria, *Baptismal, Marriage, and Death Records, 1849–1934*.

43 St Andrew's Catholic Church, Victoria, *Baptismal, Marriage, and Death Records, 1849–1934*. See also Sellers, "'Wearing the Mantle,'" 12–13.

44 For these events, see St Andrew's Catholic Church, Victoria, *Baptismal, Marriage, and Death Records, 1849–1934*.

45 Evelyn Bligh, "The Witty Family," in Helgesen, ed., *Footprints*, 277.

46 "Mrs. Witty, Dead," *Victoria Colonist*, 7 August 1900; Charlotte Witty, "Will," 20 July 1900, in British Columbia, Supreme Court, *Probated Wills*, box 51.

47 Evelyn Bligh, "The Witty Family," in Helgesen, ed., *Footprints*, 274–90.

48 Canada, *Census of Canada, 1891*.

49 Canada, *Census of Canada, 1901*.

50 "Witty in St Mary's Churchyard."

51 St Andrew's Catholic Church, Victoria, *Baptismal, Marriage, and Death Records, 1849–1934*. Charlotte's father is named as Enos Thibault in Evelyn Bligh, "The Witty Family," in Helgesen, ed., *Footprints*, 275–6.

52 Therese's Iroquois descent is recorded in "C2 Cariboo, Williams Lake, Canoe Creek, Household 1," in Canada, *Census of Canada, 1881*. Her birthplace is given in the Laing Meason family tree, courtesy of Frances Haines.

53 "C2 Cariboo, Williams Lake, Canoe Creek, Household 1," in Canada, *Census of Canada, 1881*.

54 Canada, *Census of Canada, 1901*.

55 Laing, *Colonial Farm Settlers*, 275, 282, 283, 310.

56 St Joseph's Mission, Williams Lake, *Baptisms, 1866–1901*.

57 William Laing Meason to Thomas Elwyn, Lesser Dog Creek, 30 August 1884, in BC Archives, Add. Ms. 218.

58 Canada, *Census of Canada, 1891*; Canada, *Census of Canada, 1901*.

59 "Marriage Registration No. 85-09-175254," in British Columbia, Division of Vital Statistics, *Birth, Baptismal, Marriage, and Death Records*.

60 See McKelvie and Ireland, "Victoria Voltigeurs."

61 I am grateful to Barbara Sheppard for her assistance respecting the Alexcee family. Fredrick Alexcee's sister, Mary Ann, was born a year later, in 1854, and died in 1952, and his brother, Joseph, was born in 1857 and died in 1928.

62 William Beynon to Marius Barbeau, Port Edward, 7 November 1944, in Barbeau, *Marius Barbeau Fonds*, B-F-159, box B14.

63 McCormick, "'Neither One,'" 69–71, based on her close reading of the Fort Simpson post journal. See also Tasitayerie's biography in Watson, *Lives Lived*.

64 William Beynon to Marius Barbeau, Port Edward, 7 November 1944, in Barbeau, *Marius Barbeau Fonds*, B-F-159, box B14.

65 Crosby's years on the North Coast are chronicled in Hare and Barman, *Good Intentions Gone Awry*.

66 For a recent interpretation of Alexcee's art, which also tracks his personal life and assesses other scholars on the topic, see McCormick, "'Neither One.'"

67 William Beynon to Marius Barbeau, Port Edward, 7 November 1944, in Barbeau, *Marius Barbeau Fonds*, B-F-159, box B14.

68 Barbeau, "Frederick Alexie, a Primitive," in Barbeau, *Marius Barbeau Fonds*, B-F-550, box B35. For details on the exhibit and generally, see McCormick, "'Neither One.'" On the 1916 visit, see Barbeau, "Frederick Alexie, a Primitive," in *Canadian Review of Music and Art*.

69 William Beynon to Marius Barbeau, Port Edward, 7 November 1944, in Barbeau, *Marius Barbeau Fonds*, B-F-159, box B14.

70 Barbeau, "Frederick Alexie, a Primitive," in Barbeau, *Marius Barbeau Fonds*, B-F-550, box B35. Alexcee's son Frank described his father on his death certificate as a "fisherman."

71 Ibid.

72 Charles Doy Farrington, conversation with author, 19 July 2008.

73 One of the most complete accounts, alternatively well researched and romanticized, is Olsen, "Face of Tomo Antoine."

74 Owen, "Adam Grant Horne Family," sec. 3, 6.

75 For examples, see "Record of Prisoners at Work," September 1860, in British Columbia, Attorney General, *Victoria Gaol Records*; Horace Smith, Superintendent of Police, Victoria, to William A.G. Young, Colonial Secretary, 16 June 1863, in Police Department, Victoria, file 1388, in British Columbia, *Colonial Correspondence*; and "Charge of Murder Dismissed," *Victoria Colonist*, 14 August 1863.

76 Among others who turned to Ouamtany was HBC employer Adam Horne in 1855 for an expedition circumnavigating Vancouver Island, detailed in Walkem, *Stories of Early British Columbia*, 37–50; and in Owen, "Adam Grant Horne Family."

77 Entry of 9 June 1864, in Brown, *Robert Brown and the Vancouver Island*, 44, 49.

78 Brown, "First Journey," part 2, 274, italics in original.

79 Entry of 9 June 1864, in Brown, *Robert Brown and the Vancouver Island*, 49.

80 Undated agreement, in Brown, *Robert Brown Collection*, vol. 1, file 5.

81 Entries of 9 and 10 June 1864, in Brown, *Robert Brown and the Vancouver Island*, 49, 52.

82 Entry of 13 September 1864, in ibid., 135.

83 Entry of 8 September 1864, in ibid., 133.

84 Brown, *Races of Mankind*, vol. 1, 1432. See also the interpretation and excerpt in Brown, *Robert Brown and the Vancouver Island*, 178–96.

85 "The Exploring Expedition," *Vancouver Times*, 9 April 1865.

86 See Barman, "Taming Aboriginal Sexuality."

87 "Inspector of Gaols," in British Columbia, Attorney General, *Victoria Gaol Records*, vol. 7.

88 "Calendar of Prisoners Confined in Victoria Gaol," 4 February 1860 to 19 September 1867, in ibid.

89 Owen, "Adam Grant Horne Family," sec. 3, 6.

90 Bate, "Men Who Helped"; *Sooke Story*, 94.

91 St Andrew's Catholic Church, Victoria, *Baptismal, Marriage, and Death Records, 1849–1934*.

92 Therese's death is evidenced by the description of Lazard Onearste as the widower of "Therese Satagarata" when he received a two-week "leave of absence" on 12 June 1854 to wed a Nass woman named Rosalie in Victoria. Entries of 3 and 15 June 1854, in HBC, Nanaimo Archives, *Nanaimo Journal*. See also St Andrew's Catholic Church, Victoria, *Baptismal, Marriage, and Death Records, 1849–1934*.

93 "Murder at Sooke," *Evening Express* (Victoria), 26 October 1863; "Regina vs Lazar," *Victoria Colonist*, 23 December 1863.

94 "Police Court," *Vancouver Times*, 19, 21, and 28 February 1865, 12 and 14 March 1865; "Serious Accident," *Vancouver Times*, 29 December 1865; "Released," *Vancouver Times*, 27 September 1867; "Lazar of Sooke," March 1865, in British Columbia, Attorney General, *Documents*, no. 419, box 4, file 66/13.

95 "The Shooting Case at Sooke," *Vancouver Times*, 12 March 1865.

96 Johnson, *That Was Our Way*, 4.

97 St Andrew's Catholic Church, Victoria, *Baptismal, Marriage, and Death Records, 1849–1934*. Johnson, *That Was Our Way*, calls her Mary. Her surname is taken from children's baptisms.

98 Johnson, *That Was Our Way*, 4; *Sooke Story*, 175.

99 Andrew Lascar [*sic*], in "Meeting with Sooke Tribe on Sooke No. 1 Reserve," 11 June 1913, in British Columbia, "Royal Commission," 4, 6. See also *Sooke Story*, 178.

100 Conversation with author, Sooke Museum, 1–2 August 1978.

101 Elizabeth [Hunt] Wilson to Marius Barbeau, Fort Rupert, [1947], in Barbeau, *Marius Barbeau Fonds*, B-F-270, box B20.

102 See Myers, "Deep Ties."

CHAPTER SEVEN

1 Edward Moberly, 29 August 1980, quoted in Murphy, "Homesteading in the Athabasca," 148n4. Contemporaries variously spelled the surnames Karakontie, Waniyandie, and Joachim, putting down on paper what they heard orally. As well as in contemporary documents, the above spellings were preferred in 180 scrip records held in Library and Archives Canada that I examined in respect to the three families. See North-West Territories, *Scrip Applications*.

2 Letter of Pierre-Jean De Smet, Fort Jasper, 16 April 1846, in De Smet, *Life, Letters and Travels*, vol. 2, 536.

3 North West Company, HBCA, *Ledger (Account Books), 1811–1821*; North West Company, HBCA, *Iroquois Accounts, 1819*.

4 North West Company, HBCA, *Iroquois Accounts, 1819*; HBCA, *Fort Chipewyan, Alberta: Account Books, 1821–1822*, Iroquois and Freemen's Book. See also "Dunvegan Post Journal," cited in Nicks, "Demographic Anthropology," 140.

5 Letter of Pierre-Jean De Smet, 10 June 1849, in De Smet, *Life, Letters and Travels*, vol. 3, 1187. The other two were a family of seven "half-breeds" and "a Sioux with his wife and children," neither further identified.

6 Letter of Pierre-Jean De Smet, Fort Jasper, 16 April 1846, in De Smet, *Life, Letters and Travels*, vol. 2, 536–7.

7 Letter of Pierre-Jean De Smet, 6 May 1846, in ibid., 537–8.

8 Pierre-Jean De Smet to Jean Baptiste Thibault, 8 May 1846, in Missionary Oblates, *Grandin Archives*. I am grateful to Diane Lamoureux for drawing my attention to the letter and for providing me with a transcript and to Angie Friesen, both at the Provincial Archives of Alberta, for arranging a copy of the original.

9 Entry of 6 June 1817, in Cox, *Adventures on the Columbia River*, vol. 2, 205.

10 James Hector, "Journal," 12 January 1859, in Spry, *Papers of the Palliser Expedition*, 360–1.

11 Pierre-Jean De Smet to Jean Baptiste Thibault, 8 May 1846, in Missionary Oblates, *Grandin Archives*.

12 Masson, *Bourgeois*, vol. 1, 396; North West Company, *Men's Names*.

13 North West Company, HBCA, *Ledger (Account Books), 1811–1821*.

14 HBC, "St Mary's Post Journal, 1818–19," cited in Nicks, "Demographic Anthropology," 140; Nicks and Morgan, "Grande Cache," 165, 167; Deenik, Guest, and Wuorinen, *Legends of Grande Cache*, 65; Berry, "Recovered Identities," 328–9n50.

15 On Lisette Court-Oreille's Odawa background, see Berry, "Recovered Identities," 41–2.

16 North West Company, HBCA, *Ledger (Account Books), 1819–1821*; North West Company, HBCA, *Servant Balances, 1821*; HBCA, *Fort Chipewyan, Alberta: Account Books, 1821–1822*, Athabasca General Accounts. See also Nicks and Morgan, "Grande Cache," 167; and Nicks, "Demographic Anthropology," 138.

17 Also baptized were four children of a deceased Baptiste Gauche who were likely

part of the Gaucher family otherwise mentioned only in passing. On Calliou's origins, see Masson, *Bourgeois*, vol. 1, 398; and his initial employment contract, reproduced in Macpherson, *Sun Traveller*, 5–6. Calliou has been repeatedly conflated with Ignace Karakontie, who departed Lac des Deux Montagnes four years later than Calliou left Caughnawaga. For examples of this fusion, see Frisch, "Some Ethnological and Ethnohistoric Notes," 54–6, 60–2; Macpherson, *Sun Traveller*; Anderson, *First Metis*; Belcourt, *Walking in the Woods*; and the many online websites constructed on this premise. This linkage is discounted in Nicks, "Louis Callihoo"; and in Deenik, Guest, and Wuorinen, *Legends of Grande Cache*, 40–1, 72–3. As Macpherson, *Sun Traveller*, details, Calliou and Karakontie pursued very different life courses, with Calliou and then his son Michel favouring ongoing or intermittent fur trade employment across future Alberta and for a time legal status as Indigenous persons. For an oral account of 1903 originating with the family, see Gibbons, "Iroquois."

18 Colin Robertson to Andrew Colville and John Halkett, 31 January 1820, in Robertson, *Colin Robertson's Correspondence Book*, 109.

19 Ignace Giasson to Colin Robertson, 29 March 1820, in ibid., 272.

20 See HBC, "St Mary Post Journal," cited in Nicks, "Demographic Anthropology," 140. See also Nicks and Morgan, "Grande Cache," 165, 167; Deenik, Guest, and Wuorinen, *Legends of Grande Cache*, 65; Berry, "Recovered Identities," 328–9n50; and Wuorinen, *History of Grande Cache*, 38.

21 Entry of 9 June 1817, in Ross, *Adventures of the First Settlers*, 214.

22 Drummond, "Sketch," 192–3, 201, also 189.

23 Drummond, "From Mr Drummond," 112.

24 Entries of 1–3 October 1827, in HBCA, *Jasper House, Alberta: Post Journals, 1827–1831*, with added punctuation.

25 Entries of 4, 5, and 31 October 1827, in ibid., with added punctuation. The size of neither group is given in journal entries.

26 Entries of 24 and 26 April 1828, in ibid.

27 Entry of 24 October 1829, in ibid., with added punctuation.

28 Entries of 2–4 November 1829, in ibid., with added punctuation.

29 Entry of 19 October 1830, in ibid.

30 Entries of 14 and 16 December 1830, in ibid., with added punctuation.

31 Entries of 21–23 April 1831, in ibid., with added punctuation; Taylor, *Jasper*, 17.

32 Albert Lacombe, quoted in Johnstone, *Winter and Summer Excursions*, 110.

33 Albert Lacombe, quoted in ibid., 107–8.

34 Nicks, "Demographic Anthropology," 143.

35 De Smet was born in 1800 and Lacombe in 1827. The two encountered each other at Fort Edmonton in 1845. MacGregor, *Father Lacombe*, 80.

36 Albert Lacombe, quoted in Johnstone, *Winter and Summer Excursions*, 108.

37 Albert Lacombe, quoted in ibid.

38 See Moberly, *When Fur Was King*, 95.

39 Ibid., 32. Moberly may have become aware of these Iroquois's presence there while stationed as an apprentice clerk at nearby Rocky Mountain House in

1854–55 or at Fort Edmonton in 1855–56. The probable sequence of events is taken from Moberly's biographical sheet, in HBCA, *Biographical Sheets*; and from Murphy, "Homesteading in the Athabasca," 126–7.

40 Sawchuk, Sawchuk, and Ferguson, *Metis Land Rights*, 216.

41 Nicks, "Demographic Anthropology," 12, also 165.

42 Moberly, *When Fur Was King*, 62, 69–70, 94; James Hector, "Journal," 8 February 1859, in Spry, *Papers of the Palliser Expedition*, 377.

43 Moberly, *When Fur Was King*, 4–5, also 52 describing "Iroquois encamped" along the way.

44 Ibid., 94.

45 James Hector, "Journal," 9 February 1859, in Spry, *Papers of the Palliser Expedition*, 377–8.

46 Moberly, *When Fur Was King*, 95, also 96.

47 James Hector, "Journal," 29 January and 18 February 1859, in Spry, *Papers of the Palliser Expedition*, 370–3, 377–82, based in part on conversations with Moberly. Lynx were also sought, as noted in ibid., 371–2.

48 James Hector, "Journal," 20 April 1859, in ibid., 392.

49 Edward Moberly, 29 August 1980, quoted in Murphy, "Homesteading in the Athabasca," 131. On Suzanne Moberly's parentage, see ibid., 127.

50 Moberly, *When Fur Was King*, 48, with added punctuation.

51 Ibid. In his memoir, Moberly linked his departure to his resignation from the HBC on the death of his "friend and patron, Sir George Simpson." Ibid., 109.

52 Ron Pelletier, 15 February 2007, quoted in Taylor, *Jasper*, 21. See also Ouellet, "Tales of Empowerment," 54–6; and "Jasper Homesteaders 100 Years Later," *Jasper Fitzhugh*, 2 February 2011.

53 Edward Moberly, 29 August 1980, quoted in Murphy, "Homesteading in the Athabasca," 131.

54 James Hector, "Journal," 30 January 1859, in Spry, *Papers of the Palliser Expedition*, 367.

55 Erasmus, *Buffalo Days*, 92.

56 James Hector, "Journal," 31 January 1859, in Spry, *Papers of the Palliser Expedition*, 370–1.

57 Ibid., 372.

58 James Hector, "Journal," 2 February 1859, in ibid., 372–3.

59 Entries of 20 and 30 May and 4 June 1859, in Southesk, *Saskatchewan*, 28, 31, 35, 89. See also entries of 4 and 15 July, in ibid., 89, 90.

60 Entries of 9 and 24 August 1859, in ibid., 144–5, 173. See also entry of 28 August 1859, in ibid., 182.

61 Entry of 25 August 1859, in ibid., 176.

62 Entry of 28 August 1859, in ibid., 182.

63 See Frisch, "Some Ethnological and Ethnohistoric Notes," 58; and Berry, "Recovered Identities," 40–1.

64 Entries of 27 and 28 August 1859, in Southesk, *Saskatchewan*, 180–1.

65 The various items Southesk collected were auctioned in 2006, whereupon the Royal Alberta Museum acquired a good number of them with the assistance of

provincial government funding. See "Stories" and "Jasper's 'First Tourist' Returns," *Jasper Fitzhugh*, 20 May 2010.

66 Berry, "Recovered Identities," 39–43.

67 Entry of 28 August 1859, in Southesk, *Saskatchewan*, 182.

68 Entry of 29 August 1859, in ibid., 184.

69 Berry, "Recovered Identities," 44–5, makes this point respecting the Waniyandies.

70 Payne, "Fur Trade on the Upper Athabasca," 23–4.

71 Entry of 19 August 1859, in Southesk, *Saskatchewan*, 166–7.

72 Milton and Cheadle, *North-West Passage*, 243; entries of 15 and 18 July 1863, in Cheadle, *Cheadle's Journal*, 181, 184; Berry, "Recovered Identities," 44.

73 Moberly, *Rocks and Rivers*, 90–1.

74 Ibid., 94–5.

75 Entry of 28 July 1872, in Grant, *Ocean to Ocean*, 45, 48, 56, 58, 65.

76 Entry of early September 1872, in ibid., 237–8.

77 See Payne, "Fur Trade on the Upper Athabasca," 24; Pelletier and Ouellet, "Moberly Descendants Ignored."

78 Coleman, *Canadian Rockies*, 293.

79 Edmonton, "Correspondence Books," cited in Nicks, "Demographic Anthropology," 143.

80 Albert Lacombe, quoted in Johnstone, *Winter and Summer Excursions*, 110.

81 See Ouellet, "Tales of Empowerment," 71, 81–2; and Albert Norris, recorded by George Camp, cited in Taylor, *Jasper*, 27.

82 North-West Territories, *Scrip Applications*.

83 "An Act to Amend and Consolidate the Several Acts Respecting the Public Lands of the Dominion," 15 May 1879, sec. 125e, in *Consolidated Dominion Lands Act, 1879*.

84 See Ens and Sawchuk, *From New Peoples*, 131–216; and Sawchuk, Sawchuk, and Ferguson, *Metis Land Rights*, 92–158.

85 For the early definition, see "An Act to Remove Doubts as to the Construction of Section 31 of the Act 33 Victoria, Chapter 3," 3 May 1873, sec. 1, in *Acts of the Parliament*, 120

86 For a list of locations visited, see Nicks, "Demographic Anthropology," 87.

87 For two succinct summary statements, see Frisch, "Iroquois in the West," 544–5; and Buresi, "'Rendezvous' for Renewal," 72.

88 North-West Territories, *Scrip Applications*.

89 *Edmonton Bulletin*, 17 July 1899, quoted in Leonard, *Delayed Frontier*, 85. See also Mair, *Through the Mackenzie Basin*, 69–70. The unfortunate consequence is the omission of descendants no longer carrying one of the three surnames.

90 Nicks, *Iroquois Fur Trappers*, 22–5, tracks the pesence of the three core families, along with the Callious, among scrip applicants.

91 Louis, Patrick, and Madeleine Joaquim files, in North-West Territories, *Scrip Applications*, reels 14977, 14978.

92 Adam, Martin, and Marie Joaquim files, in ibid.

93 Notation on Louis Joaquim file, in ibid., reel 14977.

94 Baptiste Wan-yadie [Waniyandie] file, in ibid., reel 15009.

95 On Pierre Delorme's possible Iroquois descent and first family, see Deenik, Guest, and Wuorinen, *Legends of Grande Cache*, 77.

96 Baptisms included in Pierre Delorme file, in North-West Territories, *Scrip Applications*, reel 14962.

97 Suzanne Joaquim Delorme file, in ibid. See also Phillip and Pierre Delorme files, in ibid.

98 Simon Karaconti [Karakontie] file, in ibid., reel 15009.

99 James Waniyande [Waniyandie] file, in ibid. See also Peggy Karaconti [Karakontie] file, in ibid.

100 Pierre Grey, quoted in Pierre Delorme file, in ibid., reel 14962.

101 Isabelle Laurion Wun-yadie [Waniyandie] file, 1 June 1900, in ibid., reel 15010.

102 François Berland, respecting the scrip application of Martin Joaquim, in North-West Territories, *Scrip Applications*, reel 14977.

103 George Dawson, "Map Showing the Distribution of the Indian Tribes of British Columbia," 1884, in Bouchard and Kennedy, "DFN: Ethnohistorical Review," 110, also 111 for an image of the map itself.

104 Bouchard and Kennedy, "DFN: Ethnohistorical Review," 110, respecting the Treaty 8 map of 1900.

105 Summaries of applications, and also some complete files, can be searched on the Library and Archives Canada website. Nicks, "Demographic Anthropology," 140, makes the same point respecting frequent intermarriage across the generations.

106 For example, see Wuorinen, *History of Grande Cache*, 17. This topic is taken up generally in Barman, *French Canadians*.

107 Pike, *Barren Ground*, 253; Leonard, *Last Great West*, 61.

108 Pike, *Barren Ground*, 258, 294. Pike visited the branch of the family living in Hudson Hope in northeastern British Columbia.

109 Bouchard and Kennedy, "DFN: Ethnohistorical Review," iv, 6, 73, 79, 82–97.

110 Napoleon, ed., *Bushland Spirit*, 16–19, 31; Bouchard and Kennedy, "DFN: Ethnohistorical Review," 7.

111 Entry of 8 November 1897, in Moodie, "Instructions," 24.

112 Calverley, "Napoleon Thomas"; Calverley, "What Price Integration?"

113 Canada, Dominion Lands Branch, *British Columbia Township General Register*, documents respecting Napoleon Thomas; British Columbia, Land Title Registry, *Dominion Government Fiats*, documents respecting Napoleon Thomas.

CHAPTER EIGHT

1 Murphy, "Homesteading in the Athabasca," 150n26; J. Shand-Harvey, Park Ranger, to Forestry Branch, Department of the Interior, 21 October 1912, reproduced in Ouellet, "Tales of Empowerment," 116. This Cree descent is noted proudly in Aseniwuche Winewak Nation of Canada, "Our Story."

2 Havard, "French Half-Breeds," 318.

3 Gibbons, "Iroquois," 126.

4 Albert Lacombe, quoted in Johnstone, *Winter and Summer Excursions*, 110.

5 Buresi, "'Rendezvous' for Renewal," 168.

6 Adam Wenyandie, homestead application, 3 July 1905, in Alberta, *Homestead Records*.

7 Albert Lacombe, quoted in Johnstone, *Winter and Summer Excursions*, 110.

8 Edward Moberly, 29 August 1980, quoted in Murphy, "Homesteading in the Athabasca," 136.

9 Augustine Waniande, homestead application, 18 December 1901, in Alberta, *Homestead Records*.

10 Coleman, *Canadian Rockies*, 278.

11 Deenik, Guest, and Wuorinen, *Legends of Grande Cache*, 47; James Shand-Harvey to Mrs Peterson, 23 January 1967, in Shand-Harvey, *Papers*.

12 MacGregor, *Overland by the Yellowhead*, 123.

13 On uncertainty over the precise location, see C. Peterson to James Shand-Harvey, 29 October 1967, and James Shand-Harvey to Mrs Peterson, 14 November 1967, in Shand-Harvey, *Papers*. Isadore Findlay's grandfather was Jaco Finlay, prominent in the Pacific Northwest fur trade. See Barman, *French Canadians*.

14 Albert Lacombe, quoted in Johnstone, *Winter and Summer Excursions*, 110–11.

15 Murphy, "Homesteading in the Athabasca," 149n23; Landry, *"Grande Cache,"* 7. The residential school was in St Albert, and its Montreal successor was Collège Sainte-Thérèse.

16 Landry, *"Grande Cache,"* 8.

17 Coleman, *Canadian Rockies*, 276. Lewis Swift married Suzette Chalifoux in 1897 in the Edmonton area. Although Swift's year of arrival is sometimes given as 1893, he used 1894 in talking to Coleman. Ibid., 276. On Swift's background, see MacGregor, *Overland by the Yellowhead*, 124–5.

18 Coleman, *Canadian Rockies*, 278.

19 Ibid., 279, italics in original.

20 Ibid., 285.

21 Schäffer, *Old Indian Trails*, 307, 319. Her source of information was "Yellowhead Pass Route," written by James McEvoy and published by the Geological Survey of Canada in 1900. Ibid., 307n1. For Schäffer's background, see Beck, *No Ordinary Woman*.

22 Schäffer, *Old Indian Trails*, 317–18.

23 Edward Moberly, 29 August 1980, quoted in Murphy, "Homesteading in the Athabasca," 141.

24 Schäffer, *Old Indian Trails*, 327.

25 Coleman, *Canadian Rockies*, 302.

26 Ibid., 302–3.

27 Albert Moberly, cited in Murphy, "Homesteading in the Athabasca," 150n26.

28 Coleman, *Canadian Rockies*, 302–3.

29 Ibid., 303–4.

30 Ibid., 305–6.

31 Ibid., 307–8.

32 Ibid., 285.

33 Edward Moberly, 29 August 1980, quoted in Murphy, "Homesteading in the Athabasca," 133, 146.

34 Edward Moberly, quoted in ibid., 132–5.

35 Edward Moberly, quoted in ibid., 134, 137.

36 Schäffer, *Old Indian Trails*, 359.

37 Coleman, *Canadian Rockies*, 346.

38 For comparisons, see Barman, *Stanley Park's Secret*; Spence, *Dispossessing the Wilderness*; and Sandlos, "Not Wanted."

39 Taylor, *Jasper*, 40. See also Pelletier and Ouellet, "Moberly Descendants Ignored."

40 Taylor, *Jasper*, 40.

41 Murphy, "'Following the Base of the Foothills,'" 87–90.

42 Edward Moberly, 29 August 1980, quoted in Murphy, "Homesteading in the Athabasca," 137.

43 Binnema and Niemi, "'Let the Line Be Drawn Now,'" 734.

44 MacLaren, ed., *Culturing Wilderness*, xxvi. More generally, see also Spence, *Dispossessing the Wilderness*, on the removal of Indigenous peoples from American national parks.

45 Shand-Harvey, interview, in Hart, *History of Hinton*, 32. See also Shand-Harvey's written declaration, in ibid. Murphy, "Homesteading in the Athabasca," 128, emphasizes Swift's opposition to eviction.

46 Shand-Harvey, interview and written declaration, in Hart, *History of Hinton*, 32.

47 Edward Moberly, 29 August 1980, quoted in Murphy, "Homesteading in the Athabasca," 131.

48 Names and amounts are taken from a carbon copy of Minister of the Interior to Governor General, 6 April 1810, reproduced in Ouellet, "Tales of Empowerment," 119–20.

49 Edward Moberly, 29 August 1980, quoted in Murphy, "Homesteading in the Athabasca," 136.

50 MacLaren, ed., *Culturing Wilderness*, xln30. According to MacLaren, Swift's claim to the 151 acres he occupied is thought to have been filed by March 1910, with the grant itself dated 19 September 1911.

51 Taylor, *Jasper*, 29–33, 44–5. On Swift's having long "reigned the monarch of the lonely mountain empire," see Washburn, *Trails Trappers, and Tenderfeet*, 177, also 178, 187–99, 290–301.

52 Ron Pelletier, quoted in "Tell the Tale," *Jasper Fitzhugh*, 28 July 2010.

53 Hart, *History of Hinton*, 54.

54 Ibid., 54–5; Edward Moberly, 29 August 1980, quoted in Murphy, "Homesteading in the Athabasca," 131.

55 Quoted in ibid., 138–9.

56 MacGregor, *Pack Saddles*, 165, also 213–14 on Vincent Waniyandie's background.

57 James Shand-Harvey, quoted in ibid., 170.

58 Hart, *History of Hinton*, 54; Wuorinen, *History of Grande Cache*, 19.

59 Samuel Elliott Fay, 25 July 1914, quoted in Helm and Murtha, eds, *Forgotten Explorer*, 30–2.

60 Samuel Elliott Fay, 26 July 1914, quoted in ibid., 30–2.

61 Samuel Elliott Fay, 27 July 1914, quoted in ibid., 33, 32. The Smoky River was in flood. Ibid., xxiii.

62 Nicks, "Demographic Anthropology," 123.

63 Oral history, as detailed in Ouellet, "Tales of Empowerment," 82, also passim on the archeological dig.

64 MacLaren, "Rejuvenating Wilderness," 352, 368n66. The enigmatic Gaucher family was also named as not being compensated.

65 For families' location, see Hart, *History of Hinton*, 50.

66 Homestead applications of Modisti Wanyandie, 8 April 1913, Louis Wanyandi, 14 July 1913, and Isabelle Wanyandi, 24 December 1914, in Alberta, *Homestead Records*.

67 MacLaren, ed., *Culturing Wilderness*, xxvii. For more detail, see MacLaren, "Rejuvenating Wilderness," 352, 366–8.

68 J. Shand-Harvey, Park Ranger, to Forestry Branch, Department of the Interior, 21 October 1912, reproduced in Ouellet, "Tales of Empowerment," 117–18.

69 Ibid., 116.

70 On the pair's identity, see Pierre Delorme and Joseph Gaucher files, North-West Territories, *Scrip Applications*, reels 14962, 14971. On Pauline, see also Ewan Moberly, representing thirty-three families, including Pauline Joaquim, to Deputy Minister, Department of the Interior, 8 March 1917, reproduced in Ouellet, "Tales of Empowerment," 129–31.

71 See Pierre Delorme file, North-West Territories, *Scrip Applications*, reel 14962.

72 J. Shand-Harvey, Park Ranger, to Forestry Branch, Department of the Interior, 21 October 1912, reproduced in Ouellet, "Tales of Empowerment," 116.

73 Ibid., 117–18.

74 R.M. Brown, Forest Supervisor, to District Inspector of Forest Services, 1 November 1912, reproduced in Ouellet, "Tales of Empowerment," 118.

75 J. André Doucet, *Timber Conditions in the Smoky River Valley and Grande Prairie Country* (Forestry Branch Bulletin no. 53, 1915), 46, quoted in Nicks, "Demographic Anthropology," 183n46, also 141; Nicks and Morgan, "Grande Cache," 170.

76 Deenik, Guest, and Wuorinen, *Legends of Grande Cache*, 49–50; Wuorinen, *History of Grande Cache*, 34, 38.

77 C. McFayden to District Supervisor of Forestry Reserves in Calgary, 15 January 1916, reproduced in Ouellet, "Tales of Empowerment," 123.

78 Ibid.

79 Ibid., 123–4.

80 Deenik, Guest, and Wuorinen, *Legends of Grande Cache*, 45.

81 C. McFayden to District Supervisor of Forestry Reserves in Calgary, 15 January 1916, reproduced in Ouellet, "Tales of Empowerment," 125.

82 MacGregor, *Pack Saddles*, 227–8.

83 This action is reported in Ewan Moberly, representing thirty-three families, to Deputy Minister, Department of the Interior, 8 March 1917, reproduced in Ouellet, "Tales of Empowerment," 129.

84 Short & Cross to Secretary of the Department of the Interior, 30 December 1916, reproduced in Ouellet, "Tales of Empowerment," 126, 128.

85 Family heads are named in Ewan Moberly, representing thirty-three families, to Deputy Minister, Department of the Interior, 8 March 1917, reproduced in Ouellet, "Tales of Empowerment," 129–31.

86 C. McFayden to District Supervisor of Forestry Reserves in Calgary, 15 January 1917, reproduced in Ouellet, "Tales of Empowerment," 123–4.

87 Ewan Moberly, representing thirty-three families, to Deputy Minister, Department of the Interior, 8 March 1917, reproduced in Ouellet, "Tales of Empowerment," 130; and partly reproduced as Ewan Moberly et al. to Minister Roche via W.A. Cory, [March 1917], Library and Archives Canada, RG39, vol. 265, file 39578, in MacLaren, ed., *Culturing Wilderness*, xxix.

88 Dolphus Moberly to the Secretary of the Department of the Interior, 14 October 1920, reproduced in Ouellet, "Tales of Empowerment," 132.

89 W.W. Badgley, Forest Supervisor, Rocky Mountain Forest Reserve, to Federal Director of Forest Services, 18 January 1921, reproduced in Ouellet, "Tales of Empowerment," 133–4.

90 Ibid., 134.

91 For more contemporary examples, see "Jasper Homesteaders 100 Years Later," *Jasper Fitzhugh*, 2 February 2011.

92 District Forest Inspector for Alberta to Federal Director of Forest Services, 28 March 1921, reproduced in Ouellet, "Tales of Empowerment," 135.

93 R.E. Palmer, District Fire Ranger, to District Forest Inspector in Calgary, 26 January 1922, reproduced in Ouellet, "Tales of Empowerment," 137.

94 James Shand-Harvey, quoted in MacGregor, *Pack Saddles*, 229.

95 Murphy, "Homesteading in the Athabasca," 128. See also Ouellette, "Tales of Empowerment," 48.

96 See Nadasdy, *Hunters and Bureaucrats*, for a similar sequence of events.

97 Glen, *Mountain Trails*, 39–40.

98 Ibid., 68.

99 Edward Moberly, 29 August 1980, cited in Murphy, "Homesteading in the Athabasca," 138–40; Edward Moberly, cited in Hart, *History of Hinton*, 53–6.

100 MacLaren, ed., *Culturing Wilderness*, xxii.

101 MacGregor, *Pack Saddles*, 149.

102 Edward Moberly, 29 August 1980, quoted in Murphy, "Homesteading in the Athabasca," 130.

103 See Hart, *History of Hinton*, 45, 48–9, 55–6, including accounts of famous visitors; and Deenik, Guest, and Wuorinen, *Legends of Grande Cache*, 79–80, 179–80. The movie, in which Felix Waniyandie and Joe Moberly also appeared, was director Otto Preminger's *River of No Return* (1954).

104 Kreg O. Sky Fonds, *Taped Interviews*.

105 Oliver Travers, interview, in ibid., with ellipses in the original indicating hesitations.

106 Frank Burstrom, interview, in ibid.

107 Ken Allen, interview, in ibid.

108 Mark and Agnes Truxler, interview, in ibid. Eugene Merrill was similarly accepting of Edward Moberly.

109 Sharlow and Wuorinen, *Grande Cache*, 118–19.

110 Deenik, Guest, and Wuorinen, *Legends of Grande Cache*, 64.

111 Wilson and Morrison, "Grande Cache," 365.

112 James Shand-Harvey, quoted in MacGregor, *Pack Saddles*, 230.

113 Ibid., 221.

114 Nicks and Morgan, "Grande Cache," 170–1.

115 MacGregor, *Pack Saddles*, 222. On women as trappers, see Ouellet, "Life and Death," 62, 64.

116 On this point, see Sawchuk, Sawchuk, and Ferguson, *Metis Land Rights*, 187, also 187–239 for their excellent analysis of the topic generally.

117 Ens and Sawchuk, *From New Peoples*, 382.

118 Sawchuk, Sawchuk, and Ferguson, *Metis Land Rights*, 218–20.

119 By the mid-1970s these voters were part of the newly minted community of Grande Cache and were listed without occupations, as had become routine on voters' lists. See Canada, *Voters Lists, 1935–1980*.

120 Wuorinen, *History of Grande Cache*, 20–1; Deenik, Guest, and Wuorinen, *Legends of Grande Cache*, 72. Possibly due to the remoteness of the location, numerous Kakwa residents had returned south by the end of the 1960s.

121 *Along the Wapiti*, 13, also 12–15.

122 Mable Moberly Tennant, interview, 2002, in Kakwa/Two Lakes Oral Histories, *Taped Interviews*.

123 Morrison, "Stress," 131, 219, also 282 and for a chronology of events to 1972, 418–24.

124 Provincial Planning Board, "Report and Recommendations to the Lieutenant Governor in Council for the New Town Status of Cache Creek, Alberta," August 1966, reproduced in Morrison, "Stress," 425–51, with the reference at 438.

125 Wilson and Morrison, "Grande Cache," 365, 369.

126 Sawchuk, Sawchuk, and Ferguson, *Metis Land Rights*, 224; Morrison, "Stress," 157–9.

127 Nicks, "Demographic Anthropology," 122–3; Morrison, "Stress," 159, 294; Wilson and Morrison, "Grande Cache," 369–71.

128 Nicks and Morgan, "Grande Cache," 163–4.

129 Morrison, "Stress," 160; Wilson and Morrison, "Grande Cache," 370–3.

130 Frisch, "Some Ethnological and Ethnohistoric Notes," 58.

131 Anderson, *First Metis*, 64.

132 Douglas Tennant, interview, 2002, in Kakwa/Two Lakes Oral Histories, *Taped Interviews*.

133 Morrison, "Stress," 219.

134 Ouellet, "Tales of Empowerment," 82. See also Sawchuk, Sawchuk, and Ferguson, *Metis Land Rights*, 226.

135 Morrison, "Stress," 180, also 187.

136 On the ensuing complications respecting provision of schooling, see ibid., 293, 304–6, 343–4.

137 Ibid., 162, 282.

138 For details on the sequence of events, see Sawchuk, Sawchuk, and Ferguson, *Metis Land Rights*, 226–40; Morrison, "Stress," 283–326; and Wilson and Morrison, "Grande Cache," 371–2.

139 The two individuals were Allen Joaquim and Kelly Joaquim, as noted in Sawchuk, Sawchuk, and Ferguson, *Metis Land Rights*, 229.

140 Morrison, "Stress," 325. See also Wilson and Morrison, "Grande Cache," 372–6.

141 On aspects of this point, see Sawchuk, Sawchuk, and Ferguson, *Metis Land Rights*, 228, 230, 232. For some comparable historical uses of adverse possession, see Barman, *Stanley Park's Secret*, 124–7, 175–8, 207–11, passim.

142 The signatories to the six agreements were as follows: for Grande Cache Lake Enterprises and Kamisak Development Co., Walter Moberly, Collin Moberly, Joe Karakontie, Milton Joachim, and Bellamy Joachim, as well as six minor Joachims, along with eight other adults, two of whom signed with their marks, and fourteen minors; for Joachim Enterprises, Alice Joachim with her mark, Victoria Joaquim, Audrey Mary Joachim with her mark, Leola Moberly with her mark, along with three minor Moberlys; for Susa Creek Co-operative Limited, Dean Wanyandie and Malcom Moberly; for Wanyandie Co-operative Limited, Kelly Joachim and Tom Wanyandie; for Muskeg Seepee Co-operative Limited, Paul Moberly and Delorme Findlay; and for Victor Lake Co-operative Limited, Charles Delorme and Dan Hicock[?]. The contracts are reproduced in Morrison, "Stress," 366–404.

143 Wilson and Morrison, "Grande Cache," 374.

144 Deenik, Guest, and Wuorinen, *Legends of Grande Cache*, 46. For an example of one of the leases, see Sawchuk, Sawchuk, and Ferguson, *Metis Land Rights*, 262–4.

145 Nicks, *Iroquois Fur Trappers*, 29. See also Wilson and Morrison, "Grande Cache," 374–6; and for a map, Morrison, "Stress," 315.

146 *Along the Wapiti*, 14.

147 Nicks, *Iroquois Fur Trappers*, 29–30; Nicks, "Demographic Anthropology," 138, also figure at 139; Nicks and Morgan, "Grande Cache," 167–8. Nicks, "Demographic Anthropology," 138, includes the Delormes and McDonalds, to make five originating families, which is numerically countered by her limiting Karconti descendants to the Moberlys. When unions did not occur with each other, Nicks notes, they "were most often with descendants of other fur company employees or freemen," and only from the 1950s were they sometimes with outsiders.

148 Morrison, "Stress," 219.

149 See Landry, "*Grande Cache*," 5, 18.

150 Wuorinen, *History of Grande Cache*, 88; Deenik, Guest, and Wuorinen, *Legends of Grande Cache*, 79.

151 Landry, *"Grande Cache,"* 2–3, 8–9, 11, 13.

152 Nicolas Roué, quoted in Landry, *"Grande Cache,"* 13–15, italics in original. Nose Creek had two family heads. One was Alex Moberly, who was married to Emily Joaquim, a daughter of Dave and Adelaide Joaquim. Alex and Emily had ten children. The other family head, Peter Karakontie, was a widower with a large number of children, some already adults, and with a brother, Albert, who lived on his own. Ibid., 14–16.

153 Morrison, "Stress," 281–2.

154 Landry, *"Grande Cache,"* 5–6.

155 See Ouellet, "Tales of Empowerment," 79–104, which includes oral testimony toward this end.

156 Dale Desjarlais, quoted in "Stories Seldom Told," *Jasper Fitzhugh*, 30 June 2010.

157 Deenik, Guest, and Wuorinen, *Legends of Grande Cache*, 39.

158 Doire, "Descendant from the Fur Trade," 11. On families' continuity, see Wuorinen, *History of Grande Cache*, 30.

159 *Along the Wapiti*, 13, referring to Joaquims, Karakonties, and Moberlys at Nose Creek.

RESEARCH NOTE

1 For examples of French usage, see "Treaty of Peace between the Iroquois and Governor de Tracy," 25 May 1666, in Brodhead, ed., *Documents*, vol. 3, 121–5; Monsieur de Denonville to Governor Edmund Andros, 23 October 1688, in Brodhead, ed., *Documents*, vol. 3, 569; and "Interpretation of Three Belts Sent by the Five Nations to the Governor of Canada," January 1693, in Brodhead, ed., *Documents*, vol. 4, 79.

2 On the various names by which Caughnawaga was known, see Jennings et al., eds, *History and Culture*, 217. On St Régis's origins, see Reid, *Khanawà:ke*, 12.

3 For early English use of "Mahauke," see "Relation of the March of the Governor of Canada into New-York," [1666], in Brodhead, ed., *Documents*, vol. 2, 118–19. For early English use of "Mowhawke" and "Mohawke," see Samuel Willis to Colonel Nicolls, 11 June 1666, in Brodhead, ed., *Documents*, vol. 2, 120–1. For early English use of "Mohawk," see Colonel Nicolls to the Council of Massachusetts, 6 July 1666, in Brodhead, ed., *Documents*, vol. 2, 120. For Dutch use of "Mohawk," see La Montagne and Jeremias van Reneslaer to P. Stuyvesant, 14 July 1664, in Brodhead, ed., *Documents*, vol. 2, 371–2. For Dutch use of "Mohakuaas," "Mahakas," and "Mohawk," see John Megapolensis, "A Full Account of the Maquaas Indians," 1644, in Hazard, *Historical Collections*, vol. 1, 520, 522.

4 For an early example of English use of "Five Nations," see "Propositions of the Schaghticoke and Five Nations of Indians, etc.," in Brodhead, ed., *Documents*, vol. 4, 40, 42, 44. For English use of "League," see "Conference between the

Governor of Pennsylvania and the Five Nations," 7 September 1722, in Brodhead, ed., *Documents*, vol. 5, 678. For English use of "League" and "Six Nations,"
see Brodhead, ed., *Documents*, vol. 5, 687. For English use of "Confederacy," see
"Conference between Major-General Johnson and the Indians," 21 June 1755,
in Brodhead, ed., *Documents*, vol. 6, 964–88; and Brodhead, ed., *Documents*,
vol. 7, 13–28.

5 Reverend Father Millet to the Reverend Mr. Dellius, 31 July 1693, in Brodhead,
ed., *Documents*, vol. 4, 49.

6 Earl of Bellomont to Count de Frontenac, 13 August 1698, in Brodhead, ed.,
Documents, vol. 4, 367.

7 Colden, *History of the Five Indian Nations*, xvi.

8 Governor [William] Tryon to the Earl of Dartmouth, 5 January 1773, in
Brodhead, ed., *Documents*, vol. 8, 344.

9 The designations are taken from Canada, Department of Indian Affairs,
Annual Reports, 1864–1990. Lozier, "In Each Other's Arms," 165, argues against
such usage.

10 See Sossoyan, "Kahnawake Iroquois," 18. On the current preference for the
term "Mohawk," see Alfred, *Heeding the Voices*. On its use retrospectively, see
Shannon, *Indians and Colonists*.

11 Lozier, "In Each Other's Arms," 165, argues against such usage.

12 Watson, *Lives Lived*; Voyageur Contracts Database. The database is introduced
in St-Onge, "Early Forefathers"; St-Onge, "'He Was Neither'"; and Grabowski
and St-Onge, "Montreal Iroquois *Engagés*."

13 As well as the Hudson's Bay Company, among North West Company share-
holder offshoots or competitors hiring Iroquois on surviving contracts nota-
rized in Montreal were Alexander Mackenzie & Co.; Charles Oakes Ermatinger;
McTavish, Frobisher & Co., which as of 1788 controlled half of the NWC
shares; McTavish, Frobisher & Co. et John Ogilvy et Thomas Thain; McTavish,
McGillivrays & Co., being the former McTavish, Frobisher & Co.; McTavish,
McGillivrays & Co. and Alexander McKenzie; McTavish, McGillivrays & Co.
and Kenneth McKenzie; McTavish, McGillivrays & Co. et John Ogilvy and
Thomas Thain; McTavish, McGillivrays & Co. & Pierre de Rocheblave;
McTavish, McGillivrays & Co. et Thomas Thain and Alexander MacKenzie;
Mess. De la Compagnie de Michilimackinac; New North West Company;
Parker Gerrard Ogilvy & Co.; Stansfield et Ross; Thomas Thain; Thomas
Thain Ecuier; and XY Company. Company names are taken from the Voyageur
Contracts Database.

14 Given that the Voyageur Contracts Database is searchable online by name, further information is readily accessible on these persons or on others mentioned
in the text, so separate endnotes are not provided for this information unless a
contract is directly quoted.

15 North West Company, Hudson's Bay Company Archives (HBCA), *Ledger
(Account Books), 1811–1821*.

16 North West Company, HBCA, *Ledger (Account Books), 1819–1821*.

17 HBCA, *Fort Chipewyan, Alberta: Account Books, 1821–1825*, Athabasca District.

18 HBCA, *Fort George, Oregon: Account Books, 1820–1822*.
19 HBCA, *Fort Victoria, British Columbia: Correspondence Books, 1864–1870*; HBC, *Fort Langley Journals*; HBCA, *Fort St James, British Columbia: Post Journals, 1820–1856*; HBCA, *Jasper House, Alberta: Post Journals, 1827–1831*; HBC, *Journal of Occurrences at Fort Nisqually*; HBC, Nanaimo Archives, *Nanaimo Correspondence*; HBC, Nanaimo Archives, *Nanaimo Journal*; HBCA, *Snake Country, Idaho, Montana, and Oregon: Post Journal, 1824*.
20 See Alfred, *Heeding the Voices*, 200nn3–4.
21 Greer, *Mohawk Saint*, xi, makes this point respecting surnames.
22 Caughnawaga, *Census, 1825*; Caughnawaga, *Census, 1831*; Oka, *Census, 1825*; St Régis, *Census, 1825*. No 1831 census survives, or one was not taken, for St Régis (Akwesasne).

Bibliography

Acts of the Parliament of the United Kingdom of Great Britain and Ireland. Ottawa: Brown Chamberlin, 1873.

Alberta. *Homestead Records, 1870–1930*. https://search.ancestry.com/search/db.aspx?dbid=60865.

Alfred, Gerald Taiaiake. *Heeding the Voices of Our Ancestors: Kahnawake Mohawk Politics and the Rise of Native Nationalism*. Toronto: Oxford University Press, 1995.

Allan, George T. "Reminiscences of Fort Vancouver on Columbia River, Oregon, as It Stood in 1832." In *Transactions of the Ninth Annual Reunion of the Oregon Pioneer Association for the Year 1881*, 75–80. Salem, OR: E.M. Waite, Steam Printer and Bookbinder, 1882.

Along the Wapiti. Grand Prairie, AB: Wapiti River Historical Society, 1981.

Andersen, Chris. *"Métis": Race, Recognition, and the Struggle for Indigenous Peoplehood*. Vancouver: UBC Press, 2014.

Anderson, Anne. *The First Metis: A New Nation*. Edmonton: Uvisco, 1985.

Anderson, William Marshall. *The Rocky Mountain Journals of William Marshall Anderson: The West in 1834*. Ed. Dale L. Morgan and Eleanor Towles Harris. San Marino, CA: Huntington Library, 1967.

Aquila, Richard. *The Iroquois Restoration: Iroquois Diplomacy on the Colonial Frontier*. Detroit: Wayne State University Press, 1983.

Armour, David Arthur. "The Merchants of Albany, New York: 1686–1760." PhD diss., Northwestern University, 1965.

Aseniwuche Winewak Nation of Canada. "Our Story." https://www.aseniwuche.ca/our-story.

Barbeau, Marius. "Frederick Alexie, a Primitive." *Canadian Review of Music and Art* 3, nos 11–12 (1945): 19–22.

– *Marius Barbeau Fonds*. Canadian Museum of History.

Barman, Jean. *Abenaki Daring: The Life and Writing of Noel Annance, 1792–1869*. Montreal and Kingston: McGill-Queen's University Press, 2016.

– *French Canadians, Furs, and Indigenous Women in the Making of the Pacific Northwest*. Vancouver: UBC Press, 2014.

– *Stanley Park's Secret: The Forgotten Families of Whoi Whoi, Kanaka Ranch, and Brockton Point*. Madeira Park, BC: Harbour, 2005.

– "Taming Aboriginal Sexuality: Gender, Power, and Race in British Columbia, 1850–1900." *BC Studies: The British Columbian Quarterly*, nos 115–16 (1997–98): 237–66.

Barman, Jean, and Bruce McIntyre Watson. *Leaving Paradise: Indigenous Hawaiians in the Pacific Northwest, 1787–1898*. Honolulu: University of Hawai'i Press, 2006.

Barr, Daniel P. *Unconquered: The Iroquois League at War in Colonial America*. Westport, CT: Praeger, 2006.

Bate, Mark. "The Men Who Helped to Build Nanaimo." *Nanaimo Free Press*, 23 March 1907.

Beck, Janice Sanford. *No Ordinary Woman: The Story of Mary Schäffer Warren*. Calgary: Rocky Mountain Books, 2001.

Béchard, Henri. *Original Caughnawaga Indians*. Montreal: International Publishers, 1967.

Belcourt, Herb. *Walking in the Woods: A Métis Journey*. Victoria, BC: Brindle and Glass, 2006.

Benn, Carl. *Mohawks on the Nile: Natives among the Canadian Voyageurs in Egypt, 1884–1885*. Toronto: Dundurn, 2009.

Berreman, J.Y. "Field Notes and Various Documents: Research Concerning Cultural Adjustments of the Grand Ronde Indian Tribes Obtained during the Summer of 1924." Typescript. National Archives Regional Facility, Seattle.

Berry, Susan. "Recovered Identities: Four Métis Artists in Nineteenth-Century Rupert's Land." In Sarah Carter and Patricia A. McCormack, eds, *Recollecting: Lives of Aboriginal Women of the Canadian Northwest and Borderlands*, 29–59, 321–40. Edmonton: Athabasca University Press, 2011.

Berton, Pierre. *Pierre Berton's War of 1812*. Toronto: Anchor, 2011.

Bidwell, John. "The First Emigrant Train to California." *Century Illustrated Magazine* 41, no. 1 (1890): 106–29.

Bigart, Robert, and Clarence Woodcock, eds. *In the Name of the Salish and Kootenai Nation: The 1855 Hell Gate Treaty and the Origin of the Flathead Indian Reservation*. Pablo, MO: Salish Kootenai College Press, 1996.

Binnema, Ted, and Gerhard J. Ens, eds. *Edmonton House Journals, Correspondence, and Reports, 1806–1821*. Edmonton: Alberta Records Publication Board, 2012.

Binnema, Ted, and Melanie Niemi. "'Let the Line Be Drawn Now': Wilderness, Conservation, and the Exclusion of Aboriginal People from Banff National Park in Canada." *Environmental History* 11, no. 4 (2006): 724–50.

Blanchard, David. "Entertainment, Dance and Northern Mohawk Showmanship." *American Indian Quarterly* 7, no. 1 (1983): 2–26.

– "High Steel: The Kahnawake Mohawk and the High Construction Trade." *Journal of Ethnic Studies* 11, no. 2 (2003): 41–60.

– "Patterns of Tradition and Change: The Re-creation of Iroquois Culture at Kahnawake." PhD diss., University of Chicago, 1982.

Boas, Franz, and James Teit. *Coeur d'Alene, Flathead and Okanogan Indians*. 1930. Reprint, Fairfield, WA: Ye Galleon, 1985.

Bonaparte, Darren. "The History of Akwesasne from Pre-Contact to Modern Times." *Wampum Chronicles*. http://www.forgottenwaronline.org/?p=811.

Bouchard, Randy, and Dorothy Kennedy. "DFN: Ethnohistorical Review." In *Site C Clean Energy Project: Volume 5, Appendix A07, Part 5*. Vancouver: BC Hydro Power

and Authority, 2013. https://www.ceaa-acee.gc.ca/050/documents_staticpost/
63919/85328/Vol5_Appendix-Duncan.pdf.

Brandâo, José António. *"Your Fyre Shall Burn No More": Iroquois Policy toward New
France and Its Native Allies to 1701.* Lincoln: University of Nebraska Press, 1997.

British Columbia. *Colonial Correspondence.* BC Archives, GR1372.

– "Royal Commission on Indian Affairs for the Province of British Columbia, 1913–
16." Typescript. Coqualeetza Education Centre, Chilliwack, British Columbia.

British Columbia, Attorney General. *Documents.* BC Archives, GR419.

– *Victoria Gaol Records.* BC Archives, GR308, vols 3, 7, 9, 10.

British Columbia, Department of Lands and Works. *Pre-emption Records for West
Coast Land, 1861–1886.* BC Archives, GR766.

British Columbia, Division of Vital Statistics. *Birth, Baptismal, Marriage, and Death
Records.* BC Archives, GR2951.

British Columbia, Land Title Registry. *Dominion Government Fiats, 446074–450655.*
LTSA5604, documents respecting Napoleon Thomas.

British Columbia, Supreme Court. *Probated Files.* BC Archives, GR1304.

– *Probated Wills.* BC Archives, GR1052.

Brodhead, John Romeyn, ed. *Documents Relative to the Colonial History of the State
of New-York.* 15 vols. Albany, NY: Weed, Parsons and Company, 1853–87.

Brosnan, Cornelius J. *Jason Lee: Prophet of the New Oregon.* New York: Macmillan,
1932.

Brown, Ellsworth Howard. "The History of the Flathead Indians in the Nineteenth
Century." PhD diss., Michigan State University, 1975.

Brown, Robert. "The First Journey of Exploration across Vancouver Island." 4 parts.
In H.W. Bates, ed., *Illustrated Travels: A Record of Discovery, Geography, and Adventure,* 254–5, 274–6, 302–4, 349–51. London: Cassell, Petter and Galpin, n.d.

– *The Races of Mankind: Being a Popular Description of the Characteristics, Manners
and Customs of the Principal Varieties of the Human Family.* 4 vols. London:
Cassell, Petter and Galpin, 1873–76.

– *Robert Brown and the Vancouver Island Exploring Expedition.* Ed. John Hayman.
Vancouver: UBC Press, 1989.

– *Robert Brown Collection.* BC Archives, MS-0794.

Bruemmer, Fred. "The Caughnawagas." *The Beaver,* no. 296 (1965): 4–11.

Buckley, Cornelius M. *Nicolas Point: His Life and Northwest Indian Chronicles.*
Chicago: Loyola University Press, 1989.

Buresi, Jessica Anne. "'Rendezvous' for Renewal at 'Lake of the Great Spirit': The
French Pilgrimage and Indigenous Journey to Lac Ste. Anne, Alberta, 1870–1896."
MA thesis, University of Calgary, 2012.

Butler, William Francis. *The Great Lone Land: A Narrative of Travel and Adventure
in the North-West of America.* 7th ed. London: Sampson Low, Martson, Low, and
Searle, 1875.

Calverley, Dorothea. "Napoleon Thomas – First Settler in the Dawson Creek District." South Peace Historical Society. http://calverley.ca/article/4-001-napoleon-
thomas-first-settler-in-the-dawson-creek-district/.

– "What Price Integration? Napoleon Thomas' Hassle with White Red Tape." South Peace Historical Society. http://calverley.ca/article/01-128-what-price-integration-napoleon-thomas-hassle-with-white-red-tape/.

Campbell, Robert. "A Narrative of Col. Robert Campbell's Experiences in the Rocky Mountain Fur Trade from 1825 to 1835." Missouri Historical Society.

Campbell, William J. *Speculators in Empire: Iroquoia and the 1768 Treaty of Fort Stanwix.* Norman: University of Oklahoma Press, 2012.

Canada. *Census of Canada, 1881.* Online at Library and Archives Canada.

– *Census of Canada, 1891.* Online at Library and Archives Canada.

– *Census of Canada, 1901.* Online at Library and Archives Canada.

– "Report of the Special Commissioners Appointed on the 8th of September, 1856, to Investigate Indian Affairs in Canada." In *Journal of the Legislative Assembly of the Province of Canada,* vol. 16, 1858, appendix.

– *Voters Lists, 1935–1980.* https://search.ancestry.ca/search/db.aspx?dbid=2983.

Canada, Department of Indian Affairs. *Annual Reports, 1864–1990.* Online at Library and Archives Canada.

Canada, Dominion Lands Branch. *British Columbia Township General Register Covering West of the 8th Meridian, Range 16, Township 77, to Range 16, Township 88, 1885–1930.* Library and Archives Canada, GR 8435, series 2, vol. 31, documents respecting Napoleon Thomas.

Canada, Indian Department. *Pre-Confederation Records.* Library and Archives Canada, RG10.

Carey, Charles Henry. "The Mission Record Book of the Methodist Episcopal Church, Willamette Station, Oregon Territory, North America, Commenced 1834." *Oregon Historical Review* 23, no. 3 (1922): 230–66.

Carriker, Robert C. *Father Peter John De Smet: Jesuit in the West.* Norman: University of Oklahoma Press, 1995.

Catlin, George. *Letters and Notes of the Manners, Customs, and Conditions of the North American Indians.* 2 vols. Philadelphia: J.W. Bradley, 1859.

Caughnawaga. *Census, 1825.* Online on FamilySearch under Canada, Lower Canada Census, 1825, Huntingdon, Sault St Louis. https://www.familysearch.org/search/collection/1834346.

– *Census, 1831.* Online on FamilySearch under Canada, Lower Canada Census, 1831, Laprairie, Caughnawaga. https://www.familysearch.org/search/collection/1834329.

Chamberlain, Alexander F. "Iroquois in Northwestern Canada." *American Anthropologist,* n.s., 6, no. 4 (1904): 459–63.

Cheadle, Walter B. *Cheadle's Journal of Trip across Canada, 1862–1863.* 1931. Reprint, Edmonton: M.G. Hurtig, 1971.

Colden, Cadwallader. *The History of the Five Indian Nations of Canada.* London: T. Osborne, 1747.

Coleman, A.P. *The Canadian Rockies: New and Old Trails.* London: T. Fisher Unwin, 1911.

Consolidated Dominion Lands Act, 1879. http://eco.canadiana.ca/view/oocihm.9_03749/3?r=0&s=1.

Coues, Elliott, ed. *New Light on the Early History of the Greater Northwest: The Manuscript Journals of Alexander Henry and of David Thompson.* 2 vols. New York: Francis P. Harper, 1897.

"Courts of Justice for the Indian Country." In Douglas Brymner, *Report on Canadian Archives, 1892,* 136–46. Ottawa: S.E. Dawson, 1893.

Courville, Serge. *Entre ville et campagne: L'essor du village dans les seigneuries du Bas-Canada.* Quebec City: Les Presses de l'Université Laval, 1990.

Cox, Ross. *Adventures on the Columbia River.* 2 vols. London: Henry Colburn and Richard Bentley, 1831.

De Kay, James E. *Zoology of New York, or The New York Fauna.* Part 1. New York: n.p., 1842.

De Smet, Pierre-Jean. *Life, Letters and Travels of Father Pierre-Jean De Smet, S.J., 1801–1873.* Ed. Hiram Martin Chittenden and Alfred Talbot Richardson. 4 vols. 1905. Reprint, New York: Arno Press and the New York Times, 1969.

Deenik, J., R. Guest, and R. Wuorinen. *Legends of Grande Cache and the Yellowhead.* Grande Cache, AB: Grande Cache Historical Society, 2002.

Demos, John. *The Unredeemed Captive: A Family Story from Early America.* New York: Alfred A. Knopf, 1994.

Dempsey, Hugh A. "David Thompson's Journeys in Idaho." *Washington Historical Quarterly* 11, nos 2–3 (1920): 97–103, 163–73.

Dennis, Matthew. *Cultivating a Landscape of Peace: Iroquois-European Encounters in Seventeenth-Century America.* Ithaca, NY: Cornell University Press, 1993.

Devine, E.J. *Historic Caughnawaga.* Montreal: Messenger, 1922.

Doire, Edna. "A Descendant from the Fur Trade Joins the Willmore Foundation." In Wilmore Wilderness Foundation, Grande Cache, Alberta, *Annual Newsletter,* 2014, 11.

The Donation Land Claim Act (1850). College of Education, University of Oregon. http://pages.uoregon.edu/mjdennis/courses/hst469_donation.htm.

Drummond, Thomas. "From Mr Drummond." *Edinburgh Journal of Science* 6 (1827): 110–13.

– "Sketch of a Journey to the Rocky Mountains and to the Columbia River of North America." *Botanical Miscellany* (London) 1 (1830): 178–219.

Engelbrecht, William. *Iroquoia: The Development of a Native World.* Syracuse, NY: Syracuse University Press, 2003.

Ens, Gerhard J., and Joe Sawchuk. *From New Peoples to New Nations: Aspects of Métis History and Identity from the Eighteenth to Twenty-First Centuries.* Toronto: University of Toronto Press, 2016.

Erasmus, Peter. *Buffalo Days and Nights.* Calgary: Fifth House, 1999.

Ermatinger, Francis. *Fur Trade Letters of Francis Ermatinger.* Ed. Lois Halliday McDonald. Glendale, CA: Arthur H. Clark, 1980.

Evans, Mike, Jean Barman, Gabrielle Legault, and Erin Dolmage. "Métis Networks in British Columbia: Examples from the Central Interior." In Nicole St-Onge, Carolyn Podruchny, and Brenda Macdougall, eds, *Contours of a People: Métis Family, Mobility, and History,* 331–67. Norman: University of Oklahoma Press, 2012.

Ewers, John C. *Gustavus Sohon's Portraits of Flathead and Pend d'Oreille Indians, 1854.* Washington, DC: Smithsonian Institution, 1948.

– "Iroquois Indians in the Far West." *Montana: The Magazine of Western History* 13, no. 2 (1963): 2–10.

Fahey, John. *The Flathead Indians.* Norman: University of Oklahoma Press, 1974.

Fenton, William N. *The Great Law and the Longhouse: A Political History of the Iroquois Confederacy.* Norman: University of Oklahoma Press, 1988.

Ferris, Warren Angus. *Life in the Rocky Mountains.* Ed. Leroy A. Hafen. Denver: Rosenstock, 1983. Originally published as a serial in *Western Literary Messenger* (Buffalo), 13 July 1842 to 4 May 1844.

Francis, Daniel, and Toby Morantz. *Partners in Furs: A History of the Fur Trade in Eastern James Bay, 1600–1870.* Montreal and Kingston: McGill-Queen's University Press, 1983.

Franklin, John. *Sir John Franklin's Journals and Correspondence: The Second Arctic Land Expedition, 1825–1827.* Ed. Richard C. Davis. Toronto: Champlain Society, 1998.

Frisch, Jack A. "Iroquois in the West." In Bruce G. Trigger, ed., *Handbook of North American Indians,* vol. 15, *Northeast,* 544–6. Washington, DC: Smithsonian Institution, 1978.

– "Revitalization, Nativism, and Tribalism among the St Regis Mohawks." PhD diss., Indiana University, 1970.

– "Some Ethnological and Ethnohistoric Notes on the Iroquois in Alberta." *Man in the Northeast* 12 (1976): 51–64.

– "Tribalism among the St Regis Mohawks: A Search for Self-Identity." *Anthropologica,* n.s., 12, no. 2 (1970): 207–19.

Fulford, Ted. "Spell of Metchosin." *Victoria Colonist,* 7 January 1962.

Gandy, Shawna Lea. "Fur Trade Daughters of the Oregon Country: Students of the Sisters of Notre Dame de Namur, 1850." MA thesis, Portland State University, 2004.

Garraghan, Gilbert J. *Catholic Beginnings in Kansas City, Missouri: An Historical Sketch.* Chicago: Loyola University Press, 1920.

– *The Jesuits of the Middle United States.* Vol. 2. New York: America Press, 1938.

Gass, Henry. "A Proud Tradition Goes Up in Smoke." *Globe and Mail,* 24 August 2013.

Gates, Charles M., ed. *Five Fur Traders of the Northwest.* St Paul: Minnesota Historical Society, 1965.

Gervais, Joseph. *Letters, 1836–1837.* Oregon Historical Society Research Library, mss 83.

Gibbons, James. "Iroquois in the North West Territories." *Annual Archaeological Report* (Toronto), 1903, 125–6.

Glen, Jack, Sr. *Mountain Trails: Memoirs of an Alberta Forest Ranger in the Mountains and Foothills of the Athabasca Forest, 1920–45.* Hinton, AB: Foothills Research Institute, 2008.

Gordon, Irene Tiernier. *The Laird of Fort William: William McGillivray and the North West Company.* Vancouver: Heritage House, 2013.

Grabowski, Jan. "Searching for the Common Ground: Natives and French in

Montreal, 1700–1730." *Proceedings of the Meeting of the French Colonial Historical Society* 18 (1993): 59–73.

Grabowski, Jan, and Nicole St-Onge. "Montreal Iroquois *Engagés* in the Western Fur Trade, 1800–1821." In Theodore Binnema, Gerhard J. Ens, and R.C. Macleod, eds, *From Rupert's Land to Canada*, 23–58. Edmonton: University of Alberta Press, 2001.

Grant, George M. *Ocean to Ocean: Sandford Fleming's Expedition through Canada in 1872*. Toronto: Belford Brothers, 1877.

Graymont, Barbara. *The Iroquois in the American Revolution*. Syracuse, NY: Syracuse University Press, 1972.

Green, Gretchen Lynn. "A New People in an Age of War: The Kahnawake Iroquois, 1867–1760." PhD diss., College of William and Mary, 1991.

Greene, John, Marc Lapprand, Gérald Moreau, and Gérald Ricard. *French Presence in Victoria B.C., 1843–1991*. Victoria: L'Association Historique Francophone de Victoria, 1991.

Greer, Allan. "Conversion and Identity: Iroquois Christianity in Seventeenth-Century New France." In Kenneth Mills and Anthony Grafton, eds, *Conversion: Old Worlds and New*, 175–98. Rochester, NY: University of Rochester Press, 2003.

– *Mohawk Saint: Catherine Tekakwitha and the Jesuits*. New York: Oxford University Press, 2005.

– ed. *The Jesuit Relations: Natives and Missionaries in Seventeenth-Century North America*. Boston: Bedford/St Martin's, 2000.

Hare, Jan, and Jean Barman. *Good Intentions Gone Awry: Emma Crosby and the Methodist Mission on the Northwest Coast*. Vancouver: UBC Press, 2006.

Harmon, Daniel Williams. *Sixteen Years in the Indian Country: The Journal of Daniel William Harmon*. Ed. W. Kaye Lamb. Toronto: Macmillan, 1957.

Hart, Hazel. *History of Hinton*. Edmonton: Friesen, 1980.

Hauptman, Laurence. *Conspiracy of Interests: Iroquois Dispossession and the Rise of New York State*. Syracuse, NY: Syracuse University Press, 1999.

– *The Iroquois in the Civil War: From Battlefield to Reservation*. Syracuse, NY: Syracuse University Press, 1993.

– *Seven Generations of Iroquois Leadership: The Six Nations since 1800*. Syracuse, NY: Syracuse University Press, 2008.

Havard, Gilles. *Empire et métissages: Indiens et Français dans le Pays d'en Haut, 1660–1715*. Sillery, QC: Septentrion, 2003.

– *The Great Peace of Montreal of 1701: French-Native Diplomacy in the Seventeenth Century*. Trans. Phyllis Aronoff and Howard Scott. Montreal and Kingston: McGill-Queen's University Press, 2001.

– *Histoire des coureurs de bois: Amérique du Nord, 1600–1840*. Paris: Les indes savants, 2016.

Havard, Vincent. "The French Half-Breeds of the Northwest." In Smithsonian Institution, *Annual Report*, 1879, 309–27.

Hazard, Ebenezer. *Historical Collections; Consisting of State Papers and Other Authentic Documents; Intended as Materials for an History of the United States of America*. 2 vols. Philadelphia: T. Dobson, 1792–94.

Helgesen, Marion I., ed. *Footprints: Pioneer Families of the Metchosin District*. Victoria: Morriss Printing for the Methcosin School Museum Society, 1983.

Helm, Charles, and Mike Murtha, eds. *The Forgotten Explorer: Samuel Prescott Fay's 1914 Expedition to the Northern Rockies*. Calgary: Rocky Mountain Books, 2009.

Henry, Alexander. *The Journal of Alexander Henry the Younger, 1799–1814*. Ed. Barry M. Gough. 2 vols. Toronto: Champlain Society, 1988–92.

Hind, Henry Youle. *Narrative of the Canadian Red River Exploring Expedition of 1857 and of the Assiniboine and Saskatchewan Exploring Expedition of 1858*. 2 vols. London: Long, Green, Longman and Roberts, 1860.

Hines, Clarence. "The Erection of Fort Nez Perce." *Oregon Historical Review* 40, no. 4 (1939): 327–35.

Holland, Clive. "Sir John Franklin." *Dictionary of Canadian Biography*. Online.

Holmgren, Eric J. "Ross Cox." *Dictionary of Canadian Biography*. Online.

Hopkins, Kelly Yvonne. "A New Landscape: Changing Iroquois Settlement Patterns, Subsistence Strategies, and Environmental Use, 1630–1783." PhD diss., University of California, Davis, 2010.

Hough, Franklin B. *A History of St Lawrence and Franklin Counties, New York*. Albany: Little and Co., 1853.

Huck, Barbara. *Exploring the Fur Trade Routes of North America*. Winnipeg: Heartland, 1992.

Hudson's Bay Company (HBC). *The Fort Langley Journals, 1827–30*. Ed. Morag Maclachlan. Vancouver: UBC Press, 1998.

– *Fort Nisqually: Servants' Accounts, 1841–68*. Vol. 10. Huntington Library, San Marino, California, FN 1239.

– *The Journal of Occurrences at Fort Nisqually, Commencing May 30, 1833, Ending September 27, 1859*. Ed. George Dickey. Tacoma, WA: Fort Nisqually Association, 1989.

Hudson's Bay Company (HBC), Nanaimo Archives. *Nanaimo Correspondence*. A/C/20.1/N15.

– *Nanaimo Journal, 14 August 1852 to 27 September 1864*. Written by Joseph McKay. Nanaimo Archives. http://www.nanaimoarchives.ca/transcripts-recordings/hbc-mckay-joumal-1852-1854.

Hudson's Bay Company Archives (HBCA), Archives of Manitoba. *Biographical Sheets*. https://www.gov.mb.ca/chc/archives/hbca/biographical/index.html.

– *Fort Chipewyan, Alberta: Account Books, 1821–1825*. Athabasca District, B.39/d/12-14, reel 1M438.

– *Fort Chipewyan, Alberta: Account Books, 1821–1822*. Athabasca General Accounts, B.39/d/12, reel 1M437.

– *Fort Chipewyan, Alberta: Account Books, 1821–1822*. Iroquois and Freemen's Book, B.39/d/14, reel 1M437.

– *Fort George, Oregon: Account Books, 1820–1825*. B.76/d/4, 9-10, reel 1M480.

– *Fort St James, British Columbia: Post Journals, 1820–1856*. B.188/a/1-21, reels 1M128, 1M129, 1M130.

– *Fort Victoria, British Columbia: Correspondence Books, 1864–1870*. B.226/b/2, reel 1M233.

– *Fort Victoria, British Columbia: Post Journals, 1846–1850*. B.226/b/1, reel 1M149.
– *Jasper House, Alberta: Post Journals, 1827–1831*. B.94/a/1-3, reel 1M65.
– *Snake Country, Idaho, Montana, and Oregon: Post Journal, 1824*. B.202/a/1-2, reel 1M142.
– *Stikine, Alaska: Post Journals, 1840–1842*. B.209/a/1, reel 1M144.
Hulbert, Archer Butler, and Dorothy Printup Hulbert, eds. *The Oregon Crusade: Across Land and Sea to Oregon*. Denver: Stewart Commission of Colorado College and Denver Public Library, 1935.
Irving, Washington. *The Adventures of Captain Bonneville, U.S.A.* 1837. Rev. ed., New York: George P. Putnam, 1868.
– *Astoria*. New York: Thomas Crowell, 1842.
Jackson, John C. *Children of the Fur Trade: Forgotten Métis of the Pacific Northwest*. Missoula, MT: Mountain, 1995.
Jameson, Jennifer E. "Iroquois of the Pacific Northwest Fur Trade: Their Archaeology and History." MA thesis, Oregon State University, 2007.
Jennings, Francis. *The Ambiguous Iroquois Empire: The Covenant Chain Confederation of Indian Tribes with English Colonies from Its Beginning to the Lancaster Treaty of 1744*. New York: Norton, 1984.
Jennings, Francis, and William N. Fenton, with Mary A. Druke and David R. Miller, eds. *The History and Culture of Iroquois Diplomacy: An Interdisciplinary Guide to the Treaties of the Six Nations and Their League*. Syracuse, NY: Syracuse University Press, 1985.
Johnson, Alice M., ed. *Saskatchewan Journals and Correspondence: Edmonton House, 1795–1800, Chesterfield House, 1800–1802*. London: Hudson's Bay Company Record Society, 1967.
Johnson, Susan Lazzar. *That Was Our Way of Life*. Sooke, BC: Sooke Region Museum, 1990.
Johnson, William. *The Papers of Sir William Johnson*. 14 vols. Albany: University of the State of New York, 1921–65.
Johnstone, C.L. *Winter and Summer Excursions in Canada*. London: Digby, Long, and Co., 1894.
Jones, Robert F., ed. *Annals of Astoria: The Headquarters Log of the Pacific Fur Company on the Columbia River, 1811–1813*. Fordham, NY: Fordham University Press, 1999.
Kakwa/Two Lakes Oral Histories. *Taped Interviews*. South Peace Regional Archives, Grande Prairie, Alberta, fonds 133.
Kane, Paul. *Wanderings of an Artist among the Indians of North America*. London: Longman, Brown, Green, Longmans, and Roberts, 1859.
Karamanski, Theodore J. "The Iroquois and the Fur Trade of the Far West." *The Beaver* 312, no. 4 (1982): 5–13.
Kreg O. Sky Fonds. *Taped Interviews*. BC Archives, PR-1812.
Laing, F.W. *Colonial Farm Settlers on the Mainland of British Columbia, 1858–1871*. Victoria: n.p., 1939.
Landry, Marcel. *"Grande Cache Is Always in My Heart."* Edmonton: Missionary Oblates of Mary Immaculate, 1992.

Leavelle, Tracy Neal. "'We Will Make It Our Own Place': Agriculture and Adaptation at the Grande Ronde Reservation, 1856–1887." *American Indian Quarterly* 22, no. 4 (1998): 433–56.

Lee, Daniel, and Joseph Frost. *Ten Years in Oregon*. 1844. Reprint, Fairfield, WA: Ye Galleon, 1968.

Leonard, David W. *Delayed Frontier: The Peace River Country to 1909*. Calgary: Detselig, 1995.

– *The Last Great West: The Agricultural Settlement of the Peace River Country to 1914*. Calgary: Detselig, 2005.

Lewis, Meriwether, and William Clark. *Journals of the Lewis and Clark Expedition*. Lincoln: University of Nebraska Press / University of Nebraska–Lincoln Libraries– Electronic Text Center, 2005. https://lewisandclarkjournals.unl.edu/journals/ contents.

Long, John. *Voyages and Travels of an Indian Interpreter and Trader*. London: n.p., 1791.

Lounsbury, Floyd. "Iroquoian Languages." In Bruce G. Trigger, ed., *Handbook of North American Indians*, vol. 15, *Northeast*, 334–43. Washington, DC: Smithsonian Institution, 1978.

Lowe, Thomas. *Private Journal Kept at Fort Vancouver, Columbia River, 1843–50*. BC Archives, E/A/L95A.

Lozier, Jean-François. "In Each Other's Arms: France and the St Lawrence Mission Villages in War and Peace, 1630–1730." PhD diss., University of Toronto, 2012.

Lunn, Jean. "The Illegal Fur Trade out of New France, 1713–60." *Report of the Annual Meeting of the Canadian Historical Association* 18, no. 1 (1939): 61–76.

MacGregor, James G. *Father Lacombe*. Edmonton: Hurtig, 1975.

– *Overland by the Yellowhead*. Saskatoon: West Producer, 1974.

– *Pack Saddles to Tête Jaune Cache*. Toronto: McClelland and Stewart, 1962.

– *Peter Fidler: Canada's Forgotten Surveyor, 1769–1822*. Toronto: McClelland and Stewart, 1966.

Mackenzie, Alexander. *Voyages from Montreal on the River St Laurence through the Continent of North America to the Frozen and Pacific Oceans*. 2 vols. London: V. Cadell, 1801.

Mackenzie, Roderick. *An Account of the Athabasca Indians by a Partner of the North-west Company, 1795*. McGill Fur Trade Project, MFTP 0032. http://digital.library. mcgill.ca/nwc/search/searchfs.htm.

MacLaren, I.S. "Rejuvenating Wilderness: The Challenge of Reintegrating Aboriginal Peoples into the 'Playground' of Jasper National Park." In Claire Elizabeth Campbell, ed., *A Century of Parks Canada, 1911–2011*, 333–70. Calgary: University of Calgary Press, 2011.

– ed. *Culturing Wilderness in Jasper National Park: Studies in Two Centuries of Human History in the Upper Athabasca River Watershed*. Edmonton: University of Alberta Press, 2007.

MacLeitch, Gail D. *Imperial Entanglements: Iroquois Change and Persistence on the Frontiers of Empire*. Philadelphia: University of Pennsylvania Press, 2011.

MacLeod, D. Peter. *The Canadian Iroquois and the Seven Years' War*. Toronto: Dundurn, 1996.

Macpherson, Elizabeth. *Sun Traveller: The Story of the Callihoos of Alberta*. St Albert, A B: Heritage Museum, 1998.

Mair, Charles. *Through the Mackenzie Basin: An Account of the Signing of Treaty No. 8 and the Scrip Commission, 1899*. Edmonton: University of Alberta Press, 1999.

Malone, Michael P., Richard B. Roeder, and William L. Lang. *Montana: A History of Two Centuries*. Rev. ed. Seattle: University of Washington Press, 1991.

Maloney, Alice Bay. "Fur Brigade to the Bonaventura: John Work's California Expedition of 1832–33 for the Hudson's Bay Company." *California Historical Society Quarterly* 23, no. 1 (1944): 19–40, and 23, no. 2 (1944): 123–46.

Masiewicz, John. *Gervase Macomber and His 26 Children in Kahnawake (Caughnawaga)*. Self-published, 2015.

Masson, L.R. *Les bourgeois de la Compagnie du Nord-Ouest*. 2 vols. Quebec City: L'Imprimerie Générale A. Coté et Cie, 1889–90.

Mathis, Bill. "A Timeline of the Life and Times of William L. (Niwentenhroa) Gray and John (Ignace Hatchiorauquasha) Gray." Typescript. Kansas Genealogical Society.

McCormick, Kaitlin. "'Neither One, Nor the Other': The Unique Oeuvre of Freddie Alexcee." M A thesis, Carleton University, 2010.

McDonald, Angus. "The Dying Voyageur of Columbia." University of Montana Archives, ms 344.

McKelvie, B.A., and Willard E. Ireland. "The Victoria Voltigeurs." *British Columbia Historical Quarterly* 20 (1956): 221–39.

McLean, John. *John McLean's Notes of a Twenty-Five Years' Service in the Hudson's Bay Territory*. Ed. W.S. Wallace. Toronto: Champlain Society, 1932.

McLoughlin, John. *Letters of Dr John McLoughlin Written at Fort Vancouver, 1829–1832*. Ed. Burt Brown Barker. Portland: Binfords and Mort for Oregon Historical Society, 1948.

– *The Letters of John McLoughlin from Fort Vancouver to the Governor and Committee, 1st series, 1825–38*. Ed. E.E. Rich. London: Champlain Society for Hudson's Bay Company Record Society, 1941.

– *The Letters of John McLoughlin from Fort Vancouver to the Governor and Committee, Second Series, 1839–44*. Ed. E.E. Rich. London: Champlain Society for Hudson's Bay Company Record Society, 1943.

– *The Letters of John McLoughlin from Fort Vancouver to the Governor and Committee, Third Series, 1844–46*. Ed. E.E. Rich. London: Champlain Society for Hudson's Bay Company Record Society, 1944.

Mellis, John C. "Coyote People and the Black Robes: Indigenous Roots of Salish Christianity." PhD diss., Saint Louis University, 1992.

– "Ignace Portui: Iroquois Evangelist to the Salish, ca. 1780–1837." *International Journal of Missionary Research* 33, no. 4 (2009): 212–15.

Mengarini, Gregorio. "Recollections of the Flathead Mission Containing Brief Observations Both Ancient and Contemporary Concerning This Particular Nation."

1848. In Gloria Ricci Lothrop, "Father Gregory Mengarini, an Italian Jesuit Missionary in the Transmontaine West: His Life and Memoirs," 174–314. PhD diss., University of Southern California, 1970.

M'Gillivray, Duncan. *The Journal of Duncan M'Gillivray of the North West Company at Fort George on the Saskatchewan, 1794–5.* Ed. Arthur S. Morton. Toronto: Macmillan, 1929.

Milton, William Fitzwilliam, and Walter B. Cheadle. *The North-West Passage by Land.* London: Cassell, Petter and Galpin, 1865.

Missionary Oblates. *Grandin Archives.* Provincial Archives of Alberta.

Mitchell, Elaine Allan. *Fort Timiskaming and the Fur Trade.* Toronto: University of Toronto Press, 1977.

Moberly, Henry John. *When Fur Was King.* London: J.M. Dent and Sons, 1929.

Moberly, Walter. *The Rocks and Rivers of British Columbia.* London: H. Blacklock and Co., 1885.

Mohawk Council of Kahnawake. *Seigneury of Sault St Louis.* Kahnawake, QC: Mohawk Council of Kahnawake, 2004.

Moodie, D. Wayne. "The Trading Post Settlement of the Canadian Northwest, 1774–1821." *Journal of Historical Geography* 13, no. 4 (1987): 360–74.

Moodie, J.D. "Instructions to, and Diary of, Inspector J.D. Moodie in Charge of Patrol from Edmonton to the Yukon, 1897." In *Report of the North-West Mounted Police, 1898.* Ottawa: S.E. Dawson, 1890.

Morgan, Dale L. *Jedediah Smith and the Opening of the West.* Lincoln: University of Nebraska Press, 1953.

Morrison, Jean. *Superior Rendezvous-Place: Fort William in the Canadian Fur Trade.* 2nd ed. Toronto: Natural Heritage Books, 2007.

Morrison, R. Bruce. "Stress and Socio-Cultural Change in a New Town." PhD diss., University of Alberta, 1977.

Morse, Eric W. *Fur Trade Canoe Routes of Canada Then and Now.* Ottawa: Parks Canada, 1979.

Mullan, John. *Report on the Construction of a Military Road from Fort Walla-Walla to Fort Benton.* Washington, DC: Government Printing Office, 1863.

Munnick, Harriet D., ed. *Catholic Church Records of the Pacific Northwest: Grand Ronde.* Portland, OR: Binford and Mort, 1987.

– ed. *Catholic Church Records of the Pacific Northwest: St Paul, Oregon, 1839–1898.* St Paul, OR: French Prairie, 1972.

– ed. *Catholic Church Records of the Pacific Northwest: Vancouver* and *Stellamaris Mission.* St Paul, OR: French Prairie, 1972.

Murphy, Peter J. "'Following the Base of the Foothills': Tracing the Boundaries of Jasper Park and Its Adjacent Rocky Mountains Forest Reserve." In I.S. MacLaren, ed., *Culturing Wilderness in Jasper National Park: Studies in Two Centuries of Human History in the Upper Athabasca River Watershed,* 71–121. Edmonton: University of Alberta Press, 2007.

– "Homesteading in the Athabasca Valley to 1910." In I.S. MacLaren, ed., *Culturing Wilderness in Jasper National Park: Studies in Two Centuries of Human History in the Upper Athabasca River Watershed*, 123–53. Edmonton: University of Alberta Press, 2007.

Myers, Carey. "Deep Ties to Native Community." *Vancouver Sun*, 30 September 2008.

Nadasdy, Paul. *Hunters and Bureaucrats: Power, Knowledge, and Aboriginal-State Relations in Southwest Yukon*. Vancouver: UBC Press, 2003.

Napoleon, Art, ed. *Bushland Spirit: Our Elders Speak*. Moberly Lake, BC: Twin Sisters, 1988.

Nicks, John. "David Thompson." *Dictionary of Canadian Biography*. Online.

Nicks, Trudy. "Demographic Anthropology of Native Populations of Western Canada, 1800–1975." PhD diss., University of Alberta, 1980.

– "The Iroquois and the Fur Trade in Western Canada." In Carol M. Judd and Arthur J. Ray, eds, *Old Trails and New Directions: Papers of the Third North American Fur Trade Conference*, 85–101. Toronto: University of Toronto Press, 1980.

– *Iroquois Fur Trappers and Their Descendants in Alberta*. Edmonton: Provincial Museum of Alberta, March 1979.

– "Louis Callihoo." *Dictionary of Canadian Biography*. Online.

Nicks, Trudy, and Kenneth Morgan. "Grande Cache: The Historic Development of an Indigenous Alberta Métis Population." In Jacqueline Peterson and Jennifer S.H. Brown, eds, *The New Peoples: Being and Becoming Métis in North America*, 163–81. Winnipeg: University of Manitoba Press, 1985.

Nisbet, Jack. *The Mapmaker's Eye: David Thompson on the Columbian Plateau*. Pullman: Washington State University Press, 2005.

Norcross, E. Blanche. *Nanaimo Retrospective: The First Century*. Nanaimo: Nanaimo Historical Society, 1979.

North West Company. *Men's Names at the Athabasca River Department, 1805*. McGill Fur Trade Project, MFTP 0031. http://digital.library.mcgill.ca/nwc/search/searchfs.htm.

North West Company, Hudson's Bay Company Archives (HBCA), Archives of Manitoba. *Account Books, 1819–1821*. Athabasca, F.4/37, reel 5M9.

– *Account Books, 1819–1821*. Memo of English River Men Who Wish to Go Down, F.4/36, reel 5M9.

– *Account Books, 1820–1821*. F.4/41, reel 5M10.

– *Account Books, 1820–1821*. Cash Disbursements to North West Company Employees, F.4/43, reel 5M10.

– *Iroquois Accounts, 1819*. F.4/35, reel 5M9.

– *Ledger (Account Books), 1811–1821*. F.4/32, reels 5M7, 5M8.

– *Ledger (Account Books), 1819–1821*. F.4/36, F.4/43, reels 5M9, 5M10.

– *Servants' Accounts, 1820–1821*. Cash Disbursements to North West Company Employees, F.4/43, reel 5M10.

– *Servant Balances, 1821*. F.4/46, reel 5M11.

– *Servants' Contracts, 1811–1822*. F.5/1-3, reel 5M13.

North-West Territories. *Scrip Applications*. Library and Archives Canada, RG15, reels 14962, 14971, 14977, 14978, 15009, 15010, with some applications online at Library and Archives Canada.

Norton, Thomas Elliott. *The Fur Trade in Colonial New York, 1686–1776*. Madison: University of Wisconsin Press, 1974.

Oberg, Michael Leroy. *Peacemakers: The Iroquois, the United States, and the Treaty of Canandaigua, 1794*. New York: Oxford University Press, 2016.

Officer, Charles, and Jake Page. *A Fabulous Kingdom: The Exploration of the Arctic*. 2nd ed. New York: Oxford University Press, 2012.

Ogden, Peter Skene. *Peter Skene Ogden's Snake Country Journals, 1824–25 and 1825–26*. Ed. E.E. Rich. London: Hudson's Bay Company Record Society, 1950.

– *Peter Skene Ogden's Snake Country Journals, 1827–28 and 1828–29*. Ed. Glynder Williams. London: Hudson's Bay Company Record Society, 1971.

Oka (Kanesatake/Lac des Deux Montagnes/Lake of Two Mountains). *Census, 1825*. Online on FamilySearch under Canada, Lower Canada Census, 1825, Lac des Deux Montagnes (mission). https://www.familysearch.org/search/collection/1834346.

– *Census, 1831*. Online on FamilySearch at Canada, Lower Canada Census, 1831, Deux Montagnes, Lac des Deux Montagnes. https://www.familysearch.org/search/collection/1834329.

Olsen, W.H. "The Face of Tomo Antoine." *Ladysmith Chronicle*, 10, 17, 24, 31 January 1963; 7, 14, 21, 28 February 1963; 7, 14, 21, 28 March 1963; 4 April 1963.

Olson, June L. *Living in the Great Circle: The Grand Ronde Indian Reservation, 1855–1905*. Clackamas, OR: A. Menard, 2011.

Ouellet, Richard. "The Life and Death of the Council of Elders of the Descendants of Jasper Park." PhD diss., University of British Columbia, 2016.

– "Tales of Empowerment: Cultural Continuity within an Evolving Identity in the Upper Athabasca Valley." MA thesis, Simon Fraser University, 2006.

Owen, John. *The Journals and Letters of Major John Owen*. Ed. Seymour Dunbar. 2 vols. New York: Edward Eberstadt, 1927.

Owen, Olga Blanche. "The Adam Grant Horne Family." BC Archives, Add. Ms. 1157.

Palladino, L.B. *Indian and White in the Northwest: A History of Catholicity in Montana, 1831 to 1891*. 1894. Reprint, Lancaster, PA: Wickersham, 1922.

Parker, Samuel. *Journal of an Exploring Tour beyond the Rocky Mountains under the Direction of the A.B.C.F.M. [American Board of Commissioners for Foreign Missions] Performed in the Years 1835, '36, and '37*. 1st ed. Ithaca, NY: n.p., 1838.

Parmenter, Jon. *The Edge of the Woods: Iroquoia, 1534–1701*. East Lansing: Michigan State University Press, 2010.

Payne, Michael. "The Fur Trade on the Upper Athabasca River, 1810–1920." In I.S. MacLaren, ed., *Culturing Wilderness in Jasper National Park: Studies in Two Centuries of Human History in the Upper Athabasca River Watershed*, 1–39. Edmonton: University of Alberta Press, 2007.

Pederson, Nora K. "Identity Politics at Grande Ronde: Toward an Ethnohistory of the Tribes of the Willamette Valley, 1855–1901." MA thesis, Western Washington University, 2010.

Peers, Elida. "A Grandmother of the West." *Sooke Mirror*, 24 June 1992.

Pelletier, Rick, and Rick Ouellet. "Moberly Descendants Ignored in Totem Dispute." *Jasper Fitzhugh*, 13 May 2010.

Peterson, Jacqueline, with Laura Peers. *Sacred Encounters: Father De Smet and the Indians of the Rocky Mountain West*. Norman: University of Oklahoma Press, 1993.

Peterson, Jan. *Black Diamond City: Nanaimo, the Victorian Era*. Surrey, BC: Heritage House, 2002.

Phillips, Paul C. "Family Letters of Two Oregon Fur Traders, 1828–1856." In John W. Hakola, ed., *Frontier Omnibus*, 29–40. Missoula: Montana State University Press, 1962.

Pierce, Jason E. *Making the White Man's West: Whiteness and the Creation of an American West*. Boulder: University Press of Colorado, 2016.

Pike, Warburton. *The Barren Ground of Northern Canada*. New York: E.P. Dutton and Company, 1917.

Podruchny, Carolyn. *Making the Voyageur World: Travelers and Traders in the North American Fur Trade*. Toronto: University of Toronto Press, 2006.

Point, Nicolas. *Wilderness Kingdom: Indian Life in the Rocky Mountains, 1840–1847: The Journals and Paintings of Nicolas Point, S.J.* Ed. Joseph P. Donnelly. New York: Holt, Rinehart and Winston, 1967.

Preston, David L. *The Texture of Contact: European and Indian Settler Communities on the Frontiers of Iroquoia, 1667–1793*. Lincoln: University of Nebraska Press, 2009.

Reid, Gerald F. *Khanawà:ke: Factionalism, Traditionalism, and Nationalism in a Mohawk Community*. Lincoln: University of Nebraska Press, 2004.

Reid, John Phillip. *Forging a Fur Empire: Expeditions in the Snake River Country, 1809–1824*. Norman, OK: Arthur H. Clark, 2011.

Reid, Russell, and Clell G. Gannon, eds. "Journal of the Atkinson-O'Fallon Expedition." *North Dakota Historical Quarterly* 4, no. 1 (1929): 5–56.

Richter, Daniel K. "Iroquois versus Iroquois: Jesuit Missions and Christianity in Village Politics, 1642–1686." *Ethnohistory* 32, no. 1 (1985): 1–16.

– *The Ordeal of the Longhouse: The Peoples of the Iroquois League in the Era of European Colonization*. Chapel Hill: University of North Carolina Press, 1992.

Robertson, Colin. *Colin Robertson's Correspondence Book, September 1817 to September 1822*. Ed. E.E. Rich. London: Champlain Society for Hudson's Bay Company Record Society, 1939.

Ronan, Peter. *History of the Flathead Indians*. 1890. Reprint, Minneapolis: Ross and Haines, 1965.

Ross, Alexander. *Adventures of the First Settlers on the Oregon or Columbia River*. London: Smith, Elder and Co., 1849.

– *The Fur Hunters of the Far West*. 2 vols. Ed. Milo Milton Quaife. London: Smith, Elder and Co., 1855.

– *The Fur Hunters of the Far West*. Ed. Kenneth A. Spaulding. Norman: University of Oklahoma Press, 1956.

– "Journal of Alexander Ross – Snake Country Expedition, 1824." Ed. T.C. Elliott. *Oregon Historical Quarterly* 14, no. 4 (1913): 366–85.

– *Snake Country, Idaho, Montana, and Oregon: Post Journal, 1824*. Hudson's Bay Company Archives, Archives of Manitoba, B.202/a/1, reel 1M142.

Rueck, Daniel. "Enclosing the Mohawk Commons: A History of Use-Rights,

Landownership, and Boundary Making in Kahnawá:ke Mohawk Territory." PhD
    diss., McGill University, 2013.
Russell, Osborne. *Journal of a Trapper.* Ed. Aubrey L. Haines. Lincoln: University of
    Nebraska Press, 1955. First published from the original manuscript as *Journal of a
    Trapper: Or, Nine Years in the Rocky Mountains, 1834–1843* (Boise, ID: Syms-York,
    1914).
Sandlos, John. "Not Wanted in the Boundary: The Expulsion of the Keeseekoowenin
    Ojibway Band from Riding Mountain Park." *Canadian Historical Review* 89, no. 9
    (2008): 189–221.
Satakarata, Louis. "Contract with Hudson's Bay Company, 1841." BC Archives,
    E/A/Sa3.
Sawaya, Jean-Pierre. "Les Sept-Nations du Canada et les Britanniques, 1759–1774:
    Alliance et dépendance." PhD diss., Université Laval, 2001.
Sawchuk, Joe, Patricia Sawchuk, and Theresa Ferguson. *Metis Land Rights in Alberta:
    A Political History.* Edmonton: Metis Association of Alberta, 1981.
Schäffer, Mary T.S. *Old Indian Trails.* New York: G.P. Putnam's Sons, 1911.
Selkirk, Thomas Douglas, Earl of. *Lord Selkirk's Diary, 1803–1804: A Journal of His
    Travels in British North America.* Ed. Patrick C.T. White. Toronto: Champlain
    Society, 1958.
Sellers, Marki. "'Wearing the Mantle on Both Shoulders': An Examination of the
    Development of Cultural Change, Mutual Accommodation, and Hybrid Forms at
    Fort Simpson/Laxigu'alaams, 1834–1862." MA thesis, Simon Fraser University, 2005.
Shand-Harvey, James. *Papers.* Jasper Yellowhead Museum and Archives, Jasper,
    Alberta.
Shannon, Timothy J. *Indians and Colonists at the Crossroads of Empire: The Albany
    Congress of 1754.* Ithaca, NY: Cornell University Press, 2000.
– *Iroquois Diplomacy on the Early American Frontier.* New York: Viking, 2008.
Sharlow, Jo, and Richard Wuorinen. *Grande Cache: The People.* Grande Cache, AB:
    Grande Cache Historical Society, 1999.
Simpson, Audra. *Mohawk Interruptus: Political Life across the Borders of Settler States.*
    Durham, NC: Duke University Press, 2014.
– "To the Reserve and Back Again: Kahnawake Mohawk Narratives of Self, Home
    and Nation." PhD diss., McGill University, 2003.
Simpson, Charles E. "The Snake Country Freemen: British Free Trappers in Idaho."
    MA thesis, University of Idaho, 1990.
Simpson, George. *Fur Trade and Empire: George Simpson's Journal.* Ed. Frederick
    Merk. 1931. Rev. ed., Cambridge, MA: Belknap, 1968.
– *Journal of Occurrences in the Athabasca Department by George Simpson, 1820 and
    1821, and Report.* Ed. E.E. Rich. London: Champlain Society for Hudson's Bay
    Company Record Society, 1938.
– *London Correspondence Inward from George Simpson, 1841–42.* Ed. Glyndwr
    Williams. London: Hudson's Bay Company Record Society, 1973.
– *Part of Dispatch from George Simpson Esquire, Governor of Rupert's Land.* Ed. E.E.
    Rich. London: Champlain Society for Hudson's Bay Company Record Society,
    1947.

Slacum, William. "Slacum's Report on Oregon, 1836–37." *Oregon Historical Quarterly* 13, no. 2 (1912): 175–224.

Snow, Dean. *The Iroquois*. Cambridge, MA: Blackwell, 1994.

The Sooke Story: The History and the Heartbeat. 2nd ed. Sooke, BC: Sooke Region Museum, 2004.

Sossoyan, Matthieu. "The Kahnawake Iroquois and the Lower-Canada Rebellions, 1837–1838." MA thesis, McGill University, 1999.

– "Note de recherché: Les Indiens, les Mohawks et les Blancs." *Recherches amerindiennes au Québec* 39, nos 1–2 (2009): 159–71.

Southesk, James Carnegie, Earl of. *Saskatchewan and the Rocky Mountains*. Toronto: James Campbell and Son, 1875.

Spence, Mark David. *Dispossessing the Wilderness: Indian Removal and the Making of the National Parks*. New York: Oxford University Press, 1999.

Spry, Irene M. *The Papers of the Palliser Expedition, 1857–1860*. Toronto: Champlain Society, 1968.

St Andrew's Catholic Church, Victoria. *Baptismal, Marriage, and Death Records, 1849–1934*. BC Archives, Add. Ms. 1.

St Joseph's Mission, Williams Lake. *Baptisms, 1866–1901*. Computerized list compiled by Brother Eddy Sykes, St Joseph Oblate House, Williams Lake.

St-Onge, Nicole. "Early Forefathers to the Athabasca Métis: Long-Term North West Company Employees." In Ute Lischke and David T. McNab, eds, *The Long Journey of a Forgotten People: Métis Identities and Family Histories*, 109–61. Waterloo, ON: Wilfrid Laurier University Press, 2007.

– "'He Was Neither a Soldier nor a Slave; He Was under the Control of No Man': Kahnawake Mohawks in the Northwest Fur Trade, 1790–1850." *Canadian Journal of History* 51, no. 1 (2016): 1–32.

St Régis (Akwesasne). *Census, 1825*. Online on FamilySearch under Canada, Lower Canada Census, 1825, Huntingdon, St Régis, Village and Indian Lands. https://www.familysearch.org/search/collection/1834346.

Stanley, George F.P., ed. *Mapping the Frontier: Charles Wilson's Diary of the Survey of the 49th Parallel, 1858–1862*. Toronto: Macmillan, 1970.

Steigmeyer, Rick. "Entiat Woman Says Ancestor Guided Columbia Pioneer." *Wenatchee World*, 15 July 2011.

Surtees, Robert J. "The Iroquois in Canada." In Francis Jennings and William N. Fenton, with Mary A. Druke and David R. Miller, eds, *The History and Culture of Iroquois Diplomacy: An Interdisciplinary Guide to the Treaties of the Six Nations and Their League*, 67–83. Syracuse, NY: Syracuse University Press, 1985.

Taylor, C.J. *Jasper: A History of the Place and Its People*. Markham, ON: Fifth House, 2009.

Thompson, David. *David Thompson's Narrative of His Explorations in Western America, 1784–1812*. Ed. J.B. Tyrrell. Toronto: Champlain Society, 1916.

– *The Travels of David Thompson, 1784–1812*. 2 vols. Ed. Sean T. Peake. Bloomington: iUniverse, 2011.

– *The Writings of David Thompson*. 2 vols. Ed. William E. Moreau. Montreal and Kingston: McGill-Queen's University Press, 2009 and 2015.

Thwaites, Reuben Gold, ed. *The Jesuit Relations and Allied Documents: Travels and Explorations of the Jesuit Missionaries in New France, 1610–1791.* 73 vols. Cleveland, OH: Burrows Brothers, 1896–1901.

Tolmie, William Fraser. *The Journals of William Fraser Tolmie: Physician and Fur Trader.* Vancouver: Mitchell, 1963.

Tooker, Elisabeth. "Iroquois since 1820." In Bruce G. Trigger, ed., *Handbook of North American Indians,* vol. 15, *Northeast,* 449–65. Washington, DC: Smithsonian Institution, 1978.

Townsend, John Kirk. *Narrative of a Journey across the Rocky Mountains, to the Columbia River.* Philadelphia: Henry Perkins, 1839.

Trelease, Allen W. "The Iroquois and the Western Fur Trade: A Problem in Interpretation." *Mississippi Valley Historical Review* 49, no. 1 (1962): 32–51.

Trudel, Marcel. "Samuel de Champlain." *Dictionary of Canadian Biography.* Online.

United States. *Journal of the Senate, 1852–55.* https://memory.loc.gov/ammem/amlaw/lwsjlink.html.

United States, Bureau of Indian Affairs. *Correspondence Respecting Funds Derived from Selling Surplus Land on the Grand Ronde Reservation, 1905.* Portland, OR: Bureau of Indian Affairs, Northwest Regional Office.

– *Grand Ronde Reservation Census, 1886–1901.* Portland, OR: Bureau of Indian Affairs, Northwest Regional Office.

– *Indian Census Rolls, 1885–1940.* Washington, DC: Bureau of Indian Affairs. https://search.ancestry.com/search/db.aspx?dbid=1059.

Utley, Robert M. *After Lewis and Clark: Mountain Men and the Paths to the Pacific.* 1997. Reprint, Lincoln: University of Nebraska Press, 2004.

Victor, Frances Fuller. *The River of the West: Life and Adventure in the Rocky Mountains and Oregon.* Hartford, CT: Columbian Book Company, 1870.

Voyageur Contracts Database. Compiled by Nicole St-Onge, Nicole Fortier, and Robert Engelbert. Centre du patrimoine, Société historique de Saint-Boniface. http://shsb.mb.ca/en/Voyageurs_database.

Walkem, W. Wymond. *Stories of Early British Columbia.* Vancouver: News Advertiser, 1914.

Warre, H.J. *Overland to Oregon in 1845.* Ed. Madeleine Major-Frégeau. Ottawa: Public Archives of Canada, 1976.

Washburn, Stanley. *Trails, Trappers, and Tenderfeet in the New Empire of Western Canada.* London: Andrew Melrose, 1913.

Watson, Bruce McIntyre. *Lives Lived West of the Divide: A Biographical Dictionary of Fur Traders Working West of the Rockies, 1793–1858.* 3 vols. Kelowna, BC: Centre for Social, Spatial, and Economic Justice Press, University of British Columbia, 2010.

Weisel, George F., ed. *Men and Trade on the Northwest Frontier as Shown by the Fort Owen Ledger.* Missoula: Montana State University Press, 1955.

Wells, Merle. "Ignace Hatchiorauquasha (John Grey)." In LeRoy Hafen, ed., *The Mountain Men and the Fur Trade of the Far West,* vol. 4, 161–75. Glendale, CA: Arthur H. Clark, 1965–72.

– "Pierre Tevanitagon (Old Pierre, the Iroquois)." In LeRoy Hafen, ed., *The Mountain Men and the Fur Trade of the Far West*, vol. 4, 351–7. Glendale, CA: Arthur H. Clark, 1965–72.

Wicks, Thomas P. "Louie Otoihkori." In *Pioneer Reminiscences of Thos. P. Wicks, British Columbia Coast, 1882*. Vancouver Archives, FC 3823.1 P55.

Williams, Christina MacDonald McKenzie. "The Daughter of Angus MacDonald." *Western Historical Quarterly* 13, no. 2 (1922): 107–17.

Willmott, Cory. "From Stroud to Strouds: The Hidden History of a British Fur Trade Textile." *Textile History* 36, no. 2 (2005): 196–234.

Wilson, C. Roderick, and R. Bruce Morrison. "Grande Cache: Another Land Claims Model." In Jim Freedman and Jerome H. Barkow, eds, *Proceedings of the Second Congress, Canadian Ethnology Society*, vol. 2, 365–77. Ottawa: Univerity of Ottawa Press, 1975.

"Witty in St Mary's Churchyard, Metchosin, British Columbia." MetchosinCentral. com. http://metchosincentral.com/stmarys/details.php?surname=WITTY.

Work, John. "Journal of John Work, November and December, 1824." Ed. T.C. Elliott. *Washington Historical Quarterly* 3, no. 3 (1912): 198–228.

– *The Snake Country Expedition of 1830–1831: John Work's Field Journal*. Ed. Francis D. Haines Jr. Norman: University of Oklahoma Press, 1971.

Wuorinen, Richard. *A History of Grande Cache*. Grande Cache, AB: Grande Cache Historical Society, 1997.

Wyeth, Nathaniel J. *The Correspondence and Journals of Captain Nathaniel J. Wyeth, 1831–6*. Ed. F.G. Young. Eugene: University of Oregon Press, 1899.

Zenk, Henry Benjamin. "Chinook Jargon and Native Cultural Persistence in the Grand Ronde Indian Community, 1856–1907: A Special Case of Creolization." PhD diss., University of Oregon, 1984.

Index

Waniyandie family, 195, 210, 217, 225, 230–1, 277n119
Wanyandie, Daniel, 233
Wanyandie, Dean and Tom, 230, 278n142
Wanyandie Co-operative, 230, 278n142
Wanyandie Flats, 213, 226
War of 1812, 35, 37, 118, 119
Warre, Henry James, 144, 175
wars, 35, 37, 118, 119, 211, 225
Watièce, George, 153
Watson, Bruce McIntyre, 128, 238, 263n1; *Lives Lived West of the Divide*, 237, 240, 263n1

Wells, Merle, 114
Whitman, Marcus and Narcissa, 63, 147
Wicks, Thomas, 243n8
Willamette Valley, 62, 135–41, 136, 146–7, 149, 152–3, 158
Wilson, C. Rodrick, 227
Witty, Charlotte Aaroniaton/Karohuhana and John, 154–7, 265n36, 265n51
Work, John, 108–9

XY Company, 41–2, 237, 280n13

Yocantez, Thomas, 38